À L'AVENTURE

AN INTRODUCTION TO FRENCH LANGUAGE AND FRANCOPHONE CULTURES

Annotated Instructor's Edition

Evelyne Charvier-Berman
El Camino College

Anne C. Cummings
El Camino College

JOHN WILEY & SONS, INC.

New York • Chichester • Brisbane • Toronto • Singapore • Weinheim

ACQUISITIONS EDITOR: Carlos Davis
SENIOR DEVELOPMENT EDITOR: Nancy Perry
SUPPLEMENTS EDITOR: Andrea Bryant
MARKETING MANAGER: Leslie Hines
SENIOR PRODUCTION EDITOR: Jeanine Furino
BOOK DESIGNER: Levavi/Levavi
ASSISTANT MANUFACTURING MANAGER: Mark Cirillo
PHOTO EDITOR: Hilary Newman
SENIOR ILLUSTRATION COORDINATOR: Anna Melhorn
COVER PHOTO: S. B. Photography/Tony Stone Images/New York, Inc.

This book was set in ITC Garamond Light by University Graphics, Inc. and
printed and bound by R. R. Donnelley & Sons. The cover was printed by
Phoenix Color.

Recognizing the importance of preserving what has been written, it is a
policy of John Wiley & Sons, Inc. to have books of enduring value published
in the United States printed on acid-free paper, and we exert out best
efforts to that end.

Note: This book is a joint work of the two authors. To emphasize this, we have listed the author's names
in alphabetical order on the title page and in the Library of Congress cataloguing data, and in reverse
alphabetical order on the cover.

ISBN 0-471-30935-4

Printed in the United States of America

10 9 8 7 6 5 4 3 2 1

TO THE INSTRUCTOR

À l'aventure is a first-year college program designed to help you create maximum opportunities for your students to discover the language and culture of the French-speaking world in a varied and stimulating environment.

The vehicle for presenting vocabulary, culture, and grammatical structures is the story line. We have made a conscious decision to use simple yet authentic French to challenge and pique the students' interest in the French-speaking world. Remind students that their knowledge and previous experiences, their willingness to take educated guesses, and the colorful art panels that accompany the story line will help them bridge the comprehension gap. You may also want to explain to students that the art, in the style of **la bande dessinée,** is an authentic and intrinsic part of French culture, used to communicate humorous as well as serious messages to readers of all ages.

How to teach a typical chapter

You may find that your class schedule does not permit you to do all of the items listed below. You will make your selections based on the number of hours that you teach, as well as your personal preferences and those of your students. You may wish to concentrate on vocabulary, structures and basic communicative activities, or put more emphasis on the cultural aspects of the text.

Chapter elements	Approach(es)	Scheduling
Story	Students read the story, in class with teacher's guidance, or at home. May be done orally or silently.	At the beginning of each episode.
Avez-vous compris?	Students answer questions orally or in writing, as homework or as a warm-up for the next class meeting.	After reading the story.
Et vous?	Students answer questions related to the story line, drawing upon their personal experiences.	After reading the story and answering **Avez-vous compris?**
Vous êtes branchés!	Assign reading in class or as homework to develop cultural awareness.	May be done anytime before the end of the chapter.

Chapter elements	Approach(es)	Scheduling
Votre Q. I. culturel	Students complete questions alone, in pairs, or in groups. After discussion, students may present their opinions to the rest of the class.	After completion of **Vous êtes branchés!**
Structures	Students familiarize themselves with grammatical structures and related vocabulary in the **Pour s'exprimer** boxes.	Generally best after reading story.
Activités	Students practice structures and vocabulary alone, in pairs, in groups.	On a daily basis.
Il y a un problème: qu'en pensez-vous?	Students discuss various options provided and/or develop other solutions to story-related problems.	After reading the episode in which the problem occurs.
À vous de jouer	Students imagine how they would deal with a given situation.	After the **Il y a un problème** section.
Lecture	Students follow the reading strategies, do the reading, and answer the questions orally or in writing.	Best to do towards the end of the chapter.
À vos stylos	Students follow the writing strategies, examine the models provided, and complete the writing assignment. May be done at home or in class.	Best to do towards the end of the chapter.
Rencontres	Students look at the map and statistics provided for each country, then read interviews with people from the area. Students answer questions and discuss what they have learned.	Best done after reading the episode which introduces a new francophone character.
Révision éclair et activités	Students review vocabulary, and structures and complete activities in groups, pairs, or individually. May be done in class or at home.	At the end of each chapter.

Chapter elements	Approach(es)	Scheduling
Prononciation	Students practice the sounds and rhythms of spoken French, by listening to their teacher or lab tape or CD. May be done in class, in the lab.	May be done anytime.
Vocabulaire actif	Students review vocabulary.	At the end of each chapter.

Sample Lesson Plans and Syllabi

À l'aventure is a first-year text designed to be completed in three quarters or two semesters. Every chapter of *À l'aventure* presents vocabulary, grammar, and activities in manageable units that will allow your students to build their speaking, reading, listening, and writing skills in a personalized, yet authentic, cultural environment.

This program offers myriad possibilities to suit different learning and teaching styles, much as the menu at an excellent restaurant provides a variety of tempting choices. Instructors can select and use only those sections of the text that best suit their students' interests and needs. In our sample lessons and syllabi, you will find some examples of how you could make and implement such choices.

Sample lesson plans for two consecutive days

Day one

A typical 50-minute class may be composed as follows:

1. Read through the **Premier Épisode** with students. Answer any comprehension/vocabulary/pronunciation questions they have. (10 min.)
2. Choose several questions from **Avez-vous compris?** for students to answer. (5 min.)
3. Choose one or two personalized questions from **Et vous?** You may ask several students the same question. (5 min.)
4. Move to the grammar explanation, saving the cultural section, **Vous êtes branchés!**, for the next day. Ask students to read it and prepare **Votre Q. I. culturel** questions at home. (15 min.)
5. Go over **Pour s'exprimer** vocabulary. (5 min.)
6. **Activités.** Choose two or three pair/individual class activities. (10 min.)

Total class time: 50 min.

Assignment: Assign written follow-up activities from workbook. Have students read **Vous êtes branchés!** and prepare **Votre Q. I. culturel.** Have students scan **Épisode 2.**

Day Two

1. Discuss **Vous êtes branchés!** and orally answer **Votre Q. I. culturel** (10 min.)
2. Have students do one of the activities not assigned from the first episode to check comprehension and to review. (5 min.)
3. Reading of **Épisode 2.** Do in pairs if it is a dialog or have student volunteers read aloud. (5 min.)
4. Have students do **Avez-vous compris?** in pairs or one student will read questions aloud and pick someone to answer them. If you do all the questions, you may wish to skip **Et vous?** (5 min.)
5. Have students do **Et vous?** with a partner or read silently, then volunteer to read questions of their choice. (5 min.)
6. **Il y a un problème:** Have students pick the best answer and justify their choice. Justification may be in English or French depending on language skills and teacher preference. May be done individually or in groups. (10 min.)
7. Introduction to structure of **Épisode 2.** (15 min.)

Total class time: 50 min.

Assignment: Written activities for **Épisode 2** in workbook and reading of **Épisode 3** story with selected questions from **Avez-vous compris?** and **Et vous?** written.

Sample Syllabi

Semester System

45 contact hours; each class is 50 minutes and meets three times a week for fifteen weeks.

The following first-semester syllabus is predicated upon completion of all structures and active vocabulary presented in *À l'aventure.*

Week 1: **Chapitre Préliminaire** and **Chapitre 1:** Greeting people, counting, days of the week, talking about the weather, useful expressions and classroom commands. **Structures IA–IB, Vous êtes branchés!**

Week 2: **Structure II, Il y a un problème, Structures III–IV, Révision éclair.**

Week 3: **Chapitre 2: Vous êtes branchés!, Structure IA,** courses of study, **Structure IB,** school supplies, **Structures IIA–IIB.**

Week 4: Color and clothing, **Structure III, Il y a un problème/À vous de jouer, Structure IV, Révision éclair, Lecture** (optional).

Week 5: **Chapitre 3: Vous êtes branchés!, Structures IA–IB,** in and around the house **Structure II,** members of the family.

Week 6: **Il y a un problème, Structure III,** physical descriptions, **Structures IVA–IVB, À vos stylos** (optional).

Week 7: **Chapitre 4:** Telling time, **Structure I, Vous êtes branchés!, Structures IIA–IIB,** day, months, and seasons.

Week 8: **Structures IIIA–IIIB,** professions, **Structures IVA–IVB,** neighborhood locales, **Lecture** (optional), **Révision éclair.**

Week 9: **Chapitre 5:** Nationalities, countries, and continents, **Structure IA,** stores and services, **Structure IB, Vous êtes branchés!, Structures IIA–IIB,** means of transportation.

Week 10: **Structures IIIA–IIIB,** back to school, **Structure IV,** giving directions, **Lecture** (optional), **Rencontres.**

Week 11: **Chapitre 6: Structure I,** drinks and snacks, **Vous êtes branchés!,** meals and everyday food, **Structures II–III.**

Week 12: Numbers, **Il y a un problème/À vous de jouer, Structure IV, À vos stylos** (optional), **Révision éclair.**

Week 13: **Chapitre 7: Vous êtes branchés!, Structure I,** things you say, write, and read, **Structure II, Il y a un problème/À vous de jouer, Structure III.**

Week 14: French-speaking countries and nationalities, **Structure IV, Lecture** (optional), **Rencontres, Révision éclair.**

Week 15: May be used for review before final exam or for test days* during the semester.

Note that this sample syllabus can be trimmed to cover only 12 or 13 chapters by omitting certain structures such as the conditional, the relative pronoun **dont,** and the superlative. These structures can be covered easily in second year. If such a decision is made, instructors can spend more time on a wider variety of chapter sections, as well as maximize the use of components in the ancillary package, such as the video and the multi-media reading shell.

Semester system

60–75 contact hours; each class meets 4–5 times per week.

The above syllabus can easily be adapted to a class with more contact hours or that meets four or five days a week. A more in-depth study of vocabulary and structures may be implemented. Additionally, time may be spent on the story, **Vous êtes branchés!,** reading and writing strands, **Rencontres** and **Révision éclair,** and/or web sites indicated by the Wiley *À l'aventure* home page address: **http://www.wiley.com/aventure.html.** As a result, students will have the opportunity to deepen their understanding of the French-speaking world.

Quarter system

40 contact hours with 10 weeks per quarter; each class meets 4 times a week for 50 minutes per class.

Week 1: **Chapitre Préliminaire** and **Chapitre 1:** Greeting people, counting, days of the week, talking about the weather, useful expressions and classroom commands. **Structures IA–IB.**

---

*Test days and methods of evaluation have not been specified within the syllabi since testing is largely a matter of individual preference.

Week 2: **Vous êtes branchés!, Structure II, Il y a un problème, Structures III–IV, Révision éclair.**

Week 3: **Chapitre 2: Vous êtes branchés!, Structure IA,** courses of study, **Structure IB,** school supplies, **Structures IIA–IIB.**

Week 4: Color and clothing, **Structure III, Il y a un problème/À vous de jouer, Structure IV, Révision éclair, Lecture.**

Week 5: **Chapitre 3: Vous êtes branchés!, Structures IA–IB,** in and around the house, **Structure II,** members of the family.

Week 6: **Il y a un problème, Structure III,** physical descriptions, **Structures IVA–IVB, À vos stylos.**

Week 7: **Chapitre 4:** Telling time, **Structure I, Vous êtes branchés!, Structures IIA–IIB,** day, months, and seasons.

Week 8: **Structures IIIA–IIIB,** professions, **Structures IVA–IVB,** neighborhood locales, **Lecture, Révision éclair.**

Week 9: **Chapitre 5:** Nationalities, countries, and continents, **Structure IA,** stores and services, **Structure IB, Vous êtes branchés!, Structures IIA–IIB.**

Week 10: Means of transportation, **Structures IIIA–IIIB,** back to school, **Structure IV,** giving directions, **Lecture, Rencontres.**

À L'AVENTURE

AN INTRODUCTION TO FRENCH LANGUAGE AND FRANCOPHONE CULTURES

À L'AVENTURE

AN INTRODUCTION TO FRENCH LANGUAGE AND FRANCOPHONE CULTURES

Evelyne Charvier-Berman
El Camino College

Anne C. Cummings
El Camino College

JOHN WILEY & SONS, INC.

New York • Chichester • Brisbane • Toronto • Singapore • Weinheim

ACQUISITIONS EDITOR: Carlos Davis
SENIOR DEVELOPMENT EDITOR: Nancy Perry
SUPPLEMENTS EDITOR: Andrea Bryant
MARKETING MANAGER: Leslie Hines
SENIOR PRODUCTION EDITOR: Jeanine Furino
BOOK DESIGNER: Levavi/Levavi
ASSISTANT MANUFACTURING MANAGER: Mark Cirillo
PHOTO EDITOR: Hilary Newman
SENIOR ILLUSTRATION COORDINATOR: Anna Melhorn
COVER PHOTO: S. B. Photography/Tony Stone Images/New York, Inc.

This book was set in ITC Garamond Light by University Graphics, Inc. and printed and
bound by R. R. Donnelley & Sons. The cover was printed by
Phoenix Color.

Note: This book is a joint work of the two authors. To emphasize this, we have listed the author's names
in alphabetical order on the title page and in the Library of Congress cataloguing data, and in reverse
alphabetical order on the cover.

Library of Congress Cataloging-in-Publication Data
Charvier-Berman, Evelyne.
    À l'aventure : an introduction to French language and francophone
  culture / Evelyne Charvier-Berman, Anne C. Cummings.
        p.   cm.
    Includes index.
    ISBN 0-471-30943-5 (cloth : alk. paper)
    1. French language—Textbooks for foreign speakers—English.
  I. Cummings, Anne C.   II. Title.
  PC2129.E5C55   1997
  448.2'421—dc20   96-44828
                                                                    CIP

Printed in the United States of America

10 9 8 7 6 5 4 3 2 1

PREFACE

Bienvenus and welcome to *À l'aventure,* a new first-year French program, developed by a French-American team with over 35 years combined experience in the classroom. This book is the result of our desire to help prepare students for the linguistic and cultural challenges they will face in traveling around the French-speaking world. We have drawn upon our experiences in each other's cultures and the experiences of real students who have studied abroad to present a wide variety of realistic and practical contexts that students are likely to encounter.

You might be asking yourself "Why choose *À l'aventure* for my classes?" The answers are simple:

◆ *À l'aventure* is a unique program that offers a fully-integrated approach in which language and culture merge in a continuous storyline, providing a stimulating learning environment for students.
◆ *À l'aventure* offers a four-skill approach and frequent recycling throughout the text. Each skill is specifically developed throughout the book to help students learn vocabulary and grammar, understand written and spoken language, and to use the language to express their views and ideas in speaking and writing.
◆ The carefully crafted **Épisodes** of each chapter provide comprehensible input, with a great deal of visual support, as well as a natural context for the study of culture, language functions, vocabulary, and grammar.
◆ *À l'aventure* will broaden students' experiences and introduce them to the many facets of French language and francophone cultures as they encounter a variety of characters from the French-speaking world.

Highlights of the *À l'aventure* Program _____

◆ *An innovative visual approach, presented in the classic form of a French* **bande dessinée** *created specially for the book by a native French cartoonist.* Each **Épisode** is illustrated by four colorful panels that help explain the story while providing a culturally authentic environment.
◆ *Myriad opportunities to develop cultural understanding.* Often seeded in the story, cultural information about daily life in France is developed through **Vous êtes branchés** sections, while a broader view of Francophone countries and cultures is found in the **Rencontres** sections.
◆ *A clear, easy-to-use presentation of langauge structures that students can use on their own.*

◆ *Thematic vocabulary, which is acquired through multiple progressive uses.* Enticing illustrations introduce much of the new vocabulary and give students contexts in which to practice it. A set of transparencies, provided for classroom use, enlivens presentations. Vocabulary seeded in the story and/or presented in **Pour s'exprimer** and **Mots à utiliser** sections is used by students in communicative activities, interviews, or follow-up written assignments.

◆ **Il y a un problème** *and* **À vous de jouer** *sections that allow students to develop critical thinking skills as they make choices that are culturally and linguistically authentic.*

◆ *A completely integrated program of print and other media.* **À l'aventure** offers great flexibility and is designed to bring diversity to each class period. It provides stimulating pacing and rhythm through teacher-student interaction, pair work, and group work.

How Does a Chapter Work?

The consistent chapter organization of *À l'aventure* will help instructors decide on the best choices for individual classes. Each of the 15 chapters contains the following elements:

◆ **Présentation Éclair.** Each chapter begins with **Présentation éclair** to introduce the communicative goals **(Pour communiquer)**, the grammatical structures **(Pour y arriver)**, and cultural vignettes **(Pour s'adapter à la culture)**.

◆ **Épisodes.** There are four **Épisodes** of the continuing story in each chapter, each of which is followed by cultural information, communicative functions, grammar, new vocabulary, and activities. Students will gain a feeling of success as they complete each of these easily teachable units. (See below for more on how an **Épisode** works.)

◆ **Il y a un problème: qu'en pensez-vous?** and **À vous de jouer.** Appearing once a chapter, these critical thinking exercises allow students to use language they know as they decide how to solve problems emerging from the storyline.

◆ **Lecture.** In every chapter, a reading section provides strategies to enhance students' abilities to comprehend and analyze authentic texts ranging in complexity from advertisements and brochures to literary selections.

◆ **À vos stylos.** Occurring in Chapters 3, 6, 9, 12 and 15, a writing section provides strategies to enhance students' abilities to produce practical, everyday documents such as personal and business letters, notes, persuasive arguments, and three-part outlines.

◆ **Rencontres.** Found in Chapters 5, 7, 9, 11, 13 and 15, this section profiles a Francophone region, country, or **département** and through interesting interviews allows students to get a glimpse of the life of one of its inhabitants.

◆ **Révision éclair et activités.** For easy student review, a summary page of all structures and functions provides cross-references to the presentations in every chapter. Activities enable students to review and to check mastery of the material they have just studied. These culminating activities help students to synthesize themes, functions, cultural information, grammar, vocabulary and to discover just how far they have come in their study of French. **Mon journal,** a written activity in each chapter, provides students with the opportunity to further pursue and deepen their understanding of cultural differences and similarities while improving their writing skills.

◆ **Prononciation.** The sounds, rhythms, and other distinctive features of French pronunciation are presented in non-technical explanations in each chapter. They are followed by brief activities for learners to practice and check mastery of the points presented.

◆ **Vocabulaire actif.** All the active words and expressions are organized thematically at the end of every chapter for easy student reference.

How Does an *Épisode* Work? ───────────────

Each of the four **Épisodes** per chapter has the following components:

1. **Story.** This section, written in authentic language, presents one **Épisode** of the continuing story in a dialogue, narrative, or letter form that students can read or role-play. As students follow the adventures of recurring characters, they begin to develop an understanding of vocabulary, themes, cultural highlights, in an easy-to-understand format. The story is recorded in the audio program and its illustrations are available on overhead transparencies.

2. **Avez-vous compris?** and **Et vous?** Immediately following the **Épisode,** a set of questions serves as a quick comprehension check before students go on to the next section. Next, **Et vous?** questions allow the students to draw upon their personal experiences and relate them to the topics of the chapter.

3. **Vous êtes branchés!** Students explore some of the relevant cultural information of the chapter and test their cultural I. Q. **(Q. I. culturel)** in this section. Some World Wide Web addresses are provided via the John Wiley and Sons/À l'aventure home page so that students can deepen their cultural understanding and improve their language skills while exploring some Francophone sites.

4. **Functions and grammatical structures.** The new linguistic component of the **Épisode** is presented with ample examples and a clear explanation, followed by charts and other visual aids. Simply presented, the grammar explanations allow students to use the structures immediately with the vocabulary and activities that follow. Frequent recycling within the chapter and in subsequent chapters ensures mastery.

5. **Pour s'exprimer** and **Mots à utiliser.** Vocabulary presentation is first seeded in the continuing story and comprehension is supported by lively accompanying art. Then, active words and expressions are grouped thematically or functionally under **Pour s'exprimer** or **Mots à utiliser** headings, often presented through art. Students immediately use their newly acquired vocabulary in the activities that follow.

6. Activités. Highly contextualized communicative activities allow students to internalize what has been presented. Activities are organized in such a way that learners move from the simple to the complex, from carefully directed exercises to personalized expression. Controlled activities are designed for quick mastery of the structure and vocabulary presented, and prepare students for the more complex task of open-ended communication. These goals may be achieved individually, in pairs or in groups.

Other Components

The *À l'aventure* complete first-year program includes:

- The *main student textbook* of 15 chapters, containing notes to the students explaining how elements of the book work as they encounter each one.
- A *free student audio tape/CD,* shrinkwrapped with the student text, which includes all episodes of the story.
- An *Annotated Instructor's Edition,* which includes suggestions and tips for presenting and reinforcing the materials. Sample syllabi are also provided.
- More than *85 full-color transparencies* illustrating the continuing story, as well as maps and selected drawings from activities throughout the book.
- A *workbook/lab manual* to reinforce classroom activities and to develop writing and listening skills.
- An *audio program for the laboratory.*
- A *tapescript for audio materials.*
- A *testing program* that tests chapter structures, vocabulary, and cultural information.
- A *50-minute video cassette with a video guide,* tailored to the main text, to enhance students' awareness of French cultural situations.
- A *software drill-and-practice program* to supplement classroom and workbook activities, available in PC and Mac formats.
- An *interactive multi-media PC and Mac reading shell* containing readings from the book and an additional selection of literary readings from the Francophone world. All readings are classified according to level of difficulty and are supported with glossing and visual aids such as photos, video, and art.

Maintenant à vous de partir **À l'aventure.** *Bonne route!*

E. C.-B.
A. C. C.

ACKNOWLEDGMENTS

There are many individuals whose professional and personal support, suggestions, and insights have proved invaluable in the development of this text.

Un gros merci à

Our students who inspired us to write this text.

Mary Jane Peluso, who made our dream of writing this book possible.

Jean-Paul Buquet, wonderful French cartoonist and artist, whose lively illustrations in each **Épisode** and throughout the text make authentic French language and culture come alive for our readers.

Kristina Baer and Peggy Potter for the editing that helped shape this book.

Andréa Charvier and Christiane Girard for their indefatigable work in France.

Our friend and colleague Charles Donovan for his careful reading of the manuscript and for his many helpful remarks.

We are indebted to the Wiley team, whose experience, insights, and hours and hours of dedication made this book a reality:

Francine Banner, Andrea Bryant, Mark Cirillo, Carlos Davis, Jeanine Furino, Leslie Hines, Karin Kincheloe, Anna Melhorn, Hilary Newman, Nancy Perry, Matthew VanHattem, Jennifer Williams.

We would like to express our appreciation to the many reviewers who provided us with helpful suggestions and comments for several versions of the manuscript. Many thanks go to

Jean-Luc Desalvo, *San Jose State University;* Christiane Fleig-Hamm, *Queen's University;* Carole Hofmann, *University of Southern California;* Hannelore Jarausch, *University of North Carolina;* John Kane, *Kent State University;* Karen Kelton, *University of Texas at Austin;* Richard Ladd, *Northern Essex Community College;* Steven Loughrin-Sacco, *Boise State University;* James Mall, *Temple University;* Laurey Martin-Berg, *University of Wisconsin-Madison;* Joseph Murphy, *West Virginia University;* Demetra Palamari, *California State University-Los Angeles;* Ester Ratner, *Brandeis University;* Marco Roman, *University of Central Oklahoma;* Charline Sacks, *Nassau Community College;* Ellen Silber, *Marymount College;* Mary Ann Stadler-Chester, *Simmons College;* Alice Strange, *Southeast Missouri State University.*

A. C. C.
E. C.-B.

CONTENTS

	Pour communiquer *Communicative goals*

Contents

	Pour communiquer
	Communicative goals

Contents

Contents

KEY TO SYMBOLS THAT APPEAR IN À L'AVENTURE

 Paired or Group Conversational Activity

 Writing Activity

 Material recorded on the student tape or audio CD that accompanies each text

 Readings

 Material relating to the Francophone world.

 Material recorded in the audio program for the laboratory

Dear Student,

Bienvenu and welcome to *À l'aventure,* an exciting new first-year French program. If you have never studied French before, (or even if you have!) you may find the following suggestions helpful.

◆ Attend class regularly and be ready to participate fully. It may seem obvious to say "Do your homework!," but it is one of the most important factors in your success in French class. Keeping up with assignments is essential if you are going to be prepared to speak, work with partners, and answer the questions your teacher may ask.

◆ Be prepared to spend at least one hour outside of class for every hour in the classroom. This does not mean five hours the night before the test! Study a little bit every day and your results will be much better.

◆ Make use of all the materials that are available with the text. The CD/tape and video provided with the text will give you the opportunity to experience French outside the classroom. Check the Wiley home page on the Internet (http://www.wiley.com/aventure.html) for extra cultural information.

◆ Familiarize yourself with the features of *À l'aventure* that will help you succeed in this course. (You will find an in-depth presentation of these and other features in the preface and within the chapters.)

   La bande dessinée: Every chapter offers 16 color cartoon panels that you can use to check and/or improve your comprehension of French. **La bande dessinée** is an authentic and intrinsic part of French culture used to communicate humorous as well as serious messages to readers of all ages.

   L'histoire: You will learn authentic French structures and vocabulary in the natural setting of a story, the way French students learn their own language. You will quickly develop your reading skills, increase vocabulary, and familiarize yourself with good written and spoken French, since you will have the opportunity to practice them at least four times per chapter. Using what you have learned about French culture and language from the story, you will be able to talk about your own experiences and ideas.

   Vocabulaire Actif: For your convenience, this section at the end of every chapter provides you with a comprehensive list of words and phrases you need to know.

   Révision éclair: You will be able to quickly locate and review the major points of each chapter by referring to the first page of the **Révision élair** section. The activities that follow will help you check your knowledge and/or prepare for a test.

Now join in the fun and begin *À l'aventure!*

Evelyne Charvier-Berman
Anne C. Cummings

LA MER DU NORD

L'ANGLETERRE

LES PAYS-BAS

L'ALLEMAGNE

LA MANCHE

Calais

Lille

LA BELGIQUE

LE LUXEMBOURG

NORD-PAS-DE-CALAIS

Le Havre

HAUTE-NORMANDIE

Rouen

PICARDIE

Reims

LORRAINE

Brest

BASSE-NORMANDIE

La Seine

Paris

ÎLE-DE-FRANCE

CHAMPAGNE-ARDENNES

La Seine

Strasbourg

Les Vosges

ALSACE

BRETAGNE

PAYS DE LA LOIRE

Orléans

La Loire

CENTRE

BOURGOGNE

FRANCHE-COMTÉ

Le Jura

Nantes

Dijon

LA FRANCE

LA SUISSE

L'OCÉAN ATLANTIQUE

La Rochelle

POITOU-CHARENTES

LIMOUSIN

Clermont-Ferrand

Lyon

Le Massif

Bordeaux

La Garonne

AUVERGNE

Central

RHÔNE-ALPES

Grenoble

L'ITALIE

Les Alpes

Le Rhône

AQUITAINE

MIDI-PYRÉNÉES

LANGUEDOC-ROUSSILLON

PROVENCE-ALPES-CÔTE D'AZUR

Avignon

Aix-en-Provence

Marseille

Nice

Cannes

MONACO

Les Pyrénées

ANDORRE

L'ESPAGNE

LA MER MÉDITERRANÉE

LA CORSE

Ajaccio

La France et ses régions

0		100		200 Milles

0	100		200 Kilomètres

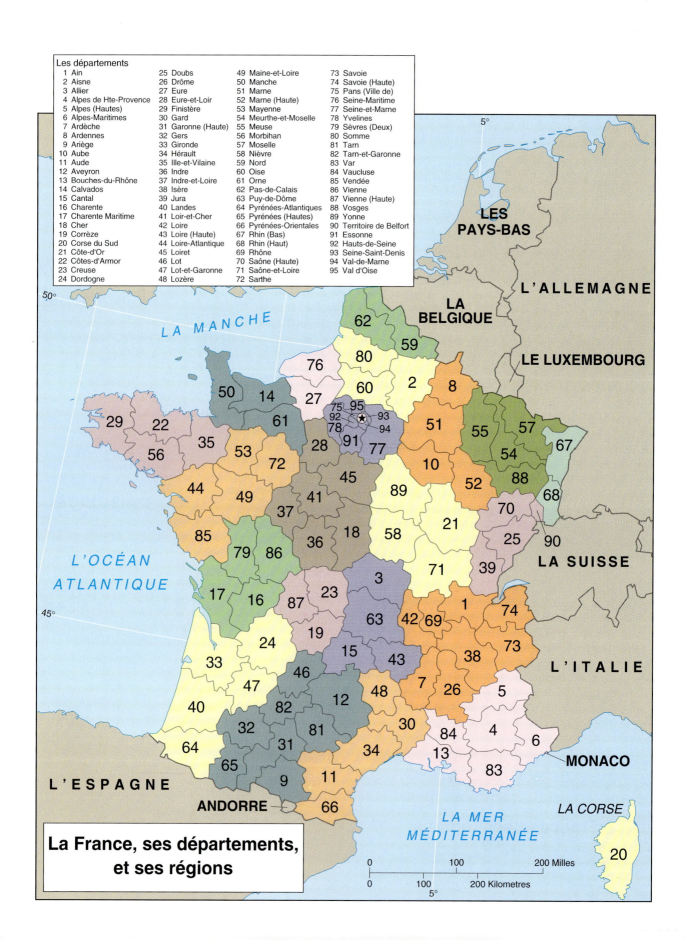

Les départements

1 Ain	25 Doubs	49 Maine-et-Loire	73 Savoie
2 Aisne	26 Drôme	50 Manche	74 Savoie (Haute)
3 Allier	27 Eure	51 Marne	75 Pans (Ville de)
4 Alpes de Hte-Provence	28 Eure-et-Loir	52 Marne (Haute)	76 Seine-Maritime
5 Alpes (Hautes)	29 Finistère	53 Mayenne	77 Seine-et-Marne
6 Alpes-Maritimes	30 Gard	54 Meurthe-et-Moselle	78 Yvelines
7 Ardèche	31 Garonne (Haute)	55 Meuse	79 Sèvres (Deux)
8 Ardennes	32 Gers	56 Morbihan	80 Somme
9 Ariège	33 Gironde	57 Moselle	81 Tarn
10 Aube	34 Hérault	58 Nièvre	82 Tarn-et-Garonne
11 Aude	35 Ille-et-Vilaine	59 Nord	83 Var
12 Aveyron	36 Indre	60 Oise	84 Vaucluse
13 Bouches-du-Rhône	37 Indre-et-Loire	61 Orne	85 Vendée
14 Calvados	38 Isère	62 Pas-de-Calais	86 Vienne
15 Cantal	39 Jura	63 Puy-de-Dôme	87 Vienne (Haute)
16 Charente	40 Landes	64 Pyrénées-Atlantiques	88 Vosges
17 Charente Maritime	41 Loir-et-Cher	65 Pyrénées (Hautes)	89 Yonne
18 Cher	42 Loire	66 Pyrénées-Orientales	90 Territoire de Belfort
19 Corrèze	43 Loire (Haute)	67 Rhin (Bas)	91 Essonne
20 Corse du Sud	44 Loire-Atlantique	68 Rhin (Haut)	92 Hauts-de-Seine
21 Côte-d'Or	45 Loiret	69 Rhône	93 Seine-Saint-Denis
22 Côtes-d'Armor	46 Lot	70 Saône (Haute)	94 Val-de-Marne
23 Creuse	47 Lot-et-Garonne	71 Saône-et-Loire	95 Val d'Oise
24 Dordogne	48 Lozère	72 Sarthe	

La France, ses départements, et ses régions

Le Canada

LE YUKON

LES TERRITOIRES DU NORD-EST

LA BAIE D'HUDSON

LA TERRE-NEUVE

LA COLOMBIE BRITANNIQUE

L'ALBERTA

LE LABRADOR

LA SASKAT-CHEWAN

LE MANITOBA

LE QUÉBEC

Edmonton

Calgary

Saskatoon

Regina

ST PIERRE-ET-MIQUELON (FR)

Vancouver

L'ONTARIO (m)

LE NOUVEAU-BRUNSWICK

Seattle

Winnipeg

Le Missouri

Le Saint-Laurent

Québec

Halifax

L'ÎLE DU PRINCE-EDOUARD

Montréal

L'OCÉAN PACIFIQUE

Ottawa

LA NOUVELLE-ÉCOSSE

Toronto

Boston

L'OCÉAN ATLANTIQUE

Minneapolis

Le Lac Supérieur

Le Lac Michigan

Le Lac Huron

Le Lac Ontario

Le Lac Érié

New York

Le Mississippi

Chicago

0   250   500 Milles

0   250   500 Kilometres

LE QUÉBEC

SAINT-PIERRE-
ET-MIQUELON

LA LOUISIANE

LA NOUVELLE-
ANGLETERRE

LA GUADELOUPE

LA MAURITANIE

HAÏTI

LA MARTINIQUE

LE SÉNÉGAL

LA GUINÉE

LA GUYANE
FRANÇAISE

LA POLYNÉSIE FRANÇAISE

Le Monde Francophone

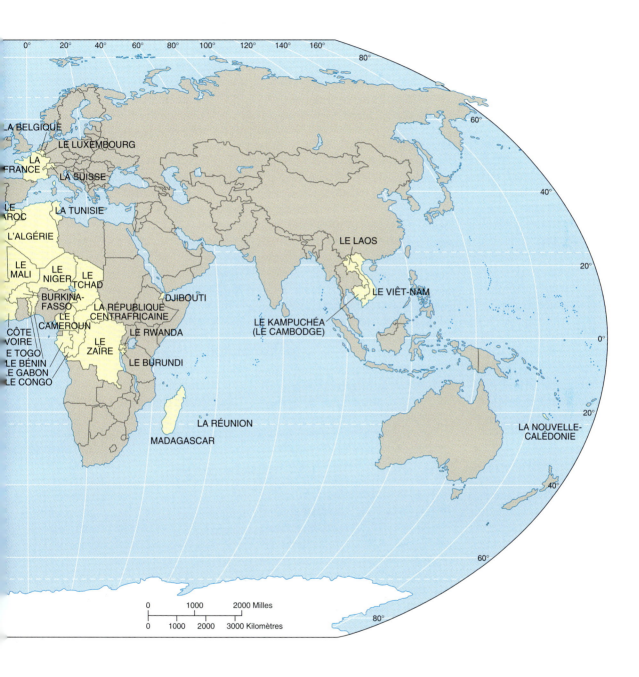

LA BELGIQUE
LE LUXEMBOURG
LA
FRANCE
LA SUISSE
LE
AROC
LA TUNISIE
L'ALGÉRIE
LE
MALI
LE
NIGER
LE
TCHAD
BURKINA-
FASSO
LA RÉPUBLIQUE
CENTRAFRICAINE
DJIBOUTI
LE
CAMEROUN
CÔTE
VOIRE
E TOGO
LE BÉNIN
E GABON
LE CONGO
LE RWANDA
LE
ZAÏRE
LE BURUNDI
LE LAOS
LE VIÊT-NAM
LE KAMPUCHÉA
(LE CAMBODGE)
LA RÉUNION
MADAGASCAR
LA NOUVELLE-
CALÉDONIE

0°   20°   40°   60°   80°   100°   120°   140°   160°
80°
60°
40°
20°
0°
20°
40°
60°
80°

0   1000   2000 Milles
0   1000   2000   3000 Kilomètres

xxvii

Chapitre préliminaire ◆ BONJOUR TOUT LE MONDE!

PRÉSENTATION ÉCLAIR

Les salutations
L'alphabet
Les nombres de 0 à 31
L'heure

Les jours de la semaine
Le temps
La salle de classe: vocabulaire pratique

JE VOUS PRÉSENTE... T5

BENJAMIN: Salut°, les étudiants°. Ça va?°
Je m'appelle° Benjamin. Je vous présente° mon
amie° Julie.

Salut *Hi* / **les étudiants** *students* / **Ça va?** *How's it
going?* / **Je m'appelle** *My name is* / **Je vous présente**
Let me introduce you to / **mon amie** *my (female) friend*

JULIE: Bonjour tout le monde°. Comment
allez-vous?° Moi, je vais bien.° Je m'appelle Julie
Lavalette et j'habite à° Monterey.

Bonjour tout le monde *Hello everybody* / **Comment
allez-vous?** *How are you?* / **Moi, je vais bien.** *I'm fine.* /
et j'habite à *and I live in*

The preliminary chapter of *À l'aventure* will
provide you with a brief introduction to the
vocabulary and culture you will need to make a
smooth entrance into the French-speaking
world. You will learn to greet people, make
small talk about time and weather, and learn
basic classroom vocabulary and commands.
Much of what you discover in the **Chapitre
préliminaire** will be re-explained and re-used
in subsequent chapters.

JULIE: Cette année°, Benjamin et moi, nous sommes° étudiants en France.

Cette année *This year* / **Benjamin et moi, nous sommes** *Benjamin and I are*

JULIE: Benjamin étudie° à Grenoble, et moi, j'étudie à Rouen. Et vous?°

étudie *studies* / **Et vous?** *And what about you?*

Here you meet two of the main characters in a story that continues throughout the text. Illustrated in the time-honored style of French cartoons, the story introduces you to the language and culture you will study. Look for the 🎧 symbol; it indicates which material is recorded on the student CD/tape.

I LES SALUTATIONS *(Greetings)*

Culture. In French, as in English, you need to be aware of both formal and informal levels of speech and you need to be able to use each when it is appropriate. For example, you don't address your best friend the way you address your boss. While you talk in a familiar/informal way to your friends *(Hi! How's it going?)*, you need to use proper form *(Good morning, Mr. Smith)* to address an older person, teacher, or boss.

Salut, ça va?

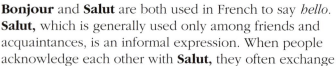

Bonjour. Comment allez-vous?

Bonjour and **Salut** are both used in French to say *hello*. **Salut,** which is generally used only among friends and acquaintances, is an informal expression. When people acknowledge each other with **Salut,** they often exchange at least two kisses (sometimes three or four depending on the region) or a simple wave of the hand. **Bonjour** is frequently accompanied by a handshake, a formal way of greeting an equal or a superior.

Greetings are usually followed by a term of direct address: either a person's name or a word such as **Monsieur, Madame,** or **Mademoiselle.** When you greet someone using **Bonjour, Monsieur** *(Hello/Good morning/Good afternoon, sir)* or **Bonjour, Madame** *(Hello/Good morning/Good afternoon, ma'am),* you should *not* include the person's family name the way you would in English *(Hello, Mrs. Walker).*

Bonjour, monsieur.

Ça va? and **Comment allez-vous?** are both used to ask *How are you?* **Ça va?** is informal and is used with the same people whom you greet with **Salut. Comment allez-vous?** is more formal. **Quoi de neuf?** is an additional greeting to find out what's new with your close friends.

When saying *goodbye,* you may use either **Salut** or **Au revoir** for close friends. **Au revoir, Madame / Monsieur** is more appropriate for less personal relationships.

Bonjour, madame.

Pour s'exprimer. New words and expressions are provided for you in list form, together with their English equivalents. Study them; they will be part of your active French vocabulary.

POUR S'EXPRIMER *(EXPRESSING YOURSELF)*

Les salutations

◆ To greet someone, say

FORMAL:	Bonjour, Monsieur.	*Good morning, Mr. Dupont.*
	Bonjour, Madame.	*Hello, Mrs. Durand.*
	Bonjour, Mademoiselle.	*Good afternoon, Miss Duprès.*
INFORMAL:	Salut, Paul!	*Hi, Paul!*

◆ To ask and give someone's name, say

FORMAL:	Comment vous appelez-vous?	*What's your name?*
	Je m'appelle Martin, Henri Martin.	*My name is Henri Martin.*
INFORMAL:	Comment t'appelles-tu?	*What's your name?*
	Je m'appelle Sara.	*My name is Sara.*

◆ To ask and tell how someone is, say

FORMAL:	Comment allez-vous?	*How are you?*
	Je vais bien, merci beaucoup. Et vous?	*I'm fine, thank you very much. And you?*
	Très bien, merci.	*Very well, thank you.*
INFORMAL:	Comment ça va?	*How's it going?; How are you doing?*
	Ça va bien, merci. Et toi?	*I'm doing fine, thanks. And you?*
or	Ça va?	*How's it going?; How are you doing?*
	Oui, ça va.	*Fine, thanks.*

◆ To introduce someone, say

FORMAL:	Je vous présente mon ami. Il s'appelle Benjamin.	*Let me introduce you to my friend. His name is Benjamin.*
INFORMAL:	Je te présente mon amie. Elle s'appelle Adèle.	*This is my friend. Her name is Adèle.*
	Voilà Adèle.	*This is Adèle.*

In either case, when you are introduced, you can say **Enchanté(e).** *Pleased to meet you.*

◆ To ask where someone lives, say

| FORMAL: | Où habitez-vous? | |
| INFORMAL: | Où habites-tu? | *Where do you live?* |

The answer is

| | J'habite à Montréal. | *I live in Montreal.* |

◆ To say goodbye, say

| FORMAL: | Au revoir, monsieur / madame / mademoiselle. | *Goodbye, Mr./Mrs./Ms. Smith; Goodbye, sir/ma'am/miss.* |
| INFORMAL: | Salut, Paul! | *Bye, Paul!* |

Au revoir, tout le monde.

ACTIVITÉS

1. Il dit bonjour à... Benjamin had several conversations this morning. For each exchange, tell who he was talking to: une femme? Julie? un professeur?

■ **WORD TO USE: une femme** *a woman*

1. —Salut! Ça va?
    —Oui, ça va. Et toi?
    —Bien!

3. —Bonjour, Monsieur. Comment allez-vous?
    —Très bien. Merci beaucoup.

2. —Bonjour, Madame. Comment allez-vous?
    —Très bien. Merci.

2. Je vous présente... Choose a couple of classmates that your partner doesn't know and introduce them to him or her. Also introduce your teacher formally to him or her. Your partner will respond appropriately.

MODÈLE: FORMEL: **Je vous présente mon ami Paul / M. Jones.**
  FAMILIER: **Voilà Paul.**

3. Dites bonjour à vos voisins! Greet the people around you. Don't forget to shake their hand. Say hello, ask for their names, find out how they are and where they live, then say goodbye.

II   L'ALPHABET

Listen to your professor or your lab tape and repeat the name of each letter.

A B C D E F G H I J K L M N O P Q R S T U V W X Y Z

III   LES NOMBRES DE 0 À 31

POUR S'EXPRIMER			
Les nombres de 0 à 31			
0 zéro	10 dix	20 vingt	30 trente
1 un	11 onze	21 vingt et un	31 trente et un
2 deux	12 douze	22 vingt-deux	
3 trois	13 treize	23 vingt-trois	
4 quatre	14 quatorze	24 vingt-quatre	
5 cinq	15 quinze	25 vingt-cinq	
6 six	16 seize	26 vingt-six	
7 sept	17 dix-sept	27 vingt-sept	
8 huit	18 dix-huit	28 vingt-huit	
9 neuf	19 dix-neuf	29 vingt-neuf	
3 + 6 = 9 Trois plus six font neuf.			

Now may be a good time to have students spell some of the words they have learned up to now, for example: **Monsieur, Mademoiselle, Madame, bonjour, merci.**

Extension. You may also wish to introduce **accent grave, accent aigu, accent circonflexe,** and **cédille** and to give students examples of how they affect the sounds of the letters: **é, è, â, ç.**

Pronunciation. Point out that in the numbers 21–29, the **t** in **vingt** must be clearly and distinctly pronounced.

ACTIVITÉS

4. Et les mathématiques! It's time to show your math skills. See how well you can add in French. Say the complete problem aloud as you solve it.

MODÈLE: 2 + 4 =

Deux plus quatre font six.

1. 1 + 3 = **5.** 5 + 7 = **9.** 12 + 19 =
2. 6 + 9 = **6.** 8 + 13 = **10.** 26 + 4 =
3. 10 + 14 = **7.** 11 + 15 =
4. 20 + 5 = **8.** 2 + 16 =

 5. Votre numéro de téléphone, s'il vous plaît! Ask three people in your class for their names and telephone numbers in case you miss an assignment. Write the information down.

■ **WORDS TO USE: Épelez** *spell* / **s'il vous plaît** *please* / **votre** *your*

MODÈLE: —**Comment vous appelez-vous?**
—**Je m'appelle Dubuis, Evelyne Dubuis.**
—**Épelez Dubuis, s'il vous plaît.**
—**D.U.B.U.I.S.**
—**Votre numéro de téléphone, s'il vous plaît.**
—**555-9853.**

IV L'HEURE `T 6`

A detailed explanation of telling time will be given in Chapter 4, p. 114.

POUR S'EXPRIMER

L'heure

◆ To ask and tell the time, say

Quelle heure est-il? *What time is it?*
Il est une heure. *It's one o'clock.*

Il est cinq heures.

Il est cinq heures et quart.

Il est cinq heures vingt-cinq.

Il est cinq heures et demie.

Il est six heures moins vingt.

Il est six heures moins le quart.

Il est minuit.

Il est midi.

You may want to have students write the problems on the board or their own papers while another student dictates them.

For extra number practice, you may wish to teach **moins** and **fois** and ask students to quiz each other on simple mathematical problems.

Culture. Tell students that French phone numbers are usually made up of eight digits and read in pairs. However, for **Activité 5,** have students read each number separately.

Quelle heure est-il?

Presentation. Have students look at each clock in the presentation and read the time. Have them also compare the spelling of **heures** in these examples with the spelling in the examples **Quelle heure est-il?** and **Il est une heure.**

ACTIVITÉ

 6. Quelle heure est-il? For each clock, ask your partner what time it is. Your partner will tell you.

MODÈLE:

—Quelle heure est-il?
—Il est trois heures moins le quart.

1.   2.   3.   4.

5.   6.  7.  8.

V LES JOURS DE LA SEMAINE *(The days of the week)*

POUR S'EXPRIMER

Les jours de la semaine

◆ To ask and tell what day it is today, say

Quel jour est-ce aujourd'hui?	*What day is it today?*
C'est lundi.	*It's Monday.*

◆ To ask and tell what the date is, say

Quelle est la date aujourd'hui?	*What is the date today?*
C'est le 12.	*It's the 12th.*

Note:
1. The first day of the week on a French calendar is **lundi.**
2. Contrary to English, days of the week are not capitalized in French.

12 lundi	Monday
13 mardi	Tuesday
14 mercredi	Wednesday
15 jeudi	Thursday
16 vendredi	Friday
17 samedi	Saturday
Sunday	dimanche 18

ACTIVITÉ

 7. Quel jour est-ce? You are trying to figure out on which days of the week your appointments fall. Ask your partner, who will respond.

MODÈLE: —Quel jour est le 15?
—C'est un jeudi.

You will learn how to give a complete date in Chapter 4, p. 120.

1. le 24?   4. le 2?   7. le 12?
2. le 13?   5. le 16?   8. le 8?
3. le 9?   6. le 21?

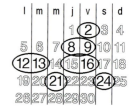

POUR S'EXPRIMER

Le temps `T 7`

◆ To ask and tell about the weather today, say

Aujourd'hui, quel temps fait-il à Dakar?	*Today, what's the weather like in Dakar?*
Aujourd'hui, il fait chaud à Dakar.	*Today, it's hot in Dakar.*

Il fait du soleil.
Il fait beau.

Il pleut.
Il fait mauvais.

Il fait chaud.

Il neige.
Il fait froid.

Il fait du vent.

http://www.wiley.com/aventure.html

ACTIVITÉS

  8. Aujourd'hui, quel temps fait-il à...? You are thinking about taking a trip soon and are curious about the weather in various places around the world.

Point out to students that the cities in **Activité 8** are found all around the French-speaking world.

MODÈLE: Dakar

—**Aujourd'hui, quel temps fait-il à Dakar?**
—**Aujourd'hui, il fait beau à Dakar.**

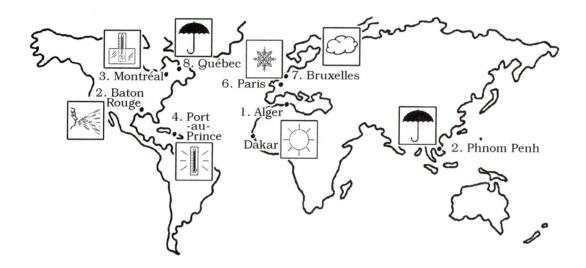

9. Moi, j'adore... Tell your partner two places you adore and describe what the weather is like there at this time of year.

■ **WORDS TO USE: maintenant** *now*/**moi** *I*

MODÈLE: Moi, j'adore Paris et Londres. Il fait froid à Paris maintenant. Il pleut à Londres.

POUR S'EXPRIMER

Dans la salle de classe `T 8`

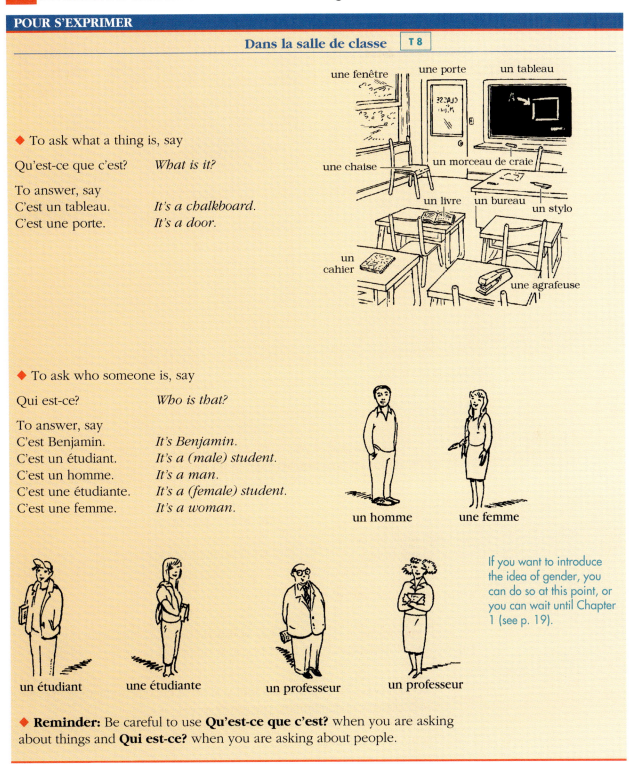

◆ To ask what a thing is, say

Qu'est-ce que c'est?   *What is it?*

To answer, say
C'est un tableau.   *It's a chalkboard.*
C'est une porte.   *It's a door.*

une fenêtre   une porte   un tableau

une chaise   un morceau de craie

un livre   un bureau   un stylo

un cahier

une agrafeuse

◆ To ask who someone is, say

Qui est-ce?   *Who is that?*

To answer, say
C'est Benjamin.   *It's Benjamin.*
C'est un étudiant.   *It's a (male) student.*
C'est un homme.   *It's a man.*
C'est une étudiante.   *It's a (female) student.*
C'est une femme.   *It's a woman.*

un homme   une femme

un étudiant   une étudiante   un professeur   un professeur

If you want to introduce the idea of gender, you can do so at this point, or you can wait until Chapter 1 (see p. 19).

◆ **Reminder:** Be careful to use **Qu'est-ce que c'est?** when you are asking about things and **Qui est-ce?** when you are asking about people.

Expressions utiles dans la classe

Learning the following phrases will help you participate effectively in class.

oui	*yes*
non	*no*
s'il vous plaît	*please*
un mot	*a word*
Entrez.	*Come in.*
Sortez.	*Leave; Go out.*
Ouvrez votre livre.	*Open your book.*
Fermez votre livre.	*Close your book.*
Allez au tableau.	*Go to the board.*
Écrivez votre nom.	*Write your (last) name.*
Rendez vos devoirs.	*Turn in your homework.*
Écoutez.	*Listen.*
Effacez le tableau.	*Erase the board.*
Épelez.	*Spell.*
Ensemble.	*Together.*
Répétez s'il vous plaît.	*Repeat, please.*
Je ne sais pas.	*I don't know.*
Je ne comprends pas.	*I don't understand.*

Dans la salle de classe.

Pronunciation practice. Write many of these terms on the board. Teach the word **mot** and then erase one word at a time, asking, **Quel mot est-ce que j'ai effacé?** Students must say aloud each erased word.

ACTIVITÉS

10. En français! If you were a French teacher, what would you tell your students if you wanted them to do the following?

1. listen
2. repeat
3. open their books
4. go to the board
5. write their name
6. leave; get out
7. come in
8. close their books

What should you say when . . . ?

9. you don't know
10. you don't understand
11. you want to know who someone is
12. you want to know what something is

11. À vous! *Your turn!* Now that you have become familiar with some basic classroom commands, get ready to become the teacher. Your partner is your student. Give your partner commands and ask questions. Then exchange roles.

◆ V O C A B U L A I R E   A C T I F ◆

Vocabulaire actif. Each chapter ends with a list of the new words and expressions from this chapter; these should now be part of your active French vocabulary.

Les salutations *Greetings*

Au revoir   *Goodbye*
Bonjour   *Hello*
Monsieur   *Sir, Mr. + last name*
Madame   *Ma'am, Mrs. + last name*
Mademoiselle   *Miss, Ms. + last name*
Salut   *Hi*
Comment allez-vous?   *How are you?* (formal)
Je vais bien, merci.   *I'm fine, thanks.*
Comment ça va?   *How are you?* (informal)
Ça va bien, merci.   *Fine, thanks.*

(Comment) ça va?   *How's it going?*
Ça va très bien!   *It's going very well.*
Quoi de neuf?   *What's new?*
Comment vous appelez-vous?   *What's your name?* (formal)
Comment t'appelles-tu?   *What's your name?* (informal)
Je m'appelle...   *My name is . . .*
Il / Elle s'appelle...   *His/Her name is . . .*
Je vous présente mon amie.   *Let me introduce you to my friend; I'd like you to meet my friend.* (formal)

Je te présente mon ami Paul.   *I'd like you to meet my friend Paul.* (informal)
Voilà mon ami Paul.   *Here's my friend Paul.* (informal)
Enchanté(e).   *Pleased to meet you.*
Où habitez-vous?   *Where do you live?* (formal)
Où habites-tu?   *Where do you live?* (informal)
J'habite à...   *I live in . . . (city)*

Les nombres

les nombres de 0 à 31
see p. 6

plus   *plus* (in math)

font   *are* (in math)

L'heure *Time*

Quelle heure est-il?   *What time is it?*
Il est midi.   *It's noon.*
Il est minuit.   *It's midnight.*

Il est une heure.   *It's one o'clock.*
et quart   *quarter past*
et demi(e)   *half past*

moins vingt   *twenty (minutes) to*
moins le quart   *quarter to*

Les jours de la semaine *The days of the week*

lundi   *Monday*
mardi   *Tuesday*
mercredi   *Wednesday*
jeudi   *Thursday*
vendredi   *Friday*

samedi   *Saturday*
dimanche   *Sunday*
aujourd'hui   *today*
Quel jour est-ce?   *What day is it?*

C'est lundi.   *It's Monday.*
Quelle est la date aujourd'hui?   *What's the date today?*
C'est le 12.   *It's the 12th.*

Le temps *Weather*

Quel temps fait-il? *What's the weather (like)?*
Il fait beau. *It's nice (out).*
Il fait chaud. *It's hot.*

Il fait froid. *It's cold.*
Il fait mauvais. *It's nasty, bad weather.*
Il fait du soleil. *It's sunny.*

Il fait du vent. *It's windy.*
Il neige. *It's snowing.*
Il pleut. *It's raining.*

Dans la salle de classe

Qu'est-ce que c'est? *What is it?; What's that?*
C'est un / c'est une... *It's a . . .*
une agrafeuse *a stapler*
un bureau *a desk*
un cahier *a notebook*
une chaise *a chair*
une fenêtre *a window*
un livre *a book*
un morceau de craie *a piece of chalk*
un mot *a word*
une porte *a door*
un stylo *a pen*
un tableau *a chalkboard*

Qui est-ce? *Who is it?; Who is that?*
C'est... *It's . . . , He is . . . , She is . . .*
un ami *a (male) friend*
une amie *a (female) friend*
un étudiant *a (male) student*
une étudiante *a (female) student*
une femme *a woman*
un homme *a man*
un professeur *a teacher (male or female)*
Allez au tableau. *Go to the board.*
Écoutez. *Listen.*
Écrivez votre nom. *Write your (last) name.*
Effacez le tableau. *Erase the board.*

Ensemble. *Together.*
Entrez. *Come in.*
Épelez, s'il vous plaît. *Spell (it), please.*
Fermez votre livre. *Close your book.*
Je ne sais pas. *I don't know.*
Je ne comprends pas. *I don't understand.*
Ouvrez votre livre. *Open your book.*
Rendez vos devoirs. *Turn in your homework.*
Répétez. *Repeat.*
Sortez. *Leave; Go out.*

Autres mots et expressions *Other words and expressions*

beaucoup *a lot, very much*
et *and*
et toi? *and you?*
et vous? *and you?*
maintenant *now*

moi *me*
non *no*
où *where*
oui *yes*

s'il vous plaît *please*
très *very*
voilà *here's*
votre *your*

Chapitre 1 ◆ **L'ARRIVÉE**

PRÉSENTATION ÉCLAIR

POUR COMMUNIQUER

Describing people and identifying location
Describing people and identifying nationality
Identifying things
Ordering drinks and snacks
Talking about your activities

A photograph and the chapter title set the scene for you in each chapter of *À l'aventure.* Use these elements and the lists of goals in the **Présentation éclair** *(Quick Presentation)* as a road map to the French language and culture you will learn in the chapter.

POUR Y ARRIVER

Les pronoms personnels sujets
Le verbe **être**
Les adjectifs qualificatifs
L'article indéfini
Les verbes réguliers en **-er**

POUR S'ADAPTER À LA CULTURE

Les gares de Paris et le TGV
La télécarte

PREMIER ÉPISODE T9

Benjamin est° un étudiant américain. Il est grand° et blond.

est *is* / **Il est grand** *He is tall*

Il est sympathique°, optimiste, et énergique mais° un peu paresseux.°

sympathique *nice* / **mais** *but* / **un peu paresseux** *a little lazy*

Épisodes. The story continues, now in four **Épisodes** per chapter. Use the art to help you understand the new language you are learning; English translations for words that may not be understood from the art are provided. As you get to know the characters and you become more skilled in French, you'll have the opportunity to give your opinion on the issues they face in daily life. The   symbol tells you that this material is part of the student CD/tape. Listening to the native French speaker's pronunciation and intonation as the story unfolds can help you understand and remember the text better.

AVEZ-VOUS COMPRIS?

(Did you understand?)

What have you learned about Benjamin? Answer the questions using either **oui** or **non.** Try to answer without looking back at the text.

1. Benjamin est un étudiant français?
2. Il est grand?
3. Il est blond?
4. Il est pessimiste?
5. Il arrive à Paris?
6. Il cherche Monsieur Bouverot?
7. Madame Bouverot est la mère de Benjamin?

Il arrive à la gare° de Grenoble.

—————
gare *station*

Il cherche° Mme Bouverot. Qui est-ce? C'est sa mère française.° Où est-elle?°

—————
Il cherche *He's looking for* / **C'est sa mère française.**
She's his French mother. / **Où est-elle?** *Where is she?*

ET VOUS?

(And you?)

1. Vous êtes *(You are)* optimiste?
2. Vous êtes pessimiste?
3. Vous êtes énergique?

Following each **Épisode** is **Avez-vous compris?**, a quick exercise to help you see if you have understood the material and **Et vous?**, a set of questions that give you the chance to talk about your own situation.

Presentation and Extension. Avez vous compris? and **Et vous?** Start each of these activities by having students answer using **oui** or **non.** Then, if you wish, model how to answer more completely using information found in the question or in the **Épisode.** For **Et vous?**, you may wish to teach **je suis** and have students ask and answer these questions in pairs.

VOUS ÊTES BRANCHÉS! *(You're in the know!)*

Les gares de Paris et le TGV

When your flight lands in Paris at Roissy-Charles-de-Gaulle or at Orly, you can take the bus, a taxi, or the RER **(Réseau Express Régional),** a suburban train line, to one of Paris's many train stations. Paris is at the hub of a vast network of train lines that link the various regions of France. Depending on your final destination, you will go to the **Gare d'Austerlitz,** the **Gare du Nord,** the **Gare de l'Est,** the **Gare Mont-parnasse,** the **Gare St-Lazare,** the **Gare Aéroport Charles-de-Gaulle,** or the **Gare de Lyon.** If you are headed for Grenoble, located 400 miles southeast of Paris, you will board your **TGV** train either at the **Gare de Lyon** or the **Gare Aéroport Charles-de-Gaulle.**

A high speed train that now connects most of France's major cities to Paris, the **TGV (train à grande vitesse)** was started in the early eighties by the **SNCF (Société nationale des chemins de fer**

Le TGV.

français). It travels 200–300 kilometers per hour (between 125 and 190 miles per hour) and has considerably shortened travel time to many destinations throughout France.

You can easily spot a **TGV;** it is orange, blue, or gray and the locomotive has a unique aerodynamic design.

VOTRE Q. I. CULTUREL *(Your cultural I.Q.)*

Before beginning, review the numbers 0 through 10. This will help students correct the false statement in item 1.

Est-ce vrai ou faux? *Is it true or false?* Tell whether each statement is true or false. Try to correct any false statement.

■ WORDS TO USE: **vrai** *true* / **faux** *false*

1. Il y a six gares principales à Paris.
2. Roissy-Charles-de-Gaulle est un aéroport à Paris.
3. Le TGV est un train à grande vitesse.
4. Le TGV voyage à 400 kilomètres à l'heure *(per hour).*

La Gare du Nord.

http://www.wiley.com/aventure.html

Vous êtes branchés! These brief notes give you glimpses of French culture. They are in English so that you can begin on your own to become familiar with aspects of contemporary French culture related to the theme of the unit. The French words are not meant to be part of your active vocabulary unless they have also been presented in a **Pour s'exprimer** vocabulary box or a *Words to use* **(mots à utiliser)** section. Read the culture notes carefully and then test **Votre Q. I. culturel** by answering the follow-up questions.

■ POUR COMMUNIQUER

Describing people and identifying location

I A LES PRONOMS PERSONNELS SUJETS

Benjamin est américain. **Il** est à la gare.
Mme Bouverot est française. **Elle** cherche Benjamin.

Les pronoms personnels sujets			
je (j')	*I*	nous	*we*
tu	*you*	vous	*you*
il	*he*	ils *(m)*	*they*
elle	*she*	elles *(f)*	*they*
on	*one/we/people*		

◆ A subject pronoun can replace a noun (a person, thing, or concept) as the subject of a sentence.

> Benjamin arrive à Grenoble. **Il** cherche Mme Bouverot.
> La gare de Lyon est immense. **Elle** est à Paris.

◆ When **je** occurs before a verb beginning with a vowel or a mute **h** (which is silent), it is shortened to **j'**.

> **Je** déteste Los Angeles, mais **j'**adore New York.
> **J'h**abite à Grenoble.

◆ **Tu** is used to address a person you know well, a child, or a pet. It never combines with a vowel and never takes an apostrophe.

> **Tu** adores Tahiti?

◆ **Vous** is used in two situations:

1. to refer to more than one person
2. to show respect to an individual such as your boss, your teacher, or an older person.

> PLURAL: **Vous** êtes contents?   *Are you happy?*
> RESPECT: **Vous** êtes Mme Bouverot?   *Are you Mrs. Bouverot?*

◆ In French, all people and things have feminine (*f*)[1] or masculine (*m*) gender. **Il** is used for masculine gender, and **elle** is used for feminine gender. Both can also mean *it*. **Ils** and **elles** are the plural forms that mean *they*.

---

[1]In this book, the symbols (*f*) and (*m*) are sometimes used to tell you when a word is feminine or masculine.

Pour communiquer. This section begins with a close look at the language you are studying—the grammatical building blocks and the purposes for which the language is used. Study the sample sentences, grammar charts, and explanations carefully. All the vocabulary in the grammar charts is considered part of your active vocabulary. Then master the new material by completing the activities that follow.

Extension. You may wish to explain that in rapid conversation, French speakers sometimes contract **tu** and a following vowel: **T'es français?**

Benjamin est à la gare. **Il** est américain.
Mme Bouverot habite à Grenoble. **Elle** est française.
Le train arrive à la gare. **Il** est rapide.
La gare est à Paris. **Elle** est immense.
Pierre et Jean-Claude? **Ils** sont (*are*) à la pharmacie.
Anne et Christine? **Elles** sont à la gare.
Les stylos? **Ils** sont sur (*on*) la table.
Les tables? **Elles** sont dans (*in*) la classe.

Note: For mixed groups (both masculine and feminine), **ils** is used.

Alain, Marie, et Sylvie? **Ils** sont à la banque.
Les stylos (*m*) et la craie (*f*)? **Ils** sont dans la classe.

◆ **On** is an impersonal pronoun used to refer to a person or people in general. In English, we say *one, you,* or *they*. **On** is also used to mean *we* in informal conversation.

On écoute quand le professeur parle.	*You listen when the teacher speaks.*
On parle français au Sénégal.	*They speak French in Senegal.*
On y va!	*Let's go!*
On mange ici?	*Shall we eat here?*

1B LE VERBE ÊTRE

C'**est** Mme Bouverot.
Elle **est** française.
Benjamin et Mme Bouverot **sont** à Grenoble.
Ils **sont** énergiques.

◆ **Être** (*to be*) is an irregular verb. An irregular verb is a verb that does not follow a predictable pattern. **Être** is used mainly to identify, describe, or situate people or things.

être			
je **suis**	*I am*	nous **sommes**	*we are*
tu **es**	*you are*	vous **êtes**	*you are*
il **est**	*he is*	ils **sont**	*they are*
elle **est**	*she is*	elles **sont**	*they are*
on **est**	*one is*		
	we are		
	people are		

◆ **C'est** (*it is, that is, he/she is*) and **ce sont** (*these are, those are, they are*) are used to identify people and things.

Qui est-ce?
— **C'est** Pierre.
— **Ce sont** mes amis.

Who is that?
— It's Pierre.
— Those are my friends.

Qu'est-ce que c'est?
— **C'est** une chaise.
— **Ce sont** mes clés.

What is that?
— It's a chair.
— Those are my keys.

◆ **C'est** may be followed by an adjective or an adverb to describe a general idea, but not to describe a specific noun.

Benjamin est inquiet?
— **C'est** possible.

Is Benjamin worried?
— It's possible.

Mme Bouverot est contente?
— **C'est** bien.[2]

Is Mrs. Bouverot happy?
— That's good.

POUR S'EXPRIMER

Adjectifs et adverbes souvent utilisés avec le verbe être (*Adjectives and adverbs commonly used with* être)

ADJECTIFS		
américain[3]	agréable	*pleasant*
calme	content(e)	*happy*
énergique	désagréable	*unpleasant*
irrésistible	français(e)	*French*
moderne	formidable	*great*
modeste	grand(e)	*big, tall*
optimiste	honnête	*honest*
pessimiste	mince	*thin*
simple	paresseux / paresseuse	*lazy*
	pauvre	*poor*
	petit(e)	*small, short*
	sévère	*strict*
	sympathique	*nice*
	timide	*shy*
	triste	*sad*

ADVERBES			
toujours	*always*	quelquefois	*sometimes*
souvent	*often*	rarement	*rarely*

[2]In this idiomatic expression, the adverb **bien** acts like an adjective.
[3]The endings of many adjectives differ in their masculine and feminine forms; see p. 27.

see p. 27.

Pour s'exprimer. New words and expressions are accompanied by illustrations or are provided for you in list form, together with their English equivalents. Use these words and expressions in the **Activités** that follow and make them part of your active French vocabulary; you will use them to express yourself in conversation and writing throughout the course.

Cognates. Notice that the adjectives in the left column are not translated. They resemble and have identical meanings to English words you know. Such words are called *cognates*. English and French have thousands of words in common. You already know a lot of French!

ACTIVITÉS

 1. C'est vrai? Ask your partner to confirm the following information.

■ **WORDS TO USE: Mais oui! / Mais non!** *Yes! / No!* (emphatic)

MODÈLES: Benjamin est sympathique? —Mais oui, _____ est sympathique.
—Mais oui, il est sympathique!

Benjamin est pessimiste? —Mais non, _____ est optimiste!
—Mais non, il est optimiste!

1. Benjamin est américain? —Mais oui, _____ est américain!
2. Mme Bouverot est française? —Mais oui, _____ est française!
3. Catherine et Mme Bouverot sont grandes? —Mais non, _____ sont petites!
4. Vous êtes optimiste? —Mais oui, _____ suis optimiste!
5. Vous êtes désagréables? —Mais non, _____ sommes timides!
6. Les étudiants sont paresseux? —Mais non, _____ sont énergiques!
7. Je suis dans la classe de français? —Mais oui, _____ es dans la classe de français.
8. Anne et Jacqueline sont pessimistes? —Mais non, _____ sont optimistes.

 2. Où sont-ils? Tell your partner where the following people are.

 MODÈLE: Alain / à Dakar
Alain est à Dakar.

1. Pierre / à Paris
2. John et Louis / à Aix-en-Provence
3. Tu / en classe à Québec
4. Vous (le professeur) / à Casablanca
5. Nous / à Fort-de-France
6. Je / à Saint-Denis

POUR S'EXPRIMER	
Quelques destinations	
à l'aéroport	*at the airport*
à la banque	*at the bank*
à la gare	*at the station*
à la maison	*at home*
à la pharmacie	*at the drugstore*
à l'université	*at school*
en classe, en cours	*in class*
dans la classe	*in the classroom*

3. Mais où sont-ils? You can't get anyone on the phone today. Imagine where they are, using some destinations from the **Pour s'exprimer** on p. 22.

MODÈLE: le professeur
Le professeur est dans la classe.

1. Mme Bouverot
2. tu
3. vous
4. M. et Mme Dubois
5. elles
6. Mon ami(e)

4. Comment sont-ils? *What are they like?* In a letter to the Bouverots, Benjamin described his family members and himself. Finish the descriptions using adjectives from the **Pour s'exprimer** on p. 21.

■ WORD TO USE: **mais** *but*

MODÈLE: maman / calme et...
Elle est calme et formidable.

1. papa / honnête et...
2. Michael / timide mais...
3. Slipper / irrésistible mais...
4. Michael et moi, nous / pauvres mais...
5. Michael et papa / formidables et...
6. moi, je / mince et...

Warm-up/follow-up. As a warm-up group activity, have students suggest adjectives to describe people. Provide translations for words they do not know in French. Then have them complete the sentences using the adjectives they have selected. As a follow-up activity, they may add an adverb such as **toujours, souvent, quelquefois,** or **rarement** to the sentence.

5. Je suis... Describe yourself in at least five sentences to your partner. Use adjectives from the **Pour s'exprimer** box on page 21 as well as the adverbs **toujours, souvent, quelquefois,** and **rarement.** The adverbs come right after the verb! Be prepared to describe your partner to the class.

MODÈLE: —**Je suis souvent optimiste. Et toi?**
—**Moi, je suis rarement optimiste. Je suis souvent pessimiste.**

Extension. Remind the students that the phrase **moi, je** is used to emphasize the subject just as intonation is used in English.

DEUXIÈME ÉPISODE

🎧 **T 10**

Benjamin est à la gare. Madame Bouverot n'est pas là.°

BENJAMIN: Où est Madame Bouverot? Elle est à la banque? Elle est à la pharmacie? Elle est à la maison? Où est-elle?

_____

n'est pas là *isn't there*

Benjamin cherche Madame Bouverot. Personne!° Que faire?°

BENJAMIN: Je cherche un taxi? Trop cher!° Je cherche un bus? Quel° bus?

_____

Personne! *No one (is there)!* / **Que faire?** *What should I do?* / **Trop cher!** *Too expensive!* / **quel** *which*

Remind students what **cherche** *means by pretending to look for something in the classroom.*

AVEZ-VOUS COMPRIS?

1. Madame Bouverot est à la gare?
2. Madame Bouverot est à la banque?
3. Benjamin téléphone à sa *(his)* maman?
4. Est-ce que[4] Benjamin est calme?
5. Est-ce que Benjamin cherche un taxi?

[4]**Est-ce que** is a marker that is used to ask *yes/no* questions. See p. 71.

BENJAMIN: Je téléphone à ma maman? Quel bébé!° Je téléphone au directeur du programme? C'est stupide! Je téléphone à Madame Bouverot?

BENJAMIN: Où est le téléphone?

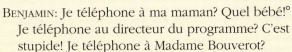

Quel bébé! *What a baby!*

ET VOUS?

Ask and answer these questions with a partner. Be prepared to tell the class what you learn about your partner.

1. Est-ce que vous êtes à la gare ou dans la classe?
2. Moi, je téléphone quelquefois. Est-ce que vous téléphonez souvent ou rarement?
3. Est-ce que vous téléphonez souvent à la gare? à l'aéroport?
4. En général, est-ce que vous êtes calme? énergique?
5. Est-ce que vous êtes optimiste?

Students may answer **oui** or **non** or in complete sentences such as **Je ne sais pas.**

Variation. You may wish to have students ask these questions in the **tu** form. Show them how to do so. Also tell students how to report their findings to the class.

IL Y A UN PROBLÈME: QU'EN PENSEZ-VOUS?

Il y a un problème: Qu'en pensez-vous? / À vous de jouer. Here is your chance to give advice on a particular problem. Using the French you've learned in each chapter, state your opinion on how a storyline character should resolve a difficult situation. As your language skills grow, you'll find yourself discussing the pros and cons of the various options in French.

Il y a un problème and **À vous de jouer.** (1) For these sections, students may work individually, in pairs, in groups, or as a class. If students work in pairs or groups, you may ask them to report the solution they choose to the class. (2) For the final choice **(Une autre solution?)** have students brainstorm French vocabulary to use in their answers and justifications. If you like, have them brainstorm other solutions and/or vote on the best solution. (3) In the first few chapters, you may allow students to use English for the discussion, but you may wish to repeat their ideas in simple French whenever possible.

Benjamin arrive à la gare de Grenoble. Mme Bouverot n'est pas là. Que faire? Benjamin devrait (*should*)

a. attendre (*wait for*) Mme Bouverot à la gare.

b. prendre (*take*) un taxi.

c. téléphoner au directeur du programme.

d. téléphoner à sa maman.

À VOUS DE JOUER!

Votre train arrive à la gare et votre ami n'est pas là. Que faites-vous? (*What do you do?*)

a. Moi, j'attends.
b. Moi, je prends un taxi.
c. Moi, je téléphone à maman.
d. Une autre solution?

Justifiez votre choix (*Justify your choice*).

Describing people and identifying nationality

II LES ADJECTIFS QUALIFICATIFS

> Benjamin est **américain.** Il est **grand** et **sympathique.** Il est
> **célibataire** (*single*).
> Mme Bouverot est **française.** Elle est **mariée** (*married*). Elle est
> **petite** et **optimiste.**

◆ Adjectives are used to describe people and things. In French, adjectives
agree in gender (masculine or feminine) and number (singular or plural) with
the noun they describe.

Adjectifs qualificatifs réguliers		
	masculin	*féminin*
SINGULIER	sympathique	sympathique
	grand	grand**e**
	marié	marié**e**
PLURIEL	sympathique**s**	sympathique**s**
	grand**s**	grand**es**
	marié**s**	marié**es**

◆ To show in writing that an adjective is feminine, you usually add an **-e** to the
masculine form. If the masculine form already ends in **e,** it remains unchanged.

masculin	*féminin*
américain	américain**e**
optimiste	optimist**e**

◆ To show in writing that an adjective is plural, you usually add an **-s** to the
singular form. Pronunciation, however, does not change from singular to plural.
If an adjective already ends in **s** or **x,** it remains unchanged.

SINGULIER	français	paresseux	française
PLURIEL	français	paresseux	française**s**

◆ Pronunciation often varies between masculine and feminine adjectives.
Masculine forms often end in a vowel sound, while feminine forms end in a
consonant sound.

grand [gRã]   grande [gRãd]

The International
Phonetic Alphabet (IPA)
will be used throughout
the book to indicate the
pronunciation of sounds,
words, and phrases.

◆ If an adjective ends in a vowel other than **e,** the feminine form is written by adding an **e,** but the pronunciation does not change.

      Benjamin est mari**é**? —Mais non! Madame Bouverot est mari**ée.**

◆ Some adjectives are irregular.

Adjectifs qualificatifs irréguliers				
	SINGULIER		**PLURIEL**	
	masculin	*féminin*	*masculin*	*féminin*
-F	acti**f**	acti**ve**	acti**fs**	acti**ves**
-EUX	paress**eux**	paress**euse**	paress**eux**	paress**euses**
-IEN	ital**ien**	ital**ienne**	ital**iens**	ital**iennes**
-EL	sensationn**el**	sensationn**elle**	sensationn**els**	sensationn**elles**

POUR S'EXPRIMER		
Adjectifs		
(m)	*(f)*	
célibataire	célibataire	*single*
divorcé	divorcée	*divorced*
fiancé	fiancée	*engaged*
marié	mariée	*married*
veuf	veuve	*widowed*

The formation of irregular adjectives is presented on p. 60.

Warm-up. As a warm-up for the following activities, have the students listen to and repeat some adjective pairs to hear the pronunciation difference between masculine and feminine forms: **grand, grande; petit, petite; français, française; américain, américaine; intelligent, intelligente.**

Students cannot hear the difference (masculine/feminine/singular/plural) for some of the adjectives in **Activité 6.** It is important, however, that they realize that they sound the same even though they are spelled differently. You may ask your students to spell out the adjectives or write them on the board. You could also assign this as a written activity.

ACTIVITÉS

6. La lettre de Madame Bouverot. Benjamin remembers a letter he received from his French family that included information about each family member. Complete the sentences using the appropriate form of each adjective.

MODÈLE: Madame Bouverot / marié / petit
    Madame Bouverot est mariée. Elle est petite.

1. Dominique / fiancé / français
2. Pierre et Catherine / célibataire / sensationnel
3. Tante (*aunt*) Cécile / veuf / paresseux
4. Monsieur et Madame Bouverot / marié / actif
5. Oncle (*uncle*) Georges / divorcé / grand

Quelques adjectifs de nationalité

(m)	(f)		(m)	(f)	
russe	russe	*Russian*	sénégalais	sénégalaise	*Senegalese*
suisse	suisse	*Swiss*	chinois	chinoise	*Chinese*
allemand	allemande	*German*	italien	italienne	*Italian*
marocain	marocaine	*Moroccan*	canadien	canadienne	*Canadian*
mexicain	mexicaine	*Mexican*	vietnamien	vietnamienne	*Vietnamese*
anglais	anglaise	*English*	coréen	coréenne	*Korean*
japonais	japonaise	*Japanese*			

Note: In French, adjectives of nationality are not capitalized.

7. D'où viennent-ils? Where are the following people from? What is their nationality?

MODÈLE: Hélène / français
Hélène est française.

1. Maria / mexicain
2. Gertrude / allemand
3. nous (*f*) / canadien
4. vous (*m, pl*) / suisse
5. je (*f*) / chinois
6. tu (*m*) / italien
7. Tomiko et Takiko (*f*) / japonais
8. les Burke / anglais

8. Quelle est sa nationalité? During the first day of class, Benjamin tries to guess his classmates' nationalities. Play the role of Benjamin and your partner will correct you.

MODÈLE: Anna / sénégalais / canadien
BENJAMIN: **Anna est sénégalaise?**
PARTENAIRE: **Mais non! Elle est canadienne!**

1. Karl et David / américain / anglais
2. Toufik (*m*) / suisse / marocain
3. vous (*f, pl*) / mexicain / russe
4. tu (*f*) / vietnamien / japonais
5. Yukio (*f*) et toi, vous / coréen / américain
6. tu (*f*) / marocain / sénégalais

9. Qui est-ce? On a piece of paper, write three sentences with adjectives that describe yourself. Exchange descriptions with other people. Each class member will read aloud the description he or she has received. The rest of the class will try to guess who the person is.

Follow-up/Warm-up:
As a written follow-up activity, ask student to choose six people in the class and write up six questions like Benjamin's in **Activité 8.** Next class session, have students ask their partner/class these questions as a warm-up.

Tell students they may invent a new persona if they wish when answering personal questions in **Activité 9.** Explain that it is impolite to ask a new French acquaintance questions about age, marital status, money matters, religion, or sexual preference.

🎧 TROISIÈME ÉPISODE `T 11`

BENJAMIN: Ah! Voilà un téléphone! Je suis sauvé!° Je téléphone à Mme Bouverot!

sauvé *saved*

BENJAMIN: Quel est le numéro de téléphone de la famille Bouverot? Oh, c'est le 76-13-24-30.

Culture. Explain to students that French phone numbers are read in pairs and that there are eight numbers in all. The first two numbers also indicate the region in which the phone is located. Tell students the first number is *soixante-seize*. As of fall 1996, France Télécom is planning to modify the system.

AVEZ-VOUS COMPRIS?

Answer the following questions using **oui** or **non,** or a complete sentence.

1. Est-ce que Benjamin téléphone à Monsieur Bouverot?
2. Est-ce que le téléphone français est comme (*like*) un téléphone américain?
3. Est-ce que le téléphone fonctionne avec un dollar?

BENJAMIN: Mais ce téléphone est bizarre! Bizarre! Bizarre! Bizarre! Il fonctionne avec° une carte! Zut!° Que faire?

──────────
fonctionne avec *operates with* / **Zut!** *Darn!*

UNE FEMME: Monsieur? Je peux vous aider?°

──────────
Je peux vous aider? *May I help you?*

ET VOUS?

1. Est-ce que vous téléphonez souvent à des amis?
2. En général, est-ce que vous téléphonez souvent, quelquefois, ou rarement?

VOUS ÊTES BRANCHÉS!

La télécarte

In France most public phones now operate with a **télécarte** that can be purchased at post offices and selected stores. The **télécarte** is a "debit card" that is worth a fixed number of **unités** (*time units*). When you make a call from **une cabine téléphonique** you must first insert the **télécarte** to verify electronically if you have enough **unités** to place your call. Don't discard your **télécarte** once you have used it up. Some cards become collectors' items because of their beautiful or unusual designs.

On téléphone avec une télécarte.

VOTRE Q. I. CULTUREL

Est-ce vrai ou faux? Tell whether each of the statements is true **(vrai)** or false **(faux).** If it is false, try to correct it.

1. Une télécarte est utilisée pour la télévision.
2. On achète (*buys*) une télécarte au bureau de poste (*at the post office*).
3. Certaines personnes collectionnent les télécartes.

http://www.wiley.com/aventure.html

■ POUR COMMUNIQUER

Identifying things

Ordering drinks and snacks

III L'ARTICLE INDÉFINI

C'est **un** téléphone bizarre.
Je voudrais (*would like*) **une** limonade, s'il vous plaît.
Ce sont **des** sandwichs au jambon (*ham*).

◆ When identifying things and people with nouns, it is often necessary to use an indefinite article before the noun.

Les articles indéfinis

	masculin	*féminin*	
SINGULIER	un	une	*a, an*
PLURIEL	des	des	*some, any*

◆ Remember that all nouns have feminine or masculine gender in French. To determine whether to use **un** or **une** with a noun, you must memorize the noun's gender.

C'est **un** téléphone.　　*This is a telephone.*
C'est **une** télécarte.　　*This is a phone card.*

◆ In English, the plural indefinite article is sometimes left out; **des** is required in French. **Des** can also be translated as *some* or *any*.

Vous avez **des** sandwichs au jambon?　　*Do you have (any) ham sandwiches?*

Ce sont **des** sandwichs au jambon.　　*These are ham sandwiches.*

POUR S'EXPRIMER

LES BOISSONS *drinks*

une bière	*a beer*
un café	*(a cup of) coffee*
un chocolat chaud	*(a cup of) hot chocolate*
un Coca	*a Coke/cola*
une eau minérale	*(a glass of) mineral water e.g., Perrier, Evian, Vittel*
un jus d'orange	*(a glass of) orange juice*
une limonade	*a lemon-lime soda*
une menthe à l'eau	*a water and mint syrup drink served with ice*
un thé	*(a cup of) tea*
un verre de lait	*a glass of milk*

LES EN-CAS *snacks*

un croissant	
un croque-monsieur	*a toasted ham and cheese sandwich*
une omelette	
une pizza	
un sandwich (au jambon)	

POUR COMMANDER ET PAYER (*to order and pay*)

Je voudrais un croissant.	*I would like a croissant.*
C'est combien un café?	*How much is a (cup of) coffee?*
C'est huit francs.	*It's eight francs.*

Culture. Explain that drinks consisting of fruit syrups and water are commonly served in French cafés. Also explain that milk is rarely drunk by adults and less by French children than American children.

T 12

10. Vous désirez? How would Benjamin ask for the following items in the station snack bar?

MODÈLE: **Un café, s'il vous plaît!**

Un thé et un croissant, s'il vous plaît!

1.   2.   3.

4.   5.   6.

Café Orbital

internet access

Le premier cybercafé de Paris - e-mail : info@orbital.fr

Un accès à tous les services d'Internet

Netscape : porte ouverte sur le monde

Naviguer sur Internet à la recherche de toutes les informations dont vous pouvez rêver, images, séquences animées et sons à la clef, sur le World Wide Web (bases de données reliées entre elles par des liens hypertextes).

News : les forums internationaux

Quels sont les services du Café Orbital?

11. C'est combien une bière? You are at a café and ask the server the price of different items. With a partner, role-play your conversation using the menu.

MODÈLE: coffee
>—**C'est combien un café?**
>—**Un café, c'est 8 francs.**

1. tea
2. lemon-lime soda
3. cola
4. beer
5. mint syrup drink

6. hot chocolate
7. toasted ham and cheese sandwich
8. omelette
9. sandwich

BUFFET DE LA GARE

Boissons

café	8F
thé	12F
chocolat	13F
bière	16F
limonade	12F
menthe à l'eau	10F
jus d'orange	15F
citron pressé	15F
eau minérale	12F
Coca	12F

En-cas

croque-monsieur	25F
sandwich au jambon	22F
pizza	15F
omelette	26F

 12. Moi, je voudrais... In a small group, take turns saying what you would like to order from the café menu. After everyone has ordered, one person will play the role of waiter **(le garçon)** and recap all the orders.

MODÈLE: —**Je voudrais un café.**
>—**Je voudrais une bière.**
>>LE GARÇON: **Un café, un coca, une limonade, deux thés, et une bière.**

QUATRIÈME ÉPISODE T 13

UNE FEMME: Monsieur? Je peux vous aider?°
BENJAMIN: Oh oui, je téléphone à ma mère française.

Je peux vous aider? *Can I help you?*

UNE FEMME: Votre mère française?
BENJAMIN: Oui, je suis étudiant à Seaside College et je suis ici pour étudier° à l'université Stendhal cette année.° Je m'appelle Benjamin.

---
je suis ici pour étudier *I'm here to study* / **cette année** *this year*

AVEZ-VOUS COMPRIS?

1. Est-ce que Benjamin désire téléphoner à M. Bouverot?
2. Benjamin est étudiant où? à UCLA? à Boston College?
3. Qui rencontre (*who meets*) Benjamin?
4. Est-ce que Mme Bouverot est en avance (*early*) ou en retard?
5. Benjamin est triste ou content?

UNE FEMME: Benjamin? Benjamin Wilson? C'est incroyable!° Je suis Madame Bouverot. Je suis en retard.° Je suis désolée!°

BENJAMIN: Ouf!° je suis bien content.

---

incroyable *incredible* / **en retard** *late* / **désolée** *sorry* / **Ouf!** *Whew!* (*Thank goodness!*)

MADAME BOUVEROT: Moi aussi°, je suis ravie.° Alors, rentrons à la maison!°

---

aussi *also, too* / **ravie** *delighted* / **Alors, rentrons à la maison!** *Well then, let's go home!*

ET VOUS?

1. Est-ce que vous êtes professeur ou étudiant?
2. Comment vous appelez-vous? Comment s'appelle le professeur?
3. En général, est-ce que vous êtes en avance, en retard ou à l'heure *(on time)* en classe?
4. Aujourd'hui, est-ce que vous êtes triste ou content(e)?

Talking about your activities

IV LES VERBES RÉGULIERS EN -ER

J'**étudie** (*I'm studying*) à l'université de Grenoble cette année.
Nous **rentrons** (*We're returning*) à la maison aujourd'hui.
Elles **parlent** (*talk*) souvent au téléphone.
Vous **mangez** rarement au buffet de la gare. *You rarely eat at the café in the station.*

◆ Every regular **-er** verb follows the same pattern. There are thousands of verbs in French that follow this model.

Les verbes réguliers en -er	
DANSER	
je dans**e**	nous dans**ons**
tu dans**es**	vous dans**ez**
il / elle / on dans**e**	ils / elles dans**ent**

Note: The endings for **je** and **il / elle / on** are the same.

◆ In English, there are several forms for these verbs in the present tense depending on the situation. In French, there is only one form. For example:

Elles parlent au téléphone. *They are talking on the telephone./ They (do) talk on the phone.*

◆ When learning **-er** verbs, remember that only two of the five endings are pronounced: **-ons** and **-ez.** All the others are silent.

◆ To keep the **g** sound soft, verbs ending in **-ger** add an **e** before the **-ons** endings in the **nous** form.

Nous mang**e**ons au restaurant. *We eat at the restaurant.*

Extension. Explain to your students that in English a hard **g** is the sound they hear in *go* and a soft **g** is the sound they hear in *George.* Point out that the same pronunciation difference occurs in French: compare **mongol** (*Mongolian*) and **mangeons.**

Adverbes					
QUAND (*when*)		COMMENT (*how*)		COMBIEN (*how much*)	
en avance	*early*	bien	*well*	assez	*enough; quite; fairly*
en retard	*late*	mal	*badly*	trop	*too much*
à l'heure	*on time*				

Verbes réguliers en -er

adorer	aimer	*to like*	nager	*to swim*
arriver	chanter	*to sing*	parler	*to speak*
danser	chercher	*to look for*	regarder	*to look at*
détester	étudier	*to study*	rentrer	*to return*
skier	fumer	*to smoke*	travailler	*to work*
téléphoner	habiter	*to live*	trouver	*to find*
	jouer (au golf)	*to play (golf)*	voyager	*to travel*
	manger	*to eat*		

ACTIVITÉS

13. Quelques activités des Bouverot. Benjamin learns certain things about his new family members and they ask him about himself. Complete the following sentences.

MODÈLE: M. Bouverot / danser / très mal
M. Bouverot danse très mal.

1. Mme Bouverot / danser / rarement
2. Dominique et M. Bouverot / chanter / souvent
3. Catherine / parler / très bien anglais
4. nous / voyager / quand nous sommes riches
5. Pierre / skier / très mal
6. vous / jouer au golf / quelquefois?
7. oui, je / adorer / le golf

 14. Non, non et non!!! Each time your partner asks you if you are doing a particular activity, say **non** and tell him or her what you are doing instead. Use the list of verbs in the **Pour s'exprimer** above. Ask at least five questions.

MODÈLE: —**Tu travailles?**
—**Non, j'étudie!**

 15. Toujours, souvent, quelquefois, ou rarement? With a partner or group, take turns asking how often your classmates do certain things. Answer using **souvent, assez souvent, très souvent, rarement, assez rarement, très rarement, toujours** and **quelquefois.**

MODÈLE: —**Tu travailles souvent?**
—**Oui, je travaille très souvent.**
OU —**Non, je travaille (très) rarement.**

 16. Tu chantes mal? Talk to at least three classmates and find out two things they do well, two things they do often, two things they always do and two things they do badly. Be prepared to report your findings to the class.

To teach the **-er** verbs you may want to use charades and miming. Give each student one of the verbs on a slip of paper and have him or her act it out for the class or for his or her partner.

Tell students to use intonation questions, e.g., **Tu danses bien?** or **Tu nages souvent?.** They may also use **ou** as in **bien ou mal?.**

📖 LECTURE

Quelle... *Whatever speed / can*

even
train

LE TÉLÉPHONE DANS LE TGV

Reading Strategy: Using cognates to help you understand a text

Cognates are words that look nearly the same *and* have the same meaning from one language to another. When you read a passage in French, look for words that you recognize from your own language, and you will probably be able to understand quite a bit of vocabulary without using a dictionary or asking for translations. Look over the paragraph below (adapted from a brochure about the TGV) to see how many cognates you can find. If you like, make a list and jot down the meanings, then compare with your classmates. Hint: There are 15–20 cognates in this paragraph.

Tous les TGV sont équipés de téléphone. Quelle que soit° la vitesse° du train, vous pouvez° établir une communication téléphonique, privée ou professionelle, en Europe, en Amérique du Nord, ou même° au Japon. Chaque rame° est équipée de trois cabines téléphoniques: une en première classe, une en seconde, et une dans la voiture-bar. Ces téléphones fonctionnent avec votre télécarte habituelle (50 ou 120 unités).

Le téléphone dans le TGV.

Answer the following questions.

1. Est-ce que les TGV sont équipés de télévisions ou de téléphones?
2. Est-ce que les communications privées sont possibles ou impossibles en TGV?
3. Où sont les cabines téléphoniques dans le TGV?
4. Comment fonctionnent les téléphones dans le TGV?

RÉVISION ÉCLAIR

Describing people and identifying location   **Voir p. 19.**

> **Je suis** énergique.
> Robert et Jean **sont** à Paris.

Describing people and identifying nationality   **Voir p. 27.**

> Tu es **grand.**
> Je suis **marié.**
> Elle est **française.**

Identifying things   **Voir p. 32.**
Ordering drinks and snacks

> Qu'est-ce que c'est? **C'est une** banque.
> **Un** café, s'il vous plaît.

Talking about your activities   **Voir p. 38.**

> Ils **regardent** la télévision.
> Nous **mangeons** au restaurant.

> **Révision éclair**
> gives you a quick reference to the pages where new grammar has been presented in the chapter, and more contextualized examples of that grammar. Activities follow that will help you check your mastery of the important language of the chapter.

ÊTES-VOUS BRANCHÉS? _____

 Mon journal. Jot down what you know about the TGV, Parisian train stations, and French public phones. Compare the French train and phone systems to what you have experienced in your own country.

Y ÊTES-VOUS ARRIVÉS? _____

 A. Interview. You want to know more about your partner. Take turns asking and answering these questions. Be ready to report what you learned about your partner to the class.

1. Comment vous appelez-vous?
2. Quelle est votre nationalité?
3. Vous êtes marié(e)? célibataire?

In the first few chapters you may want students to write their journal entries in English because they lack the necessary vocabulary and/or structures to clearly express their thoughts. As they learn more, you may ask them to switch to French. You may decide not to put a letter grade at first or decide to grade these paragraphs holistically.

4. Vous êtes énergique ou souvent paresseux(-se)?

5. En général, quand arrivez-vous en classe? à l'heure? en retard? en avance?

6. Est-ce que vous travaillez beaucoup?

7. Vous regardez souvent la télévision?

8. Est-ce que vous mangez souvent au restaurant?

9. Est-ce que vous voyagez beaucoup?

10. ?

You may wish to assign **Activité B** as a written exercise.

 B. Moi, je suis... Find a new partner and introduce yourself. Describe yourself physically and psychologically; tell your nationality and your marital status; say what you do often or rarely. Remember, you may make up a new persona if you wish.

 C. Voilà les participants. In groups of three, take turns playing game-show host and contestants. The host greets the contestants and asks them five questions, for example, if they are single or married, what their outlook on life is, if they work/play/travel a lot, and what things they do well or badly.

 # PRONONCIATION

LA LIAISON

Prononciation explains differences and/or similarities between French and English sounds and provides practice designed to help you sound like a native speaker.

One of the things that makes French so pleasant to listen to is the linking together of certain sounds. This is called **liaison.** As you hear more and more French, you will learn exactly where to make (or avoid) **liaison. Liaison** occurs only when a word ending in a consonant (usually **s, x,** or **t**) precedes a word beginning with a vowel or a mute **h,** as in the word **heure** *(hour).* The final **s** or **x** sounds like **[z]** in liaison. The phrases below illustrate **liaison.**

Point out to your students that the **liaison** symbol is not part of the word's spelling but is used here simply to help them learn correct pronunciation.

1. Pronounce these phrases after your professor or lab tape.

a. Les étudiants sont tristes.

b. Il est ici.

c. Vous êtes coréen?

d. Ce sont des activités.

e. Je suis étudiant.

f. Il est six heures.

2. Pronounce each phrase, being careful to make the **liaison.** Then listen to your professor or lab tape to check your pronunciation.

a. Tu es une femme intelligente.

b. Il est anglais.

c. Ils sont italiens.

d. Il est deux heures.

e. Nous préparons des exercices difficiles.

f. Dansent-ils?

g. Les hôtels sont grands.

Vocabulaire actif. The list of active vocabulary, which ends each chapter, includes only the new words and expressions that have been presented in grammar boxes, **Pour s'exprimer** boxes, and *Words to use* (**Mots à utiliser**) sections. Words and expressions are grouped within categories that will make studying, remembering, and using the vocabulary easier for you.

Pronoms personnels sujets

je	*I*	elle	*she; it*			vous	*you*
tu	*you*	on	*one; we; people*			ils	*they* (*m, pl* or *m* and *f* together)
il	*he; it*	nous	*we*			elles	*they* (*f, pl*)

Adjectifs

LES ADJECTIFS QUALIFICATIFS

actif, active	*active*	honnête	*honest*	pessimiste	*pessimistic*
agréable	*pleasant*	irrésistible	*irresistible*	petit(e)	*little; short*
calme	*calm*	mince	*thin*	sévère	*strict*
content(e)	*happy*	moderne	*modern*	simple	*simple; plain*
désagréable	*unpleasant*	modeste	*modest*	sympathique	*nice*
énergique	*energetic*	optimiste	*optimistic*	timide	*shy*
formidable	*great*	paresseux, paresseuse	*lazy*	triste	*sad*
grand(e)	*big; tall*	pauvre	*poor*		

L'ÉTAT CIVIL

célibataire	*single*	fiancé(e)	*engaged to be married*	veuf, veuve	*widowed*
divorcé(e)	*divorced*	marié(e)	*married*		

QUELQUES ADJECTIFS DE NATIONALITÉ

allemand(e)	*German*	coréen(ne)	*Korean*	mexicain(e)	*Mexican*
américain(e)	*American*	français(e)	*French*	russe	*Russian*
anglais(e)	*English*	italien(ne)	*Italian*	sénégalais(e)	*Senegalese*
canadien(ne)	*Canadian*	japonais(e)	*Japanese*	suisse	*Swiss*
chinois	*Chinese*	marocain(e)	*Moroccan*	vietnamien(ne)	*Vietnamese*

Adverbes

ADVERBES DE FRÉQUENCE

quelquefois	*sometimes*	souvent	*often*	toujours	*always*
rarement	*rarely*				

à l'heure   *on time*   en retard   *late*   quand   *when*
en avance   *early*

ADVERBES DE MANIÈRE ET DE QUANTITÉ

assez   *enough; quite; fairly; rather*   combien   *how much*   mal   *badly*
bien   *well*   comment   *how*   trop   *too much*

Noms

LES BOISSONS

une bière   *a beer*   une eau minérale   *a (glass of)*   une menthe à l'eau   *a drink*
un café   *a (cup of) coffee*   *mineral water*   *made of mint syrup and water*
un chocolat chaud   *a (cup of)*   un jus d'orange   *a (glass of)*   un thé   *a (cup of) tea*
    hot chocolate   *orange juice*   un verre de lait   *a glass of milk*
un Coca   *a coke*   une limonade   *a lemon-lime*
                                        soda

LES EN-CAS

un croissant   *a crescent-shaped*   une omelette   *an omelet*   un sandwich (au jambon)
    roll   une pizza   *a pizza*   *a (ham) sandwich*
un croque-monsieur   *a toasted*
    ham, cheese, and béchamel
    sauce sandwich

Verbes

adorer   *to adore*   être   *to be*   regarder   *to look at*
aimer   *to like*   fumer   *to smoke*   rentrer   *to return*
arriver   *to arrive*   habiter   *to live*   skier   *to ski*
chanter   *to sing*   jouer   *to play*   téléphoner   *to telephone*
chercher   *to look for*   manger   *to eat*   travailler   *to work*
danser   *to dance*   nager   *to swim*   trouver   *to find*
détester   *to hate*   parler   *to speak, to talk*   voyager   *to travel*
étudier   *to study*

Autres mots et expressions utiles

à l'aéroport   *at the airport*   à l'université   *at school*   mais   *but*
à la banque   *at the bank*   en classe, en cours   *in class*   mais oui!   *yes!*
à la gare   *at the station*   dans (la classe)   *in (the classroom)* mais non!   *no!*
à la maison   *at home*   faux   *false*   vrai   *true*
à la pharmacie   *at the drugstore* je voudrais   *I would like*

Chapitre 2 ◆ JULIE S'INSTALLE

PRÉSENTATION ÉCLAIR

POUR COMMUNIQUER

Referring to people and things
Talking about possessions
Saying no
Describing people and things
Expressing preferences
Asking questions

POUR Y ARRIVER

L'article défini
de + l'article défini
La négation
La place de l'adjectif
Les verbes de préférence en **-er**
L'interrogation

POUR S'ADAPTER À LA CULTURE

La ville de Rouen
La consommation de tabac en France

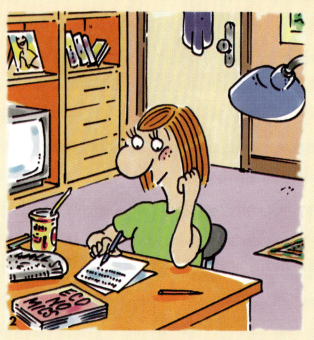

1 Voilà Julie. Elle est américaine. Elle étudie aussi à Seaside College. C'est une amie de Benjamin. Elle est assez grande et brune° avec des taches de rousseur°.

---

brune *a brunette* / **avec des taches de rousseur** *with freckles*

2 Julie est intelligente, travailleuse°, et curieuse, mais elle n'est pas° très patiente. Elle étudie l'économie—et le français, bien sûr°.

---

travailleuse *hard-working* / **n'est pas** *isn't* / **bien sûr** *of course*

Culture. The French term **foyer** does not have an exact English equivalent. In the university setting, a **foyer** is a group home for students, a cross between a dormitory and a hotel. A **résidence universitaire,** located near a campus, is close to the American idea of a dorm.

AVEZ-VOUS COMPRIS?

1. Est-ce que Julie est américaine ou française?
2. Est-ce qu'elle est brune ou blonde? grande ou petite? travailleuse ou paresseuse? patiente ou impatiente?
3. Est-ce que Julie étudie le français et les mathématiques?
4. Est-ce que Julie aime le rock? la pizza? le chocolat?
5. En France, est-ce qu'elle habite dans un appartement?

3

Elle aime la musique classique, mais elle déteste le rock. Elle adore le bon° chocolat, mais elle déteste la pizza.

---
bon *good*

4

Quand Julie arrive en France, elle s'installe dans un foyer° à Rouen. Mais, est-ce qu'elle va aimer° cette° résidence?

---
s'installe dans un foyer *settles in a residence hall* /
est-ce qu'elle va aimer *is she going to like* / **cette** *this*

ET VOUS?

1. Est-ce que vous êtes blond(e)? brun(e)? grand(e)? petit(e)?
2. Est-ce que vous étudiez les maths? l'anglais? l'économie? la psychologie?
3. Quelle *(What)* musique aimez-vous? le rock? le jazz? le rap? la musique classique?
4. Est-ce que vous aimez la pizza? le chocolat?
5. Vous habitez dans un appartement? dans un foyer? dans une maison *(house)*?
6. Est-ce que vous habitez à Paris? à New York? à Los Angeles? Où?

VOUS ÊTES BRANCHÉS

Rouen, la ville aux cent clochers

Rouen, the capital of **la haute Normandie,** a province in the northwest of France, has a history dating back to the Viking era. Its Gothic cathedral, built between the 14th and 16th centuries, inspired a series of paintings by the Impressionist painter, **Claude Monet** (1840–1926). The many churches and abbeys scattered throughout the city and surrounding area prompted writer **Victor Hugo** (1802–1885) to call Rouen "the city of 100 spires." Famous historical and literary figures from **Jeanne d'Arc,** who was burned at the stake there in 1431, to **Madame Bovary,** heroine created by **Gustave Flaubert** (1821–1880), are also associated with Rouen.

La cathédrale de Rouen par Claude Monet.

La cathédrale le soir.

VOTRE Q. I. CULTUREL

Glissez le bon mot à sa place. Find the right word to complete the phrases below.

1. _____ est la capitale de la Haute Normandie.
2. Le peintre impressioniste de la cathédrale s'appelle _____ .
3. _____ est l'héroïne de Gustave Flaubert.

http://www.wiley.com/aventure.html

■ POUR COMMUNIQUER

Referring to people and things

IA   L'ARTICLE DÉFINI

L'amie de Benjamin s'appelle Julie.
Julie étudie **le** français et l'économie.
Les étudiants habitent dans **la** résidence Victor-Hugo.

◆ To refer to a specific person, thing, or concept use the definite article: **le, la, l', les** *(the)*.

Voilà **la** résidence.   *There's the dorm.*
Les étudiants sont ici.   *The students are here.*

L'article défini	*masculin*	*féminin*
SINGULIER	**le** livre	**la** résidence
SINGULIER + VOYELLE (OU H MUET)	**l'**homme	**l'**étudiante
PLURIEL	**les** étudiants	**les** maisons

◆ In French, the definite article marks the number and gender of the noun it precedes. When a masculine or feminine singular noun begins with a vowel sound, however, use **l'** in place of **le** or **la. Les** is used for all masculine and feminine plural nouns.

◆ When a noun is used in a general sense, the definite article is omitted in English but is required in French.

Tell students that general nouns are usually used as the subject of a sentence or as the object of a verb of preference. Both uses are illustrated in the examples.

Le français est amusant.   *French is fun.*
J'adore **la** pizza.   *I love pizza.*

ACTIVITÉS

 1. Qu'en pensez-vous? What do you think about the following items? Exchange information with your partner.

MODÈLE: café
        —J'adore le café!
  OU **—Je déteste le café! Et toi?**
        —Moi, je...

1. bière
2. limonade
3. chocolat chaud
4. Coca
5. omelettes
6. eau minérale
7. croissants
8. pizza

POUR S'EXPRIMER

Quelques disciplines

(m)	*(f)*	*(pl)*
l'allemand	la biologie	les mathématiques *(f)*
l'anglais	l'économie	les sciences politiques *(f)*
l'espagnol	la géographie	
le français	l'histoire	
l'italien	l'informatique	
le japonais	*(computer science)*	
	la littérature	
	la musique	
	la psychologie	

Note:

1. When you refer to a course someone is taking, use the definite article.
   Hélène étudie **les** mathématiques.
2. In French, mathematics and political science are always plural.
3. French students often abbreviate the names of their courses: **les maths, la psycho, la géo,** et **les sciences-po.**
4. Languages are not capitalized in French.

2. Qu'est-ce qu'ils étudient? Julie is curious about these students living at the **foyer.** Tell her their nationality and what they are studying.

MODÈLE: Maria / brésilien / informatique / français / maths
Maria est brésilienne. Elle étudie l'informatique, le français, et les maths.

1. Regina / allemand / histoire / espagnol / sciences-po
2. Takiko *(f)* / japonais / informatique / italien / économie
3. Julio / mexicain / psychologie / anglais / géographie
4. Sofia / italien / mathématiques / français / littérature
5. Boris / russe / économie / allemand / maths
6. Charlie / américain / sciences politiques / japonais / géographie
7. et moi, je / *(your nationality)* / *(your classes)*

50 cinquante

Chapitre 2

ACTIVITÉS

11. Comment sont-ils? Tell what the following people and things look like.

You may choose to assign **Activité 11** either as an oral or a written activity.

MODÈLE: beau C'est un homme.
  C'est un bel homme.

1. nouveau   Voilà une étudiante.
2. autre   Ce sont les amis de Pierre.
3. jeune   C'est une fille sympathique.
4. gros   Nous mangeons une banane jaune.
5. joli   Elles regardent les baskets.
6. vieux   Le pantalon noir est dans la chambre.
7. grand   Elle entre dans la chambre.
8. petit   Marie-Louise donne la robe à Cybille.
9. mauvais   Nous regardons souvent les films.
10. gentil   Le fiancé de Babette s'appelle Jacques.
11. bon   *Pronto* est un livre d'italien.
12. beau   Ils adorent la lampe.

 12. Je suis curieux! Find out from your partner if he or she

1. likes stylish clothes.
2. hates old clothes.
3. lives in a big or small room.
4. likes intelligent women/men.
5. speaks French with the other students in the class.
6. wears orange pants.
7. eats a big fat sandwich at noon.
8. likes good books.
9. Other questions?

TROISIÈME ÉPISODE

Ça ne va pas!° La vie° au foyer n'est vraiment° pas agréable.

Ça ne va pas! *Things aren't going well!* / **La vie** *Life* / **vraiment** *really*

JULIE: Je n'aime pas le foyer! Et je n'aime pas beaucoup ma camarade de chambre! Elle aime fumer. Moi, je ne fume pas. Je n'aime pas ça. Elle n'aime pas la musique classique. Moi, j'adore ça. Elle est désordonnée°, et en plus, elle porte ma jupe, mon short, et ma jolie robe bleue sans permission! Ah! non!

désordonnée *messy*

AVEZ-VOUS COMPRIS?

1. Est-ce que Julie est contente?
2. Comment est la vie au foyer?
3. Comparez les deux camarades de chambres.
4. Julie porte les vêtements de Françoise?
5. Est-ce que le téléphone et les douches sont dans la chambre de Julie?

JULIE: Et puis les douches° et le téléphone sont loin°, et il y a du bruit.°

_____

douches *showers* / **loin** *far (away)* / **il y a du bruit** *it's noisy*

JULIE: Bon, les douches, le téléphone, le bruit, la musique de Françoise, je peux vivre avec°, mais ses cigarettes? Ça, non!

_____

Je peux vivre avec *I can live with (them)*

ET VOUS?

1. Est-ce que vous habitez sur le campus? à la maison?
2. Et vos amis, où habitent-ils?
3. Votre chambre, elle est ordonnée ou désordonnée?
4. Est-ce que votre camarade de chambre fume? Et vous?

VOUS ÊTES BRANCHÉS!

La consommation de tabac en France

In many countries, smoking is a fact of life, despite health warnings. In France, for example, in 1992, 48% of the men and 33% of the women smoked. While more and more French restaurants are beginning to have **espaces non-fumeurs** *(no smoking areas),* smoking is still much more widespread in francophone countries than in the United States.

Aimez-vous fumer?

VOTRE Q. I. CULTUREL

Est-ce vrai ou faux?

1. 48% des Françaises fument.
2. Maintenant des espaces non-fumeurs existent dans les restaurants en France.
3. On fume beaucoup plus en France qu'aux U.S.A.

http://www.wiley.com/aventure.html

■ POUR COMMUNIQUER

Expressing preferences

III LES VERBES DE PRÉFÉRENCE EN -ER

Je **n'aime pas** le foyer!
Je **n'aime pas beaucoup** ma camarade de chambre!
J'**adore** la musique classique.
Elle **préfère** manger à la maison.

◆ To express preference or likes and dislikes, use the following verbs:

Les verbes de préférence en -er			
aimer	*to like*	adorer	*to love*
aimer beaucoup	*to like very much*	détester	*to hate*
aimer bien	*to like, enjoy*	préférer	*to prefer*
aimer mieux	*to like (something/someone) better*		

◆ The verb **préférer** is a regular **-er** verb like **aimer, adorer,** and **détester.** However, its accent pattern varies slightly.

préférer	
je préf**è**re	nous préférons
tu préf**è**res	vous préférez
il / elle / on préf**è**re	ils / elles préf**è**rent

Extension. If you wish, give students these other verbs that follow the same pattern as **préférer: espérer** (to hope), **répéter** (to repeat), **exagérer** (to exaggerate).

Note: Like the infinitive, the **nous** and **vous** forms of **préférer** are spelled with an **é** while every other form is spelled with an **è.**

◆ Verbs of preference are often followed by a definite article and a noun.

Julie **adore** le chocolat.   *Julie loves chocolate.*

◆ Verbs of preference may also be followed by an infinitive (a verb form that has no subject and means "to X") to express likes or dislikes.

Françoise **déteste** chanter.   *Françoise hates to sing.*
Julie **n'aime pas** nager.   *Julie doesn't like to swim.*

◆ The negation is generally placed around the conjugated verb even when it precedes an infinitive.

Nous **aimons regarder** la télé.   *We like to watch TV.*

    conjugated verb   infinitive

Nous **n'aimons pas** regarder la télé.   *We don't like to watch TV.*

Quelques parfums *(flavors)*

le chocolat

la vanille

la glace au chocolat

la glace à la vanille

le citron

la menthe

le sorbet au citron

le thé à la menthe

13. À chacun son goût! Françoise makes a list of things to eat and drink for a party she is planning. Say what each party-goer will dislike, like, or prefer.

MODÈLE: **Nous adorons le thé à la menthe.**

je		la glace au chocolat
nous		la glace à la vanille
Julie et Sébastien	aimer	le sorbet au citron
les étudiants	préférer	les sandwichs
Philippe	aimer beaucoup	le thé à la menthe
Céline	adorer	le café
Barbara et Laure	aimer mieux	l'eau minérale
vous	détester	les carottes
tu		le Coca lite

14. Regarde cet ensemble! *Look at that outfit!* At Françoise's party, Gina and Paul comment on everyone's clothes. Use your imagination to recreate the conversation.

MODÈLE: la robe de Marie
> **Gina: Regarde la robe de Marie!**
> **Paul: J'adore la robe de Marie.**
> OU **Je n'aime pas du tout la robe de Marie.**

> la jupe de Céleste
> **Gina: Oh là là! La jupe de Céleste!**
> **Paul: J'aime bien la jupe de Céleste.**
> OU **Je déteste la jupe de Céleste.**

1. le short de Julio
2. le tee-shirt de Sofia
3. les baskets de Roberto
4. la jupe de Françoise
5. la veste de Charlie
6. la chemise de Takiko
7. le jean de Julie

 15. Voilà ce que j'aime! Find out what activities your partner likes or dislikes.

■ WORDS TO USE: **beaucoup** *very much* / **un peu** *a little*

MODÈLE: danser / travailler
> **—Vous aimez danser?**
> **—Oui, j'aime beaucoup danser, mais je n'aime pas du tout travailler.**

	manger
	étudier
	regarder la télé
adorer	danser
aimer	écouter la radio
détester	écouter le prof
	voyager
	travailler

QUATRIÈME ÉPISODE `T 19`

Julie n'est pas contente. En fait, elle est furieuse. Elle désire étrangler Françoise.

JULIE: Écoute, Françoise, tu fumes constamment! Tu ne peux pas° fumer dehors?°

FRANÇOISE: Dehors!? Pas question! C'est ma chambre aussi!

Tu ne peux pas *You can't* / **dehors** *outside*

AVEZ-VOUS COMPRIS?

1. Est-ce que Julie est contente?
2. Est-ce qu'elle est calme?
3. Elle désire inviter Françoise à dîner?
4. Françoise aime fumer. Et Julie?
5. Est-ce que Françoise accepte ou refuse de fumer dehors?

3

4

JULIE: Bon, tu peux fumer quand je ne suis pas là.
FRANÇOISE: Et ma liberté alors?

JULIE: Elle est impossible! Que faire? Je quitte° le
foyer? Je reste° au foyer? Il faut° trouver
une solution!

Je quitte *(Shall) I leave* / **Je reste** *(Shall) I stay* / **Il faut**
I have to

ET VOUS?

1. Est-ce que vous êtes quelquefois furieux (furieuse)?
2. Quand vous êtes furieux (furieuse), est-ce que vous désirez étrangler
quelqu'un *(someone)?*
3. Est-ce que vous fumez? Si oui, est-ce que vous fumez dans la classe? à la
maison? dehors?
4. Quand il y a un problème, est-ce que vous trouvez rapidement une solution?

IL Y A UN PROBLÈME: QU'EN PENSEZ-VOUS?

For ideas on how to use this section, see the annotation in Chapter 1, p. 26.

Julie habite au foyer à Rouen. Elle n'est pas contente. Il faut trouver une solution. Que faire? Répondez avec **oui** ou **non.**

Julie devrait (*should*)

a. rester au foyer.
b. être amie avec Françoise.
c. quitter le foyer.
d. Une autre solution?

Justifiez votre choix (*Justify your choice*).

À VOUS DE JOUER

Vous habitez dans une résidence universitaire. Vous n'aimez pas beaucoup la résidence, et vous détestez votre camarade de chambre. Que faites-vous? *(What do you do?)*

a. Moi, je reste à la résidence.
b. Moi, je cherche un(e) autre camarade de chambre.
c. Moi, je quitte la résidence.
d. Une autre solution?

■ POUR COMMUNIQUER

Asking questions

IV L'INTERROGATION

Tu es furieuse**?**
Tu es furieuse, **n'est-ce pas?**
Est-ce que tu es furieuse?
Es-tu furieuse?

There are four ways to ask *yes/no* questions in French.

◆ **Intonation.** At the end of a sentence, raise your voice in a questioning tone.

Vous aimez le chocolat?   *(Do) you like chocolate?*

◆ **N'est-ce pas.** If you think the answer to your question is **oui,** use **n'est-ce pas** at the end of a sentence. The intonation rises on **n'est-ce pas.** Depending on the context, **n'est-ce pas** can mean *right?, aren't I?, can't you?, won't they?,* etc.

Julie est curieuse, **n'est-ce pas?**   *Julie is curious, isn't she?*
Julie habite en France, **n'est-ce pas?**   *Julie lives in France, right? (doesn't she?)*

◆ **Est-ce que.** To ask a *yes/no* question, use **est-ce que** at the beginning of a sentence. If **est-ce que** precedes a word beginning with a vowel sound, it is shortened to **est-ce qu'.**

Est-ce que Julie déteste la pizza?   *Does Julie hate pizza?*
Est-ce qu' elles aiment la musique   *Do they like classical music?*
    classique?

◆ **For recognition only. Inversion.** Sometimes inversion is used to ask *yes/no* questions. This means that the subject pronoun and the verb trade places. Inversion is not normally used with **je.**

Parlez-vous français?   *Do you speak French?*
Sommes-nous en retard?   *Are we late?*
But: Est-ce que je suis dans la bonne classe? *Am I in the right class?*

Asking questions using inversion will be formally presented in Chapter 3.

ACTIVITÉS

16. Hein? Comment? Takiko has trouble understanding Julie's questions, so Julie must sometimes ask them twice. With a partner, imagine their conversation.

■ **WORD TO USE: aussi** *too/also*

MODÈLE: JULIE: **Tu aimes le chocolat?**
       TAKIKO: **Comment?**
       JULIE: **Tu aimes le chocolat, n'est-ce pas?**
       TAKIKO: **Ah oui! Et toi, est-ce que tu aimes le chocolat aussi?**

1. Tu habites dans un foyer?
2. Tu aimes bien ta *(your)* camarade de chambre?
3. Elle fume des cigarettes?
4. Vous aimez manger au resto-u (restaurant universitaire)?
5. Vous mangez au resto-u demain *(tomorrow)*?
6. Tes *(your)* amis aiment manger au restaurant?

17. Elle est très égoïste, n'est-ce pas? Takiko asks Julie about Françoise. Julie answers with more information. Create their conversation with a partner.

MODÈLE: elle / être désagréable (très) —Oui,...
       TAKIKO: **Elle est désagréable, n'est-ce pas?**
       JULIE: **Oui, elle est très désagréable.**

1. elle / fumer (souvent) —Oui,...
2. elle / regarder / la télévision (à minuit) —Oui,...
3. ses *(her)* amies et elle / écouter les professeurs (ne... jamais) —Non,...
4. elle / respecter ses amies (ne... pas) —Non,...
5. ses amies et elle / être (laides) —Oui,...
6. elle / être sympathique (ne... pas du tout) —Non,...

18. Et toi alors? Find out as much as you can about your partner in a brief interview. Ask as many different questions as you can, using a variety of question forms. Then switch partners, and interview your new partner about the person he or she just spoke to. Use **être** and the verbs listed on pp. 39 and 65. (If you can't answer your partner's question about your first partner, simply answer **Je ne sais pas.**)

MODÈLE:

Vous: **Tu aimes le chocolat?**
PARTENAIRE 1: **Oui, j'aime beaucoup le chocolat.**
Vous: **Est-ce qu'il / elle aime le chocolat?**
PARTENAIRE 2: **Oui, il / elle aime beaucoup le chocolat.**
OU Vous: **Il / Elle habite dans un foyer, n'est-ce pas?**
PARTENAIRE 2: **Je ne sais pas.**

LECTURE

AU RESTAURANT

Reading Strategy: Applying prior knowledge

You already know a lot about the world around you. You can use prior knowledge to help you gain further information about items you are reading. For example, you have already eaten out at a variety of restaurants in your own city. What kind of information do restaurants typically place in their ads? Can pictures or symbols help you to determine where to eat?

Look over the restaurant ads below. Using your prior knowledge, tell at least one thing you can determine from each ad.

Now look over the ads again. Don't worry if you don't understand all the words. Take notes about the location of each restaurant, the type of food each serves, and what you think the specialties are. Then answer these questions.

1. Quelle (*what*) est l'adresse du restaurant **l'Équateur?**
2. **Tim** est quelle sorte de restaurant?
3. Quelle est une spécialité de **la Crêperie Gwenaelle?** le chocolat? le thé? la pizza?
4. À quel (*at which*) restaurant désirez-vous manger? au restaurant **Tim?** à **la Crêperie Gwenaelle?** à **l'Équateur?** Justifiez votre choix.

Referring to people and things **Voir p. 48.**

> Voici **les** étudiants.
> **Le** français est amusant.

Talking about possessions **Voir p. 51.**

> C'est **le** sac à dos **de** Marie.
> Voilà **la** porte **de la** classe.

Saying no **Voir p. 56.**

> Je **ne** fume **pas.**
> Il **n'**aime **pas du tout** la pizza.
> Elle **n'**arrive **jamais** en retard.

Describing people and things **Voir p. 59.**

> Nous portons une **jolie robe rouge.**
> C'est un **petit garçon intelligent.**

Expressing preferences **Voir p. 64.**

> Françoise **préfère** fumer.
> Julie **aime bien** la France.
> Nous **n'**aimons **pas du tout** regarder la télé.

Asking questions **Voir p. 70.**

> **Est-ce que** tu adores le chocolat?
> Julie étudie l'économie, **n'est-ce pas?**

ÊTES-VOUS BRANCHÉS? _____

Mon journal. In this chapter you have read and talked about the city of Rouen and about some French smoking habits. Choose one of the topics and write two or three similarities or differences you see in comparison to your own city or culture. Give your opinions if you wish.

Y ÊTES-VOUS ARRIVÉS? _____

A. Mes activités. With a partner, discuss your favorite and least favorite activities, using the verbs on p. 39 to get started. Ask your partner questions using **est-ce que** or **n'est-ce pas** to find out what he or she likes to do, and list the answers. Then discuss what you have in common. For example, **J'aime manger au restaurant, et tu aimes manger au restaurant aussi.**

B. Vive la différence! Find a new partner. Now look at your list from **Activité A.** Tell your new partner about the differences between you and your former partner. For example, **J'aime danser, mais Mary n'aime pas danser,** or **Je déteste parler italien, mais Raymond adore parler italien.**

 C. Se mettre sur son trente et un. *(To dress to the nines.)* You've just won 3000 francs (about $600) in the lottery **(la loterie).** Before you go on a clothes-shopping spree, tell a partner which articles of clothing you would like and what color(s) each item is. Use the list of clothing on p. 57. Have your partner do the same. For example, **Je voudrais un pantalon bleu.**

 D. Quelle collection! One student collects at least two items from three different classmates. The class tries to guess to whom each item belongs. Continue asking and answering questions until all the items have been properly identified.

MODÈLE: —**Est-ce que c'est le livre de Debbie?**
—**Oui, c'est le livre de Debbie.**
OU —**Non, ce n'est pas le livre de Debbie. C'est le livre de Tim.**

 PRONONCIATION

LES SONS [s] ET [z]

In most cases in French, the letter **s** is pronounced like the double **s** in hi**SS** ([s]). Other spellings that sound the same are **ç** or **c** before **i** or **e.** If a word contains a single **s** between two vowels, however, pronounce it like the [z] in bu**ZZ.** The letter **z** is also pronounced [z]. Final **s** is almost always silent in French.

1. Look over the words below; then repeat them after your professor or lab tape. Pay attention to spelling while you pronounce the words.

[s]	[z]
chau**ss**ettes	ro**s**e
fran**ç**ais	chemi**s**e
c'est	furieu**s**e
cinq	**z**éro
nous **s**ommes	vou**s** êtes
ils **s**ont	il**s** aiment

2. Now look over the words below. Copy the list onto a separate sheet of paper.
   Next to each word or group, mark either **[s]** or **[z]** to indicate the right sound.
   Then say all the words aloud.

a. onze

b. chemise

c. chaussure

d. monsieur

e. mademoiselle

f. veste

g. cassette

h. ça va

i. n'est-ce pas

j. maison

◆ VOCABULAIRE ACTIF ◆

Les disciplines   *School subjects*

l'allemand *(m)*   *German*
l'anglais *(m)*   *English*
la biologie   *biology*
l'économie *(f)*   *economics*
l'espagnol *(m)*   *Spanish*
le français   *French*
la géographie   *geography*

l'histoire *(f)*   *history*
l'informatique *(f)*   *computer
   science*
l'italien *(m)*   *Italian*
le japonais   *Japanese*
la littérature   *literature*

les mathématiques *(f)*
   mathematics
la musique   *music*
la psychologie   *psychology*
les sciences politiques   *political
   science*

Des objets utiles   *Useful items*

un appareil-photo   *camera*
un baladeur   *Walkman*
une calculatrice   *calculator*

une cassette   *cassette tape*
un disque compact   *compact disc*
un livre   *book*

une radio   *radio*
un sac à dos   *backpack*

Des vêtements   *Clothing*

des baskets *(f)*   *hightops*
des chaussettes *(f)*   *socks*
des chaussures *(f)*   *shoes*
une chemise   *shirt*
un collant   *tights; pantyhose*

un imperméable   *raincoat*
un jean   *pair of jeans*
une jupe   *skirt*
un pantalon   *pants*
une robe   *dress*

un short   *shorts*
un tee-shirt   *T-shirt*
des tennis *(f)*   *tennis shoes*
une veste   *jacket*

Les parfums   *Flavors*

le chocolat   *chocolate*
le citron   *lemon*

la menthe   *mint*

la vanille   *vanilla*

Noms divers

un(e) camarade de chambre *roommate*	une chambre *bedroom* la glace *ice cream*	le sorbet *sherbet* un vêtement *an article of clothing*

Les adjectifs de couleur

beige *beige* blanc(he) *white* bleu(e) *blue* brun(e) *brown* gris(e) *grey*	jaune *yellow* marron *brown* noir(e) *black* orange *orange*	rose *pink* rouge *red* vert(e) *green* violet(te) *purple*

Quelques adjectifs pour décrire les vêtements

bon marché *inexpensive* cher, chère *expensive* chic *chic*	confortable *comfortable* élégant(e) *elegant* laid(e) *ugly*	propre *clean* sale *dirty* simple *simple*

Adjectifs qui précèdent généralement le nom

autre *other* beau, bel, belle(s), beaux *handsome, beautiful* bon, bonne *good* gentil, gentille *nice, kind*	grand(e) *tall, big* gros, grosse *fat, large* jeune *young* joli(e) *pretty* mauvais(e) *bad*	nouveau, nouvel, nouvelle(s), nouveau(x) *new* petit(e) *short, small* vieux, vieil, vieille(s), vieux *old*

Des verbes de préférence

adorer *to love* aimer *to like* aimer beaucoup *to like very much*	aimer bien *to like; enjoy* aimer mieux *to like something or someone better*	détester *to hate* préférer *to prefer*

Expressions interrogatives

de quelle couleur... ? *what color . . . ?*	est-ce que... ? *(yes/no question marker)*	n'est-ce pas? *(yes/no question marker)*

Expressions de négation

ne... pas *not*	ne... jamais *never*	ne... pas du tout *not at all*

Autres mots et expressions utiles

aussi *too; also* avec *with*	un peu *a little*	porter *to wear*

Chapitre 3 ◆ À LA MAISON

PRÉSENTATION ÉCLAIR

POUR COMMUNIQUER

Talking about possessions (continued)
Talking about needs and wants
Asking questions (continued)

POUR Y ARRIVER

Le verbe **avoir**
Les expressions **il y a, voici, voilà**
Les adjectifs possessifs
Les expressions avec **avoir**

L'inversion
Quelques mots interrogatifs: **qui, que, quel(le)(s)**

POUR S'ADAPTER À LA CULTURE

Grenoble
La famille française: le mariage et les enfants

Voilà Benjamin chez° les Bouverot, sa famille française.

chez les Bouverot *at the Bouverot's house*

Il y a° six personnes dans sa famille. M. Bouverot, Jean-Claude, a 43 ans°. Il est électricien à l'EDF°. Mme Bouverot, Christine, a 45 ans. Elle est expert-comptable°.

Il y a *There are* / **a 43 ans** *is 43 years old* / **EDF** (Électricité de France) *the French state-run gas and electricity company* / **expert-comptable** *certified public accountant (CPA)*

In the **Et Vous** section, you may give your students information about your own family. In your examples, use the appropriate forms of the possessive adjectives so that students only have to repeat them in their answers.

AVEZ-VOUS COMPRIS?

1. Quel est le prénom *(first name)* de M. Bouverot? de Mme Bouverot?

2. M. Bouverot est électricien. Quelle est la profession de Mme Bouverot?

3. Qui *(who)* habite chez les Bouverot?

4. Comment s'appelle la chatte? Comment s'appelle le chien?

5. Qu'est-ce que Mme Bouverot dit *(say)* à Benjamin?

Tata° Cécile est la tante de Jean-Claude. Elle a 70 ans et elle est veuve. Il y a trois enfants dans la famille: Pierre, 18 ans; Dominique, 20 ans; et Catherine, 10 ans. Et il ne faut pas oublier° leur chien°, Dallas, et leur chatte° Barbara.

Tata *familiar for* **tante,** *aunt* / **il ne faut pas oublier** *one mustn't forget* / **leur chien** *their (male) dog* / **chatte** *(female) cat*

Tout le monde est très sympathique et Madame Bouverot dit° à Benjamin: «Fais comme chez toi.»°

dit *says* / **Fais comme chez toi.** *Make yourself at home.*

ET VOUS?

1. Est-ce que vous êtes français?
2. Dans ma famille, il y a quatre personnes. Et dans votre famille?
3. Mon père *(father)* s'appelle Pierre. Et votre père?
4. Ma mère *(mother)* s'appelle Anne. Et votre mère?
5. Il y a un chat chez moi. Il s'appelle Clifford. Et chez vous?

Let the students answer with a simple **non** if they don't have a pet. If you want them to answer in a complete sentence, help them by first modeling **Il n'y a pas de.** The negation of **il y a** is explained on p. 83.

VOUS ÊTES BRANCHÉS!

Grenoble

Located in **les Alpes** at the confluence of **le Drac** and **l'Isère** rivers, **Grenoble** is only 600 feet above sea level. However, it is well known as a winter sports center. In 1968, Grenoble hosted the Winter Olympics, and native son **Jean-Claude Killy** won three gold medals in the men's ski events.

The region around Grenoble is known for its superb cuisine, including **fondue savoyarde,** a melted cheese dish favored by skiers.

Grenoble and its suburbs are home to 400,000 people. Active industries, including a nuclear power plant, flourish along with excellent research facilities. In Grenoble, **l'Université Stendhal,** named for writer **Henri Beyle,** better known as **Stendhal,** (1783–1842), attracts scholars from all over the world.

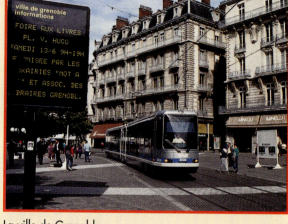

La ville de Grenoble.

The university has more than 4,000 teachers and 30,000 students.

La fondue savoyarde.

VOTRE Q. I. CULTUREL

Qu'avez-vous retenu? *What do you recall?* Answer the following questions.

1. Grenoble est dans les Pyrénées?
2. Comment s'appellent les rivières de Grenoble?
3. Comment s'appelle l'Université de Grenoble?

http://www.wiley.com/aventure.html

■ POUR COMMUNIQUER

Talking about possessions (continued)

IA LE VERBE *AVOIR*

Christine et Jean-Claude **ont** trois enfants.
Jean-Claude **a** une tante.
Nous **avons** une grande maison.
Vous **avez** un chat?

◆ The verb **avoir** *(to have)* indicates possession. When you want to talk about things you have or own, use **avoir.**

avoir	
j'**ai**	nous **avons**
tu **as**	vous **avez**
il / elle / on **a**	ils / elles **ont**

J'**ai** un chat. Il s'appelle
   Maximilien.
Cathy **a** un chien. Il s'appelle
   Médor.

I have a cat. His name is
   Maximilien.
Cathy has a dog. His name is
   Médor.

◆ When using **avoir** in the negative, change any indefinite article **un, une, des** to **de. De** becomes **d'** before a vowel sound.

Vous avez **un** chien?
Vous avez **une** télévision?
Tu as **des** amis?

—Non, je **n'**ai **pas de** chien.
—Non, nous n'avons **pas de** télévision.
—Non, moi, je **n'**ai **pas d'**amis.

ACTIVITÉS

T 21

POUR S'EXPRIMER

Informatique, vidéo, et hi-fi *(Computers, video, and stereo)*

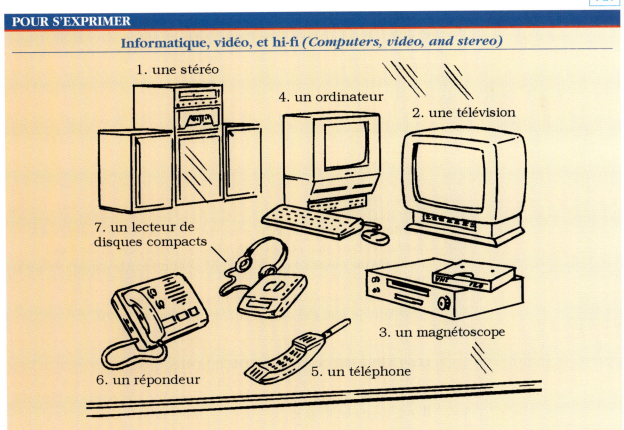

1. une stéréo
4. un ordinateur
2. une télévision
7. un lecteur de disques compacts
3. un magnétoscope
6. un répondeur
5. un téléphone

1. Il est observateur. Benjamin wants to know more about his new family so he observes what each person owns. Look at the drawing on p. 81 to complete the following statements using **avoir.**

MODÈLE: Dominique / 7
Dominique a un lecteur de disques compacts.

1. Christine / 1
2. Jean-Claude et Pierre / 5
3. Dominique et moi, nous / 2
4. Tata Cécile et toi, Catherine, vous / 3
5. Pierre / 6
6. et moi, je / 4

 2. Sondage *Survey.* Conduct a survey to see which appliances people have. In a small group, take turns asking and answering the questions. Remember to make the appropriate changes in the negative sentences.

MODÈLE: —**Vous avez une stéréo et un baladeur?** (stéréo oui, baladeur, non)
—**Oui, j'ai une stéréo, mais je n'ai pas de baladeur.**

1. Vous avez une télé et un magnétoscope? (télé oui, magnétoscope non)
2. Et vous Madame et Monsieur, vous avez une radio et une stéréo? (radio, non, stéréo, oui)
3. Et vous Mademoiselle, vous avez un ordinateur et un lecteur de disques compacts? (ordinateur, oui, lecteur, non)
4. Et vous, Monsieur, vous avez un téléphone et un répondeur (téléphone, oui, répondeur, non)
5. Est-ce que vous avez un répondeur et un lecteur de disques compacts? (répondeur, oui, lecteur de disques compacts, non)
6. Et vous, vous avez un ordinateur et un répondeur? (répondeur, non, ordinateur, oui)

 3. Mes possessions. With a partner, take turns asking each other questions about your possessions. Use the vocabulary in the **Pour s'exprimer** boxes on pp. 52 and 81. Ask at least five questions each.

MODÈLE: —**J'ai une stéréo. Est-ce que tu as une stéréo?**
—**Non, je n'ai pas de stéréo. As-tu une télévision?**

1B **LES EXPRESSIONS IL Y A, VOICI, VOILÀ**

Il y a un dictionnaire sur la table.   *There is a dictionary on the table.*
Il y a vingt étudiants ici.   *There are 20 students here.*

◆ **Avoir** is used in the expression **il y a** to say that something exists or is located somewhere. **Il y a** means *there is* or *there are.*

> **Il y a** trois chambres au premier étage.   *There are three bedrooms on the second floor.*

◆ Note the difference between **il y a** and **voilà / voici.** Both may be translated as *there is* or *there are,* but **voilà / voici** are used to point at or point out specific people or things, while **il y a** is mainly used to tell that something exists somewhere.

> **Voilà** Benjamin.   *There's Benjamin.*
> **Voici** ma chambre.   *Here's my room.*
> **Il y a** cinq stylos dans mon sac.   *There are five pens in my bag.*

◆ When using **il y a** in the negative **(il n'y a pas),** make sure to change the indefinite articles **un, une, des** to **de** or **d'.**

> Il y a **un** chat ici? —Non, il n'y a pas **de** chat ici.

Note that in French **le rez-de-chaussée** is the American *first floor,* **le premier étage** is the *second floor,* and so on.

ACTIVITÉS

T 22

POUR S'EXPRIMER

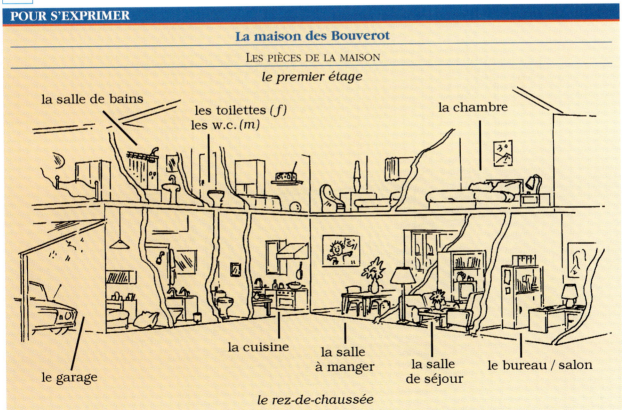

La maison des Bouverot

LES PIÈCES DE LA MAISON

le premier étage

la salle de bains
les toilettes (*f*)
les w.c. (*m*)
la chambre

la cuisine
la salle à manger
la salle de séjour
le bureau / salon
le garage

le rez-de-chaussée

un sofa

une lampe

une table basse

un fauteuil

LA CHAMBRE DE DOMINIQUE

une glace

une plante verte

un lit

une commode

une chaise

un bureau

un tapis

4. Voilà! Pierre Bouverot gives Benjamin a tour, pointing out rooms and furnishings along the way. Complete Pierre's tour information, using **voilà** or **il y a** as appropriate.

■ WORDS TO USE: **pièces** *(f) rooms* / **meubles** *(m) furniture*

_____ sept pièces dans ma maison. _____ la salle de séjour. Dans la salle de séjour, _____ un sofa et deux fauteuils confortables. _____ la salle de bains. Ah! tiens *(oh, look!)* _____ le tee-shirt de Dominique et _____ les tennis de Catherine!

Dans la salle à manger, _____ beaucoup de meubles. _____ une table, des chaises, une plante verte et une photo de famille. _____ Pierre bébé. Qu'est-ce qu'il est petit!

5. Qu'est-ce qu'il y a dans la maison de Benjamin?
Benjamin's new Moroccan friend, Larbi, wants to know about Benjamin's house in Grenoble. Refer to the picture on p. 83 and list all the rooms. Start with **Dans la maison, il y a…**

 6. Et la salle de séjour alors? Larbi wants to know exactly what Benjamin has in his living room. With a partner, imagine their conversation.

MODÈLE: LARBI: **Est-ce qu'il y a une télévision?**
                 BENJAMIN: **Oui, il y a une télévision.**

 7. Et chez vous? la salle de séjour? With a partner, talk about your (ideal) home and the living room in it.

1. Slowly list all the rooms in your (ideal) house so your partner can write them down. Have your partner do the same for you.
2. Next list all the things in the living room while your partner writes them down. Have your partner do the same for you.
3. Now ask each other questions to make sure the notes you took are accurate.

 8. Et la chambre? Look at the picture of Dominique's room on p. 84. Describe the items in her room, then ask your partner what she or he has in her or his (ideal) room.

MODÈLE: —**Dans la chambre de Dominique, il y a une commode. Et toi, est-ce que tu as une commode?**
                 —**Oui, j'ai une commode.**
          OU —**Non, je n'ai pas de commode.**

Voici la chambre de Benjamin. Il y a un petit lit, une lampe et un grand bureau. Derrière° la porte, il y a une glace.

derrière *behind*

À la maison en Californie, Benjamin a un ordinateur, une stéréo, une télévision et un téléphone. Ici°, il y a un ordinateur et un Minitel.

ici *here*

AVEZ-VOUS COMPRIS?

1. Qu'est-ce qu'il y a dans la chambre de Benjamin chez les Bouverot?
2. Chez Benjamin aux U.S.A., qu'est-ce qu'il y a?
3. Qu'est ce que c'est qu'un Minitel?
4. Est-ce que c'est difficile à utiliser?

BENJAMIN: Dis° Dominique, qu'est-ce que c'est qu'un Minitel?

DOMINIQUE: C'est une sorte d'ordinateur où on peut faire° des réservations de train, avoir les programmes de cinéma, de concert... C'est très pratique.

Dis *tell (me)* / **on peut faire** *one can make*

BENJAMIN: C'est difficile à utiliser?

DOMINIQUE: Non, c'est vraiment facile°. Regarde!°

facile *easy* / **Regarde!** *Look!*

ET VOUS?

1. Dans votre chambre, est-ce qu'il y a un petit ou un grand lit? Dans **ma** chambre il y a...
2. Est-ce qu'il y a une glace?
3. Avez-vous un téléphone? une radio? une stéréo, un ordinateur dans votre chambre? Dans **ma** chambre il y a...
4. Est-ce que vous aimez votre chambre?

Culture. Started in the early 1980s and promoted by the **France Télécom** (the French national telecommunications company), the **Minitel** provides on-line services to over six million households. It allows immediate access to banking, phone books, libraries, entertainment information, train and plane reservations, as well as chat groups and support groups.

VOUS ÊTES BRANCHÉS!

La famille française: le mariage et les enfants

Le mariage à la mairie est obligatoire.

French families are changing. People are marrying later in life, are not marrying at all, or are hesitant to remarry. In fact, over the last 20 years, the number of marriages has dropped by almost half. This is probably because under French law, one may obtain a **certificat de concubinage,** which certifies that a couple is living together as husband and wife. This document gives unmarried couples the same access to social and medical services as that enjoyed by married couples.

The birthrate in France has also declined significantly over the last fifty years. Concerned by the diminishing birthrate and the erosion of the traditional family structure, the French government devised **une politique nataliste,** a series of measures aimed at encouraging larger families and helping couples raise their children. These measures include

- free or inexpensive prenatal care
- sixteen weeks of maternity leave at full pay for working mothers.
- **allocations familiales** *(monthly allowances that start around 700F)* to families with two or more children.
- Subsidized **crèches** *(day-care centers)* and free preschools for children of working parents.

VOTRE Q. I. CULTUREL

Est-ce vrai ou faux?

1. Aujourd'hui, le mariage est moins *(less)* fréquent qu'autrefois *(before)*.
2. Un certificat de concubinage certifie qu'un couple habite ensemble.
3. La politique nataliste du gouvernement français encourage les familles à avoir des enfants.

http://www.wiley.com/aventure.html

■ POUR COMMUNIQUER

Talking about possessions (continued)

II   LES ADJECTIFS POSSESSIFS

Ma mère *(mother)* est comptable. Et **ton** père *(father)*?
Nous avons des amis sympathiques. **Nos** amis habitent à Grenoble. Et **vos** amis?

◆ To indicate ownership or relationships, use possessive adjectives. Like other adjectives, possessive adjectives agree in gender and number with the noun they describe.

Les adjectifs possessifs			
	masculin	*féminin*	*pluriel*
my	mon père	ma mère	mes enfants
your	ton père	ta mère	tes enfants
his	son père	sa mère	ses enfants
her	son père	sa mère	ses enfants
our	notre père	notre mère	nos enfants
your	votre père	votre mère	vos enfants
their	leur père	leur mère	leurs enfants

◆ **Attention!** Unlike in English, the gender of the owner does not affect the form of the possessive adjective in French. It is the possession—the noun that follows—that determines whether a possessive adjective will be masculine or feminine, singular or plural.

> Voilà Benjamin. **Sa** stéréo est super et **son** tee-shirt aussi!
> Voilà Catherine. **Sa** stéréo est super et **son** tee-shirt aussi.

Note: Mon, ton, son are used for any singular noun that begins with a vowel sound, even when the noun is feminine.

> **Mon** ami Jacques travaille à EDF.
> **Mon** ami**e** Jacqueline a une stéréo fantastique.

◆ **But:** Ma chère *(dear)* amie Jacqueline...

ACTIVITÉS

9. Qu'est-ce qu'ils ont? Show ownership by using the appropriate possessive adjectives.

■ **WORD TO USE: le chien** *(male) dog*

MODÈLE: J'ai une radio. _____ radio est sur la table.
　　　　　J'ai une radio. Ma radio est sur la table.

1. Tu as un chien. _____ chien s'appelle Dallas.
2. Dominique a un lecteur de disques compacts. _____ lecteur est superbe.
3. Tata Cécile a des cassettes. À mon avis *(in my opinion)*, _____ cassettes ne sont pas fantastiques!
4. J'ai des amis. _____ amis sont sympathiques. Et vous? Est-ce que _____ amis sont sympathiques aussi?

5. M. et Mme Bouverot ont un ordinateur. _____ ordinateur est rapide. Ils ont aussi deux autos. _____ autos sont bleues.

6. Nous avons un magnétoscope. _____ magnétoscope est excellent.

 10. C'est à qui? *Whose is it?* Catherine and Benjamin are straightening up the living room. Sometimes Benjamin doesn't know who owns one of the items he picks up. Catherine helps him out. With a partner, imagine their conversation.

MODÈLE: ton baladeur (non / le baladeur de papa)
    BENJAMIN: **C'est ton baladeur?**
    CATHERINE: **Non, ce n'est pas mon baladeur. C'est le baladeur de papa!**

    les livres de papa (oui)
    BENJAMIN: **Ce sont les livres de papa?**
    CATHERINE: **Oui, ce sont ses livres!**

1. ta lampe (non / la lampe de Dominique)
2. ton téléphone (non / le téléphone de Jean-Claude)
3. la stéréo de tes parents (oui)
4. les photos de Christine (non / les photos de Tata Cécile)
5. tes livres (non / les livres de Dominique et de Tata Cécile)
6. ton magnétoscope (non / le magnétoscope de la famille)
7. ma calculatrice (non / la calculatrice de Pierre)

ACTIVITÉS

Extension. If needed, teach **beau-frère / belle-sœur, beau-père / belle-mère, arrière grand-père / arrière grand-mère. Parrain / marraine** and **demi-sœur / demi-frère** may also be useful. Point out that **beau** and **belle** have two possible meanings: *in-law* or *step-*.

POUR S'EXPRIMER

Les membres de la famille			
le mari	*husband*	la femme	*wife*
le père	*father*	la mère	*mother*
le fils	*son*	la fille	*daughter*
le frère	*brother*	la soeur	*sister*
le grand-père	*grandfather*	la grand-mère	*grandmother*
l'oncle	*uncle*	la tante	*aunt*
le neveu	*nephew*	la nièce	*niece*
le cousin	*male cousin*	la cousine	*female cousin*

 11. La famille d'Éric Your friend Éric has found his family tree in an old box of books. With a partner, look at the tree, and ask and answer questions about the family.

MODÈLE: —**Qui est-ce?**
    —**C'est ma grand-mère.**

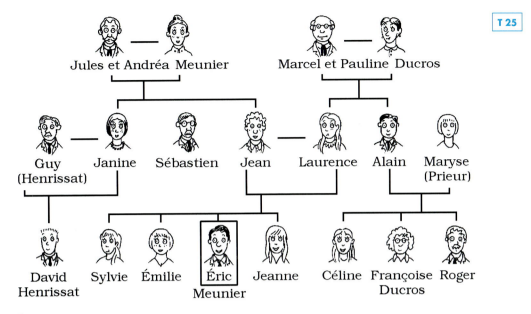

Jules et Andréa Meunier   Marcel et Pauline Ducros

T 25

Guy (Henrissat)   Janine   Sébastien   Jean   Laurence   Alain   Maryse (Prieur)

David Henrissat   Sylvie   Émilie   Éric Meunier   Jeanne   Céline   Françoise Ducros   Roger

12. Et ta famille? Ask your partner about his or her family, take notes, then share the information with another classmate. Your partner has the option of telling about his or her family or using his or her imagination.

■ WORDS TO USE: **le chat** (*male*) *cat* / **la chatte** (*female*) *cat* / **la chienne** (*female*) *dog*

MODÈLE: VOUS: **Comment s'appelle ton père?**
CHERYL: **Mon père s'appelle Paul.**
VOUS (À UN(E) AUTRE ÉTUDIANT(E)): **Le père de Cheryl s'appelle Paul.**

1. Comment s'appelle ta mère?
2. Où habitent tes parents?
3. Combien de (*how many*) frères et de sœurs as-tu?
4. Ta famille et toi, est-ce que vous habitez dans une maison? dans un appartement?
5. Comment est votre maison / appartement?
6. As-tu un chien? un chat? Comment s'appelle ton chien? ta chienne? ton chat? ta chatte?
7. Comment s'appelle ta cousine préférée? Et ton cousin préféré?

13. Ma famille Ask your partner to draw your family tree as you name members of your family (you can name as many as you wish or use your imagination). Now choose two members of your family and describe them with at least two adjectives.

MODÈLE: grand-mère
Ma grand-mère s'appelle Mary. Elle est grande et optimiste.

grand-père
Mon grand-père s'appelle John. Il est un peu gros et très sympathique.

Follow-up. Ask students to report their findings to the class. Next day, follow up by asking the class what they remember.

⌒ TROISIÈME ÉPISODE

T 26

Au début, Benjamin a du mal à° s'adapter. Il a envie de dormir° le jour, et il a sommeil° en classe.

___

a du mal à *has trouble* / **a envie de dormir** *feels like sleeping* / **a sommeil** *is sleepy*

Il a envie de parler anglais. Alors, il téléphone à ses amis. Il est constamment au téléphone.

AVEZ-VOUS COMPRIS?

1. Benjamin s'adapte facilement ou difficilement à la vie dans sa famille?
2. Qu'est-ce qu'il a envie de faire *(do)?*
3. Est-ce que Benjamin téléphone souvent ou rarement à ses amis?
4. Est-ce que Madame Bouverot est contente? Pourquoi *(why)* ou pourquoi pas?

Madame Bouverot n'est pas contente. Benjamin passe° trop de temps au téléphone. Il est désordonné et ne range° jamais sa chambre. En plus, il prend des douches° trop longues.

passe *spends* / **range** *straightens up* / **prend des douches** *takes showers*

MME BOUVEROT: Benjamin, vous avez deux minutes?
BENJAMIN: Mais bien sûr, Madame.
MME BOUVEROT: Asseyez-vous. J'ai besoin de vous parler°.

J'ai besoin de vous parler. *I need to speak to you.*

ET VOUS?

1. Est-ce que vous avez envie de dormir en classe? Si oui, dans quelle(s) classe(s)?
2. Est-ce que vous parlez souvent au téléphone? Avec qui?
3. Est-ce que vous êtes désordonné(e) *(messy)?* Et votre frère? votre sœur? vos parents?
4. Est-ce que vous rangez souvent votre chambre?

IL Y A UN PROBLÈME: QU'EN PENSEZ-VOUS?

Benjamin comprend que Madame Bouverot n'est pas contente.
Benjamin devrait (*should*)

a. refuser de parler avec Mme Bouverot.
b. demander à *(ask)* Mme Bouverot «Quel est le problème?»
c. téléphoner à ses amis pour parler de Mme Bouverot.
d. Avez-vous une autre solution?

Justifiez votre choix.

À VOUS DE JOUER

Vous habitez avec une famille en France. Mme Moreau, votre «mère» française, n'est pas contente. Qu'est-ce que vous faites *(do)*?
Moi, je

a. change de famille.
b. parle du problème à mes amis.
c. téléphone chez moi.
d. Avez-vous une autre solution?

Justifiez votre réponse.

■ POUR COMMUNIQUER

Talking about needs and wants

III   LES EXPRESSIONS AVEC AVOIR

Benjamin **a sommeil.**	*Benjamin is sleepy.*
Il **a envie de** parler anglais.	*He feels like speaking English.*
J'**ai besoin de** vous parler.	*I need to speak to you.*

◆ Many useful French expressions contain the verb **avoir.** Note that these expressions always use **avoir** in French even though they are frequently translated as *to be* in English.

Des expressions avec avoir

avoir besoin de	*to need (to)*	avoir sommeil	*to be sleepy*
avoir envie de	*to feel like*	avoir 10 ans	*to be 10 years old*
avoir honte (de)	*to be ashamed*	avoir de la chance	*to be lucky*
avoir peur (de)	*to be afraid (of/to)*	avoir du mal à	*to have trouble (doing something)*
avoir raison (de)	*to be right*	avoir tort (de)	*to be wrong*
avoir chaud	*to be hot*	avoir froid	*to be cold*
avoir faim	*to be hungry*	avoir soif	*to be thirsty*

◆ The expressions **avoir envie** and **avoir besoin** are always followed by **de +** a noun or **de +** an infinitive.

Nous **avons envie (besoin) de** chocolat.	*We would like (need) some chocolate.*
Nous **avons envie (besoin) de regarder** cette émission.	*We would like (need) to watch this program.*

◆ The **de** in **avoir besoin de** does not change before a plural noun, and it is shortened to **d'** before a vowel sound.

J'ai besoin **de** courage.   J'ai besoin **de** vacances.   J'ai besoin **d'**amis.

◆ The expressions **avoir honte, avoir peur, avoir raison,** and **avoir tort** may be used with or without **de +** infinitive. **Avoir peur** may also be followed by **de +** a noun.

Catherine **a honte.** Elle **a honte de fumer.**	*Catherine is ashamed. She is ashamed of smoking.*
J'**ai peur.** J'**ai peur d'être** ici.	*I'm afraid. I'm afraid to be here.*
Dallas **a peur de** Benjamin.	*Dallas is afraid of Benjamin.*

◆ **Avoir du mal à** is always followed by an infinitive.

Benjamin **a du mal à s'adapter.**	*Benjamin is having trouble adjusting.*

◆ To find out how old someone is, ask **Quel âge avez-vous?** or **Quel âge as-tu?** To answer this question, use the verb **avoir** followed by a number + **ans.** Unlike in English, the number is always followed by **ans** to express age.

Quel âge avez-vous?	*How old are you?*
J'**ai 18 ans.**	*I am 18 (years old).*
Christine **a** 45 **ans.**	*Christine is 45 (years old).*

Grammar. The expression **avoir besoin de** + infinitive is commonly used in everyday French. If you prefer not to use it, you may teach **devoir** + infinitive instead.

Extension. Tell students that if they don't add **ans** to the number, a French speaker will expect another noun.

ACTIVITÉS

14. Qu'est-ce qu'ils ont? *What's the matter with them?* Describe each drawing using the most appropriate expression with **avoir.**

T 27

Modèle: Il a froid.

1   2

3   4   5   6   7

15. J'ai envie de danser. Tell about the desires and duties of the people below. Follow the model.

■ **WORDS TO USE: difficile** *difficult* / **ranger** *to straighten up; to tidy up*

MODÈLE: (je) regarder la télévision/étudier
> **J'ai envie de regarder la télévision, mais j'ai besoin d'étudier.**

1. (tu) nager / préparer le dîner
2. (nous) manger au restaurant / rester à la maison
3. (Mme Bouverot) regarder un film / travailler
4. (ils) voyager / écouter une cassette au laboratoire
5. (vous) jouer au tennis / chercher un appartement
6. (Benjamin) visiter Grenoble / ranger sa chambre
7. (je) parler au téléphone / préparer un examen difficile
8. (Cathy et Pierre) danser / parler à leurs parents

16. ...parce que j'ai soif. Complete the following sentences with a plausible explanation using **parce que** *(because)* and an expression with **avoir.** Follow the model.

MODÈLE: Elles portent un short parce qu'elles...
> **Elles portent un short parce qu'elles ont chaud.**

1. Ils sont au restaurant parce qu'ils...
2. Tu as un pullover et des gants parce que tu...
3. Je suis au lit *(in bed)* parce que je...
4. Nous avons envie d'un Coca parce que nous...
5. Je suis à la bibliothèque *(library)* parce que je...
6. Cathy tremble parce qu'elle...
7. Jean-Claude et Christine travaillent parce qu'ils...
8. Tu as un million de dollars parce que tu...

Extension. Tell students to use the definite article **les** when describing hair and eyes. Explain that **roux** (never **rouge**) must be used for hair color. If you wish, add **longs / courts** and **bouclés / frisés / raides** for hair styles. You may also wish to teach **marron** *(dark brown)* for eyes. Note that both **noisette** and **marron** are invariable.

ACTIVITÉS

POUR S'EXPRIMER

La description physique

De quelle couleur sont les yeux et les cheveux de Robert?

Il a les yeux bleus et les cheveux gris.

De quelle couleur sont les yeux et les cheveux de Jeanne?

Elle a les yeux verts et les cheveux roux.

De quelle couleur sont les yeux et les cheveux de Patrick?

Il a les yeux noirs et les cheveux blonds.

De quelle couleur sont les yeux et les cheveux de Jeanne?

Elle a les yeux noisette et les cheveux bruns.

17. Interview. Find out from your partner

1. the color of his or her friend's eyes.
2. the color of his or her friend's hair.
3. the color of his or her mother's hair and eyes.
4. what his or her English professor looks like.
5. what his or her ideal man or woman looks like.

 18. Qui est-ce? Write a short description of one of your classmates including height, hair and eye color, and clothing. Give it to a different classmate who will try to guess the identity of the person from your description.

POUR S'EXPRIMER		
Les nombres de 32 à 70		
32 trente-deux	50 cinquante	60 soixante
40 quarante	51 cinquante et un	61 soixante et un
41 quarante et un	52 cinquante-deux	62 soixante-deux
42 quarante-deux		70 soixante-dix

 19. Ils ont quel âge? Look at Dominique's family photo album. With a partner, take turns asking about, identifying, and guessing the age of the people in each photo.

■ WORD TO USE: **là** *here; there*

MODÈLE: Tata Cécile.
—**Qui est-ce?**
—**C'est Tata Cécile.
Là, elle a 30 ans.**

20. Mon acteur favori. Now you can fully describe just about anyone. Pick your favorite actor or actress and describe him or her, and say how old he or she is. If you don't know his or her age, guess it.

Tell students to pay special attention to *seventy*, which combines *sixty* and *ten*.

Culture. Tell your students the expressions **se mettre sur son trente et un** *(to dress to the nines; to put on one's Sunday best)*, and **trente-six** *(lots of, umpteen)* as in **Je te l'ai déjà dit trente-six fois!** Ask if they can think of any English expressions that also use numbers.

Follow-up. You may ask students to identify the family relationships in the pictures for **Activité 19** if you want them to review the possessive adjectives. For example, they could answer, **«C'est ma tante Cécile.»**, or **«C'est mon frère.»**

Benjamin et Mme Bouverot entrent dans le salon. Catherine écoute à la porte. Dominique et Pierre arrivent.

DOMINIQUE: Mais qu'est-ce que tu fais° ici, Cathy?
CATHERINE: Chut!° J'écoute!
DOMINIQUE: Qui est dans le salon?
CATHERINE: C'est Benjamin.
DOMINIQUE: Qu'est-ce qu'il fait?
CATHERINE: Rien°. Il écoute maman.

---

fais *are doing* / **Chut!** *Ssshhh!* / **Rien.** *Nothing.*

AVEZ-VOUS COMPRIS?

1. Qui entre dans le salon?
2. Où est Cathy?
3. Qu'est-ce que Mme Bouverot dit *(say)* à Benjamin?
Elle dit «...»
4. Quand Benjamin ouvre la porte, comment est-ce que Catherine explique *(explain)* sa présence?
5. Est-ce que Benjamin est furieux? Expliquez.

DOMINIQUE: Qu'est-ce qu'elle dit?
CATHERINE: Elle dit à Benjamin de ranger sa chambre, d'utiliser le téléphone avec modération, et de prendre des douches courtes°.
PIERRE: Oh là là! Ça chauffe!° Attention! Ils arrivent!

---

courtes *short* / **Ça chauffe!** *There's trouble ahead!*

Benjamin ouvre la porte.

BENJAMIN: Qu'est-ce que tu fais° là Catherine?
CATHERINE: Eh bien, je cherche, je cherche un livre, une photo, euh...
BENJAMIN: Quel° livre? Quelle photo? Oh! la vilaine!° Elle écoute à la porte!
Benjamin rit°.
BENJAMIN: Moi, aussi, ça m'arrive d'°écouter à la porte.

---

fais *are doing* / **quel** *which (what)* / **la vilaine!** *naughty girl!* / **rit** *laughs* / **ça m'arrive d'** *I've been known to*

ET VOUS?

1. Pour une conversation privée, préférez-vous rester (*stay*) à la maison ou quitter (*leave*) la maison?
2. Quand vous êtes au téléphone à la maison, est-ce que votre famille écoute votre conversation?
3. Est-ce que vous êtes content(e) quand les autres personnes écoutent votre conversation?
4. Est-ce que vous écoutez quelquefois la conversation d'une autre personne? Si oui, quand et où?

Asking questions (continued)

IVA L'INVERSION

> Quel âge **as-tu?**
> **Avez-vous** des frères ou des sœurs?
> Qui **est-ce?**

Review. See pp. 70 and 71 to refresh your memory on how to ask questions.

Culture. Tell students that inversion is generally used in fairly formal settings, but that they may hear it in other situations. It is commonly used with questions such as **Quelle heure est-il?, Quel temps fait-il?,** and **Comment allez-vous?**

◆ You already know how to ask yes/no questions using intonation, **est-ce que,** and **n'est-ce pas.** You also have learned that inversion of the subject and verb is sometimes used to do the same thing. Compare the examples below:

> **Est-ce que** vous parlez français?
> **Parlez-vous** français?

◆ If the subject is a noun, the correct word order is noun + verb + pronoun. The pronoun must correspond to the noun. This applies to both people and things.

> Les étudiants sont intelligents.
> **Les étudiants** sont-**ils** intelligents?

◆ When **il, elle,** or **on** is the subject, and the verb ends in a vowel, you must insert **t** between the verb and subject for easier pronunciation.

> Il arrive à la gare de Grenoble.
> Arrive-**t**-il à la gare de Grenoble?

Attention: Inversion is not normally used with **je.** Use **est-ce que** instead.

> Est-ce que j'arrive en retard?

◆ Inversion is frequently used for certain common questions such as:

Comment allez-vous? (Comment vas-tu?)	*How are you?*
Quel temps fait-il?	*How's the weather?*
Quelle heure est-il?	*What time is it?*
Quel âge avez-vous? (Quel âge as-tu?)	*How old are you?*

ACTIVITÉS

 21. Et ta famille? Find out as much as you can about your partner's friends and family. Use the cues below to ask questions using inversion.

MODÈLE: ta sœur / être / intelligent
—**Et ta sœur, est-elle intelligente?**
—**Oui, elle est assez intelligente.**

1. tes frères / manger / beaucoup
2. ton amie / skier / mal
3. ton ami / étudier / bien
4. tes parents / nager / souvent
5. ton professeur / avoir peur de / ton chien
6. ta mère / écouter / ses amis
7. tu / chercher / ton ordinateur
8. ton père / regarder / la télévision

 22. Interview. With a partner, play the roles of a journalist and a celebrity. Find out, for example, if the celebrity is married, has children, likes to watch television, travels a lot, and often listens to the radio. Use inversion for all your questions. Then reverse roles.

IVB QUELQUES MOTS INTERROGATIFS: QUI, QUE, QUEL(LE)(S)

Qui est dans le salon?
Que dit-elle à Benjamin?
Quel livre cherches-tu?

◆ When you want or need specific information, use the following interrogative expressions:

Mots interrogatifs	
qui	who? whom?
que	what?
quel(le)(s)	which? what?

◆ **Qui** is a pronoun used to ask a question about a person. It may replace the subject of a verb, or the object of a verb or preposition.

Qui est là?	*Who's there?*
Qui admires-tu?	*Whom do you admire?*
À qui parlez-vous?	*To whom are you speaking?*

◆ **Que** is a pronoun used to ask a question about a thing. It may replace the object of a verb. Use inversion after **que** or use the alternate form **qu'est-ce que** + subject + verb.

> **Que** mangez-vous?
> **Qu'est-ce que** vous mangez?

◆ **Quel(le)(s)** is an adjective used to identify a specific thing or person. It agrees in number and gender with the noun it modifies. Inversion is frequently used in questions with **quel(le)(s)**. All forms are pronounced the same way, unless there is **liaison** (see Chapter 1).

> **Quel** professeur aimez-vous?
> **Quels** livres préférez-vous?
> **Quels artistes** aimes-tu?
> **Quelle** classe détestez-vous?
> **Quelles** femmes sont dans ta classe?
> **Quelles amies** sont ici?

Attention! When writing, choose the correct form of **quel.** It should agree with the noun that follows, even if it is separated from the noun by the verb **être.**

> **Quelle** est **la date** aujourd'hui?   *What is the date today?*

◆ **For recognition only.** When a preposition such as **avec, de, à** or **dans** is used with **qui, que** or **quel(le)(s)**, the question begins with the preposition. Also note that **que** changes to **quoi** in questions beginning with a preposition.

> **De quoi** parlez-vous?   *What are you talking about?*
> **À qui** écrit-il?   *To whom is he writing?*
> **Dans quel** restaurant mange-t-elle?   *In which restaurant is she eating?*

ACTIVITÉS

 23. Qui fait quoi? Benjamin asks M. Bouverot some questions. Play the roles with a partner.

MODÈLE: jouer au golf (Cathy)
>   BENJAMIN: **Qui joue au golf?**
>   M. BOUVEROT: **Cathy joue au golf.**

1. avoir un dictionnaire anglais (Dominique)
2. travailler au bureau (je)
3. être étudiant (Pierre et Dominique)
4. aimer le chocolat noir *(dark)* (ma femme et moi, nous)
5. parler français avec un accent (tu)

24. Et toi alors? Find out who in your class is involved in the activities listed below by asking at least five questions using **qui.** You may add other activities to the list if you wish. Be prepared to report your findings to the class.

Follow-up. You may wish to have students do **Activité 24** in groups and then report to the class what they have learned.

■ WORD TO USE: **seul(e)** *alone*

MODÈLE: —**Qui habite dans une maison?**
       —**Paul habite dans une maison.**
   OU —**Moi, j'habite dans une maison.**

1. parler une autre langue
2. manger souvent au restaurant
3. manger au restaurant universitaire
4. habiter dans un appartement / une maison / une résidence universitaire
5. habiter seul(e) / avec un(e) camarade de chambre / avec sa famille
6. regarder les émissions *(programs)* de sport à la télé
7. détester les examens
8. voyager souvent
9. chanter bien
10. danser comme Janet Jackson
11. aimer bien le professeur de français

 25. Mais qu'est-ce que tu fais? Catherine is feeling overly energetic today. She's running through the house opening doors to find out what everyone's doing. Use **qu'est-ce que** to say what Catherine asks each family member. Your partner will give the probable response.

Follow-up. Have weaker students ask the class questions with **qu'est-ce que** using the verbs in **Activité 25.** Ask for volunteers to come up with original responses.

MODÈLE: Benjamin mange un sandwich.
       CATHERINE: **Qu'est-ce que tu manges?**
       BENJAMIN: **Je mange un sandwich.**

1. M. et Mme Bouverot regardent la télé.
2. Tata Cécile mange une carotte.
3. Dominique écoute un CD.
4. Pierre range sa chambre.
5. Benjamin étudie son français.
6. Dallas et Barbara mangent les chaussures de Tata Cécile.

 26. Quels sont tes goûts *(tastes)***?** Tell your partner what you like. Then find out what he or she likes. Use **quel(le)(s).**

Follow-up. Ask students to report on their partner's tastes and/or their own preferences. If reporting on themselves, ask them to give reasons. For example, **J'aime Diana's Greek Café parce que les gyros sont très bons.**

MODÈLE: —**J'aime la musique punk. Et toi, quelle musique aimes-tu?**
       —**Je préfère les films (m) de Spielberg. Et toi, quels films préfères-tu?**

les films   le restaurant
la musique (le jazz? le reggae?)   le professeur
les musiciens / les musiciennes   les acteurs / les actrices
le cours de français

DÉCORER SA MAISON

Reading Strategy: Locating topic sentences and supporting details

Topic sentences give a reader the main idea of a paragraph and are often followed by detailed information that supports the main idea. In each of the two paragraphs, find the topic sentence and two supporting details for each topic sentence. Compare your choices with a partner's to see if you agree. Then answer these questions before rereading the passage.

1. Which objects in your room at home reveal your personality?
2. What style of furniture does your family have at home? Are all the rooms decorated in the same style?
3. Are any of the rooms in your home used for more than one purpose? If so, why?

son... *one's home*

affiche... *shows off*

chez... *at the antique dealer* / **assortir...** *match*
ne... guerre... *hardly allow*

share / *same*

Décorer son chez soi°

La maison affiche° d'abord la personnalité de ses occupants et leur sens du confort. Les Français ont une certaine préférence pour les meubles anciens, copies ou authentiques, hérités de la famille ou trouvés chez l'antiquaire°. Ils n'hésitent pas à assortir° les meubles avec quelques objets contemporains ou modernes.

Les petits appartements ne permettent guère° d'avoir une pièce pour toutes les activités: la salle de séjour est quelquefois la salle à manger, le salon, ou le bureau...; deux enfants partagent° souvent la même° chambre.

Source: Adapted from *Chez vous en France* by Geneviève Brame.

Now answer these questions.

1. Quel style de meubles les Français préfèrent-ils?
2. Aiment-ils aussi les objets modernes?
3. Est-ce qu'il y a toujours une pièce différente pour toutes les activités? une chambre pour chaque enfant?

À VOS STYLOS!

UNE LETTRE

Writing Strategy: Making lists and adding information

When you want to write a letter, you must think about the things that you want or need to tell your correspondent. Making a list is a good way to start. Next you can fill in or add more information about each topic you have chosen. Before you begin writing, read the letter you have just received from Michèle, your new penpal who lives in the **Île de la Réunion.**

> Chère Peggy,
>
> Je m'appelle Michèle. J'ai 20 ans. Il y a quatre personnes dans ma famille. J'habite dans une maison avec mes parents, mes deux frères, et mon chien, Médor.
> Je suis étudiante à l'Université de la Réunion. J'ai trois cours° intéressants et deux cours très difficiles. J'étudie beaucoup, mais je préfère danser et sortir° avec mes amis. J'ai de la chance. J'ai un ordinateur et une stéréo chez moi. J'aime écouter la musique antillaise° et américaine. Et toi, qu'est-ce que tu aimes? Écris-moi vite.°
>
> Ton amie,
>
> *Michèle*

classes

to go out

antillaise *from the Antilles*
Écris... *Write to me fast*

Using Michèle's letter as a guide, follow the steps below.

1. Look over Michèle's letter. Make a general list of the things that she writes about (e.g., name, age, family information, studies, possessions). Then, make your own general list of topics to write about in your reply. You do not need to include everything on Michèle's list, and may add other topics if you wish.

2. Now look at the specifics of Michèle's letter. What precise information does she provide in her letter? Write down names, ages, possessions, likes and dislikes, and so on, for each of the general topics you listed earlier. Do the same for your own list.

3. Now you have everything you need to start writing. The final step in your letter is to organize the ideas you have listed into a reply to Michèle. **À vos stylos!**

RÉVISION ÉCLAIR

Talking about possessions (continued)   **Voir pp. 80 et 82.**

> **J'ai** beaucoup de livres.
> **Il y a** un crayon, un livre, et des papiers sur la table.

Talking about possessions (continued)   **Voir p. 88.**

> **Ma** maison est grande, mais **ton** appartement est petit.
> **Mes** amis sont gentils; **vos** amis sont gentils aussi.

Talking about needs and wants   **Voir p. 94.**

> **Vous avez faim** quand vous ne mangez pas assez.
> **Nous avons envie de** manger.

Asking questions (continued)   **Voir pp. 100 et 101.**

> **Êtes-vous** fatigués?
> **Qui** parle arabe?
> **Qu'est-ce que** tu as?
> **Quel** est ton film favori?

ÊTES-VOUS BRANCHÉS? ───────────────

Mon journal. In your journal, write two facts you have learned about the city of Grenoble, and two facts you have learned about French marriages and French families. Compare the French customs and ceremonies to what you are used to at home. For example, if you were getting married, how would you like to do *your* ceremony?

Y ÊTES-VOUS ARRIVÉS? ───────────────

A. Je sais poser des questions! For each of the cues below, see how many ways (including intonation, **n'est-ce pas,** and **est-ce que**) you can ask a yes/no question. Your partner will answer.

1. (tu) regarder souvent MTV
2. (elles) téléphoner à leurs amis
3. (je) dîner au restaurant
4. (nous) voyager au Japon
5. (il) jouer au golf
6. (vous) être timide
7. (tu) avoir soif
8. (Dominique) avoir sommeil
9. (M et Mme Wilson) avoir une maison en Californie
10. (Anne et toi) skier bien

B. Madame Rapide. You have a friend who always finishes your sentences before you have a chance to complete your thoughts. How would your friend finish the phrases you have started? Work with a partner.

MODÈLE: —**J'ai peur quand...**
—**...quand tu n'as pas tes devoirs?**

1. Le professeur a peur...
2. Nous avons faim...
3. Vous avez soif...
4. J'ai sommeil...
5. Benjamin a honte...
6. Les étudiants ont besoin d'étudier...

 C. On déménage! *Let's move!* Pierre is helping his friend Jean-Paul move out of his room at the **résidence universitaire.** Jean-Paul has already packed four boxes, and Pierre wants to know what is in each one. Recreate their conversation with a partner, using the items from the list below.

MODÈLE: —**Qu'est-ce qu'il y a dans le carton numéro 2?**
—**Numéro 2? Euh, il y a un baladeur, des cassettes, et mes disques compacts.**

chaussettes	appareil-photo	magnétoscope
baladeur	répondeur	sac à dos
pantalon	petite lampe	cahier
stéréo	tee-shirts	devoirs
livres	cassettes	plante

 D. En week-end. The Bouverot family is getting ready to leave on a weekend trip and Mme Bouverot is checking to see if all the family members have what they need. Ask Mme Bouverot's questions, and your partner will answer.

MODÈLE: Jean-Claude / tu / livre
—**Jean-Claude, tu as ton livre?**
—**Oui, bien sûr, j'ai mon livre.**

1. Benjamin / vous / baladeur
2. Dominique et Catherine / vous / shorts
3. Pierre / tu / compacts
4. Jean-Claude et moi / nous / passeports
5. Tata Cécile / elle / aspirine
6. et moi / je / magazines

E. Interview. Find out from your partner

1. who arrives late for class.
2. who never listens to the teacher.
3. who is tall/short.
4. what your partner is studying.
5. what he or she hates to watch on television.
6. what he or she has at home.
7. which musical group he or she likes.
8. which restaurant he or she prefers.
9. which class he or she loves/hates.

 PRONONCIATION

LES VOYELLES NASALES

By now you probably have noticed that French has certain sounds that do not exist in English. The nasal vowels may be the most obvious of these sounds. There are several nasal vowels in French. They are generally indicated by **m** or **n** in spelling.

- If an **m** or **n** is doubled after a vowel or is followed by a vowel, the preceding vowel is not nasalized. Examples include **homme, immortel, imiter, bonnet, italienne, initial.**

1. Look over the words below to find the nasal vowels. Then listen to your professor or lab tape and repeat the words.

[ã]	[ɛ̃]	[ɔ̃]
gra**nd**	vi**ng**t	**on**ze
fra**n**çais	mi**n**ce	c**om**ptable
da**ns**	b**ain**	s**on**
ge**n**til	ci**nq**	m**on**de
enfant	électrici**en**	av**on**s
cha**m**bre	chi**en**	rép**on**deur

2. For words spelled with **-um** or **-un,** some native speakers will pronounce the sound as [ɛ̃] (see above), and some will pronounce it [œ̃]. Listen closely to your professor or lab tape and imitate the sound you hear in the following words.

un   l**un**di   br**un**   parf**um**   comm**un**   h**um**ble

3. Look over the groups of words below. In each group, there are three words with a nasal vowel, and one word where the vowel is *not* nasal. Decide which word does not belong, then pronounce the remaining words. Then listen to your lab tape to check your answers.

a. salon   compact   bonnet   maison
b. minuit   mince   impossible   cinq
c. Jean   soixante   ranger   Anne

◆ V O C A B U L A I R E   A C T I F ◆

La maison   *The house*

le bureau *office*	le premier étage *second floor*	la salle de séjour *living room*
la chambre *bedroom*	le rez-de-chaussée *first floor*	le salon *den*
la cuisine *kitchen*	la salle à manger *dining room*	les toilettes *(f)* *restroom, bathroom*
le garage *garage*	la salle de bains *bathroom*	les W.C. *(m)* *toilet*
une pièce *room*		

Les meubles *(m)*   *Furniture*

une commode *dresser*	une lampe *lamp*	un sofa *sofa*
un fauteuil *armchair*	un lit *bed*	une table basse *coffee table*
une glace *mirror*	une plante (verte) *plant*	un tapis *rug*

Informatique, vidéo, et hi-fi

un lecteur de disques compacts *CD player*	un ordinateur *computer*	un téléphone *phone*
un magnétoscope *VCR*	un répondeur *answering machine*	une télévision *television*
	une stéréo *stereo*	

Les membres de la famille

un cousin *cousin*	une grand-mère *grandmother*	une nièce *niece*
une cousine *cousin*	un grand-père *grandfather*	un oncle *uncle*
une femme *wife*	un mari *husband*	un père *father*
une fille *daughter*	une mère *mother*	une sœur *sister*
un fils *son*	un neveu *nephew*	une tante *aunt*
un frère *brother*		

La description physique

les cheveux *hair*	Quel âge avez-vous (Quel âge as-tu)? *How old are you?*	J'ai... ans. *I am . . . years old.*
les yeux *eyes*		
roux *red*		

Les nombres

les nombres de 32 à 70
See p. 97.

See p. 97.

Les adjectifs possessifs

mon, ma, mes *my*	son, sa, ses *his; her*	votre, vos *your*
ton, ta, tes *your*	notre, nos *our*	leur, leurs *their*

Avoir et ses expressions

avoir *to have*	avoir envie de *to feel like*	avoir raison (de) *to be right*
avoir... ans *to be . . . years old*	avoir faim *to be hungry*	avoir soif *to be thirsty*
avoir besoin de *to need (to)*	avoir froid *to be cold*	avoir sommeil *to be sleepy*
avoir chaud *to be hot*	avoir honte (de) *to be ashamed*	avoir tort (de) *to be wrong*
avoir de la chance *to be lucky*	avoir peur (de) *to be afraid,*	il y a *there is/are*
avoir du mal à *to have trouble*	*scared (of/to)*	
(doing something)		

Autres mots utiles

le chat *(male) cat*	difficile *difficult*	là *here; there*
la chatte *(female) cat*	que *what*	ranger *to straighten up; to tidy up*
le chien *(male) dog*	quel(le)(s) *what, which*	seul(e) *alone*
la chienne *(female) dog*	qui *who, whom*	voici *here is/are*

Chapitre 4 ◆ À LA RECHERCHE D'UN APPARTEMENT

PRÉSENTATION ÉCLAIR

POUR COMMUNIQUER

Telling time
Describing your schedule
Talking about your activities (continued)
Asking questions (continued)
Adding emphasis
Situating people and things

POUR Y ARRIVER

L'heure
Les jours, les mois, et les saisons

Le verbe **faire** et quelques expressions
Les mots interrogatifs: **où, quand, comment, pourquoi**
Les pronoms accentués
Les prépositions
Le verbe **mettre**

POUR S'ADAPTER À LA CULTURE

Les jours de fête en France
Les appartements en France

1

Julie parle à son amie Florence.

JULIE: Ça ne va vraiment pas avec Françoise. Aujourd'hui, c'est décidé, je cherche un appartement!

2

FLORENCE: Quelle sorte d'appartement?

JULIE: Oh... un grand appartement calme à partager° avec une personne sympa qui ne fume pas!

_____
partager *to share*

AVEZ-VOUS COMPRIS?

1. Avec qui est-ce que Julie parle?
2. Qu'est-ce que Julie cherche aujourd'hui?
3. Quel type d'appartement est-ce que Julie cherche?
4. Quel est le programme de Julie pour la matinée?
5. Qu'est-ce que Florence propose à Julie?

FLORENCE: Mais, tu vas faire comment?°

JULIE: J'ai un plan. Voilà mon programme de la matinée°. Je suis au CROUS° à dix heures, à la fac° à onze heures et demie, et à la poste pour téléphoner à une heure moins le quart...

Mais, tu vas faire comment? *But, how are you going to do that?* / **matinée** *morning* / **CROUS** (Centre régional d'œuvres universitaires et scolaires) *local center to help students with various aspects of student life* / **fac (faculté)** *university*

FLORENCE: Moi aussi, j'ai une idée. Passe au kiosque, achète° le journal et regarde les petites annonces!°

---

achète *buy* / **petites annonces** *classified ads*

ET VOUS?

1. Où habitez-vous?
2. Est-ce que vous aimez votre appartement ou votre maison?
3. Où est-ce que les étudiants cherchent un appartement dans votre ville *(city)*?
4. Et vous, où est-ce que vous cherchez un appartement?

Extension. Some students may wonder about **matin** versus **matinée.** Provide them with other similar pairs **(soir / soirée, an / année)** and tell them that the suffix **-ée** indicates the passage of time as opposed to a block of time.

Telling time

▮ L'HEURE

Il est une heure. Il est deux heures et quart. Il est six heures vingt. Il est sept heures moins vingt-cinq.

Il est neuf heures et demie. Il est minuit. Il est dix heures moins le quart. Il est midi.

Julie est au CROUS **à dix heures.**
Elle lit *(reads)* le journal **à onze heures et quart.**
Elle est à la fac **à onze heures et demie.**
Elle est en classe **à midi.**
Elle téléphone **à trois heures moins le quart.**

◆ **Quelle heure est-il?** means *What time is it?*

◆ To find out what time something happened or will happen, ask **À quelle heure?** The answer will begin with **à.**

> **À quelle heure** est-ce que Julie est au café?
> Elle est au café **à onze heures et quart.**

◆ To indicate that an action occurs over several hours, use **de... à.**

> Julie travaille **de** trois heures **à** six heures.

You may want to compare and contrast the spelling of **demi** in **minuit et demi** and in **une heure et demie.** Ask students to try to figure out why there is a spelling change. In addition, point out that most people do not say **douze heures.**

◆ French has special expressions for quarter hours and half hours.

Il est huit heures **et quart.**	*It is a **quarter past** eight.*
Il est neuf heures **et demie.**	*It is **half past** nine.*
Il est dix heures **moins le quart.**	*It is **a quarter to** ten.* or *It is nine forty-five.*

◆ a.m. and p.m. times are indicated as follows:

Il est huit heures **du matin.**	*It's 8:00 a.m.*
Il est deux heures **de l'après-midi.**	*It's 2:00 p.m.*
Il est huit heures **du soir.**	*It's 8:00 p.m.*

Note: Another way of indicating a.m. and p.m. is by using a 24 hour clock. All timetables, schedules and official business make use of **l'heure officielle.** 24-hour time does not use **et quart, et demi(e)** or **moins le quart.**

Il est quatorze heures.	*It's 2:00 p.m.*
Il est quatorze heures quinze.	*It's 2:15 p.m.*
Il est quatorze heures trente.	*It's 2:30 p.m.*
Il est quatorze heures quarante-cinq.	*It's 2:45 p.m.*

ACTIVITÉS

1. À quelle heure? Look at Julie's calendar and tell what time Julie does each activity.

■ WORD TO USE: **la bibliothèque** *library*

1. À quelle heure est-ce que Julie est au restaurant?
2. À quelle heure est-ce qu'elle a son cours d'économie?
3. À quelle heure est-ce qu'elle dîne avec Philippe?
4. À quelle heure est-ce qu'elle nage à la piscine?
5. À quelle heure est-ce qu'elle est à son cours de philosophie?
6. À quelle heure est-ce qu'elle étudie à la bibliothèque?
7. À quelle heure est-ce qu'elle est à son cours de phonétique?

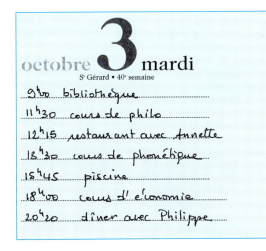

octobre **3** mardi
S¹ Gérard • 40ᵉ semaine

9ʰ00 bibliothèque
11ʰ30 cours de philo
12ʰ15 restaurant avec Annette
13ʰ30 cours de phonétique
15ʰ45 piscine
18ʰ00 cours d'économie
20ʰ20 dîner avec Philippe

 2. À quelle heure part l'avion pour... Look at the airport schedule of departing flights. Ask your partner what time each plane leaves.

MODÈLE: —À quelle heure part l'avion pour Nice?
—Il part à onze heures et demie (du matin).

DESTINATION	VOL	DÉPART
Nice	123	11:30
Londres	328	15:15
Madrid	234	15:30
New York	654	16:15
Dakar	850	17:05
Montréal	140	19:45

 3. Vous êtes où à quelle heure? Tell your partner about your schedule. Mention four different times in the day. Use **d'abord, ensuite, puis,** et **enfin.**

MODÈLE: **D'abord, j'arrive à la fac à huit heures. Ensuite, je suis en cours d'anglais à neuf heures. Puis, je suis à la bibliothèque à deux heures. Enfin je suis à la maison à cinq heures.**

🎧 DEUXIÈME ÉPISODE T 30

Aujourd'hui, c'est le 15 octobre. Nous sommes en automne. Il est quatorze heures. Il fait du soleil. Julie et Florence bavardent°.

──────────

bavardent *are chatting*

JULIE: Qu'est-ce que tu as envie de faire°
 maintenant, Florence?
FLORENCE: J'ai envie de faire une promenade° mais
 j'ai besoin de faire° mes devoirs. Et toi?

──────────

faire *to do* / **faire une promenade** *to take a walk* /
faire mes devoirs *to do my homework*

AVEZ-VOUS COMPRIS?

1. Quelle est la date dans l'histoire *(story)*?
2. Quel temps fait-il?
3. Qu'est-ce que Florence a envie de faire? Et Julie?
4. Qu'est-ce que Julie a besoin de faire? Et Florence?
5. Qu'est-ce que Julie regarde? Pourquoi?

3

JULIE: Moi, j'ai envie de faire la sieste° mais il faut faire les courses° et trouver un appartement!

_____
faire la sieste *to take a nap* / **il faut faire les courses**
I have to run errands

4

FLORENCE: Tu as le journal?
JULIE: Oui, oui bien sûr. Regarde!° il y a trois petites annonces intéressantes.
FLORENCE: Super! Téléphone vite!°

_____
regarde *look* / **vite** *quickly*

ET VOUS?

1. Quelle est la date aujourd'hui?
2. Est-ce qu'il fait beau aujourd'hui?
3. Quand il fait beau, qu'est-ce que vous aimez faire? danser? nager?
4. Cet après-midi qu'est-ce que vous avez besoin de faire? étudier? travailler? trouver un appartement?
5. Qu'est-ce que vous avez envie de faire? regarder la télévision? nager? écouter la radio? faire la sieste?

VOUS ÊTES BRANCHÉS!

Les jours de fête en France *Holidays in France*

Many countries have similar holidays. Similar holidays do not necessarily fall on the same dates, however. For example, Americans celebrate their national holiday on July 4th whereas the French celebrate **la fête nationale**—*Bastille Day*—**le 14 juillet**—on July 14th. On *Bastille Day,* most French people enjoy watching a military parade and fireworks. Then they usually go dancing in open-air **bals populaires** *(dances)* which spring up all over French cities.

In France, there are many opportunities to celebrate, for example, **le Jour de l'An, le 1er janvier** *(New Year's Day),* **la Fête du Travail, le 1er mai** *(May 1st, Labor Day),* and **la Fête des Mères** *(Mother's Day)* the last Sunday in May.

Historically a Catholic country, France celebrates **Pâques** *(Easter),* **Noël** *(Christmas),* and **la Tous-**

Noël

Ramadan

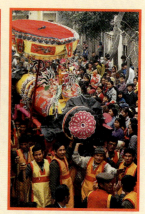

Têt

saint *(November 1st, All Saints' Day),* a day dedicated to honoring the dead. Most people also celebrate their individual **fête** (the day of the saint after whom they are named).

Religious diversity, however, is growing in France. Islam, for example, has the second largest number of adherents in France today. Religious observances and holidays celebrated by various groups in the French community include **Ramadan** (Islamic period of fasting), **Têt** (Vietnamese New Year), and **Rosh Ha-Shana** (Jewish New Year).

Rosh Ha-Shana.

VOTRE Q. I. CULTUREL

Le savez-vous? *Do you know this?*

A. Match the holiday or religious observance with its equivalent in English.

1. Ramadan	**a.** New Year's Day
2. Pâques	**b.** Mother's Day
3. La Fête des Mères	**c.** Vietnamese New Year
4. Rosh Ha-Shana	**d.** Christmas
5. La Fête du Travail	**e.** All Saints' Day
6. Le Jour de l'An	**f.** Labor Day
7. Têt	**g.** Easter
8. Noël	**h.** Jewish New Year
9. La Toussaint	**i.** Islamic fasting period

Le 14 juillet à Paris.

B. Name at least two holidays that are celebrated in the United States but not in France. Try to explain why these holidays are not celebrated by the French.

http://www.wiley.com/aventure.html

Describing your schedule

IIA **LES JOURS, LES MOIS, ET LES SAISONS** *Days, months, and seasons*

Le lundi, Julie est à l'université.
En octobre, les étudiants travaillent beaucoup.
En automne, nous cherchons un appartement.

Les jours		Les mois		Les saisons	
lundi	*Monday*	janvier	*January*	l'hiver	*winter*
mardi	*Tuesday*	février	*February*		
mercredi	*Wednesday*	mars	*March*	le printemps	*spring*
jeudi	*Thursday*	avril	*April*		
vendredi	*Friday*	mai	*May*		
samedi	*Saturday*	juin	*June*	l'été	*summer*
dimanche	*Sunday*	juillet	*July*		
		août	*August*		
		septembre	*September*	l'automne	*fall*
		octobre	*October*		
		novembre	*November*		
		décembre	*December*		

◆ The days of the week and the months are not capitalized in French.

◆ To find and tell what day it is, use the following expressions:

Quel jour est-ce (aujourd'hui)?   *What day is it (today)?*
C'est mardi.   *It's Tuesday.*

◆ To say that actions are repeated on the same day of every week, use the definite article **le** before the day.

Julie étudie **le lundi.**   *Julie studies every Monday.*
But: Lundi, Julie cherche un   *(This) Monday, Julie is looking for an*
appartement.   *apartment.*

◆ To indicate that an action occurs over a period of several days, use **du... au.**

Je travaille **du** lundi **au** vendredi. *I work (from) Monday through Friday.*

◆ The date in French is always given as **le** and the number followed *directly* by the month.

> **Quelle est la date aujourd'hui?**　　*What's today's date?*
> **C'est le** 15 octobre.　　*It's October 15.*
> **Nous sommes le** 15 octobre.　　*It's October 15.*

Note: When the date is the first of the month, use **le premier.**

> C'est **le premier** mai.　　*It's May first.*

◆ To say *in* (a month or a season), use **en.** The only exception is **au printemps.**

> **en** juin　　*in June*
> **en** hiver　　*in winter*
> **au** printemps　　*in spring*

ACTIVITÉS

4. Quelle coïncidence! Julie is mentioning that the birthdays of certain members of her family are common American holidays. Tell when each person was born.

■ WORDS TO USE: **anniversaire** *birthday* / **fête** *holiday*

MODÈLE: L'anniversaire de maman est le jour de Noël.
　　　　C'est le 25 décembre.

1. L'anniversaire d'Arthur est le jour de Halloween.
2. L'anniversaire d'Emily est la veille de Noël *(Christmas Eve)*.
3. L'anniversaire de Thom est le jour de la fête nationale américaine.
4. L'anniversaire de Big Red est le Jour de l'An.
5. Moi, mon anniversaire est le jour de la Saint Valentin.
6. L'anniversaire de papa est le jour de *April Fool's*.
7. L'anniversaire de Dave est le jour de la Saint Patrick.

5. Mon emploi du temps *My schedule*. You are looking for a part-time job. Figure out which hours you are free to work on Mondays, Wednesdays, and Fridays.

■ WORD TO USE: **libre** *free*

Follow-up. You may want students to tell what their schedule is on Tuesdays and Thursdays and/or the weekend. **Le week-end...**

MODÈLE: **Le lundi, le mercredi et le vendredi, je suis à l'université de 8 heures à 3 heures. Je suis libre de 4 heures à 6 heures.**

Talking about your activities (continued)

IIB LE VERBE FAIRE ET QUELQUES EXPRESSIONS

Qu'est-ce qu'on **fait?**
Au foyer, les étudiants **font leurs devoirs.**
À la maison, je **fais la cuisine.**
Dans la classe, vous **faites attention.**

◆ The irregular verb **faire** *(to do, to make)* is conjugated as follows.

faire	
je **fais**	nous **faisons**
tu **fais**	vous **faites**
il / elle / on **fait**	ils / elles **font**

Note: The **ai** in **faisons** is pronounced [ə] because it occurs in an unstressed syllable.

◆ Many different activities and weather conditions are expressed in idioms using **faire.** Some are listed below in the **Pour s'exprimer.**

POUR S'EXPRIMER
Quelques expressions avec faire

À LA MAISON

faire les courses	*to do shopping, errands*
faire la cuisine	*to cook*
faire la grasse matinée	*to sleep in, late*
faire son lit	*to make one's bed*
faire le ménage	*to do the housework*
faire les provisions	*to do grocery shopping*
faire la sieste	*to take a nap*
faire la vaisselle	*to do the dishes*

À L'UNIVERSITÉ

faire attention	*to pay attention*
faire ses devoirs	*to do one's homework*
faire le...	*to dial a phone number*

EN VACANCES   *on vacation*

faire du camping	*to camp, go camping*
faire la fête	*to party*
faire une promenade	*to go for a walk*
faire du ski, du tennis	*to ski, play tennis*
faire un voyage	*to take a trip*

Culture. Point out to students that **faire la fête** is the standard French expression. They can also use **faire la nouba, faire la java,** and **faire la bringue.** The first two expressions originated in Algeria. Tell students that all three should be reserved for informal, spoken French; they are slang terms and should not find their way into compositions.

6. Qu'est-ce qu'on fait? Julie and some of her American friends are visiting a friend's country house. Julie goes over the assignments and rules with everyone. Complete her statements using a form of the verb **faire.**

1. Alors, nous _____ la fête ce week-end!
2. Toi, Sandra, tu _____ les provisions avant le départ. D'accord?
3. Paul _____ la cuisine.
4. Christopher et Stéphanie, vous _____ la vaisselle.
5. Virginia et David, ils _____ les lits.
6. Et plus tard, moi, je _____ le ménage! C'est la vie!

Elle se prépare à faire la cuisine.

7. En quelle saison? Tell what Julie and her friends do at different times of the year. Choose words from each column.

Modèle: **Julie fait du ski en hiver.**
Julie fait du camping au printemps.

Julie	du ski	printemps
Loulou et André	du camping	été
Benjamin et moi, nous faire	une promenade	automne
je	la sieste	hiver
tu	un voyage	

 8. Et vous, que faites-vous? Find out from your partner what his or her activities are. Here are a few questions to get you started.

Modèle: —**Le week-end, fais-tu ton lit?**
—**Oui, je fais mon lit.**
ou —**Non, je ne fais pas mon lit, je fais une promenade.**

1. À quelle heure fais-tu tes devoirs?
2. Fais-tu du tennis? du ski? du camping?
3. Dans quel supermarché fais-tu tes provisions?
4. Qui fait la cuisine à la maison?
5. Le week-end, fais-tu la grasse matinée?
6. Imaginez une autre question.

9. Interview. Ask at least two people in your class the following questions and report your findings to a third classmate. Ask

1. at what time she or he does her or his homework.
2. whether she or he goes camping or skiing.
3. in what supermarket she or he shops.
4. who cooks in her or his family.
5. whether she or he sometimes sleeps in.

TROISIÈME ÉPISODE

Julie entre dans la cabine téléphonique. Elle a une liste de trois personnes qui ont une chambre à louer°. Elle compose° le premier numéro. La ligne est vraiment mauvaise°.

JULIE: Allô! Bonjour Madame, je m'appelle Julie Lavalette.

LA DAME: Comment? Pardon?

JULIE: Je m'appelle Julie Lavalette, et je téléphone...

LA DAME: Comment? Pourquoi est-ce que vous téléphonez?

JULIE: Je téléphone pour l'appartement.

LA DAME: Oh, je suis désolée, mais c'est déjà loué°. Au revoir!

à louer *for rent* / **compose** *dials* / **La ligne est vraiment mauvaise.** *The line is really bad.* / **c'est déjà loué** *it's already rented*

Julie est un peu° triste mais elle a un deuxième numéro°. Elle fait le 35-45-36-72. Dring! Dring!

JULIE: Allô! Bonjour, Monsieur, je m'appelle Julie Lavalette, et je téléphone pour la chambre à louer.

LE MONSIEUR: Oui, j'ai une chambre claire° et calme. Je suis fumeur et je...

JULIE: Vous fumez? Je suis désolée, Monsieur, mais je n'aime pas la fumée. Au revoir!

---

un peu *a little* / **un deuxième numéro** *a second number* / **claire** *light*

AVEZ-VOUS COMPRIS?

1. Combien de numéros de téléphone a Julie?
2. Est-ce que la première personne a une chambre pour Julie? Pourquoi ou pourquoi pas?
3. Qu'est-ce que la deuxième personne fait que Julie n'aime pas?
4. Comment s'appelle la troisième personne? Comment est son appartement?
5. Quand est-ce que Julie visite l'appartement?

124 cent vingt-quatre   **Chapitre 4**

Il reste un numéro°. Julie fait le troisième numéro.

JULIE: Allô! Je m'appelle Julie Lavalette et je cherche une chambre à louer.

CAROLINE: Bonjour. Ici Caroline Perrin. J'ai un petit appartement avec deux chambres au premier étage.

JULIE: Comment est la chambre?

CAROLINE: Elle est calme et très claire. Je cherche de préférence une jeune femme qui ne fume pas pour partager le loyer° et les charges°.

Il reste un numéro. *One number is left.* / **partager le loyer** *share the rent* / **charges** *utilities*

JULIE: Ça m'intéresse°. Quand est-ce que je peux visiter°?

CAROLINE: Venez° à onze heures demain°.

JULIE: Où se trouve° l'appartement?

CAROLINE: Voici l'adresse: 5, rue du Gros-Horloge.

JULIE: D'accord°. À demain°!

Ça m'intéresse *I'm interested* / **je peux visiter?** *can I visit?* / **venez** *come* / **demain** *tomorrow* / **Où se trouve** *Where is (it) located* / **D'accord** *OK* / **À demain!** *See you tomorrow!*

ET VOUS?

1. Quelle est l'adresse de votre appartement ou de votre maison?
2. Comment est votre chambre? votre appartement? Décrivez.
3. Est-ce que vous habitez seul(e)? avec un(e) camarade de chambre? avec vos parents? avec votre mari / femme?
4. Est-ce que votre camarade de chambre fume? Et vos parents? Et vous? Est-ce que vous aimez ça?

Tell students that the word **horloge** is feminine in modern French but that it was masculine during the Middle Ages when the street in Rouen was named.

VOUS ÊTES BRANCHÉS!

Les appartements en France

The first time you visit a French apartment, you may be surprised by some of the differences that you find. Rooms are generally smaller, and appliances such as **réfrigérateurs** *(refrigerators)* and **machines à laver** *(washing machines)* tend to be quite small compared to the ones you are used to. Upon further exploration, you may discover that **un chauffe-eau,** a small water heater, is located above the sink in the kitchen and a second small water heater might be found in the bathroom.

You might also find a **bidet,** a low wash basin for intimate personal hygiene in your bathroom, while the toilet is often located in a separate room. Another interesting feature of some French bathrooms is a **baignoire** *(bathtub)* equipped with a hand-held shower head that may sometimes be mounted on a fixture attached to the wall.

La salle de bains.

To rent an apartment in France, you may be asked for a **caution** *(security deposit)*. Generally, it is the equivalent of the first and last month's rent. As with American apartments, rents for French apartments vary depending on location, size, and amenities.

VOTRE Q. I. CULTUREL

Chassez l'intrus. Tell which part of each list does not belong, and why.

1. Dans une salle de bains, il y a une baignoire, un bidet, et une caution.
2. Dans un appartement en France, on trouve des chauffe-eaux dans la salle de séjour, la cuisine, et la salle de bains.
3. Les machines à laver, les portes, et les réfrigérateurs sont très petits en France.

■■ POUR COMMUNIQUER

Asking questions (continued)

IIIA LES MOTS INTERROGATIFS: OÙ, QUAND, COMMENT, POURQUOI

◆ **Quand** *(when)*

> **Quand** est-ce qu'elle fait ses devoirs?   **Quand** faites-vous la sieste?

◆ **Où** (*where*)

> **Où** habitez-vous?
> **Où** aiment-ils étudier?

◆ **Comment** (*how; what*)

> **Comment** fais-tu la mousse au chocolat?
> **Comment** vas-tu?

To ask what someone or something is like, use **comment.**

> **Comment** est ton professeur? *What is your professor like?*

Comment is also used in several idiomatic expressions.

> **Comment** vous appelez-vous?   *What's your name?*
> **Comment?** Pardon?   *What (did you say)? Excuse me?*

◆ **Pourquoi** (*why*)
Answer a **pourquoi** question with **parce que** (*because*).

> —**Pourquoi** regardes-tu la télévision?
> —**Parce que** j'aime les films.

◆ These question words may be followed either by **est-ce que** or inversion.

ACTIVITÉS

 10. Quelle est la question? Complete each question with the correct word: **quand, où, comment, pourquoi.** Your partner will answer.

MODÈLE: _____ fais-tu la grasse matinée? le week-end?
    —Quand fais-tu la grasse matinée?
    —Je fais la grasse matinée le samedi.

1. _____ habitez-vous? à Newport?
2. _____ écoutez-vous la radio? le soir?
3. _____ allez-vous?
4. _____ mangez-vous au restaurant? parce que vous adorez ça?
5. _____ faites-vous vos devoirs? le matin?
6. _____ préférez-vous votre café? chaud? glacé?

11. J'aimerais savoir... *I'd like to know* . . . Find someone in your class that you don't know very well and try to learn as much about him or her as possible.

MODÈLE: **Pourquoi est-ce que tu étudies ici?**

	faire	tes devoirs
quand	manger	au restaurant
où	travailler	en classe
comment	être	tes professeurs
pourquoi	étudier	ici
	habiter	tes parents

 12. Pardon, j'ai une question. You can now learn many things about people and their lives by asking questions. Use **quand, où, comment, pourquoi, qui, qu'est-ce que, quel(le)(s)** to help satisfy your curiosity about one of your classmates. Ask

1. where she or he lives.
2. when she or he studies and where.
3. what (kind of) music she or he likes.
4. with whom she or he works.
5. what his or her parents are like.
6. what she or he is studying.
7. why she or he is studying here.

Adding emphasis

IIIB LES PRONOMS ACCENTUÉS

> **Moi,** je suis désolée!
> Qui habite avec **elle?**
> **Nous,** nous aimons beaucoup notre appartement.

Les pronoms accentués			
moi	*me, I*	**nous**	*us, we*
toi	*you*	**vous**	*you*
lui	*him, he*	**eux**	*them, they (m)*
elle	*her, she*	**elles**	*them, they (f)*
soi	*one*		

◆ To emphasize a subject, use a stress pronoun in addition to the regular subject pronoun.

Lui, il est intelligent!	*He's (really) smart!*
Tu es belle, **toi!**	*You're (really) pretty!*
Moi, je suis intelligent, mais **toi,** tu es stupide!	*I'm (really) intelligent, but you're (really) stupid!*

◆ Sometimes stress pronouns are used alone or with **c'est** or **ce sont** to answer a question. **Ce sont** is used only with **eux** and **elles.** All other forms use **c'est.**

> Qui aime le chocolat?
> —**Moi!**
>
> Qui est là?
> —C'est **nous.**
>
> Qui a mon stylo?
> —Ce sont **eux!**

◆ Stress pronouns often follow prepositions.

Vous mangez **chez vous** ce soir.	*You're eating at home (at your house) tonight.*
Julie dîne **avec eux** demain soir.	*Julie is having dinner with them tomorrow night.*
Chacun **pour soi.**	*Every man for himself.*

Note: The expression **être à** indicates possession.

Cette cassette est **à moi** et ce disque est **à elle.** *This cassette is mine, and that record is hers.*

You will study prepositions on p. 134.

◆ **FOR RECOGNITION ONLY** Stress pronouns are sometimes combined with **-même(s)** to mean *-self* or *-selves.*

> Julie fait la vaisselle **elle-même.**   *Julie does the dishes herself.*

◆ Stress pronouns can be used as part of a compound subject before the subject pronoun.

Julie et **moi,** nous faisons les courses ensemble le samedi.	*Julie and I shop together every Saturday.*

ACTIVITÉS

13. Qui est responsable? Julie is running around the **foyer** to find out who broke her CD player. Everyone points out a different guilty party. Complete the conversation.

1. Brigitte, c'est toi?—Non, ce n'est pas _____ .
   Alors, c'est Laure et Christine?—Oui, ce sont _____ .
2. Laure et Christine, c'est vous?—Non, ce n'est pas _____ .
   C'est Suzanne?—Oui, c'est _____ .
3. Suzanne, c'est toi?—Non, ce n'est pas _____ .
   Alors, ce sont tes amis?—Oui, ce sont _____ .
4. Alors qui??? c'est Robert?—Non, ce n'est pas _____ .
   Il fait attention! C'est bizarre! Mystère!

14. Je suis d'accord! *I agree!* Laure agrees enthusiastically with everything people say. Imagine her responses to the following statements.

■ **WORDS TO USE: Je suis d'accord.** *I agree.* / **meilleur ami** *best friend* / **bête** *silly; dumb*

MODÈLE: J'aime bien Gérard Depardieu. (super)
—**Je suis d'accord. Lui, il est super!**

1. J'aime bien Catherine Deneuve. (belle)
2. Je déteste Robert. (bête)
3. J'adore mes amies. (sympathiques)
4. J'aime beaucoup Bach et Beethoven. (extraordinaires)
5. Nous aimons beaucoup nos amis. (amusants)
6. Nous adorons notre meilleur ami. (gentil)
7. Nous détestons ces jeunes filles. (snob)

POUR S'EXPRIMER

Quelques professions

agent d'assurance	*insurance agent*
agent immobilier	*real estate agent*
agent de police	*police officer*
agent de voyage	*travel agent*
assistant(e) social(e)	*social worker*
avocat(e)	*lawyer*
cadre	*executive*
chanteur / chanteuse	*singer*
comptable	*accountant*
écrivain	*writer*
fonctionnaire	*civil servant*
homme / femme d'affaires	*businessman/woman*
hôtesse de l'air	*flight attendant (female)*
infirmier / infirmière	*nurse*
ingénieur	*engineer*
médecin	*physician*
pharmacien / pharmacienne	*pharmacist*
plombier	*plumber*
steward	*flight attendant (male)*

Une avocate devant son Minitel.

Note: Unlike English, French does not use the indefinite article with professions.

Je suis professeur. *I am a professor.*

15. Je voudrais être... *I'd like to be . . .* Some children are looking at pictures and deciding what they want to be when they grow up. Imagine what they say.

MODÈLE: —Moi, je voudrais être pharmacienne. Et toi?
—Moi je voudrais être...

    1   2   3   4

    5   6   7

 16. Que font-ils? Ask about the professions of five people or groups that your partner is familiar with.

MODÈLE: —Que fait ta mère?
—Elle, elle est médecin.

—Que font Hootie and the Blowfish?
—Eux, ils sont chanteurs.

 17. Comment trouves-tu... ? *What do you think of . . . ?* Jot down the names of five actors, actresses, musical groups, artists, classmates, or professors. Then, with a partner, exchange opinions. If you like, you may also include your opinion of your partner and of yourself.

MODÈLE: —Comment trouves-tu Danny DeVito?
—Lui, il est très amusant.
—Moi, je trouve Danny DeVito stupide!

🎧 QUATRIÈME ÉPISODE T 33

C'est le 16 octobre. Il est onze heures. Julie arrive chez Caroline. Elle regarde bien l'immeuble° de l'extérieur. C'est super! L'arrêt de bus° est devant l'immeuble; la boulangerie° est à côté de l'épicerie° au coin° de la rue°. Elle monte° et sonne° à la porte.

---

immeuble *apartment building* / **arrêt de bus** *bus stop* / **boulangerie** *bakery* / **à côté de l'épicerie** *next to the grocery store* / **au coin** *on the corner* / **rue** *street* / **monte** *goes up* / **sonne** *rings*

JULIE: Caroline?
CAROLINE: Oui, c'est moi. Vous êtes Julie? Entrez! Voilà l'appartement. La salle à manger est confortable, mais la cuisine est petite. Julie est surprise. Elle regarde la machine à laver° et le réfrigérateur. Ils sont minuscules!

---

machine à laver *washing machine*

AVEZ-VOUS COMPRIS?

1. Quelle heure est-il quand Julie arrive chez Caroline?
2. Qu'est-ce qu'il y a près de l'immeuble?
3. Où est l'arrêt d'autobus? la boulangerie? l'épicerie?
4. Est-ce que Julie aime l'appartement?

3

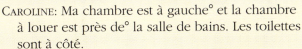

4

CAROLINE: Ma chambre est à gauche° et la chambre à louer est près de° la salle de bains. Les toilettes sont à côté.

Julie visite le reste de l'appartement.

à gauche *to the left* / **près de** *near*

JULIE: J'aime beaucoup l'appartement. Quelles sont vos conditions?

CAROLINE: Je voudrais 2500 francs de caution. Tous les mois°, on partage tous les frais°: les charges, le téléphone, le chauffage°, le loyer. Au total 3600F environ, soit, pour vous 1800F. On partage aussi toutes les tâches°: vous faites le ménage, je fais la cuisine, vous faites les courses, je mets° la table.

JULIE: Tous les jours?

CAROLINE: C'est à discuter°.

JULIE: Je vais réfléchir°.

CAROLINE: D'accord. Donnez-moi° votre réponse demain.

Tous les mois *Every month* / **frais** *expenses* / **chauffage** *heat* / **tâches** *chores* / **mets** *set* / **C'est à discuter.** *We can talk about it.* / **Je vais réfléchir.** *I'll think about it.* / **Donnez-moi** *Give me*

ET VOUS?

1. Où habitez-vous? Est-ce qu'il y a un arrêt de bus près de chez vous?
2. Est-ce qu'il y a une boulangerie au coin de votre rue? Qu'est-ce qu'il y a au coin de votre rue?
3. Votre chambre est-elle ordonnée *(tidy)* ou désordonnée?
4. Chez vous, qui fait le ménage? Qui fait les courses?
5. Dans votre ville, est-ce que les loyers sont chers?

Situating people and things

IVA LES PRÉPOSITIONS

T 34

1. La souris est
entre les deux chats.

2. La souris est
devant le chat.

3. La souris est
derrière le chat.

4. La souris est
sur le chat.

5. La souris est
sous le chat.

6. La souris est
dans le chat.

◆ Some prepositions are followed directly by a noun.

> Vous êtes **derrière** moi.
> Le professeur est **devant** la classe.

◆ Others require **de.**

Le Minitel est **près de la** lampe.	*The Minitel is near the lamp.*
La maison est **en face du** parc.	*The house is across from the park.*
Nous habitons **loin des** autres étudiants.	*We live far from the other students.*

Some of the prepositions followed by **de** are **à côté de, au coin de, au milieu de, en face de, loin de,** and **près de.** Remember to use the correct form of **de** + article (see Ch. 2, p. 51) if an article is necessary.

◆ **À côté de, au coin de, près de** and **loin de** may all be used without **de** if no noun follows them.

L'aéroport est **loin.**	*The airport is far (away).*
La boulangerie est **à côté.**	*The bakery is next door.*

◆ **Chez** means *at* or *to one's house/home*. Use a stress pronoun after **chez** to indicate ownership.

Nous mangeons **chez** nous.	*We are eating at our house.*
Elle fait ses devoirs **chez** elle.	*She does her homework at home (at her house).*

◆ **Se trouver** means *to be located*. Use this expression to ask where something is.

Où se trouve la boulangerie?	*Where is the bakery?*
Où se trouvent les toilettes?	*Where is the restroom?*

POUR S'EXPRIMER	
Dans mon quartier	*In my neighborhood*
l'arrêt de bus *(m)*	*bus stop*
la bibliothèque	*library*
la boulangerie	*bakery*
le café	*café/coffee shop*
le centre commercial	*shopping center/mall*
le cinéma	*movie theater*
l'épicerie *(f)*	*grocery store*
l'immeuble *(m)*	*apartment building*
le parc	*park*
le parking	*parking lot*
la poste	*post office*
le restaurant	*restaurant*
le supermarché	*supermarket*
le théâtre	*theater*

ACTIVITÉS

18. Comment est le quartier? Julie asks Caroline about the neighborhood. With a partner, play the roles, asking **Où se trouve** and answering with the locations indicated.

MODÈLE: la boulangerie / près de / la poste
        —**Où se trouve la boulangerie?**
        —**La boulangerie est près de la poste.**

1. l'arrêt de bus / devant / l'immeuble
2. le CROUS / loin de / l'appartement
3. l'épicerie / au coin de / la rue
4. le campus / près de / le centre commercial
5. le parking / derrière / l'immeuble
6. le café / entre / le cinéma et le restaurant
7. le théâtre / en face de / la bibliothèque
8. le supermarché / devant / le parc
9. la boulangerie / près de / chez moi

Pierre

19. Une soirée Julie has moved in, and Caroline is having a party. Since Julie doesn't know anyone, Caroline discreetly points out her guests. Look at the drawing and tell what she says.

MODÈLE: Pierre
—**Voilà Pierre. Il est à côté de la lampe.**

Élisabeth

Sébastien

Jules / David

Benoît

Marie / Françoise

1. Benoît
2. Élisabeth
3. Marie et Françoise

4. Sébastien
5. Jules et David

 20. Ils sont loin d'elles? With a partner, use the lists below and ask and answer as many questions as possible about the locations of the partygoers. Be sure to use a stress pronoun in the answer.

MODÈLE: Jules et David   loin de   Marie
—**Jules et David sont loin de Marie?**
—**Oui, ils sont loin d'elle.**

Françoise	près de	Sébastien
Marie	devant	Françoise et Benoît
Elizabeth	derrière	moi
Benoît	être	à côté de	toi
nous	entre	Françoise et Elizabeth
tu	en face de	Jules et David

21. Dans la salle de classe. You would like to improve your memory for names. Ask a partner to tell you the names of at least five students in your class and where they are sitting. Draw a chart as your partner uses **devant, derrière, entre, à côté de, près de,** or **loin de** in his or her descriptions. When you have finished, show your partner the chart to verify the seating arrangement.

Situating people and things (continued)

IVB LE VERBE METTRE

Je **mets** mon livre dans mon sac.
Julie **met** la table.
Quand il fait chaud, Caroline et Julie **mettent** un bikini.
Pour écouter la musique, nous **mettons** la radio.

mettre	
je **mets**	nous **mettons**
tu **mets**	vous **mettez**
il, elle, on **met**	ils, elles **mettent**

◆ The irregular verb **mettre** has several meanings:

to put, to place:	Je **mets** le livre sur le bureau.
to put on:	Tu **mets** une jupe.
to set the table:	Julie **met** la table pour le dîner.
to turn on (the television, the radio, the lights, etc.):	Mon ami et moi, nous **mettons** la télévision à six heures.

◆ Other verbs conjugated like **mettre** include

permettre (à quelqu'un de faire quelque chose) *to permit (someone to do something)*

Mes parents **permettent** à mon frère de fumer.

promettre (à quelqu'un de faire quelque chose) *to promise (someone to do something)*

Vous **promettez** au professeur de faire vos devoirs.

ACTIVITÉS

22. Qu'est-ce que je mets? Before the party, everyone wonders what to wear. Help them decide what to put on.

Benoît		un smoking *(tuxedo)*
Françoise		un bikini
Marie et Julie		une jupe élégante
David	mettre	une robe chic
nous		un jean
je		un sweatshirt
vous		un short
tu		un pantalon

23. Vous faites la même chose? Ask if your partner does the same things as you. Find out

1. what he or she puts on when he or she is on vacation.
2. when he or she turns on the radio or TV.
3. if he or she ever sets the table and if so, when.
4. if he or she promises his or her mother to do the housework.
5. if he or she promises the French teacher to study five hours a day.
6. if he or she allows his or her dog to eat the sofa.
7. who he or she allows to enter his or her room.
8. any other information about putting or placing things, making promises, or giving permission.

IL Y A UN PROBLÈME: QU'EN PENSEZ-VOUS?

Julie cherche un appartement. Caroline propose une chambre et une liste de conditions.
   Julie devrait…

a. accepter les conditions.
b. négocier.
c. refuser les conditions et chercher un autre appartement.
d. Avez-vous une autre solution?

Justifiez votre réponse.

À VOUS DE JOUER

Vous cherchez un appartement. La personne qui propose son appartement fume. Que faites-vous?
   Moi, j(e)…

a. refuse son offre.
b. accepte l'appartement si la personne fume seulement dans sa chambre.
c. demande un espace non-fumeur dans l'appartement.
d. accepte son offre.
e. Avez-vous une autre solution?

Justifiez votre réponse.

LES PETITES ANNONCES

Reading Strategy: Guessing from context

When you use the words and phrases that surround an unfamiliar word or passage to help shed light on its meaning, you are using <u>context</u> to fill in the missing information. For example, in the sentence "Peter popped the juicy red **klunk** in his mouth and promptly broke his tooth on the pit," you might guess from the context that a **klunk** is a cherry. As your knowledge of French grows, you will be able to use context more and more often to understand new words and ideas. Try using this strategy with the following reading.

1.

■ PLEIN CENTRE studio libre en septembre, cuisine aménagée tout confort, loyer 2300F charges et chauffage compris, Ag Isère tél 76.84.43.31

2.

■ Studio Rue Clos Bey, 25m2, 3e ét., ds. imm. gd. standing, kitch. équip., libre, 2600F, caut. 5000, ag. Duval Immobilier 76.46.55.71

3.

■ AV J. PERROT, 1 p + c 28m2 hab, salon 14m2 cuis 8m2 + hall, exp ouest, chauffage à prévoir, 1.950F, chges comprises, 76.24.56.17

1. Look over the ads above and see how many of the abbreviations you can figure out. (You may want to look back at the vocabulary in **Épisodes 2** and **3** before studying the ads.) Jot down any items that are not clear and ask a partner what he or she thinks they mean. Try to answer any questions your partner may have. Then answer the questions below.

a. Quel appartement est libre en septembre?
b. Quel appartement n'a pas de chauffage?
c. Quel appartement est au troisième étage?
d. Quelle est la caution pour l'appartement 2?
e. Où est l'appartement 3?
f. Est-ce que les charges de l'appartement 3 sont comprises dans le loyer?

Culture. French apartments are measured in **mètres carrés** *(square meters)* rather than square feet. One **mètre carré** is approximately nine square feet. Thus, 60 m² would be about 540 square feet.

2. Which of the apartments advertised would you like to rent if you were studying in France? Write down at least three reasons for your choice, in French.

MODÈLE: **Je voudrais louer l'appartement deux parce que...**

RÉVISION ÉCLAIR

Telling time   **Voir p. 114.**

Quelle heure est-il? Il est **huit heures et quart.**

Describing your schedule   **Voir p. 119.**

Je suis à l'université **du lundi au vendredi.**

Talking about your activities (continued)   **Voir p. 121.**

Je **fais la cuisine** tous les jours.

Asking questions (continued)   **Voir p. 126.**

Pourquoi mangez-vous à la cafétéria?

Adding emphasis   **Voir p. 128.**

Moi, je danse comme Patrick Swayze.

Situating people and things   **Voir pp. 134 et 137.**

Julie **met** ses clés dans son sac.
Julie trouve un appartement **près de** la boulangerie.

ÊTES-VOUS BRANCHÉS?

 Mon journal. Having friends at our homes to celebrate special occasions and holidays is something we all enjoy. Describe in your journal some holidays you might celebrate in France, but not in the United States, and vice versa. Then, in a separate entry, describe some of the differences and similarities you would find when comparing French and American apartments or houses.

Y ÊTES-VOUS ARRIVÉS?

 A. Une semaine typique. Your friend will be visiting you next week and would like to know your weekly schedule so you can plan your time together. Write your friend a letter explaining what you do during the week, and what your weekend is like. Remember to include the times you do different activities. Look at p. 105 in Chapter 3 for a model of an informal letter.

 B. Et chez toi? You know what goes on in your own home. Now find out from your partner what happens in her or his house. Ask, for example, who does the dishes, the cooking, who sleeps late, and who skis or plays tennis, and the times and days when they do these activities.

C. Où sommes-nous? Using the locations from the **Pour s'exprimer** on p. 135, draw a map of the different shops and businesses near your home (or school) for your partner, leaving all but one of the labels off the map. If you like, you may also use proper names of restaurants, shops, or businesses. Beginning with the location you have labeled, tell your partner the names of the other shops and businesses and where they are located in relationship to each other. See if your partner can label them. If he or she makes a mistake, correct him or her. When your map is finished, reverse roles.

MODÈLE: **La boulangerie se trouve à côté de la bibliothèque.**

D. Mon nouveau quartier. Imagine you must move to another neighborhood. When you find a good real estate agent, you have all sorts of questions to ask. Write a short list of questions to find out as much as you can about the new area, including which businesses are there, what people do for sports or other activities, and where you can shop. Use **qui, qu'est-ce que, où, quand, quel(le)(s), comment, pourquoi,** as well as **est-ce que.**

E. Ma nouvelle adresse est... Julie has decided to move in with Caroline. Imagine you are Julie, and write a letter to your friends from French class to let them know your new address. In your letter, describe your house-hunting and some of the things you have discovered about French apartments and neighborhoods.

 PRONONCIATION

LES SONS [ɛ] ET [e]

The sound [ɛ], similar to the sound of **e** in the English word *bet,* can be represented several ways: **ê** (with an **accent circonflexe**), **è** (with an **accent grave**), **ai, es,** or **e** in a syllable ending in a pronounced consonant.

The sound [e] is similar to the sound of **ai** in the English word *bait.* This sound may be represented by the written combination **er** or **ez** or by **é** (with an **accent aigu**).

1. Listen to your professor or lab tape and say the words below, concentrating on the vowel sound of the highlighted letters.

[ɛ]

fête	semaine	elle	fenêtre
septembre	mettre	accepte	toilettes
faire	est-ce	derrière	

[e]

élégant	télévision	Sébastien	aéroport
décembre	décider	côté	répétez

2. Each pair of words contrasts the sounds [ɛ] and [e]. Pronounce each word carefully. Then listen to your professor or lab tape and check your pronunciation.

a. thé / tête
b. faites / fée
c. décembre / septembre
d. dernier / dernière

e. première / premier
f. Claire / clé
g. ôter / hôtel

◆ VOCABULAIRE ACTIF ◆

L'heure   *Time*

Quelle heure est-il? *What time is it?*	À quelle heure? *At what time?*	de l'après-midi *in the afternoon (p.m.)*
Il est... heures. *It is . . . o'clock.*	à... heures *at . . . o'clock* du matin *in the morning (a.m.)*	du soir *in the evening (p.m.)*

Les jours de la semaine   *The days of the week*

lundi *Monday*	jeudi *Thursday*	samedi *Saturday*
mardi *Tuesday*	vendredi *Friday*	dimanche *Sunday*
mercredi *Wednesday*		

Les mois   *The months*

janvier *January*	mai *May*	septembre *September*
février *February*	juin *June*	octobre *October*
mars *March*	juillet *July*	novembre *November*
avril *April*	août *August*	décembre *December*

Les saisons   *The seasons*

le printemps *spring*	l'automne (m) *autumn*	l'hiver (m) *winter*
l'été (m) *summer*		

Les fêtes   *Holidays*

un anniversaire *a birthday*	le Jour de l'An *New Year's Day*	Têt *Vietnamese New Year*
une fête *a Saint's Day, a holiday*	Noël *Christmas*	la Toussaint *All Saint's Day*
la Fête des Mères *Mother's Day*	Pâques *Easter*	les vacances (d'été) *(summer) vacation*
la Fête du Travail *Labor Day*	Ramadan *Islamic fasting period*	
	Rosh Ha-Shana *Jewish New Year*	

Quelques professions

un agent d'assurance *insurance agent*

un agent de police *police officer*

un agent de voyage *travel agent*

un agent immobilier *real estate agent*

un(e) assistant(e) social(e) *social worker*

un(e) avocat(e) *lawyer*

un cadre *executive*

un chanteur / une chanteuse *singer*

un comptable *accountant*

un écrivain *writer*

un fonctionnaire *civil servant*

un homme / une femme d'affaires *businessman/woman*

une hôtesse de l'air *flight attendant (female)*

un infirmier / une infirmière *nurse*

un ingénieur *engineer*

un médecin *physician*

un pharmacien / une pharmacienne *pharmacist*

un plombier *plumber*

un steward *flight attendant (male)*

Mon quartier *My neighborhood*

l'arrêt de bus (m) *bus stop*

la bibliothèque *library*

la boulangerie *bakery*

le café *café/coffee shop*

le centre commercial *shopping center/mall*

le cinéma *movie theater*

l'épicerie (f) *grocery store*

l'immeuble (m) *apartment building*

le parc *park*

le parking *parking lot*

la poste *post office*

le restaurant *restaurant*

le supermarché *supermarket*

le théâtre *theater*

Les activités

faire *to do, to make*

faire attention *to pay attention*

faire le... *to dial a number*

faire du camping *to camp*

faire les courses *to do the shopping*

faire la cuisine *to cook*

faire ses devoirs *to do one's homework*

faire la fête *to party*

faire la grasse matinée *to sleep in, late*

faire son lit *to make one's bed*

faire le ménage *to do the housework*

faire une promenade *to go for a walk*

faire les provisions *to do grocery shopping*

faire la sieste *to take a nap*

faire du ski / du tennis *to ski, to play tennis*

faire la vaisselle *to do the dishes*

faire un voyage *to take a trip*

Les mots interrogatifs

comment *how*

où *where*

pourquoi *why*

quand *when*

Les pronoms accentués

moi *me, I*

toi *you*

elle *her, she*

lui *him, he*

soi *one*

nous *us, we*

vous *you*

elles *them, they (f)*

eux *them, they (m)*

Les prépositions

à côté (de)   *next to, next door*
au milieu (de)   *in the middle (of)*
au coin (de)   *at the corner (of)*
chez   *at/to one's house*
dans   *in*

derrière   *behind*
devant   *in front of*
en face (de)   *across from, facing*
entre   *between*

loin (de)   *far (from)*
près (de)   *near (to)*
sous   *under*
sur   *on*

Autres expressions

à la maison   *at home*
bête   *silly; dumb*
d'abord   *first*
en vacances   *on vacation*
enfin   *finally*
ensuite   *next; then*
je (ne) suis (pas) d'accord
   I (don't) agree

libre   *free*
meilleur(e) ami(e)   *best friend*
mettre   *to put; put on*
parce que   *because*
permettre (à quelqu'un de faire
   quelque chose)   *to permit
   (someone to do something)*

promettre (à quelqu'un de faire
   quelque chose)   *to promise
   (someone to do something)*
puis   *then*
se trouver   *to be located; found*

Chapitre 5 ◆ # GRENOBLE, ME VOILÀ!

PRÉSENTATION ÉCLAIR

POUR COMMUNIQUER

Telling where you are going
Making plans
Talking about transportation
Expressing choices and making purchases
Talking about places already mentioned

POUR Y ARRIVER

Le verbe **aller**
À + l'article défini

Le futur proche
Le verbe **prendre**
Les adjectifs démonstratifs
Le verbe **acheter**
Le pronom adverbial **y**

POUR S'ADAPTER À LA CULTURE

Les transports en commun
Au café

Benjamin est dans sa chambre. Il pense°.

BENJAMIN: Bon, il fait beau aujourd'hui. J'ai envie de faire des courses et j'ai besoin de stylos, de papier, de livres, de déodorant, et de shampooing. J'ai aussi envie d'explorer Grenoble et d'aller prendre° un café.

---

pense *is thinking* / **d'aller prendre** *to go and have*

Benjamin sort de° sa chambre et demande des conseils° à Mme Bouverot.

BENJAMIN: Madame, où est-ce qu'il faut aller° pour acheter° du papier, des stylos, des livres, du déodorant, et du shampooing?

MME BOUVEROT: C'est très facile!° Tu vas au centre ville°. Il y a d'excellentes librairies°. Ensuite, va aux Galeries Lafayette pour le reste.

---

sort de *leaves* / **demande des conseils** *asks for advice* / **où est-ce qu'il faut aller** *where should one go* / **acheter** *to buy* / **facile** *easy* / **centre ville** *downtown* / **librairies** *bookstores*

AVEZ-VOUS COMPRIS?

1. Où est Benjamin?
2. À qui parle-t-il?
3. Qu'est-ce qu'il a envie de faire?
4. De quoi a-t-il besoin?
5. Où est-ce qu'il y a d'excellentes librairies?
6. Qu'est-ce que Benjamin achète pour Mme Bouverot?

MME BOUVEROT: Benjamin, est-ce que tu peux me rendre un petit service?° J'ai beaucoup à faire aujourd'hui, et je n'ai pas le temps° d'aller en ville.

BENJAMIN: Bien sûr!°

---

est-ce que tu peux me rendre un petit service? *can you do me a little favor?* / **temps** *time* / **Bien sûr!** *Of course!*

MME BOUVEROT: Nos amis Maurice et Janine vont dîner° avec nous ce soir. Tu peux aller à la pâtisserie acheter une tarte?

BENJAMIN: Mais oui!

MME BOUVEROT: Pour aller plus vite°, prends le tram!° N'oublie pas d'aller au bureau de tabac° acheter un carnet de tickets!°

BENJAMIN: D'accord! À tout à l'heure!°

---

vont dîner *are going to have dinner* / **plus vite** *faster* / **prends le tram** *take the tram/trolley* / **bureau de tabac** *tobacco store* / **carnet de tickets** *book of tickets* / **À tout à l'heure!** *See you later!*

ET VOUS?

1. Aujourd'hui qu'est-ce que vous avez envie de faire? La sieste? Une promenade?
2. En ce moment, de quoi avez-vous besoin?
3. Est-ce que vous préférez faire les courses au centre ville ou dans un centre commercial?
4. Quand préférez-vous faire les courses? Quand il pleut? Quand il fait beau?

Culture. In a **bureau de tabac,** you can buy newspapers, magazines, and cigarettes. You can also find stamps, telephone cards, and often books of bus tickets. Cigarettes can only be purchased in a **bureau de tabac** and are not available at supermarkets, drugstores, or gas stations.

■ POUR COMMUNIQUER

Telling where you are going

IA LE VERBE ALLER

Aujourd'hui, Benjamin **va** au centre de Grenoble. Il **va** à la pâtisserie.
Et vous, **allez-vous** souvent à la pâtisserie?
Après la classe, où **vont** les étudiants?
Comment ça **va?**

◆ **Aller** *(to go)* is an irregular verb commonly used with **à** to indicate destination.

aller	
je **vais**	nous **allons**
tu **vas**	vous **allez**
il / elle / on **va**	ils / elles **vont**

Je **vais** à Paris.   *I go to Paris.*
Nous **allons** à la banque.   *We're going to the bank.*

◆ To talk about going to a particular place, use the following forms:
aller à + cities

     Je vais **à** New York.

aller en + feminine countries, countries beginning with a vowel sound, and continents

     Nous allons **en** France, **en** Israël, et puis **en** Amérique du Sud.

aller au + masculine countries beginning with a consonant

     Les étudiants vont quelquefois **au** Mexique pour les vacances.

aller aux + countries that are plural.

     Daniel va **aux** États-Unis l'été.

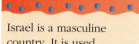

Israel is a masculine country. It is used without an article: **Israël est un beau pays.**

◆ In the expressions **Comment allez-vous?** *(How are you?)* and **Je vais très bien** *(I'm fine)*, the verb **aller** cannot be translated literally. **Comment ça va?** is the French equivalent of *How's it going?* (See the **Chapitre préliminaire.**)

Francophone countries are studied in Chapter 7, p. 226. You may want to review masculine and feminine forms of adjectives of nationality in Chapter 1, p. 29. Tell students to use the definite article when no preposition is used (**La France est belle**) and to omit the article when referring to Israel (**Israël est un beau pays**).

POUR S'EXPRIMER

QUELQUES NATIONALITÉS ET PAYS (countries)			LES CONTINENTS
Les Canadiens		**au** Canada.	Nous allons **en** Afrique.
Les Japonais		**au** Japon.	**en** Amérique du Nord.
Les Mexicains		**au** Mexique.	**en** Amérique du Sud.
Les Allemands		**en** Allemagne.	**en** Antarctique.
Les Anglais		**en** Angleterre.	**en** Asie.
Les Chinois		**en** Chine.	**en** Australie.
Les Espagnols		**en** Espagne.	**en** Europe.
Les Français	habitent	**en** France.	
Les Irlandais		**en** Irlande.	
Les Israéliens		**en** Israël.	
Les Italiens		**en** Italie.	
Les Russes		**en** Russie.	
Les Suisses		**en** Suisse.	
Les Américains		**aux** États-Unis.	

ACTIVITÉS

1. On y va! *Let's go!* A group of students is at the travel agency making travel arrangements. Tell where they are going.

MODÈLE: je / Paris
Je vais à Paris.

1. tu / Rome
2. vous / Tokyo
3. Pierre et moi, nous / Montréal
4. Anne / Madrid
5. elles / Honolulu
6. mes amis / Sidney
7. Paul / Dakar
8. moi, je...

2. En vacances! Imagine where the following people are going on vacation. Be sure to use the right preposition following **aller.**

MODÈLE: **Je vais en France.**   OU **Je vais en Europe.**
   OU **Je vais au Canada.**

je		Canada
mon / ma meilleur(e) ami(e)		Asie
mon professeur		Afrique
mes ami(e)s et moi, nous		Europe
vous	aller	États-Unis
tu		Espagne
le président et sa femme		Italie
elles		Allemagne
		Mexique
		Japon
		Australie
		France

3. Devinez qui je suis et où je vais! *Guess who I am and where I'm going!* Create a new identity for yourself, pick a vacation spot, and get your partner to guess who you are, and where you are going. To do this, follow these easy steps:

1. Decide secretly on a new name, nationality, and destination from the **Pour s'exprimer** above. On a small piece of paper write down your new identity.

MODÈLE: **Je m'appelle Christiane. Je suis française et je vais en vacances au Japon.**

2. Try to guess your partner's new identity by asking him or her questions.

MODÈLE: **Comment t'appelles-tu? Es-tu chinois(e) ou français(e)? Vas-tu en vacances en Espagne? En Russie? En Suisse?**

3. Don't forget to exchange roles.

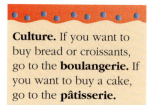

Culture. If you want to buy bread or croissants, go to the **boulangerie.** If you want to buy a cake, go to the **pâtisserie.**

POUR S'EXPRIMER	
En ville	*In town*
Où se trouve la pharmacie?	*Where is the pharmacy (located)?*
Elle est devant la banque.	*It's in front of the bank.*
la boucherie	*butcher*
le bureau de tabac	*tobacco store*
l'église *(f)*	*church*
la fromagerie	*cheese store*
le gymnase	*gymnasium*
l'hypermarché *(m)*	*giant supermarket*
la librairie	*bookstore*
le musée	*museum*
la pâtisserie	*bakery (pastry shop)*
la piscine	*swimming pool*
la poste, le bureau de poste	*post office*
le stade	*stadium*
l'université *(f)*, la faculté, la fac	*university*
la ville	*city*

4. Qu'est-ce que c'est? With a partner, look at the pictures and identify the places.

MODÈLE: —Qu'est-ce que c'est?
—C'est un bureau de tabac.

le bureau de tabac

1

2

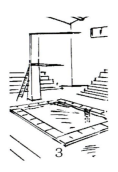

3

4

5

6

5. Où se trouve... ? You are in a new city and you need to run some errands. Look at the map and, with your partner, take turns explaining to each other where each shop is located.

■ WORDS TO USE: **Voyons** *Let's see* / **Je pense que** *I think that* / **penser** *to think*

MODÈLE: —**Je voudrais aller à la pâtisserie. Mais où se trouve-t-elle?**
—**Voyons... Euh! Je pense que le parking est derrière la poste.**

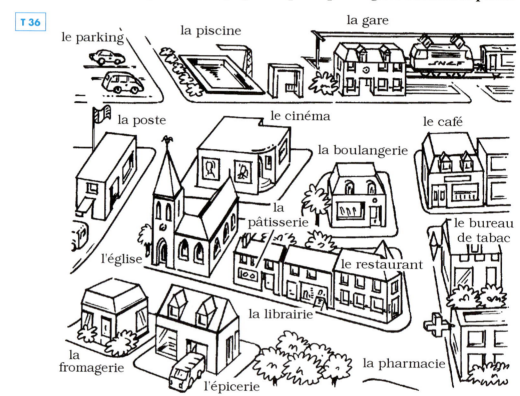

T 36

1. la gare
2. l'épicerie
3. la pharmacie

4. le restaurant
5. la boulangerie
6.–7. À vous de choisir. (*Your choice*)

Telling where you are going (continued)

1B À + L'ARTICLE DÉFINI

Benjamin va **à la** pâtisserie pour Mme Bouverot.
Allez-vous souvent **à l'**épicerie? **à la** boulangerie?
Est-ce que vos amis dînent souvent **au** restaurant?
Vont-ils souvent **aux** fêtes organisées **à l'**université?

◆ Aller is often followed by the preposition **à** (*to; at*). When **à** is followed by **le** or **les,** a contraction is formed.

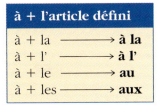

à + l'article défini	
à + la ——→	**à la**
à + l' ——→	**à l'**
à + le ——→	**au**
à + les ——→	**aux**

Je vais **à la** boucherie et Caroline va **au** restaurant.

ACTIVITÉS

6. Tout le monde *(everyone)* **fait les courses!** This week, everyone is going to help do the family shopping according to Mme Bouverot's instructions.

■ **WORDS TO USE: acheter** *to buy* / **tout le monde** *everyone*

MODÈLE: Jean-Claude / épicerie / pour acheter des fruits
Jean-Claude va à l'épicerie pour acheter des fruits.

1. Jean-Claude / poste / pour acheter une télécarte
2. Pierre / bureau de tabac / pour acheter le journal
3. Dominique et Catherine, elles / pâtisserie / pour acheter une tarte
4. Tata Cécile et Benjamin, vous / boucherie / pour acheter des steaks
5. tout le monde / magasins / pour faire des courses
6. moi, je / pharmacie / pour acheter de l'aspirine

7. En route! Everybody is busy with different errands. Follow each person around, and tell where each goes. Use **d'abord, ensuite,** and **enfin.**

MODÈLE: tu / l'université / la bibliothèque / le cours
D'abord tu vas à l'université, ensuite tu vas à la bibliothèque, et enfin tu vas aux cours.

1. tu / la banque / le supermarché / le restaurant
2. vous / l'épicerie / la boulangerie / la boucherie
3. nous / l'hypermarché / les Galeries Lafayette / le café
4. tu / la librairie / le stade / le théâtre
5. vous / le gymnase / les musées / la maison

8. Interview. Find out from your partner

1. if he or she goes to the library Monday through Friday.
2. what days his or her French class is.
3. when he or she goes to the bank.
4. if he or she shops on weekdays or weekends.
5. which supermarket he or she goes to and why.
6. if he or she often goes to the movies.
7. Ask a question of your choice.

BENJAMIN: Voyons, un peu d'organisation. D'abord, je vais au bureau de tabac, j'achète° un carnet de tickets et je prends° le tram. Ensuite, en ville, je vais aller à la librairie et aux Galeries Lafayette; enfin, je vais acheter la tarte de Mme Bouverot à la pâtisserie. Quelle heure est-il? Oh là! là! Il est trois heures et demie! Vite!° Vite! Et le tram? Il est où?

---

j'achète *I buy* / **je prends** *I take* / **vite** *quick*

Super! Il arrive!
Benjamin composte° son ticket, et il monte° dans le tram. Il regarde autour de° lui et pense: «J'aimerais° bien avoir un tram comme ça° à Seaside!»

---

composte *validates* / **monte** *gets on* / **autour de** *around* / **j'aimerais** *I'd like* / **comme ça** *like this*

AVEZ-VOUS COMPRIS?

1. Qu'est-ce que Benjamin va faire d'abord? ensuite? enfin?
2. Quelle heure est-il quand Benjamin arrive à l'arrêt de tram?
3. Comment avance le tram?
4. Qu'est ce que Benjamin pense?
5. Où est-ce que Benjamin arrive?

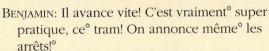

BENJAMIN: Il avance vite! C'est vraiment° super pratique, ce° tram! On annonce même° les arrêts!°

UNE VOIX°: Place° Victor-Hugo.

---

vraiment *really* / **ce** *this* / **même** *even* / **arrêts** *the stops* / **voix** *voice* / **Place** *Square*

BENJAMIN: Je suis arrivé! Grenoble, me voilà!°

---

me voilà! *here I am!*

ET VOUS?

1. Dans votre ville, est-ce qu'il y a un bon système de transport en commun? C'est un système de bus? de train? de tram?
2. Est-ce que ce système est rapide?
3. Est-ce que les transports en commun chez vous sont confortables? assez fréquents? bien organisés?

VOUS ÊTES BRANCHÉS!

Les transports en commun

In France, public transportation is very reliable. Residents of most major cities and small towns know that they can count on buses, subways, or streetcars to get them where they need to go.

Paris, Lyon, and **Marseille** have extensive subway systems that are fairly clean and cheap. In Paris, the train, le **métro** *(subway),* and bus systems allow you to get to any point in the city or the nearby suburbs quickly without needing a car. Grenoble does not have a metro, but rather relies on a modern tramway (streetcar) system combined with a bus system which transports the **Grenoblois** to work, to shopping centers, and to leisure activities. **Le tram** is a clean, fast and energy-efficient means of transportation. It offers video screens and electronic announcements and was designed with the traveller in mind.

Le tram de Grenoble.

Dans le métro.

VOTRE Q. I. CULTUREL

Est-ce **vrai** ou **faux**?

1. À Paris, il y a un système de bus, de métro, et de train très facile et pratique à utiliser.
2. À Grenoble, il y a un métro.
3. Le tram ne va pas aux centres commerciaux.

http://www.wiley.com/aventure.html

■ POUR COMMUNIQUER

Making plans

IIA LE FUTUR PROCHE

> Nous **allons monter** dans le tram.
> Tu **vas composter** ton ticket?
> Demain, les étudiants du cours de français **vont arriver** en bus.
> Moi, je **vais monter** dans l'autobus pour aller à la maison.

◆ Future plans or intentions can be expressed in French much as they are in English. To say what you *are going to do,* use the present tense of **aller** followed by an infinitive.

Je **vais composter** mon ticket.
Nous **allons aller** au cinéma
demain soir.

I'm going to validate my ticket.
We're going to go to the movies
tomorrow night.

◆ In the negative, **ne... pas** is placed around a form of **aller.**

Tu **ne** vas **pas** acheter une robe!
Les étudiants **ne** vont **pas** étudier de 8 heures à 23 heures!

◆ Inversion may also be used with the **futur proche.**

Allez-vous manger au restaurant demain?
N'allez-vous pas étudier le week-end prochain?
Les étudiants **vont-ils** danser ce soir?

The future tense is explained
in Chapter 13, p. 405.

POUR S'EXPRIMER

Quelques adverbes de temps qui peuvent indiquer le futur

aujourd'hui	*today*	en dix minutes	*within ten minutes*
avant (le cours)	*before (class)*	le mois prochain	*next month*
après (le cours)	*after (class)*	la semaine prochaine	*next week*
(à) bientôt	*(see you) soon*	le week-end prochain	*next weekend*
ce soir	*tonight*	lundi prochain	*next Monday*
dans deux semaines	*in two weeks (from now)*	plus tard	*in a while; later*
dans dix minutes	*in ten minutes (from now)*	(à) tout à l'heure	*(see you) later*
demain	*tomorrow*		

ACTIVITÉS

9. Que va-t-il arriver? Benjamin tells his friend Larbi what he and the Bouverots are going to do this weekend.

MODÈLE: M. Bouverot / regarder un match de football / dimanche prochain
M. Bouverot va regarder un match de football dimanche prochain.

1. Mme Bouverot / faire un gâteau au chocolat / ce soir
2. Dominique / préparer / un examen / demain
3. Pierre et Catherine / aller / au cinéma / demain soir
4. Dallas / manger constamment / le week-end prochain
5. et toi et moi, nous / visiter le musée Dauphinois / samedi
6. je / manger avec des amis / tout à l'heure
7. Cathy / poser des questions / après le film

Culture. Le musée Dauphinois is devoted to preserving various aspects of the life of the **Dauphiné** province. This may be a good opportunity to tell students about the difference between the **provinces** and today's **régions**. **Provinces** are historical divisions, whereas **régions** are primarily administrative and geographical divisions.

 10. Madame Soleil. Predict what your partner is going to do tonight. He or she will correct you if you guess wrong, or agree with you if you guess correctly. Choose verbs from the following possibilities: **aller au cinéma après la classe, travailler, écouter ta musique préférée, préparer un examen, faire un devoir de maths avant le dîner, danser, étudier, regarder la télé...**

(continued)

Culture. Mme Soleil was a very popular astrologer of the eighties. In everyday language, a **Mme Soleil** is anyone who tells the future.

MODÈLE: —Tu vas étudier ton français.

—Tu as tort! Je ne vais pas étudier mon français, je vais aller au cinéma.

—Tu vas regarder la télévision.

—Tu as raison! Je vais regarder la télévision.

 11. Qu'est-ce que tu vas faire ce week-end?

1. Ask your partner about his or her activities this coming weekend. Write a list of his or her activities. Your partner will do the same for you.
2. Join forces with another pair of students. All four students ask questions and respond to the group about what their partner(s) will do this coming weekend.

Talking about transportation

IIB LE VERBE PRENDRE

Benjamin **prend** le bus pour aller en ville?
Tu **prends des notes** en classe?
Est-ce que vous **prenez** un ticket quand vous montez dans le tram?

◆ **Prendre** *(to take)* is an irregular verb. Other verbs that follow the same pattern are

apprendre *to learn*
apprendre à quelqu'un *to teach someone*
comprendre *to understand*

prendre	
je **prends**	nous **prenons**
tu **prends**	vous **prenez**
il / elle / on **prend**	ils / elles / **prennent**

◆ **Prendre** is used with means of transportation. In general, use **le, l'**, or **la** after the verb.

Je prends **le** bus pour aller à l'université.
Ils prennent **l'**avion pour aller en France.
Nous prenons **un** métro et deux bus tous les jours.

Note: Some forms of transportation do not use **prendre.**

Je **vais** à l'université **à pied** *(on foot).*
Les étudiants **vont** sur le campus **à bicyclette** *(by bicycle).*

◆ **Prendre** can mean *to have* when speaking of foods and drinks.

Prenez-vous un café le matin?   *Do you have (a cup of) coffee in the morning?*

◆ **Prendre** is also used in certain common idiomatic expressions:

prendre des notes *to take notes*   **prendre du poids** *to gain weight*
prendre une décision *to make*
  a decision

POUR S'EXPRIMER

Les moyens de transports

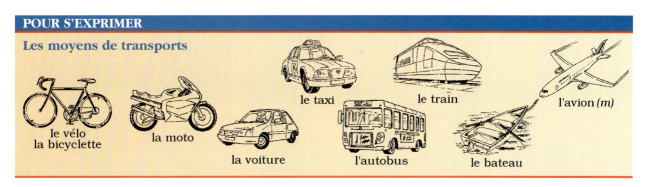

le taxi   le train   l'avion *(m)*

le vélo
la bicyclette   la moto   la voiture   l'autobus   le bateau

ACTIVITÉS

12. On y va! *Let's go!* How do the following people get to their destinations? Use the appropriate article or preposition.

■ **WORD TO USE: les gens** *(people)*

MODÈLE: pour aller à l'université, je
  Pour aller à l'université, je prends le bus.

1. Pour aller à l'université, Julie
2. Pour aller à l'appartement, Caroline et Julie
3. Pour aller à Paris, nous
4. Pour aller au cinéma le soir, je
5. Pour aller à l'aéroport, tu
6. Pour aller travailler, les gens
7. Et vous, pour aller à la fac, vous

Culture. You may wish to add **le VTT (vélo tout terrain,** *mountain bike)* and the expression **en VTT.** The sport has become increasingly popular in France.

 13. Quelles sont les habitudes de votre partenaire? *What are your partner's habits?* Find out by asking him or her these questions, and then change roles. Be ready to report your findings to the class.

■ **WORDS TO USE: à ton / votre avis** *in your opinion /* **à mon avis** *in my opinion /* **vite** *quickly /* **tout de suite** *immediately*

1. Est-ce que tu prends le bus tout de suite après la classe? Si oui, à quelle heure? Ensuite, est-ce que tu prends vite un café? un thé? un chocolat à la maison? Avec qui?
2. À ton avis, en général, es-tu un bon ou un mauvais étudiant? Prends-tu souvent des notes en cours? Pourquoi ou pourquoi pas?
3. Apprends-tu généralement tes leçons? Où? Comprends-tu tes professeurs? souvent? rarement? jamais?
4. Es-tu souvent nerveux / nerveuse avant un examen? Est-ce que tu manges beaucoup? Est-ce que tu prends du poids? Quand? Le week-end? La semaine des examens?
5. Est-ce que tu prends des décisions rapides en général? Est-ce que tes décisions sont généralement bonnes ou mauvaises?

TROISIÈME ÉPISODE

 T 38

BENJAMIN: Mme Bouverot m'a dit°: «Traverse la place, ensuite continue tout droit° et...» Oh! Zut! Je ne sais plus!° Je tourne à gauche°, je tourne à droite°, ou je continue tout droit? Aïe, aïe, aïe, je suis perdu!°

m'a dit *told me* / **tout droit** *straight ahead* / **Je ne sais plus!** *I don't know anymore!* / **à gauche** *to the left* / **à droite** *to the right* / **je suis perdu!** *I'm lost!*

Benjamin s'assied° sur un banc face à une grande place. Il regarde les gens passer, et il pense: «Qu'est-ce que cette ville est animée!° C'est incroyable!° C'est moderne, et c'est vieux...»

s'assied *sits down* / **Qu'est-ce que cette ville est animée!** *How lively this city is!* / **C'est incroyable!** *It's incredible!*

AVEZ-VOUS COMPRIS?

1. Est-ce que Benjamin est perdu?
2. Qu'est-ce qu'il fait?
3. Qui arrive?
4. Qu'est-ce que cette personne demande à Benjamin?
5. Qu'est-ce que Benjamin répond?
6. Quelle est la nationalité de ce jeune homme?
7. Où vont-ils continuer la conversation?

3

4

Un jeune homme s'approche de Benjamin.

JEUNE HOMME: Pardon monsieur, où sont les Galeries Lafayette?

BENJAMIN: Euh, euh! les Galeries Lafayette, je ne sais pas; je ne suis pas de Grenoble. Je suis un étudiant américain.

JEUNE HOMME: Ça alors, tu es américain, et tu étudies à Grenoble! Moi, je suis québécois, de Québec. Je m'appelle Joël, je viens de l'université Laval, et j'étudie aussi ici cette année. Tu veux prendre un pot°? Regarde. En face, il y a un café sympa°, non?

BENJAMIN: O.K., un café et puis, après, on va trouver les Galeries Lafayette ensemble°!

prendre un pot *to have something to drink* / **sympa** *pleasant* / **ensemble** *together*

ET VOUS?

1. Où habitez-vous?
2. Comment est votre ville? moderne? animée? vieille?
3. Avez-vous des amis étrangers *(foreign)*?
4. De quelle nationalité sont vos amis?
5. Aimez-vous aller au café avec vos amis?
6. Où aimez-vous aller avec vos amis?

Culture. This is a good place to bring up the issue of **Québécois** identity as being **«une société distincte»** from the rest of Canada. In November 1996, the **Québécois** voted to remain part of Canada by a very narrow margin. Ask students if they think that the question of **Québec** independence is now completely solved. Ask them if they think that **Québec** should split from the rest of Canada or not, and to support their position.

■ POUR COMMUNIQUER

Expressing choices and making purchases

IIIA **LES ADJECTIFS DÉMONSTRATIFS**

> **Ce** café est sympa.
> **Cet** étudiant est québécois.
> **Cette** ville est assez grande.
> **Ces** femmes sont vieilles.

◆ The demonstrative adjective **ce (cet, cette)** means *this* or *that*. The plural form **ces** means *these* or *those*.

Les adjectifs démonstratifs			
	masculin	*masculin + voyelle*	*féminin*
SINGULIER	ce	cet	cette
PLURIEL	ces	ces	ces

◆ Use the demonstrative adjectives to point out, choose, or describe specific people or things. They take the place of an article.

> Quel livre est en français? **Ce** livre est en français.
> **Ces** jeunes filles habitent à côté.

◆ Like all adjectives, the demonstratives agree in number and gender with the noun they modify.

> **Ce** café est sympa.
> **Cette** ville est très vieille.

◆ For pronunciation reasons, **cet** is the masculine singular form used before a vowel sound. It is pronounced the same as **cette.**

> **Cet homme** est canadien. *That man is Canadian.*

For recognition only: For added emphasis, or to distinguish between *this* and *that* or *these* and *those* in the same phrase or sentence, add **-ci** or **-là** to the nouns.

> J'adore ce chocolat-**ci!**   *I love this (particular) chocolate!*
> Ces enfants-**ci** sont français; ces   ***These*** *children are French;* ***those***
>   enfants-**là** sont chinois.   *children are Chinese.*

J'**achète** mes stylos à la librairie Plausole.
Nous **achetons** un café après la classe.

acheter	
j'ach**è**te	nous ach*e*tons
tu ach**è**tes	vous ach*e*tez
il / elle / on ach**è**te	ils / elles ach**è**tent

Note that like the infinitive, the **nous** and **vous** forms of the verb have *no* accent, whereas every other form is spelled with an **è** (**e** with an **accent grave**).

POUR S'EXPRIMER

La rentrée	(Back to school)
un cahier	notebook
un crayon	pencil
un (crayon) feutre	felt pen
des disquettes (f)	diskettes
une fiche, une carte	index card
une gomme	eraser
un livre	book
un papier	paper
une feuille de papier	a sheet of paper
une règle	ruler
un sac à dos	backpack
une serviette	bookbag, soft-sided briefcase
un stylo	pen
des trombones (m)	paper clips

ACTIVITÉS

14. Qu'est-ce qu'on va choisir? Joël and Benjamin go to the **Galeries Lafayette** department store to buy school supplies. Use **ce, cet, cette,** and **ces** to show the choices they make.

MODÈLE: (stylos) Je vais acheter...
    Je vais acheter ces stylos.

1. (papier) Tu as besoin de...
2. (crayons) J'ai envie d'acheter...
3. (cahier) J'ai besoin de...
4. (livres) Tu achètes...

5. (stylo) Tu as envie d'acheter...
6. (cartes) J'ai besoin de...
7. (gomme) Je vais acheter...
8. (feutre) Tu as besoin de...

15. À vous de choisir. *Your choice.* You and your friends need to shop for school supplies. From the items in the picture, ask what your friends want, need, or are going to buy. Remember to use **ce, cet, cette,** or **ces** in your questions and answers.

MODÈLE: —Tu as envie de cette gomme?
　　　　—Non, je vais acheter ces cahiers.

　　　　—Tu as besoin de ce papier?
　　　　—Non, mais j'ai envie d'acheter ce stylo.

16. Qu'est-ce qu'ils achètent? People are making purchases for their home offices. Tell what they do and do not buy.

MODÈLE: **Ces femmes achètent des cahiers, mais elles n'achètent pas de fiches.**

		cahiers
jeunes filles		crayons
femmes		agrafeuse
homme		serviette
jeune homme	acheter	fiches
nous		disquettes
vous		feutres
tu		stylos
je		trombones

17. Au centre commercial. You and your friends are at the mall. Discuss with a partner the things you're buying or not buying. You may include school supplies, clothes, electronic equipment, and furniture.

■ WORD TO USE: **vraiment** *really*

MODÈLE: —**Moi, j'achète des feutres verts et une grande serviette.**
—**Vraiment? Moi, j'achète des crayons et des trombones.**
—**Et comme vêtement, j'achète un blue jean et un blouson noir, et toi?**
—**Moi, je...**

Aux Galeries Lafayette

1

Benjamin et son nouvel ami Joël s'installent à la terrasse du café Le Cintra au milieu de la place Grenette.

JOËL: Garçon, s'il vous plaît, un café crème et un café!
GARÇON: Tout de suite°, monsieur, j'arrive!

———
tout de suite *right away*

2

JOËL: Alors, Benjamin, tu es à Grenoble depuis° quand?
BENJAMIN: J'y suis depuis fin° août, et toi?
JOËL: Moi, depuis septembre. Où habites-tu aux États-Unis?
BENJAMIN: J'habite près de Los Angeles.

———
depuis *since* / **fin** *the end of*

AVEZ-VOUS COMPRIS?

1. Où est-ce que Benjamin et Joël vont pour discuter?
2. Qu'est-ce qu'ils commandent?
3. Joël est à Grenoble depuis quand?
4. Où Benjamin habite-t-il aux États-Unis?
5. Où Benjamin a-t-il envie d'aller?
6. Quelle heure est-il quand Benjamin regarde sa montre?

JOËL: Tu as de la chance! Moi j'adore le cinéma. Tu vas souvent à Hollywood, à Universal Studios? Ça doit être° vraiment super!

BENJAMIN: Euh, eh bien… Euh non, je n'y° vais pas souvent. Enfin, j'y vais quand j'ai des invités à la maison. J'y vais avec eux. Mais Québec, dis-moi comment c'est°. J'ai bien envie d'y aller.

———————
Ça doit être *It must be* / **y** *there* / **dis-moi comment c'est** *tell me what it's like*

Tout à coup°, au milieu de la conversation, Benjamin regarde sa montre.

BENJAMIN: Mon Dieu!° il est déjà cinq heures—et la tarte! Mme Bouverot va être furieuse! Il faut y aller. Mais au fait, on est toujours perdu, alors, qu'est-ce qu'on fait?

———————
tout à coup *all of a sudden* / **Mon Dieu!** *My goodness!*

ET VOUS?

1. Où allez-vous pour parler avec vos amis?
2. De quelle(s) ville(s) sont vos ami(e)s?
3. Désirez-vous visiter une autre ville? Quelle ville?
4. Faites-vous toujours attention à l'heure?
5. Arrivez-vous quelquefois en retard? Où et pourquoi?

VOUS ÊTES BRANCHÉS

Au café

Many consider the **café** a mainstay of French social and cultural life. In some cities, you will find **cafés** on nearly every corner, and even the smallest French villages generally have at least one **café.** It is not just the coffee and a menu of light fare that draw people together for a morning break or afternoon pick-me-up. A **café** is a great place to observe people, to write, or to meet friends. **Cafés** provide a welcome haven for singles, couples, families, or groups of students. Once you have bought a drink, you may remain at your table for hours, enjoying the passing show of humanity.

However, since French life is becoming more and more hectic, and prices continue to rise, **cafés** are slowly being replaced by fast food establishments,

Au café.

which may provide the same convenience for eating but certainly not the same charm.

VOTRE Q. I. CULTUREL

Répondez aux questions suivantes.

1. Nommez trois choses à faire au café.
2. Qui fréquente les cafés?
3. Pourquoi des restaurants comme MacDonald's remplacent-ils les cafés?

http://www.wiley.com/aventure.html

■ POUR COMMUNIQUER

Talking about places already mentioned

IV **LE PRONOM ADVERBIAL Y**

Mme Bouverot va **à la banque.** Elle **y** va le vendredi.
Nous mangeons **au café.** Nous **y** mangeons avec nos amis.
Je déteste aller **chez le dentiste.** Je déteste **y** aller.

◆ The adverbial pronoun **y** means *there.* It is used to avoid repetition when you want to refer to a place you've already mentioned.

Tu es sur le campus tous les jours?—Oui, j'**y** suis.
Ma voiture est dans le garage. Elle **y** est avec mon vélo.

◆ **Y** may also be used to replace **à +** a thing or **à +** an idea. In this case, **y** means *(about) it* or *(about) them*.

Vous pensez **à vos problèmes?**
  —Oui, j'**y** pense toujours.

Are you thinking about your problems?—Yes, I think about them all the time.

Benjamin pense **à l'amour.** Il **y** pense souvent.

*Benjamin is thinking about love. He often thinks about **it**.*

◆ **Y,** like all pronouns, appears directly before the verb with which it is associated in both affirmative and negative sentences.

CONJUGATED VERB:
Tu travailles **à la bibliothèque.** Tu **y** travailles.
Tu ne travailles pas **à la bibliothèque.** Tu n'**y** travailles pas.

INFINITIVE:
Tu aimes aller **au cinéma.** Tu aimes **y** aller.
Tu n'aimes pas étudier **dans ta chambre.** Tu n'aimes pas **y** étudier.

ACTIVITÉS

18. Alors, on y va? You're working at a travel agency. With a partner, ask and confirm the departure dates and destinations of the following travelers. Be sure to use **y** in all the confirmations.

MODÈLE: —M. et Mme Dupont vont à Papeete? (28/2)
          —Oui, ils y vont le vingt-huit février.

1. Mlle Cartéron va à Rome? (22/6)
2. M. Przybos va à Prague? (13/3)
3. M. et Mme Vernon vont à Madrid? (1/8)
4. Mme Andrieu va à Genève? (24/4)
5. Mlle Duprey va à Budapest? (19/12)
6. Tu vas au congrès à Paris? (14/7)
7. Vous allez à Washington? (12/1)
8. Vos parents vont à Nice? (16/2)

19. Où est-elle? Benjamin wants to find out where the rest of the Bouverots are, but Catherine won't tell him. Using the locations indicated on p. 170, with a partner give Benjamin's questions and Catherine's answers (always negative) according to the model. Use **y** in your responses.

MODÈLE: Maman (banque)
        —Maman est à la banque?
        —Non, elle n'y est pas.

Warm-up. Before doing **Activité 18,** remind students that dates written in French show the day first and the month second: **le 5 février.** You might also want to do a quick review of the months.

Culture. In French, when writing dates, put the day, followed by the month and the year. 9/4/96 is April 9, 1996.

1. Pierre (boulangerie)
2. Dominique et maman (pâtisserie)
3. Tata Cécile (cinéma)
4. Papa (café)

5. Dominique (bureau de poste)
6. Maman et papa (restaurant)
7. Tata Cécile (épicerie)
8. Maman (pharmacie)

 20. Tiens! Voilà une star! From the lists below, decide which celebrities go where and then see if your partner agrees or disagrees with your choice.

MODÈLE: —**Arnold Schwarzenegger mange au restaurant.**
—**Oui, tu as raison. Il y mange.**
OU —**Non, tu as tort. Il n'y mange pas. Il mange au gymnase.**

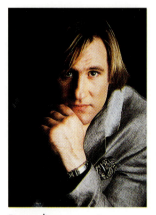

Depardieu—un acteur
formidable.

Arnold Schwarzenegger	travailler	à l'université
Gérard Depardieu	danser	à la discothèque
Julia Child	manger	au restaurant
le président	aller	au gymnase
Mel Gibson	skier	à la librairie
Michael Jordan	jouer	à la montagne
Bob Hope	étudier	au laboratoire
Alice Walker	fumer	à la poste
Madonna	chanter	à l'épicerie

 21. Tu y es? Ask at least three people in your class the following questions. Share the most interesting information you have gathered with the rest of the class. Remember to use **y** in your answers whenever possible.

1. Pourquoi est-ce que tu manges souvent au restaurant?
2. Quand étudies-tu à la bibliothèque?
3. Tu habites dans un appartement? Si oui, avec qui?
4. Dans ta chambre, est-ce que tes livres sont sur ton lit?
5. Est-ce que tu aimes aller au cinéma? Pourquoi?
6. Est-ce que tu détestes rester au lit le samedi matin?

POUR S'EXPRIMER			
Où se trouve... ?			
à droite	*right*	sur la place	*on the square*
à gauche	*left*	sur l'avenue	*on the avenue*
au coin (de)	*at the corner (of)*	sur le boulevard	*on the boulevard*
au feu	*at the light*	tournez...	*turn . . .*
continuez...	*continue . . .*	tout droit	*straight*
dans la rue	*on, in the street*	traversez...	*cross . . .*
jusqu'à (au)	*as far as*		
prenez...	*take . . .*		

l'Isère

le Musée Stendhal

Place Saint André

Voie Corato

R. Jean-Jacques Rousseau

le Jardin de Ville

Grande Rue

Bd. Édouard Rey

Place Grenette

R. de la République

Rue La Fayette

Rue Voltaire

le Musée d'Histoire Naturelle

R. Félix Poulat

R. de la Poste

Place Victor Hugo

Place de Verdun

Rue Haxo

le Jardin des Plantes

R. Fantin Latour

Rue Lesdiguières

Rue de Strasbourg

Boulevard Jean Pain

Bd. Maréchal Lyautey

l'Anneau de Vitesse

 22. Où se trouve... ? A bus tour has stopped at the place Victor-Hugo in Grenoble (marked with an arrow). Give the tourists directions to get to their destinations. Have your partner trace their route on the map.

■ WORD TO USE: **facile,** *easy*

MODÈLE: M. Perrault / l'église Saint-André

—**Pardon, monsieur, où se trouve l'église Saint André?**
—**C'est très facile. Prenez la rue Félix Poulat. Continuez tout droit jusqu'à la Place Grenette. Traversez la place et continuez tout droit. Ensuite, prenez la Grande Rue jusqu'à la Place Saint André. L'église Saint André est sur la place à gauche.**

1. M. Balay / le Musée Stendhal
2. Mlle Dupont / le Jardin des Plantes
3. M. et Mme Sarrasin / le Jardin de Ville
4. Mme Daniel / le Musée d'Histoire Naturelle
5. Mlle Choron / l'Anneau de Vitesse *(skating rink)*
6. Mme Poulet / la Place de Verdun

IL Y A UN PROBLÈME: QU'EN PENSEZ-VOUS?

Benjamin et Joël cherchent les Galeries Lafayette, mais ils ne trouvent pas le magasin. Qu'est-ce qu'ils devraient faire?

Benjamin et Joël devraient

a. rentrer à la maison et ne pas faire les courses.

b. demander leur chemin *(their way)*.

c. continuer à chercher le magasin.

d. Avez-vous une autre solution?

Justifiez votre réponse.

À VOUS DE JOUER

Vous cherchez l'appartement de votre ami(e), mais vous ne trouvez pas la bonne rue. Qu'est-ce que vous faites?

Moi, je...

a. téléphone tout de suite chez mon ami(e).

b. continue à chercher l'appartement.

c. demande la route à une personne qui passe dans la rue.

d. vais au café pour prendre quelque chose à manger.

e. Avez-vous une autre solution?

Justifiez votre réponse.

LECTURE

LE PETIT TRAIN

Reading Strategy: Scanning

One of the quickest ways to get information from printed material is to **scan** the paragraph or the page. Scanning is usually done quickly or casually to find a point of particular interest or to get a brief idea of the contents of an article or brochure. You will use this technique after answering the pre-reading questions below.

Remember that months and adjectives of nationality are not normally capitalized in French. Advertisements such as the one on p. 173, or brochures sometimes do not follow the rules.

1. Describe your travel preferences.

a. Aimez-vous voyager?

b. Aimez-vous visiter d'autres villes?

c. En général, est-ce que vous faites une visite seul(e) ou une visite guidée?

d. Quand vous visitez une ville, que visitez-vous? les musées? les églises? les discothèques? les clubs de jazz? les quartiers pittoresques?

2. Scan the brochure «*Le Petit Train de Grenoble*» and make a list of the main points such as hours and prices. Then plan a visit to Grenoble by answering the following questions.

a. En quel(s) mois fait-on la visite en train?
b. Combien de temps faut-il pour faire la visite?
c. Est-ce que la visite commentée est en français uniquement?
d. Où va-t-on pour commencer la visite?
e. À quelle heure commence la première *(first)* visite? la dernière *(last)* visite?
f. Combien coûte la visite? Est-ce qu'il y a un prix spécial pour enfants?
g. Est-ce qu'il est possible de réserver le train? Si oui, qu'est-ce qu'il faut faire?

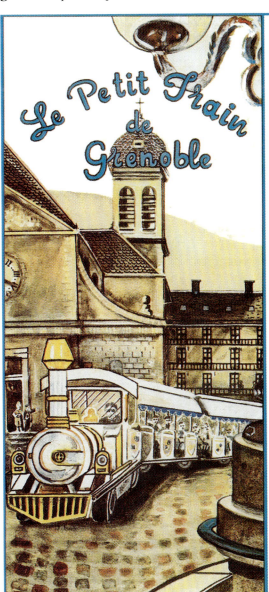

L'office de Tourisme avec

LE PETIT TRAIN DE GRENOBLE

vous propose :

De Février à Octobre de 10 h à 19 h
Visite commentée de 40 minutes
en Anglais, Allemand, Italien, Espagnol

﹏

40 minutes où vous découvrirez :
La capitale des Alpes, la vieille ville médiévale,
les Quais, les Places, monuments et personnages qui ont marqué
GRENOBLE depuis 2000 ANS

﹏

Départ de la visite : **PLACE GRENETTE**
toutes les heures : 10 h, 11 h, 12 h, 13 h, 14 h,
15 h, 16 h, 17 h, 18 h, 19 h.
Juillet - Août : nocturne à 21 h, 22 h, 23 h.

Prix / Price / Preise
30 F adultes   15 F enfants

Réservation :
Tél. 76 51 02 51 Fax. 76 01 02 33
Tarif : groupes, location, mariage, etc.
nous consulter.

R E N C O N T R E S

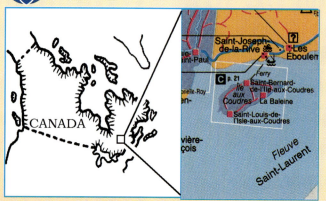

Encounters

Un Québécois qui aime bien sa région

POPULATION:	**Canada**	28 000 000
	Québec	7 000 000
SUPERFICIE:	**Canada**	9 970 610 km2
	Québec	1 667 926 km2
CAPITALE:	**Canada**	Ottawa
	Québec	Québec
LANGUES:	français, anglais, langues autochtones *(native)*	

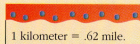

1 kilometer = .62 mile.

river
waterfall
everything I need

Décrivez-vous.

Je m'appelle Gaëtan Boileau, j'ai 49 ans et je suis veuf. Mon fils Joël est étudiant à Québec, mais moi, je préfère rester ici à Saint-Joseph-de-la-Rive où c'est calme, et je suis en pleine nature. Dans la région de Charlevoix, avec le fleuve° Saint-Laurent à côté, la chute° Cimon tout près et l'Île aux Coudres pas loin, j'ai tout ce qu'il me faut°.

make
crèches... *Nativity scenes*
oxen

Que faites-vous dans la vie?

Je fabrique° des santons, des petites figurines qui servent à décorer les crèches de Noël°. Tenez, voilà un petit Saint Joseph que je viens de finir. Il est beau, n'est-ce pas? Et regardez mes beaux bœufs°.

il... *there are only*
presque... *almost all*

XVII... *17th century*

Alors, vous êtes artisan?

Oui. Dans notre village il n'y a que° 250 résidents, et ils sont presque tous° artisans ou peintres. Par exemple, mon ami Jacques travaille à la Papeterie Saint-Gilles où l'on fait du papier grand luxe en utilisant une méthode traditionnelle qui date du XVIIème siècle°.

fishing

Que faites-vous comme passe-temps?

J'aime bien aller à la pêche° ou écouter de la musique chez moi. Gilles Vigneault est un de mes musiciens préférés.

future
gens... *people who don't know how to live*

Que pensez-vous de l'avenir°?

L'avenir? Eh bien, l'avenir c'est pour les gens qui ne savent pas vivre° au présent. Je suis très content de ma vie, et je pense rarement à demain.

QUELQUES QUESTIONS
1. Quelles sont les activités professionnelles de M. Boileau?
2. En quoi est-ce que la vie de M. Boileau est différente de la vie de son fils?
3. Y a-t-il des artisans ou artistes qui habitent près de chez vous? Si oui, aimez-vous leur art? Pourquoi ou pourquoi pas?

http://www.wiley.com/aventure.html

Rencontres. In this chapter and every other chapter thereafter, you will meet French speakers from five different continents. Learn about their lives through interviews, and by studying handy facts and maps from the French-speaking world.

Un moulin dans la région de Charlevoix.

RÉVISION ÉCLAIR

Telling where you are going   **Voir pp. 148 et 152.**

> Benjamin **va aux** Galeries Lafayette.

Making plans   **Voir p. 156.**

> Demain je **vais acheter** un cahier.

Talking about transportation   **Voir p. 158.**

> Elles **prennent** un taxi.

Expressing choices and making purchases   **Voir pp. 162 et 163.**

> J'aime bien **ce stylo** et **cette gomme.**
> Robert **achète** des trombones.

Talking about places already mentioned   **Voir p. 168.**

> Vas-tu **au cinéma** ce soir?—Bien sûr, j'**y** vais à huit heures.

ÊTES-VOUS BRANCHÉS?

Mon journal. In your journal, write two or three things that you learned about French food shopping, public transportation, or cafés. Compare what you've learned to your personal experience. For example, where do you shop? How do you get around your town? Where do you go when you want to take a break? How do you feel about these differences?

Y ÊTES-VOUS ARRIVÉS? ———————————————

 1. En weekend. Imagine that you and your friends are going away for the weekend. Tell a partner what you are going to do first, next, and last. Remember to use the verb **aller** in all your descriptions.

 2. On fait les courses. Use the map on p. 152 to tell about the errands you have to run. When possible, tell why you are going to the different destinations. Then ask a partner where he or she is going, using the same map.

 3. Allons-y! Without telling your partner(s), choose a destination and use the map to direct your partner(s) to it. Give them a starting point, then tell them to turn left, turn right, go straight, etc. Then ask them **Où êtes-vous?** to see if they have followed your directions accurately.

 PRONONCIATION
———————————————

Les sons [u] et [y] ———————————————————————————

One of the enjoyable aspects of learning any new language is trying to imitate the sounds and rhythms that you hear. Sometimes it is quite easy because the sounds are familiar; other times, you must make a real effort to produce authentic sounds. For instance, in some languages, you may need to learn to round your lips, make a click, or flap your tongue to get just the right sound.

1. The French sound **[u]** is similar to the long **u** (as in *do* and *too*) in English. In French it is represented by the spelling combination **ou**. Look over the following words. Then listen to your professor or lab tape, and repeat each one.

tout	ou	pour
loue	vous	cours
boulevard	souvent	boucherie

2. In French, the vowel **[y]** must be distinguished from **[u]**. It occurs in spellings with **u** when it is not in the combination **ou**. How can you make the correct French sound? Pucker your lips as if you were going to whistle, and put the tip of your tongue against your bottom teeth. Without moving anything say **eee. Voilà!** Now listen to your professor or lab tape and say the words below.

tu	eu	pure	plus
lu	rue	curieux	campus
bu	sur	bureau	succès

3. In each group below, one of the words doesn't fit with the others. Write it and say it aloud. Then listen to your lab tape to check your answers.

a. toujours	rouge	bureau
b. trouve	tu	rue
c. étudie	sous	coûtent
d. musée	boulevard	courses
e. où	du	étude

Quelques pays et continents

l'Angleterre *(f)* *England*	le Japon *Japan*	l'Amérique du Nord *(f)* *North America*
l'Allemagne *(f)* *Germany*	l'Irlande *(f)* *Ireland*	l'Amérique du Sud *(f)* *South America*
le Canada *Canada*	Israël *(m)* *Israel*	
la Chine *China*	l'Italie *(f)* *Italy*	Antarctique *(f)* *Antarctica*
l'Espagne *(f)* *Spain*	le Mexique *Mexico*	l'Asie *(f)* *Asia*
les États-Unis *(m)* *the United States*	la Russie *Russia*	l'Australie *(f)* *Australia*
	la Suisse *Switzerland*	l'Europe *(f)* *Europe*
la France *France*	l'Afrique *(f)* *Africa*	

Nationalitiés (Voir aussi Chapitre 1, p. 29.)

les Espagnols   *the Spanish, Spaniards*   les Irlandais   *the Irish*   les Israëliens   *Israelis*

En ville

la banque *bank*	l'hypermarché *(m)* *giant supermarket*	la piscine *swimming pool*
la boucherie *butcher shop*	la librairie *bookstore*	la poste, le bureau de poste *post office*
le bureau de tabac *tobacco shop*	le magasin *shop, store*	le stade *stadium*
l'église *(f)* *church*	le musée *museum*	l'université, la faculté, la fac *university*
la fromagerie *cheese shop*	la pâtisserie *bakery (pastry shop)*	
le gymnase *gymnasium*	la pharmacie *pharmacy*	la ville *city, town*

Quelques expressions qui peuvent indiquer le futur

à bientôt *see you soon*	dans deux semaines *in two weeks*	la semaine prochaine *next week*
à tout à l'heure *see you later*	demain *tomorrow*	ce soir *tonight*
après *after*	en dix minutes *within ten minutes*	tout à l'heure *later*
avant *before*		le week-end prochain *next weekend*
bientôt *soon*	le mois prochain *next month*	
dans dix minutes *in ten minutes*	plus tard *later*	

Quelques moyens de transport

l'avion *plane*	la moto *motocycle*	le vélo, la bicyclette *bicycle*
le bateau *boat*	le taxi *taxi*	la voiture, l'auto *car*
le bus *bus*	le train *train*	

Pour la rentrée

un cahier *notebook*	une fiche *(index) card*	un sac à dos *backpack*
un crayon *pencil*	une gomme *eraser*	une serviette *book bag, soft-sided*
une disquette *diskette*	un papier, une feuille de papier	*briefcase*
un feutre (un crayon-feutre)	*piece of paper*	un stylo *pen*
felt-tipped pen	une règle *ruler*	un trombone *paper clip*

Où se trouve... ?

à droite *right*	jusqu'à *up to*	continuez *continue*
à gauche *left*	sur l'avenue *on the avenue*	prenez *take*
au feu *at the light*	sur le boulevard *on the boulevard*	tournez *turn*
au coin (de) *at the corner (of)*	sur la place *on the square*	traversez *cross*
dans la rue *in, on the street*	tout droit *straight ahead*	

Verbes

acheter *to buy*	penser *to think*	prendre des notes *to take notes*
aller *to go*	prendre *to take, to have*	prendre du poids *to put on weight*
apprendre *to learn*	prendre une décision *to make*	tourner *to turn*
comprendre *to understand*	*a decision*	traverser *to cross*
continuer *to continue*		

Pronom adverbial

y *there*

Adjectifs démonstratifs

ce, cet, cette *this, that*　　　ces *these, those*

Quelques mots et expressions utiles

à *to, at*	facile *easy*	tout le monde *everyone*
au, aux *to (the), at (the)*	les gens *(m) people*	vite *quickly*
à mon / ton / votre avis *in my/your*	un pays *a country*	vraiment *really*
opinion	penser *to think, find*	voyons *let's see*
en *to, in*	tout de suite *immediately*	

Chapitre 6 • PREMIER WEEK-END

PRÉSENTATION ÉCLAIR

POUR COMMUNIQUER

Ordering drinks and snacks (continued)
Talking about quantities and ordering a meal
Talking about quantities (continued)
Saying no (continued)

POUR Y ARRIVER

Le verbe **boire**
Le partitif
Les expressions de quantité et les nombres
  (suite)
La négation: **ne... plus** et **ne... rien**

POUR S'ADAPTER À LA CULTURE

Les repas et l'étiquette à table
Les spécialités normandes

🎧 PREMIER ÉPISODE   `T 41`

Julie est en France depuis° deux mois. Après beaucoup de° difficultés, elle est maintenant très contente. Elle partage l'appartement de Caroline, et elle adore ça. C'est le week-end; Julie écrit° d'abord à son prof de français aux États-Unis, ensuite à Benjamin.

---

depuis *since* / **beaucoup de** *a lot of* / **écrit** *writes*

Chère Madame,

Enfin le week-end! Ici, la vie° est belle! J'habite avec Caroline dans un appartement confortable assez près de l'université. Elle est sympathique, et nous sommes maintenant amies. En plus, c'est un cordon bleu°. Elle m'apprend à faire la cuisine. Le matin, je bois° un café au lait et je prends une tartine° avec de la bonne confiture!° Miam, miam! Pour le déjeuner°, je bois de l'eau minérale. Et quand on va au restaurant pour le dîner, je bois même° un verre de vin°. Je suis une vraie Française, n'est-ce pas?

---

vie *life* / **cordon bleu** *excellent cook* / **bois** *drink* / **tartine** *slice of bread and butter* / **confiture** *jam* / **déjeuner** *lunch* / **même** *even* / **verre de vin** *glass of wine*

AVEZ-VOUS COMPRIS?

1. Comment va Julie? Est-elle triste?
2. Comment est son appartement?
3. Décrivez un peu Caroline.
4. Qu'est-ce que Julie prend pour le petit déjeuner le matin?
5. À la fac, comment sont ses cours?
6. En général, où étudie-t-elle?

Je fais souvent des promenades à pied dans la ville et je prends rarement l'autobus parce que je prends du poids.

À la fac, ça va bien. Mes cours sont assez difficiles. Je prends beaucoup de notes, j'étudie tranquillement à la maison et à la bibliothèque et, en général, je comprends assez bien ce que je fais.

Bien à vous,°
Julie

_____

Bien... , *Yours truly,*

ET VOUS?

1. Est-ce que vous aimez bien votre maison, chambre, appartement?

2. Avez-vous un(e) camarade de chambre? Si oui, est-ce que vous êtes ami(e) avec lui / elle?

3. Qu'est-ce que votre camarade de chambre ou votre meilleur(e) ami(e) aime faire?

4. Est-ce qu'il / elle fait bien la cuisine?

5. Et vous, faites-vous bien la cuisine? Quel plat *(dish)* est-ce que vous faites bien?

6. Où est-ce que vous étudiez souvent?

■ POUR COMMUNIQUER

Ordering drinks and snacks (continued)

I **LE VERBE** *BOIRE*

Caroline **boit** un café au lait le matin.
Les Français **boivent** souvent un verre de vin avec le dîner.
Et vous, qu'est-ce que vous **buvez** au petit déjeuner?

◆ **Boire** *(to drink)* is an irregular verb.

boire	
je **bois**	nous **buvons**
tu **bois**	vous **buvez**
il / elle / on **boit**	ils / elles **boivent**

◆ **Boire** is only used to talk about drinks, while **prendre** can be used to talk about food and/or drinks. **Manger** *(to eat)* is used with food, *not* with names of meals. **Déjeuner** and **dîner** are the verbs used to mean *to eat lunch* and *to eat dinner.*

Qu'est-ce que tu **bois?**	*What are you having/drinking?*
Nous **buvons** beaucoup d'eau minérale.	*We drink a lot of mineral water.*
Julie **prend** du café et un croissant le matin.	*Julie has (a cup of) coffee and a croissant in the morning.*
Je **mange** un sandwich à midi et une salade le soir.	*I eat a sandwich at noon and a salad at night.*
Je **déjeune** à midi, et je **dîne** à huit heures du soir.	*I have lunch at noon, and I have dinner at 8 p.m.*

QUELQUES BOISSONS POUR LE PETIT DÉJEUNER, LE DÉJEUNER OU LE DÎNER

un café crème

un thé citron

une orange pressée

un citron pressé

un verre de vin blanc

un verre de vin rouge

un kir

Culture. Be careful when you order! A **citron pressé** is similar to lemonade. **Limonade,** on the other hand, resembles Seven-Up.

Culture. French people tend to drink wine at meal times. Red wine is generally drunk more often than white.

A **kir** is a popular drink made of black currant liqueur and white wine. A more sophisticated version is a **kir royal** made with champagne instead of white wine.

T 42

QUELQUES EN-CAS (*Snacks*)

un sandwich au jambon

un sandwich au saucisson

un sandwich au fromage

une salade niçoise

ACTIVITÉS

1. Qu'est-ce que tu bois? Caroline, Julie, and some of their friends have gathered at a café. Tell what each person orders.

MODÈLE: Caroline / café crème (oui) / thé au citron (non)
> **Caroline boit un café crème. Elle ne boit pas de thé citron!**

1. Caroline / orange pressée (oui) / citron pressé (non)
2. Julie et Paulette / café crème (oui) / kir (non)
3. nous / verre de vin blanc (oui) / verre de vin rouge (non)
4. Jeanne et toi, vous / verre d'eau minérale (oui) / verre de lait (non)
5. tu / menthe à l'eau (oui) / Coca (non)
6. moi, je / limonade (oui) / chocolat (non)

> **Review.** You have learned that after **avoir** the negative of **un, une,** and **des** is **de.** This is also true with other verbs such as **boire, prendre,** and **manger.**

2. J'ai faim et j'ai soif! You are making a list of what your classmates want to eat and drink on the next class trip. Ask as many people as possible what they would like. Report your findings to the class.

■ **WORDS TO USE: Il faut** *We need*

To order, say

MODÈLE: —**Qu'est-ce que tu prends comme en-cas?**
> —**Je voudrais un sandwich au fromage.**
> —**Et, qu'est-ce que tu bois?**
> —**Un Coca, s'il te plaît.**

To report your findings, say

MODÈLE: **Il faut 2 Perrier**
> **3 Coca**
> **5 sandwichs au jambon...**

Brand names are usually invariable.

3. Détectives, à vos marques! *(Detectives, get ready!)* In your class find
—two people that drink **café au lait** with breakfast
—one person that drinks a glass of milk with dinner
—three people that eat a sandwich for lunch.

■ **WORD TO USE: quelqu'un** *someone*

MODÈLE: Il y a quelqu'un qui boit un thé au petit déjeuner?

DEUXIÈME ÉPISODE

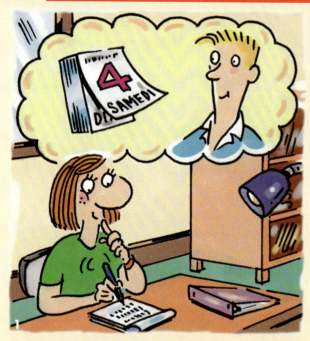

Julie est en pleine forme°. Elle écrit maintenant à Benjamin à Grenoble. Elle a envie d'inviter son ami à visiter Rouen. Peut-être° le week-end prochain...

en pleine forme *feeling great* / **peut-être** *maybe*

Salut Benjamin!

Comment vas-tu? Moi, je suis en pleine forme, et j'ai de très bonnes nouvelles°. Tu te rappelles° le foyer? Quel cauchemar!° Maintenant j'habite dans un appartement confortable, et j'ai même une amie française! Elle s'appelle Caroline, et je partage° son appartement. Elle est petite et mince, elle a les cheveux châtain¹° et de grands yeux verts. Tout à fait° le style de fille que tu aimes... Je plaisante°...

de bonnes nouvelles *good news* / **tu te rappelles** *you remember* / **Quel cauchemar!** *What a nightmare!* / **je partage** *I share* / **châtain** *brown* / **Tout à fait** *Absolutely* / **Je plaisante** *I'm kidding*

AVEZ-VOUS COMPRIS?

1. Qu'est-ce que Julie a envie de faire?
2. Quelle est la profession de Caroline?
3. Selon *(according to)* Julie, est-ce que Benjamin va aimer Caroline? Pourquoi?
4. À votre avis, pourquoi est-ce que Julie s'entend bien avec Caroline?
5. Qu'est-ce que Caroline apprend à Julie?
6. À votre avis, Benjamin va-t-il accepter l'invitation de Julie?

¹Like **marron, châtain** never changes.

Pour moi, c'est fantastique parce qu'elle est étudiante ici à Rouen comme moi, et on s'entend° très bien. Elle m'aide beaucoup à apprécier la cuisine française. Avec elle, j'apprends à manger du coq au vin° et des escargots° et même à boire du café! Tu imagines! Et toi, maintenant que tu es en France, est-ce que tu prends du chocolat avec des tartines?

---

on s'entend *get along* / **coq au vin** *chicken in wine sauce* / **escargots** *snails*

La vie° à Rouen est belle. Est-ce que tu as envie de visiter Rouen? Pourquoi pas le week-end prochain? Comme ça, tu vas rencontrer° Caroline et Minette (c'est notre chatte!), et tu vas voir° l'appartement! Téléphone-moi vite au 35-02-14-44.
Grosses bises°,
Julie

---

la vie *life* / **rencontrer** *to meet* / **voir** *to see* / **Grosses bises,** *Love, (lit: "big" kisses)*

ET VOUS?

1. Comment allez-vous aujourd'hui?
2. Qu'est-ce que vous avez envie de faire le week-end prochain?
3. Comment s'appelle votre meilleur(e) ami(e)?
4. Allez-vous inviter votre ami(e) à passer le week-end chez vous? Pourquoi ou pourquoi pas?

VOUS ÊTES BRANCHÉS!

Les repas et l'étiquette à table

The French pride themselves on their **cuisine** and have very clear ideas about the composition of their three daily meals. **Le petit déjeuner** *(breakfast)* usually consists of bread, butter, and jam served with **café noir, café au lait, thé,** or **chocolat.** Morning coffee is generally drunk with milk; later in the day, coffee is consumed black.

Le déjeuner *(lunch)* was once the big meal of the day but today, **le dîner** *(dinner)* is the time when families gather around the table. Contrary to American meals where various foods are served family style on one plate, French meals are usually served in courses over a longer period. An **hors-d'œuvre** and a main course are often followed by a salad course, a cheese course, and dessert (often a piece of fresh fruit). People dine later, around 8 p.m., and the meal is often the focal point of the evening. Wine **(le vin)** may accompany meals. Neither butter **(le beurre)** nor milk **(le lait)** usually appears at the lunch or dinner table.

When you sit down to a meal in France, the following tips will help you be a perfect guest:

À table.

- Place your bread on the table instead of on your plate. As a rule, there are no bread plates.
- Always eat cheese with your bread or with a knife and fork. Don't just pick up a piece with your fingers and eat it.
- When you are not eating, leave your hands on the table rather than in your lap.
- To refuse another serving politely, say **Merci** or **Non, merci.**

VOTRE Q. I. CULTUREL

A. Which items are not appropriate for the following meals?

1. le petit déjeuner: une tartine de confiture, un verre de vin rouge, une salade
2. le déjeuner: une tartine beurrée, un café noir, un verre de Coca
3. le dîner: un verre de vin rouge, un verre de vin blanc, un café au lait

Justify your answers.

B. Cite at least three major differences between a French dinner and an American one. Don't forget to include table manners!

http://www.wiley.com/aventure.html

POUR S'EXPRIMER

Repas *(meals)* et produits de tous les jours

MENU

Pour le petit déjeuner *For breakfast*

le croissant   *a crescent roll*
la brioche   *a cake-like bread*

le pain   *bread*
le petit pain   *a roll*

Pour le déjeuner ou dîner *For lunch or dinner*

Comme légumes (m)
As a vegetable course

les asperges (f)   *asparagus*
les carottes (f)   *carrots*
les épinards (m)   *spinach*
les frites (f)   *french fries*
les haricots verts (m)   *green beans*
les petits pois (m)   *peas*
les pâtes (f)   *pasta*
les pommes de terre (f)   *potatoes*
la salade   *salad*

Comme poisson (m)
As a fish course

le saumon   *salmon*
la truite   *trout*

Comme viande (f)
As a meat course

l'agneau (m)   *lamb*
le bœuf   *beef*
le lapin   *rabbit*
le porc   *pork*
le poulet   *chicken*
le veau   *veal*

Comme dessert (m)
For dessert

le gâteau au chocolat
    chocolate cake
la glace à la vanille
    vanilla ice cream
la mousse au chocolat
    chocolate mousse
les petits gâteaux   *pastries*
la tarte (aux pommes)
    (apple) tart

This list is purely a **point de départ.** Expand it, or tailor it to the interest and tastes of your students. Your students will be delighted to learn the vocabulary they need to order what they like and avoid what they dislike. You may wish to include such items as **cuisses de grenouille** *(frogs' legs)* and **escargots** *(snails)* to prompt some discussion and cultural awareness.

Point out to students that definite or indefinite articles are usually not included on a menu, even though they are present on ours for pedagogical reasons.

ACTIVITÉ

 4. Et toi, qu'est-ce que tu aimes? With a partner, talk about what you like and dislike eating for breakfast, lunch and dinner.

Modèle: —Qu'est-ce que tu aimes comme légumes pour le déjeuner?
   —J'adore *les* carottes.

   —Qu'est-ce que tu détestes comme légumes?
   —Je déteste *les* asperges.

1. Qu'est-ce que tu aimes beaucoup pour le petit déjeuner?
2. Qu'est-ce que tu adores comme poisson pour le déjeuner?
3. Qu'est-ce que tu aimes comme viande pour le dîner?
4. Qu'est-ce que tu aimes bien comme légumes pour le dîner?
5. Qu'est-ce que tu préfères comme dessert? pour le déjeuner? pour le dîner?

■ POUR COMMUNIQUER

Talking about quantities and ordering a meal

II LE PARTITIF

Avant les examens, les étudiants prennent **du** café.
Nous mangeons **de la** glace au cinéma.
Quand il fait chaud et qu'on a soif, on prend **de l'**eau.
Nous prenons **des** asperges pour le dîner.

◆ To say that you are eating, ordering or drinking an unspecified amount of something, use the partitive. The partitive, **du, de la, de l', des,** indicates that you are having *part of* what you are talking about; for example you will have *some* chicken for dinner, not the whole animal, and you will say:

Je mange **du** poulet, **des** carottes, et **de la** tarte.	*I eat (some) chicken, (some) carrots, and (some) pie.*

Note that the partitive markers in English *(some, any)* are not always expressed but are at least implied.

◆ The partitive varies in gender and number and will take the gender and number of the noun it precedes.

Le partitif			
	masculin	*féminin*	*devant une voyelle*
SINGULIER	**du**	**de la**	**de l'**
PLURIEL	**des**	**des**	**des**

Ils prennent **du** poulet.
Nous prenons **de la** soupe.
Tu prends **de l'**eau minérale?
Elle prend **des** asperges.

◆ In the **negative,** the partitive has one form: **de** (**d'** before a vowel sound).

Je mange **du** poulet. Je **ne** mange **pas de** poulet.
Je mange **de la** soupe. Je **ne** mange **pas de** soupe.
Il prend **de l'**eau. Il **ne** prend **pas d'**eau.
Vous prenez **des** glaces. Vous **ne** prenez **pas de** glace(s).

Repas et produits de tous les jours *(continued)*

LES FROMAGES *cheese*

le brie	*Brie*
le camembert	*Camembert*
le gruyère	*Swiss cheese*
le roquefort	*Roquefort; blue cheese*

LES FRUITS *fruit*

une banane	*a banana*
des cerises *(f)*	*cherries*
des fraises *(f)*	*strawberries*
une orange	*an orange*
une pêche	*a peach*
une pomme	*an apple*

AUTRES PRODUITS

le beurre	*butter*
la confiture	*jam*
la farine	*flour*
le lait	*milk*
les œufs	*eggs*
le poivre	*pepper*
le sel	*salt*
le sucre	*sugar*

Watch for the difference in pronunciation between **un œuf** [œf] and **des œufs** [ø].

ACTIVITÉS

5. Il faut bien manger les restes! Some of Caroline's friends had a big party. There are plenty of leftovers, so everyone decides to eat whatever they want for dinner. Tell what they have.

MODÈLE: Paul / poulet / pommes de terre
Paul prend du poulet et des pommes de terre.

1. Pierre / pain / beurre / œufs / fraises
2. Frédérique / agneau / haricots verts / brie / camembert / tarte
3. Françoise / café / glace à la vanille / mousse au chocolat
4. Jean-Paul et Dominique / eau minérale / poulet froid / salade *(f)* / pêches
5. Catherine / Coca / gâteau *(m)* / cerises

6. Êtes-vous allergique? The following people are allergic to different foods. Decide what foods they cannot purchase. There may be more than one answer for each allergy. Remember to use **de (d')** in the negative!

Encourage your students to come up with several possibilities for each item in **Activité 6.** For example, if someone is allergic to milk, they may mention milk, cheese, cream, ice cream, and cake.

MODÈLE: Marc est allergique au lait.
Il n'achète pas de glace.
Il n'achète pas de fromage.

1. Jean-Marie est allergique au poisson.
2. M. et Mme Bérard sont allergiques à la caféine.
3. Mme Bérard est allergique au sucre.
4. Sandrine est allergique au blé *(wheat)*.
5. M. Bérard et Jean-Marie sont allergiques aux œufs.
6. Sébastien est allergique au beurre.

 7. Il n'y en a plus! *There's none left!* At your favorite restaurant, you are ready to order. Unfortunately, they have run out of some items. Role play the conversations below with your partner.

■ WORDS TO USE: **Je suis désolé(e)** *I'm sorry*

MODÈLE: CLIENT: **Vous avez du saumon?**
          GARÇON / SERVEUSE: **Bien sûr, nous avons du saumon.**
          OU **Je suis désolé(e), nous n'avons pas de saumon.**

1. Vous avez de l'agneau?
2. Le chef a du lapin?
3. Vous avez des haricots verts?
4. Vous avez de l'eau minérale?
5. Est-ce qu'il y a de la tarte aux fraises ce soir?
6. Est-ce que vous avez de la glace au chocolat?
7. Est-ce que vous avez du sel? du poivre?
8. Voulez-vous manger ici ou aller ailleurs *(somewhere else)?*

8. Qu'est-ce que vous prenez pour le dîner? You are the server at a restaurant. Ask your partner what she or he wants for dinner. Then exchange roles. Use words from the two **Pour s'exprimer** boxes on p. 189 and p. 191.

MODÈLE: —**Bonjour, Monsieur / Madame. Que désirez-vous?**
—**Eh bien, comme légume, je vais prendre des asperges, et comme viande, du poulet.**
—**Et comme dessert?**
—**Euh... De la glace à la vanille.**
—**Et comme boisson?**
—**De l'eau minérale. Merci.**

Chez le fromager.

Benjamin est très content de lire° la lettre de Julie. Il pense que visiter Rouen le week-end prochain est une excellente idée.

──────────
lire *to read*

Il téléphone à Julie.
Dring! Dring! Dring!

BENJAMIN: Allô, Julie, c'est toi?
JULIE: Mais oui, Benjamin. Ça va?
BENJAMIN: Bien sûr! J'ai très envie de monter te voir° à Rouen. Mais, dis-moi° est-ce qu'il y a beaucoup de choses° à visiter?

──────────
monter te voir *come up to see you* / **dis-moi** *tell me* / **choses** *things*

AVEZ-VOUS COMPRIS?

1. Benjamin a-t-il envie de visiter Rouen?
2. À qui téléphone-t-il?
3. Qu'est-ce qu'il y a à visiter à Rouen?
4. Où Benjamin va-t-il passer le week-end?
5. Quel jour et à quelle heure va-t-il arriver à la gare?
6. Où est-ce que Julie va chercher Benjamin?
7. À votre avis, est-ce que Benjamin va passer un bon week-end? Pourquoi ou pourquoi pas?

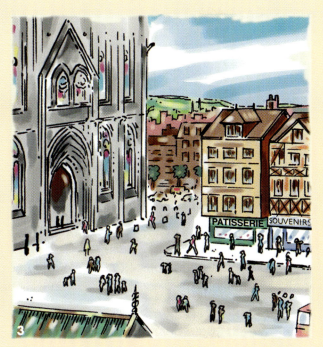

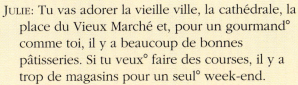

JULIE: Tu vas adorer la vieille ville, la cathédrale, la place du Vieux Marché et, pour un gourmand° comme toi, il y a beaucoup de bonnes pâtisseries. Si tu veux° faire des courses, il y a trop de magasins pour un seul° week-end.

BENJAMIN: On va passer° un week-end super! Mais au fait°, est-ce que je peux° passer le week-end chez toi?

---

gourmand *someone fond of eating* / **veux** *want* / **seul** *single* / **passer** *to spend* / **au fait** *by the way* / **je peux** *may I*

JULIE: Bien sûr! Je vais demander à Caroline, mais je suis sûre qu'il n'y a pas de problèmes! Bon, tu arrives quand?

BENJAMIN: Je vais prendre le train qui arrive à Rouen à 17h00.

JULIE: Très bien. À vendredi soir à la gare.

BENJAMIN: D'accord. Au revoir, Julie.

JULIE: Salut, Benjamin!

ET VOUS?

1. Allez-vous visiter une autre ville bientôt? Si oui, quelle ville? Pourquoi?
2. Quand vous voyagez, prenez-vous le train, l'avion ou l'autobus? Quel moyen de transport préférez-vous?
3. Quand vous voyagez, allez-vous chez des amis ou à l'hôtel?
4. Passez-vous quelquefois le week-end chez des amis?
5. Invitez-vous aussi des amis chez vous? Pourquoi ou pourquoi pas?

VOUS ÊTES BRANCHÉS

Les spécialités normandes

Rouen is located in the heart of Normandy on the Seine River. **Chef-lieu** (*county or regional seat*) of the **Haute-Normandie** region and the **département de la Seine-Maritime,** Rouen is situated in an area that is rainy much of the year. Lush green fields and meadows for grazing cattle dot the countryside, and the damp weather also provides excellent growing conditions for apples. Most of Normandy's food specialties are thus based on either dairy products or apples.

Alcoholic and non-alcoholic apple cider from Normandy is enjoyed throughout France. **Calvados,** a strong apple brandy, is world-famous. People also enjoy the apples in **tartes aux pommes** (*open-faced apple pies*) and a special apple candy, **sucre de pomme.** Other specialties from Normandy include dairy products such as **Camembert** and **Pont**

Vaches et pommiers normands.

l'Évêque cheeses, heavy cream, and butter. In spite of weather that might not be ideal, Normandy is a province worth visiting for its culinary delights.

VOTRE Q. I. CULTUREL

1. Quel fruit est associé avec la Normandie?
2. Nommez deux ou trois produits qui utilisent ce fruit.
3. Quels produits laitiers est-ce que l'on trouve en Normandie?

http://www.wiley.com/aventure.html

■ POUR COMMUNIQUER

Talking about quantities (continued)

III LES EXPRESSIONS DE QUANTITÉ

Il y a **beaucoup de** choses à visiter.
Benjamin mange **assez de** pâtisseries.
Tu poses **trop de** questions.
Je mange **quelques** fruits tous les jours.

◆ To answer the question **combien de... ?** (*how much?* or *how many?*) when you don't know the exact quantity, use the following expressions:

assez de	enough (of)	peu de	little/few
beaucoup de	a lot (of)	trop de	too much (of)/too many (of)
un peu de	a little (of)		

Note the difference in meaning between **un peu de** and **peu de.**

Pour rester mince, je mange **(très) peu de** beurre.	To stay thin, I eat (very) little butter.
Je prends **un peu de** sucre dans mon café.	I take a little sugar in my coffee.

◆ Most expressions of quantity will be followed by **de / d'** unless they are used as a one-word answer. **De** is invariable even in the plural.

—**Combien de** café bois-tu?   —Je bois **beaucoup de** café.

BUT: —**Combien d'**argent avez-vous?   —**Beaucoup!**

Ils mangent **beaucoup de** carotte**s.**

◆ **Quelques** (some, a few) is used *without* **de.**

Je prends **quelques** livres avec moi pour étudier.   *I take a few books with me to study.*

◆ Weights and measures are expressions of quantity.

un litre de	a liter of	un kilo(gramme) de	a kilo(gram) of
100 grammes de	100 grams of	une boîte de	a box or can of

Elle va acheter **250 grammes de** chocolat.

◆ Additional expressions include containers, pieces, slices, or approximate number amounts.

A kilogram = 2.2 pounds.

une bouteille de	a bottle of	un morceau de	a piece (hunk) of (cheese)
une tasse de	a cup of	une cuillerée de	a spoonful of
un verre de	a glass of	une dizaine (douzaine,	approximately 10 (12, 15, etc.)
une part de	a slice of (pie, cake)	quinzaine, etc.) de	
une tranche de	a slice of (meat, bread)		

Note: Une douzaine also means *an even dozen.*

Je voudrais **une bouteille de** bière.
Donnez-moi **une tasse de** thé.
Nous allons prendre **six tranches de** jambon.
Tu vas inviter **une dizaine d'**amis chez toi.

ACTIVITÉS

9. Nous en avons combien? You are working in a restaurant and need to take inventory of your supplies before placing next month's order. Look at the list below and use your imagination to decide on the quantities of each item.

■ **WORD TO USE: il reste...** *is/are left; there is/are . . . left*

<table>
<tr><td>nous avons
il y a
voilà
il reste</td><td>beaucoup de
un peu de
trois kilos de
assez de
une quinzaine de
10 litres de
trop de
cinq bouteilles de
sept boîtes de</td><td>ketchup
tomates
café
sucre
fruits
mayonnaise
jus d'orange
lait
carottes
eau minérale
sel
poivre</td></tr>
</table>

Il reste... never changes: **Il reste trois bouteilles de jus d'orange.** *There are three bottles of orange juice left.*

Extension. Several expressions of quantity and/or size may be combined to give more precise information: Elle a **beaucoup trop de** travail pour jouer au tennis.

10. Il faut changer de régime (diet)! Julie's friend Simone wants to improve her eating habits, so she goes to a diet center to consult a nutritionist. With a partner, play the roles of Simone and the nutritionist.

■ **WORDS TO USE: choses** *things* / **sucrées** *sweet* / **salées** *salty*

MODÈLE: —**Est-ce que vous mangez beaucoup de chocolat?**
—**Oui, je mange un peu de chocolat tous les jours.**

1. Est-ce que vous buvez assez d'eau? (Oui)
2. Est-ce que vous mangez beaucoup de légumes? (Non)
3. Combien de morceaux de fromage mangez-vous par jour? (4)
4. Combien de tasses de café buvez-vous par jour? (10)
5. Mangez-vous peu de poisson? (Non)
6. Vous mangez beaucoup de glace, n'est-ce pas? (Oui)
7. Mangez-vous trop de pain? (Non)
8. Combien de verres de vin buvez-vous par semaine? (2)
9. Est-ce que vous mangez beaucoup de choses sucrées? beaucoup de choses salées?

Variation. In **Activité 10,** have the nutritionist give advice. Remind students of the expression **il faut** (it's necessary) and model it for them: **Il faut boire beaucoup d'eau. Il ne faut pas manger de chocolat. Il faut manger beaucoup de légumes...**

11. Moi, je mange... Describe your own diet based on the questions the nutritionist asked in **Activité 10.** You may add more information if you like.

POUR S'EXPRIMER: LES NOMBRES (SUITE)

70 soixante-dix	80 quatre-vingts	90 quatre-vingt-dix
71 soixante et onze	81 quatre-vingt-un	91 quatre-vingt-onze
72 soixante-douze	82 quatre-vingt-deux	92 quatre-vingt-douze
100 cent	300 trois cents	500 cinq cents
200 deux cents	301 trois cent un	501 cinq cent un
201 deux cent un		
1 000 mille	1 000 000 un million	1 000 000 000 un milliard
2 000 mille	2 000 000 deux millions	2 000 000 000 deux milliards

Note

1. The number **quatre-vingts** ends in **s**, whereas **quatre-vingt-un** and the following numbers do not.
2. Exact multiples of **cent** end in **s.** Drop it when **cent** is followed by another number.
3. **Mille** never changes.
4. Use **un million de / un milliard de** + a plural noun:
     un million *de* **francs**
     un milliard *de* **personnes**

12. Le coût *(cost)* de la vie. People are always curious about the cost of living in different places. Use the list below to tell what things cost in Rouen. Then, tell what the same items cost where you live.

Extension. Have students practice their other numbers (73, 74, etc.). You may want to play Bingo to use numbers in a realistic context.

■ **WORD TO USE: coûter** *to cost*

MODÈLE: un croissant 5 F
     À Rouen un croissant coûte cinq francs. Chez moi, un croissant coûte deux dollars.

un sandwich au jambon	25 F	un appartement de 4 pièces	760 000 F
un café	8 F	(à acheter)	
un dîner au restaurant	95 F	un blue jean	270 F
une petite voiture neuve *(new)*	85 000 F	un livre	135 F
un appartement de 4 pièces (à louer)	4 500 F	un sac à dos	89 F

13. Mes achats. *My purchases.* Make a list of five things you have recently purchased using the vocabulary from the **Pour s'exprimer** on p. 81 and p. 163. Give the list to your partner and ask her or him to guess what each item costs. If your partner guesses wrong, tell her or him the correct price.

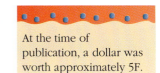

At the time of publication, a dollar was worth approximately 5F.

■ **WORD TO USE: alors** *well; then; so*

MODÈLE: une radio
     —**Combien coûte ma radio?**
     —**Voyons, euh... ta radio coûte 45 dollars.**
     —**Bravo, tu as raison. Elle coûte 44 dollars et 50 cents.**

ou—**Non, tu as tort!**
     —**Alors, combien coûte ta radio?**
     —**Elle coûte 25 dollars!**

QUATRIÈME ÉPISODE

T 45

Benjamin est très content de passer un week-end à Rouen. Il prend le train et arrive à la gare à 17h00 comme prévu°. Julie est là.

JULIE: Salut, Benjamin. Tu vas bien?

BENJAMIN: Mais bien sûr, le week-end je suis toujours en forme°.

comme prévu *as planned* / **je suis toujours en forme** *I always feel great*

JULIE: Alors, on prend quelque chose à boire, et on bavarde° un peu? Et puis, après, on rentre à l'appartement, et comme ça, tu vas rencontrer° Caroline et Minette.

BENJAMIN: Bavarder, d'accord, mais je ne veux rien° prendre. Je n'ai plus° soif; trois Orangina dans le train, ça suffit!°

on bavarde *we'll chat* / **rencontrer** *to meet* / **ne... rien** *nothing* / **ne... plus** *no longer* / **ça suffit** *that's enough*

AVEZ-VOUS COMPRIS?

1. À quelle heure et où est-ce que Julie rencontre Benjamin?
2. Qu'est-ce que Julie propose?
3. Quelle est la réaction de Benjamin?
4. Benjamin a-t-il envie de boire quelque chose? Pourquoi ou pourquoi pas?
5. Est-ce que Benjamin est curieux de rencontrer Caroline? Quelle question pose-t-il?
6. Quand ils arrivent à l'appartement, Julie commence à paniquer. Pourquoi?

3

JULIE: Bon, tu as envie de prendre le bus ou de marcher° un peu? Caroline et moi, nous ne prenons jamais le bus.

BENJAMIN: Marchons et parle-moi de Caroline. Je suis vraiment curieux de rencontrer ta nouvelle amie. Comment est-elle? Elle est jolie?

JULIE: Benjamin, tu es incorrigible!

BENJAMIN: Bon, très bien, alors on y va?

JULIE: Allons-y!°

_____

marcher *to walk* / **Allons-y!** *Let's go!*

4

Julie et Benjamin arrivent devant la porte de l'appartement. Julie regarde Benjamin, et tout à coup° elle panique.

JULIE: Aïe, aïe, aïe, que je suis bête! Caroline sait° que tu vas passer le week-end à Rouen mais... elle ne sait pas que tu vas rester dans l'appartement avec nous! J'ai oublié° de demander° à Caroline. Oh! zut! zut! zut!

_____

tout à coup *all of a sudden* / **sait** *knows* / **J'ai oublié** *I forgot* / **demander** *to ask*

ET VOUS?

1. Prenez-vous quelquefois le train pour aller voir des amis?
2. Après un voyage, avez-vous envie de boire quelque chose? Avez-vous envie de marcher un peu?
3. Aimez-vous passer le week-end chez des amis, ou préférez-vous aller à l'hôtel?
4. Demandez-vous toujours la permission à votre camarade de chambre ou à votre famille avant d'inviter quelqu'un à passer le week-end chez vous?
5. À votre avis, combien de jours au maximum un(e) invité(e) *(guest)* devrait-il / elle rester chez vous? Pourquoi?

IL Y A UN PROBLÈME: QU'EN PENSEZ-VOUS?

Julie invite Benjamin à passer le week-end chez elle à Rouen mais Caroline ne sait pas qu'il arrive. Qu'est-ce que Julie devrait faire?
Elle devrait

a. annoncer à Caroline que Benjamin passe le week-end dans l'appartement.

b. demander la permission à Caroline un peu en retard.

c. offrir de payer l'hôtel pour Benjamin.

d. Avez-vous une autre solution?

Justifiez votre choix.

À VOUS DE JOUER!

Follow-up. Have students pair up and create dialogs to illustrate the conversation between Julie and Caroline. They can then take turns playing the roles of the two roommates in front of the class. Have students vote on the most realistic or funniest dialogs and best acting.

Votre amie vous invite à passer le week-end chez ses parents. Quand vous arrivez, la maison est fermée, et votre amie n'est pas là. Que faites-vous?
Moi, je

a. rentre chez moi.

b. reste là et j'attends

c. vais à l'hôtel et je téléphone à mon amie

d. Avez-vous une autre solution?

Justifiez votre réponse.

■ POUR COMMUNIQUER

Saying no (continued)

IV LA NÉGATION: NE... PLUS ET NE... RIEN

> Je **n'**ai **plus** soif.
> Benjamin **ne** pose **plus de** questions.
> Il **n'**y a **rien à** boire.

◆ **Ne... plus** *(no more; no longer; not anymore)* is the negative form of the affirmative expressions **encore** or **toujours** *(still)*.

> Est-ce qu'elles habitent **encore / toujours** près de Rouen?
> Non, elles **n'**habitent **plus** là.

◆ **Ne... rien** *(nothing)* is the negative form of **quelque chose** *(something)* and sometimes answers questions with **Qu'est-ce que... ?**

Review. You learned how to use **ne... pas** and **ne... jamais** in Chapter 2, p. 56. You might want to review those negative expressions before you read this section.

Est-ce que tu as **quelque chose** dans ton sac?
Qu'est-ce que tu as dans ton sac?
—Je **n'**ai **rien** dans mon sac.

◆ As with other negatives, put **ne** before the verb and **plus** or **rien** immediately after the conjugated verb. In a sentence with **y,** place **n'** before **y.**

Caroline **ne** fait **plus** la grasse matinée.
Nous **n'**allons **rien** manger.
Il **n'**y a **rien** dans mon sac.

◆ Like with other negations, **ne... plus** takes **de (d')** before a noun instead of **un, une, des, du, de la,** or **de l'.**

Elle **n'**a **plus d'**amis.
Je **n'**achète **plus de** ketchup.

Ne... rien can be followed by **à + infinitif.**

Elle **n'**a **rien à** manger.

◆ Short negative questions and answers can be made using **plus de** (+ noun) or **rien.**

Plus de questions? Alors, **plus de** problèmes!
—Que fais-tu?
—**Rien.**

Grammar. Remind students that **le, la,** and **les** stay the same when used in a negative statement.

Culture. The expression **De rien** means *You're welcome.* Another expression used for the same purpose is **Je t'en prie.** The French often don't bother to say **De rien** or **Je t'en prie,** because it is not considered impolite in French to omit it.

ACTIVITÉS

 14. Rien à faire! Julie is having a bad day. She has a negative answer for everything Caroline proposes. With a partner, play both roles.

■ **WORDS TO USE: tu veux** *do you want*

MODÈLE: CAROLINE: **Tu veux regarder la télé?**
JULIE: **Il n'y a rien à regarder.**

1. Tu veux faire quelque chose?
2. Tu veux manger quelque chose?
3. Tu veux boire quelque chose?
4. Tu veux acheter quelque chose au centre commercial?
5. Tu veux écouter de la musique?
6. Tu veux lire *(read)* quelque chose?

Extension. Point out to students that **(Il n'y a) pas de quoi, Je vous en prie,** and **À votre service** are used in addition to **De rien** to mean *You're welcome.*

15. Plus de folies! Simone has a new diet thanks to her visit to the nutritionist. She tells Julie what she doesn't eat or drink anymore. With a partner, create their conversation.

MODÈLE: du chocolat

        JULIE: **Manges-tu encore du chocolat?**

    SIMONE: **Ah, non! je ne mange plus de chocolat!**

        JULIE: **Prends-tu encore du vin?**

    SIMONE: **Ah, non! je ne prends plus de vin!**

1. des pâtisseries   **5.** du café

2. de l'alcool   **6.** de la viande rouge

3. du beurre   **7.** des olives

4. du Coca   **8.** de la tarte aux pommes

 16. Le week-end. You ask a friend about his plans for next weekend. Is he going to watch something on TV? buy something at the mall? eat some chocolate? He will answer that he isn't going to watch, buy, or eat anything because he no longer does that. With a partner, create the conversation.

MODÈLE: —**Tu vas regarder quelque chose à la télé?**

       —**Non, je ne vais rien regarder.**

       —**Pourquoi pas?**

       —**Parce que je ne regarde plus la télé.**

LECTURE

UNE RECETTE

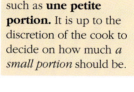

Reading Strategy: Applying prior knowledge

1. We have favorite dishes. To make them, we all follow some kind of recipe, whether it is from a cookbook or passed on by a friend or relative. Here is a recipe that uses a specialty of Normandy, **Camembert** cheese. Read the recipe below. Using your prior knowledge of cooking, decide with a partner what the following expressions mean based on how the recipe works: **couper, passer dans l'œuf, tourner dans la chapelure, faire chauffer.**

2. Look over the recipe ingredients. Then look at the shopping list provided and check off the items you will buy. (Not all of the ingredients listed will be used.) Next, decide how much of each ingredient you will need. Finally, look at the list of stores, and decide where you will buy each ingredient. You may find more than one ingredient in each store.

Camembert, berceau (*birthplace*) du camembert.

frying pan

breaded

immediately

CAMEMBERT CHAUD SUR PAIN DE SEIGLE°

Pour 4 personnes:
2 petites portions de camembert,
1 cuillerée à soupe de beurre fondu°,
1 œuf, 1 cuillerée à soupe de chapelure°, 4 petites tranches de pain de seigle° ou de pain complet°.

• Couper les portions de camembert en deux, les passer dans l'œuf, puis les tourner dans la chapelure.

• Faire chauffer le beurre dans une grande poêle°. Faire revenir rapidement des deux côtés les morceaux de fromage panés°.

• En garnir les tranches de pain et servir aussitôt°.

melted

bread crumbs
rye / **pain...** *whole-grain bread*

Du pain, du vin et du fromage.

Ingrédients

1. _____ œufs
2. _____ lait
3. _____ camembert
4. _____ chapelure
5. _____ oignon
6. _____ pain de seigle
7. _____ beurre
8. _____ sucre

Quantités

2 petites _____ de camembert
4 petites _____ de pain de seigle
1 _____ de chapelure
1 _____ de beurre
1 œuf

Magasins

la fromagerie: _____

la boulangerie: _____

l'épicerie: _____

3. Reread the recipe, then answer the questions below.

a. Combien de temps faut-il pour préparer la recette?

b. C'est pour combien de personnes?

c. Est-ce que c'est une recette que vous désirez préparer? Pourquoi ou pourquoi pas?

À VOS STYLOS!

Writing Strategy: Brainstorming, organizing, and supporting your position

The ability to persuade someone about your point of view is a very useful skill. There are several steps to follow if you want to be convincing. First, brainstorm as many ideas as possible and jot them down; for example, if you want to convince someone not to smoke, you might write:

1. **La fumée pollue l'air.**
2. **Les gens sont allergiques à la fumée.**
3. **La fumée est dangereuse pour les enfants.**
4. **La fumée est dangereuse pour l'environnement.**
5. **Les cigarettes coûtent cher.**
6. **Je n'aime pas la fumée.**

Next, organize your points. Reread your ideas and decide which ones to keep, combine, or eliminate, and choose the order in which they should be presented. For example, you might eliminate number 6, combine numbers 2 and 3, and add number 1 to number 4. Then reorder your list.

1. **La fumée est dangereuse pour l'environnement parce qu'elle pollue l'air.**
2. **La fumée est dangeureuse pour tous les gens (enfants et gens allergiques).**
3. **Les cigarettes coûtent cher.**

Finally, to be truly persuasive you must back up your arguments with supporting documents, statistics, articles or personal experiences that prove your point. For example, to support reason number three, **Les cigarettes coûtent cher,** you can say,

Un paquet de cigarettes coûte à peu près douze francs. Quand tu fumes 4 paquets de cigarettes par semaine, ça coûte 48 francs par semaine, 192 francs par mois, et 2 304 francs par an. Est-ce que tu préfères fumer ou aller à New York pour tes vacances?

Using the steps outlined above, write a persuasive argument either for or against being a vegetarian.

A. Start by brainstorming three reasons for or against.

Je mange des légumes...	Je mange de la viande...
1.	1.
2.	2.
3.	3.

B. Organize and prioritize.
C. Support your reasons with evidence.
D. Write a draft. **À vos stylos!**

Help students with vocabulary. Give them some cognates like **calories, cholestérol, vitamines,** and **énergie** and some useful words like **santé** and **matières grasses** so students can come up with sentences such as **Les légumes sont bons pour la santé. Ils sont bon marché. Il n'y a pas de cholestérol ou de matières grasses dans les légumes. Il n'y a pas beaucoup de calories dans les légumes.** Other possibilities are **J'adore la viande. La viande est excellente pour la santé. Il est possible de manger un peu de viande et d'avoir beaucoup d'énergie. Il y a beaucoup de vitamines dans la viande. J'achète de la viande avec peu de matières grasses.**

Ordering drinks and snacks (continued) **Voir p. 182.**

> Tu **bois** un café le matin?
> Il prend **un croissant.**

Talking about quantities and ordering a meal **Voir p. 190.**

> Nous prenons **des** carottes.
> Pour **le déjeuner,** je prends de la viande.

Talking about quantities (continued) **Voir p. 196.**

> Je voudrais **une tranche de** jambon.
> Elles achètent **beaucoup de** chocolat.

Saying no (continued) **Voir p. 202.**

> Il **n'**y a **plus de** pain.
> Je **ne** mange **rien** aujourd'hui.

ÊTES-VOUS BRANCHÉS?

Mon journal. What have you learned about French drinks, foods, meals, and table manners? In your journal, set up two sections: **Les Français** and **Les Américains.** Under the first heading, indicate what the French eat, drink, and do (or don't do) at various meals and times of day, and in the other section tell what typical Americans do. For example, **Les Français prennent du café au lait le matin, mais ils prennent du café noir le soir. Les Américains prennent du café au lait le matin et le soir.**

Y ÊTES-VOUS ARRIVÉS?

A. L'anniversaire de Paul. Some students plan to get together for their friend Paul's birthday. Complete the story below with **du, de la, de l', des, de,** and **d',** to find out what they are eating at the celebration.

Ce soir nous dînons au restaurant pour fêter *(celebrate)* l'anniversaire de Paul. Nous commençons par les hors-d'œuvre, et après, nous commandons le plat principal. Nous ne prenons pas (1.) _____ poisson parce que nous préférons la viande. Comme viande, il y a (2.) _____ poulet, (3.) _____ agneau, et (4.) _____ veau. Et qu'est-ce qu'il y a comme légumes? Nous prenons (5.) _____ pommes de terre, (6.) _____ haricots verts, (7.) _____ carottes ou (8.) _____ petits pois. Nous buvons aussi (9.) _____ vin rouge et (10.) _____ eau minérale. Comme dessert, nous allons prendre (11.) _____ gâteau avec (12.) _____ glace. Pour finir le repas, je prends (13.) _____ café avec (14.) _____ sucre, mais les autres prennent (15.) _____ thé. Quelle bonne soirée!

Follow-up. Activité A may be done orally or in writing. Ask students to write a similar paragraph when they have completed this activity.

B. Mon ami(e) et moi. Write the answers to the questions below. Your partner will do the same. When you have finished, ask your partner *yes–no* questions to see if you can guess how she or he has answered. You may repeat this activity with more than one partner if you like.

1. Quand vous avez très soif, qu'est-ce que vous buvez?
2. Quand vous avez envie de prendre un en-cas, qu'est-ce que vous prenez?
3. Est-ce que vous buvez beaucoup de Coca ou beaucoup d'eau?
4. Décrivez votre petit déjeuner idéal.
5. À la fac, qu'est-ce que vous prenez pour le déjeuner? Et à la maison?
6. Faites une liste de trois choses que vous ne mangez plus et que vous ne buvez plus.
7. Que faites-vous quand il n'y a rien à manger chez vous?

C. J'ai trop de travail! With two or three partners, discuss, for example, how many classes you have, approximately how many students are in each class, if you have enough time to sleep, how little or much free time you have, and if you have too many compositions. If you need to refresh your memory on expressions of quantity, see p. 196.

 PRONONCIATION

Les sons [o] et [ɔ]

1. In French, the closed [o] sound occurs in a syllable that ends in a vowel sound. The lips are rounded and slightly pushed forward, as if to kiss someone. French spelling has different combinations for the sound [o]: h**ô**tel, b**eau, aux,** gr**os.** Listen to your professor or lab tape and repeat the words below, paying special attention to the spellings in bold.

auto	f**aux**	m**o**t
b**eaux**	gr**os**	n**o**s
chât**eau**	h**au**t	r**ô**ti

2. Not all words spelled with the letter **o** are pronounced the same way. In French there is also an open **o** sound, [ɔ]. In the words below, each **o** is in a syllable ending in a consonant sound. Look over the list and say the words after listening to your professor or lab tape.

bonne	pomme	note
flotte	sommes	robe
votre	kiosque	porte

3. Look over the pairs of words on p. 209, then decide which word is pronounced open **o** [ɔ], as in **bonne,** and which is closed **o** [o], as in **faux.** Identify all the words with the open **o** sound, then say each pair of words aloud.

Pronunciation. Point out to students that the French **[o]** does not have the diphthong that is commonly part of the long **o** sound in English. Help students to compare the two sounds.

a. gomme / gros
b. lot / lotte
c. tôt / tonne
d. mode / mot
e. pot / porte

◆ V O C A B U L A I R E   A C T I F ◆

Les boissons (f)   Drinks

un café au lait *coffee with milk*	un kir *black currant liqueur with white wine*	un verre de vin blanc *a glass of white wine*
un café crème *coffee with cream*	une orange pressée *fresh-squeezed orange juice*	un verre de vin rouge *a glass of red wine*
un citron pressé *fresh-squeezed lemonade*	un thé citron *tea with lemon*	

Les en-cas (m)   Snacks

une salade niçoise *a kind of mixed salad*	un sandwich au jambon *a ham sandwich*	un sandwich au saucisson *a salami sandwich*
un sandwich au fromage *a cheese sandwich*		

Les repas (m)   Meals

le petit déjeuner *breakfast*	le déjeuner *lunch*	le dîner *dinner*

Les légumes (m)   Vegetables

des asperges (f) *asparagus*	des frites (f) *fries*	des petits pois (m) *peas*
une carotte *a carrot*	des haricots verts (m) *green beans*	une pomme de terre (f) *a potato*
des épinards (m) *spinach*		une salade *a head of lettuce*

Les viandes (f)   Meats

l'agneau (m) *lamb*	le lapin *rabbit*	le poulet *chicken*
le bœuf *beef*	le porc *pork*	le veau *veal*

Le poisson (m)   Fish

la truite *trout*	le saumon *salmon*	

Les fromages (m)   Cheese

le brie *Brie*	le gruyère *Swiss*	le roquefort *Roquefort*
le camembert *Camembert*		

Les fruits (m)   *Fruit*

une banane *a banana*	une fraise *a strawberry*	une pêche *a peach*
une cerise *a cherry*	une orange *an orange*	une pomme *an apple*

Les desserts (m)   *Desserts*

un gâteau (au chocolat) *a (chocolate) cake*	la glace à la vanille *vanilla ice cream*	la tarte (aux pommes) *(apple) tart*
un petit gâteau *an individual pastry, cookie*	la mousse au chocolat *chocolate mousse*	

Autres produits   *Other products*

le beurre *butter*	le lait *milk*	les pâtes (f) *pasta*
une brioche *a brioche (cake-like muffin)*	un œuf *an egg*	le poivre *pepper*
la confiture *jam*	le pain *bread*	le sel *salt*
un croissant *crescent roll*	un petit pain *a roll*	le sucre *sugar*
la farine *flour*		

Expressions de quantité

assez de *enough (of)*	un kilo(gramme) de *a kilo(gram) (approximately 2.2 pounds)*	peu de *little; few*
une boîte de *a can of*		quelques *some; a few*
une bouteille de *a bottle of*	un litre de *a liter of*	trop de *too much (of)*
beaucoup de *a lot of*	un morceau de *a piece of*	une tasse de *a cup of*
une cuillerée de *a spoonful of*	une part de *a piece of*	une tranche de *a slice of*
une dizaine (douzaine) de *around ten (twelve)*	un peu de *a little*	un verre de *a glass of*

Les nombres (suite) *(voir p. 199)*

cent *one hundred*	un million *one million*	un milliard *one billion*
mille *one thousand*		

Quelques négations

ne... plus *no longer; no more*	ne... rien *nothing*

Mots et expressions utiles

alors *well; then; so*	de la, du, de l', des *some; any*	quelque chose *something*
boire *to drink*	désolé(e) *sorry*	quelqu'un *someone*
une chose *a thing*	encore *still*	salé *salty*
comme (légumes)... *as a (vegetable); for*	il faut *we need; it is necessary*	sucré *sweet*
coûter *to cost*	il reste *is/are left*	tu veux *do you want*
	pour *for*	

Chapitre 7 ◆ À LA FAC!

PRÉSENTATION ÉCLAIR

POUR COMMUNIQUER

Talking about your activities (continued)
Avoiding repetition
Telling where you come from and what you have just done
Talking about the past

POUR Y ARRIVER

Les verbes **dire, écrire, lire**
Le pronom adverbial **en**
Le verbe **venir** et **venir de**
Le passé composé avec **avoir**

POUR S'ADAPTER À LA CULTURE

Le système universitaire en France
La vie universitaire

Caroline est étudiante en droit° à l'Université de Mont Saint-Aignan à Rouen. Elle étudie le droit et aussi les sciences politiques, l'économie et l'anglais, parce qu'elle a envie de travailler pour une compagnie internationale. Julie, elle aussi, travaille beaucoup, et aujourd'hui ça va mal. Elle parle de ses problèmes à Caroline.

_____
droit *law*

CAROLINE: Ça ne va pas, Julie, aujourd'hui?
JULIE: Je ne sais pas où donner de la tête°. J'ai beaucoup de choses à lire°, j'ai trois dissertations° à faire, et je ne sais pas où commencer!°

_____
où donner de la tête *what to do first* / **lire** *to read* / **dissertations** *term papers* / **où commencer** *where to begin*

AVEZ-VOUS COMPRIS?

1. Qu'est-ce que Caroline étudie? Pourquoi?
2. Caroline a-t-elle beaucoup de temps libre? Et Julie? Qu'est-ce qu'elles ont besoin de faire?
3. Quel proverbe est-ce que la mère de Caroline utilise souvent? Pourquoi?
4. Qu'est-ce que Julie pense de sa camarade de chambre? Et vous, qu'en pensez-vous?
5. Qu'est-ce que Caroline fait pour aider Julie?

CAROLINE: D'abord, du calme et ensuite de l'organisation! Ma mère dit° toujours: «Petit à petit, l'oiseau fait son nid°».

JULIE: Tu as raison. D'abord, je lis° mon français et j'écris° ma dissertation sur Pascal, puis j'étudie ma civilisation française et je fais ma dissert° pour mon cours de psychologie.

CAROLINE: C'est ça. Pas de panique à la fac. C'est toi qui dis ça en général.

---

dit *says* / **Petit à petit, l'oiseau fait son nid** *Little by little, the bird makes its nest* / **lis** *read* / **j'écris** *I write* / **dissert / dissertation** *term paper*

JULIE: Merci! C'est vraiment super d'avoir une camarade de chambre comme toi. Tu m'aides moralement° et, en plus, on partage le loyer°. Heureusement, parce qu'un appartement à Rouen pour une étudiante seule°, c'est beaucoup trop cher!

---

m'aides moralement *support me* / **partage le loyer** *split the rent* / **seule** *alone*

ET VOUS?

1. Qu'est-ce que vous étudiez ce trimestre / semestre? l'anglais? l'histoire?
2. Avez-vous beaucoup de temps libre? Que faites-vous quand vous êtes libre?
3. Comment organisez-vous vos devoirs? Que faites-vous d'abord? ensuite? enfin?
4. Habitez-vous seul(e)? avec un(e) camarade de chambre? avec votre famille?
5. Les loyers sont-ils chers dans votre ville?

À LA FAC!

VOUS ÊTES BRANCHÉS!

Le système universitaire en France

In the last year of **lycée** *(high school)*, students traditionally take a national exam called the **baccalauréat**, also known as **le bac.** After successfully completing **le bac**, students may enter the higher education system, which includes universities, **I.U.T. (Instituts universitaires technologiques),** and the **grandes écoles.**

The French university system differs from the American university system. Students have already chosen a major before entering the university and devote their time almost exclusively to their area of specialization. At the end of the first two years, students receive a **D.E.U.G. (Diplôme d'études universitaires générales);** at the end of the third year, **une licence** (roughly equivalent to a Bachelor's degree in the United States); at the end of the fourth year, **une maîtrise** *(Master's degree).*

Instead of going to a university, technologically inclined students can attend an **I.U.T.,** which offers numerous **spécialisations** *(majors)* such as engineering and electronics. After two years, students receive **un diplôme universitaire de technologie** that al-

Devant la fac.

lows them to enter the work force or specialize further.

Another possibility is the **grandes écoles,** where many French political figures have gone to school. Equivalent to the most prestigious American universities, they require students to pass extremely competitive entrance exams. They each award their own specific diploma.

Culture. Be careful of the French word **collège.** It does not refer to a university but to a school corresponding to junior high or high school in the American system.

VOTRE Q. I. CULTUREL

A. Combien de temps étudie-t-on pour avoir… ?

1. _____ un D.E.U.G.   **a.** trois ans
2. _____ une licence   **b.** quatre ans
3. _____ une maîtrise   **c.** deux ans

B. Répondez aux questions suivantes.

1. Quel diplôme faut-il pour entrer à l'université?
2. Quel diplôme les étudiants ont-ils après deux ans à l'université? après trois ans?
3. Où va-t-on pour faire des études techniques?
4. Comment s'appellent les universités françaises très prestigieuses?

Culture. You may want to give the names of some of the famous **grandes écoles (Saint-Cyr, Polytechnique, l'ENA, HEC)** and find an American equivalent for your students. **Saint-Cyr,** located close to **Versailles,** for example, is roughly equivalent to *West Point.*

http://www.wiley.com/aventure.html

Talking about your activities (continued)

I LES VERBES *DIRE, ÉCRIRE, LIRE*

Caroline et Julie **disent** toujours bonjour à leurs professeurs.
Caroline **écrit** des dissertations pour ses cours.
Elle **lit** quatre livres pour son cours de littérature.
Et vous, est-ce que vous **lisez** beaucoup? Est-ce que vous **écrivez**
beaucoup de dissertations ce semestre?

◆ **Dire** *(to say or tell)*, **écrire** *(to write)*, and **lire** *(to read)* are all irregular
verbs. **Décrire** *(to describe)* has the same forms as **écrire.**

dire	ecrire	lire
je **dis**	j'**écris**	je **lis**
tu **dis**	tu **écris**	tu **lis**
il / elle / on **dit**	il / elle / on **écrit**	il / elle / on **lit**
nous **disons**	nous **écrivons**	nous **lisons**
vous **dites**	vous **écrivez**	vous **lisez**
ils / elles **disent**	ils / elles **écrivent**	ils / elles **lisent**

POUR S'EXPRIMER

À dire, à écrire, à lire

dire au revoir	*to say goodbye*
dire bonjour (à)	*to say hi, hello (to)*
dire des bêtises	*to say silly things*
dire des mensonges	*to tell fibs, lies, stories*
dire merci	*to say thank you*
dire la vérité	*to tell the truth*
écrire une carte postale	*to write a postcard*
écrire un devoir	*to write an assignment*
écrire une dissertation	*to write a paper*
écrire une lettre	*to write a letter*
écrire un livre	*to write a book*
écrire un mot	*to write a note*
lire une bande dessinée / B.D.	*to read a comic book*
lire un livre	*to read a book*
lire un magazine	*to read a magazine*
lire une pièce de théâtre	*to read a play*
lire un poème	*to read a poem*
lire un roman	*to read a novel*

From Chapter 7 on, all direction lines will be in French. Please feel free to modify them by using the **tu** form if you feel more comfortable doing so.

Follow-up. Using elements from **Activité 1** as a starting point, ask students to come up with their own questions such as **Quand est-ce que vous dites merci au professeur?, Est-ce que vous écrivez souvent vos dissertations le week-end?, Où écrivez-vous des lettres?, À qui écrivez-vous souvent?** To help students, divide the task into four steps.

1. Have students brainstorm a list of question words, and write them on the board.
2. In the next column, set up the verbs **lire, écrire,** and **dire.**
3. Have students come up with a list of adverbs **(souvent, rarement...)** and a list of things you write, read, or say. Give a couple of examples and let students create a series of interview questions.
4. Ask them to interview a couple of people in the class.

ACTIVITÉS

1. À l'université, qu'est-ce que les gens font? Choisissez *(Choose)* un élément dans chaque colonne et dites ce que les personnes font à la fac.

MODÈLE: **Les étudiants écrivent des dissertations le week-end.**

je		un roman pour le cours de littérature
les étudiants		des dissertations le week-end
le professeur	lire	des devoirs à la bibliothèque
mon amie Caroline	dire	bonjour aux amis
nous	écrire	des lettres le soir
vous		merci au professeur
toi, tu		bonjour aux étudiants
		des examens
		un mot à leurs amis

2. Êtes-vous logique? Est-ce dire, écrire, ou lire? Choisissez le verbe qui convient *(fits)* et n'oubliez pas de faire attention aux formes des verbes.

MODÈLE: Le professeur _____ un examen.
      Le professeur lit un examen.
  OU **Le professeur écrit un examen.**

1. Les étudiants _____ une dissertation.
2. Nous _____ notre livre de français tous les soirs.
3. Est-ce que vous _____ toujours la vérité à vos parents?
4. Préférez-vous _____ des bandes dessinées ou des romans?
5. En vacances beaucoup de gens _____ des cartes postales.
6. Nous aimons _____ des romans le week-end.
7. Quand on entre, on _____ bonjour; quand on sort *(leave)* on _____ au revoir.
8. Moi, je déteste _____ à mes amis; je préfère téléphoner.

3. Et toi, que fais-tu? Demandez à votre partenaire de décrire ses activités et celles *(those)* de sa famille. Voici quelques questions pour vous aider.

■ MOTS À UTILISER: **avoir le temps** *to have the time*

1. Est-ce que tu lis souvent? Et les membres de ta famille? ta mère? ton père? tes enfants?
2. En général, as-tu le temps de lire? Qu'est-ce que tu lis? des romans? des bandes dessinées? des poèmes?
3. Préfères-tu écrire ou téléphoner? Et ta famille? Pourquoi?
4. Quand tu écris, écris-tu des cartes postales? des lettres?
5. Dis-tu toujours la vérité à tes parents? à tes professeurs?
6. Quand est-ce que tu ne dis pas la vérité? Quand est-ce que tu dis des mensonges?

C'est quoi ta note?

Caroline a besoin d'un peu plus d'argent°. Elle en a vraiment besoin. La vie° est chère, et il y a toujours quelque chose à acheter: du papier, un stylo, un livre pour l'université. Sa famille n'est pas riche. Alors, elle se demande où trouver de l'argent. Elle en parle à Julie.

un peu plus d'argent *a little more money* / **la vie** *life*

CAROLINE: Dis, Julie, j'ai besoin de gagner° un peu d'argent supplémentaire. Tu as une idée?

JULIE: Mais oui, j'en ai une! Il y a sûrement quelque chose à la fac. Tu es très bonne en droit et en anglais, non? Tu peux donner° des cours particuliers!° Beaucoup d'étudiants en donnent, pourquoi pas toi?

CAROLINE: Ça, c'est vrai!

gagner *to earn* / **peux donner** *can give* / **cours particuliers** *private lessons*

AVEZ-VOUS COMPRIS?

You will learn about **en** on p. 220. It has several meanings in English, and can usually be translated as *some, it,* or *them.*

1. De quoi Caroline a-t-elle besoin?
2. Est-ce que sa famille aide beaucoup Caroline? Pourquoi?
3. Quelle solution Julie propose-t-elle au problème de Caroline?
4. À votre avis, est-ce que c'est une bonne idée? Pourquoi ou pourquoi pas?
5. Où est-ce que Caroline met une petite annonce?
6. Qui appelle Caroline au téléphone? Pourquoi?

Caroline décide d'aller à la fac pour mettre une petite annonce:

> Étudiante en droit donne cours particuliers. Droit et anglais. Téléphonez au 35-02-14-44 après 18h00. Demandez Caroline.

Après ses cours, Caroline rentre et demande à Julie:

CAROLINE: J'ai des messages?
JULIE: Oui, écoute le répondeur. Il y en a un; un monsieur Tran qui a besoin de quelques leçons d'anglais avant un voyage d'affaires.
CAROLINE: Chic, alors, je vais l'appeler° tout de suite!

l'appeler *to call him.*

ET VOUS?

1. Avez-vous besoin de gagner un peu d'argent en ce moment?
2. Est-ce que vous travaillez pour gagner de l'argent maintenant? Si oui, combien d'heures travaillez-vous par semaine? Si non, en ce moment cherchez-vous du travail?
3. Comment est-ce que vous cherchez du travail en général? Vous regardez le journal? Vous téléphonez aux amis?

Avoiding repetition

▮ LE PRONOM ADVERBIAL *EN*

> Est-ce que Caroline cherche du travail? —Oui, elle **en** cherche.
> A-t-elle besoin d'argent? —Oui, elle **en** a besoin.
> Avez-vous un travail après l'université? —Non, je n'**en** ai pas.
> En général, avez-vous peur des examens? —Non, je n'**en** ai pas peur.

◆ A noun introduced by **un, une, des, de la, du,** or **de l'** may trigger the use of the pronoun **en.** Like **y,** it is used to avoid repeating information.

> Avez-vous **un** cours de français ce trimestre?
> COMPARE: —Oui, j'ai un cours de français ce trimestre.
>   —Oui, j'**en** ai un.

> COMPARE: —Non, je n'ai pas de cours de français ce trimestre.
>   —Non, je n'**en** ai pas.

> Y a-t-il **des** étudiants à la bibliothèque? —Oui, il y **en** a.
> Votre professeur de français a-t-il **de la** patience? —Oui, il **en** a.
> Avez-vous **de l'**argent pour votre loyer? —Oui, j'**en** ai.

◆ **En** may also replace nouns introduced by numbers or expressions of quantity such as **beaucoup de, trop de,** and **assez de.** The number or quantity must be repeated after the verb.

> Combien de romans lisez-vous? —J'**en** lis **trois.**
> Avez-vous assez de devoirs maintenant? —Oh, oui, j'**en** ai **assez.**

◆ Some verbs are followed by **de** + noun phrase **(parler de, avoir besoin de, être content de, avoir peur de, avoir envie de). En** may replace the **de** + noun.

> Parlez-vous souvent **de** vos problèmes? —Oui, nous **en** parlons souvent.

◆ When **en** is used with the immediate future or with a verb + infinitive, it usually appears before the infinitive.

> Allez-vous faire **des devoirs** ce soir? —Oui, je vais **en** faire.
> Aimez-vous écrire **des compositions?** —Oui, j'aime **en** écrire.

◆ **Note: En** can only replace nouns designating people if a quantity is mentioned. Otherwise, a **pronom accentué** is used for people.

> Avez-vous **beaucoup** d'amis? —Bien sûr, j'**en** ai beaucoup.
> Avez-vous besoin **de votre professeur?** —Oui, nous avons besoin de **lui.**

ACTIVITÉS

 4. La vie quotidienne Posez les questions suivantes *(following)* à votre partenaire qui va répondre en utilisant **en.**

■ MOTS À UTILISER: **la vie** *life* / **gagner de l'argent** *earn money* / **donner** *to give*

MODÈLE: Tes parents disent-ils des bêtises? (non)
   Non, ils n'en disent pas!

1. Est-ce que ta sœur lit de la poésie? (oui)
2. Tes amis écrivent-ils des dissertations ce semestre? (non)
3. On boit du café dans la classe? (non)
4. Est-ce que ton / ta camarade a des examens en ce moment? (oui)
5. Donnes-tu quelquefois de l'argent à tes amis?
6. En général, est-ce que tu es content(e) de ta vie? (?)

 5. Et vous, combien en avez-vous? Vous êtes toujours curieux. Posez quelques questions supplémentaires à votre partenaire selon le modèle. Répondez en utilisant un chiffre ou une expression de quantité.

■ MOT À UTILISER: **leçon** *lesson*

MODÈLE: livres—**Combien de livres as-tu?**   —**Moi, j'en ai trop!**
   —**J'en ai six. Et toi?**   OU —**J'en ai beaucoup.**

1. cours faciles	4. exercices	7. leçons faciles
2. cours difficiles	5. dissertations	8. leçons difficiles
3. professeurs difficiles	6. examens par mois	

 6. Monsieur rêveur. En groupe, répondez aux questions suivantes à tour de rôle *(one by one)*. Utilisez **en** dans vos réponses quand c'est possible.

■ MOT À UTILISER: **lunettes** *(f) glasses*

1. Est-ce que ce monsieur a beaucoup d'énergie?
2. A-t-il une télévision?
3. Est-ce qu'il a des lunettes?
4. Porte-t-il un pantalon élégant? des baskets?
5. Est-ce que les Tahitiens ont peur du chien?
6. Et vous, vous avez peur des chiens?

 7. Dites la vérité!

■ MOT À UTILISER: **oublier** *to forget*

Make sure you respond using **en** whenever possible, and be ready to report your findings to the class. Find out from your partner if she or he
   —often drinks coffee at school
   —has too much work in his or her classes this semester
   —sometimes forgets to read his or her lessons
   —is afraid of exams
   —is happy with his or her life in general

C'est l'heure de la première leçon de M. Tran. Caroline a un peu le trac°.

CAROLINE: Est-ce que je vais être un bon professeur? Est-ce que M. Tran va comprendre mes explications?°

Quelqu'un sonne°.

———
a un peu le trac *is a little nervous* / **explications** *explanations* / **sonne** *rings*

Quand Caroline ouvre°, il y a un homme d'affaires à la porte.

CAROLINE: M. Tran? Vous venez° pour votre leçon d'anglais?

M. TRAN: Mais oui. Je suis désolé d'être en retard, mais j'arrive de Notre-Dame de Bondeville de l'autre côté de Rouen.

———
ouvre *opens (the door)* / **venez** *have come*

AVEZ-VOUS COMPRIS?

1. Caroline est-elle un peu anxieuse avant la première leçon?
2. Qui sonne à la porte?
3. Pourquoi M. Tran est-il en retard?
4. Qu'est-ce que Caroline vient de faire?
5. Est-ce que M. Tran est français? Si non, d'où vient-il?
6. M. Tran est-il content de sa leçon avec Caroline? Pourquoi ou pourquoi pas?
7. Combien coûte une leçon avec Caroline? À votre avis, est-ce un prix *(price)* raisonnable?

CAROLINE: Entrez. Asseyez-vous. Je viens de faire° du café. Vous en voulez° une tasse?

M. TRAN: Oui, très volontiers°. Merci.

Pendant° la leçon, Caroline apprend que M. Tran vient du° Viêt-nam, mais il a fait ses études en France. Dans deux mois, il va faire un voyage d'affaires en Angleterre et il a besoin de perfectionner son anglais.

Je viens de faire *I've just made* / **voulez** *want* / **très volontiers** *gladly* / **pendant** *during* / **vient du** *comes from*

À la fin de la leçon, M. Tran est très content.

M. TRAN: Merci infiniment! J'ai l'impression que mon anglais commence à revenir°.

CAROLINE: Vous voyez, ce n'est pas si difficile que ça!

M. TRAN: Je vous dois combien°, mademoiselle?

CAROLINE: Cent francs, monsieur.

M. Tran cherche son portefeuille°, mais il ne le trouve pas.

M. TRAN: Oh, je suis vraiment désolé! J'ai laissé mon portefeuille° au bureau...

---

revenir *come back* / **Je vous dois combien** *How much do I owe you* / **j'ai laissé mon portefeuille** *I left my wallet*

ET VOUS?

1. Que font les étudiants américains quand ils ont besoin d'argent? Est-ce que vous faites la même chose?
2. Quelquefois prenez-vous des leçons? De quoi? de musique? de danse? Combien coûte la leçon?
3. Arrivez-vous toujours à l'heure pour vos classes? Si non, pourquoi pas?
4. En général, êtes-vous content(e) de vos cours? Quel(s) cours aimez-vous? détestez-vous? Dites pourquoi.

Culture. To learn more about **Viêt-nam,** read **Rencontres** p. 236.

M. Tran n'a pas d'argent pour payer *(to pay)* Caroline après sa leçon.
  Devrait-elle...

a. demander à M. Tran de payer plus tard.
b. mettre M. Tran à la porte.
c. demander à M. Tran de revenir dans une heure pour payer sa leçon.
d. demander à M. Tran de payer cinq leçons d'avance.
e. Avez-vous une autre solution?

Justifiez votre réponse.

À VOUS DE JOUER!

Un / une camarade de classe invite tout le monde à dîner au restaurant parce
qu'il / elle a fini *(finished)* son D.E.U.G. Quand le garçon arrive avec
l'addition *(the check)*, votre camarade va aux toilettes et ne revient pas. Que
faites-vous?
  Moi, je...

a. vais chez moi sans payer.
b. dis aux amis: «Eh bien, combien coûtent nos repas?»
c. vais chercher mon / ma camarade aux toilettes.
d. Avez-vous une autre solution?

Justifiez votre réponse.

■ POUR COMMUNIQUER

Telling where you come from and what you have just done

III *VENIR ET VENIR DE*

M. Tran **vient** chez Caroline pour sa leçon.
D'où **venez-vous?**
Nous **venons des** États-Unis.
Caroline et Julie **viennent de** faire du café.

◆ **Venir** *(to come)* is an irregular verb. Other verbs conjugated the same way
are **revenir** *(to return)* and **devenir** *(to become)*.

venir	
je **viens**	nous **venons**
tu **viens**	vous **venez**
il, elle, on **vient**	ils, elles **viennent**

◆ **Venir** is often followed by **de** to indicate where someone comes from or is coming from. If **venir** is used with a noun or a masculine or plural country, **de** is used with the definite article.

> **Venez**-vous **de la** bibliothèque?
> Je **viens du** Mexique.
> Je **viens des** États-Unis.

With most cities and with feminine countries or continents, **de** is used without the definite article.

> Je **viens de** Grenoble.
> Elles **viennent de** Belgique.
> Van **vient d'**Asie.

◆ **Le passé immédiat:** To show that you have *just finished* doing something, use **venir de (d')** + infinitive.

Il **vient de poser** une question.	*He just asked a question.*
Nous **venons d'arriver.**	*We just arrived.*
Vous **venez de comprendre** le problème.	*You just understood the problem.*

Review. You already know how to tell about things you are going to do using the immediate future (see Chapter 5, p. 156).

ACTIVITÉS

8. À quelle heure viennent-ils? Les amis de Caroline viennent travailler chez elle, mais pas au même *(same)* moment. Dites à quelle heure ils arrivent.

MODÈLE: Georges et moi / 3h00
> **Georges et moi, nous venons à trois heures.**

1. Paul / 4h30
2. Éliane et Gigi / 6h15
3. nous / 2h45
4. Virginie / 3h00
5. Claudette et toi / 5h20
6. je / 1h10
7. Jacques et Raymond / 6h30
8. tu / 5h45

Review. You may want to review locations and prepositions in Chapter 4, p. 134 and Chapter 5, p. 150 to prepare students for the activities that follow.

9. D'où viennent-ils? Tout le monde rentre après une longue journée *(day)*. D'où viennent-ils?

MODÈLE: nous / pharmacie
Nous venons de la pharmacie.

1. il / banque
2. tu / bureau de tabac
3. elles / pharmacie
4. Pierre et Caroline / boulangerie
5. je / gymnase
6. vous / piscine
7. nous / librairie
8. elle / poste

 10. Interview. Find out from at least three people in your class

1. what time they come to class every day.
2. where they come from.
3. where their parents come from.
4. if they return to campus on weekends.
5. if they are going to return to campus in ten years.

POUR S'EXPRIMER

Quelques pays francophones et quelques nationalités

l'Algérie	algérien(ne)	le Maroc	marocain(e)
la Belgique	belge	le Sénégal	sénégalais(e)
le Cameroun	camerounais(e)	la Tunisie	tunisien(ne)
la Côte d'Ivoire	ivoirien(ne)	le Viêt-nam	vietnamien(ne)

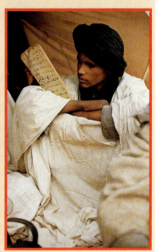

Habitants du monde francophone: une Belge, une Tahitienne et un Marocain.

11. Le monde francophone. Caroline rencontre souvent des étudiants de pays différents où l'on parle français. Savez-vous *(do you know)* d'où ils viennent?

Review. Remind students of the contracted forms of **de** + article.

MODÈLE: Marius et Jomo / sénégalais. Ils...
Marius et Jomo sont sénégalais. Ils viennent du Sénégal.

Sylvie / tunisienne. Elle...
Sylvie est tunisienne. Elle vient de Tunisie.

1. Robert et Farouk / marocains. Ils...
2. Josette / ivoirienne. Elle...
3. Émilie et Catherine / vietnamiennes. Elles...
4. Cécile / canadienne. Elle...
5. Christian / belge. Il...
6. Grégorie / camerounais. Il...
7. Fuad / algérien. Il...

12. Trop tard! Vous demandez ce que les gens vont faire, mais c'est trop tard—c'est déjà fait *(it's already been done)*!

Review. Before doing **Activité 12,** remind students that **venir de** + infinitive indicates the immediate past. Point out the similarity to **aller** + infinitive for the immediate future.

MODÈLE: —**Vas-tu déjeuner?**
—**Non, je viens de déjeuner.**

1. Vas-tu nager à la piscine?
2. Tu vas dîner avec nous?
3. Marianne va écrire sa dissertation?
4. Est-ce que Jacques et Stéphane vont manger une pizza?
5. Jean et toi, vous allez sortir *(go out)?*
6. Marthe et Sophie vont écrire à leurs cousins?
7. Tu vas téléphoner à Marguerite?
8. Paul va lire la carte postale de son amie?
9. Tu vas dire bonjour à tes amis?
10. Et vous deux, qu'est-ce que vous venez de faire?

13. On vient de... Tell your partner two things you did just before coming to class. Then guess two things your partner did immediately before class. Your partner will correct you if you guess wrong. Remember to use **venir de** in all your statements and questions.

MODÈLE: —**Tu viens de manger un sandwich et de boire un café.**
—**C'est vrai. Je viens de manger un sandwich, mais je ne viens pas de boire un café.**

🎧 QUATRIÈME ÉPISODE T 49

Julie arrive à la maison. Caroline a l'air triste. Julie regarde Caroline et demande:

JULIE: Alors, ça ne va pas?

CAROLINE: Non, pas tellement°.

JULIE: Ah bon? Pourquoi? Ton étudiant a décidé° de ne pas venir pour sa leçon?

CAROLINE: Non, ce n'est pas ça.

JULIE: Alors?

---

pas tellement *not really* / **a décidé** *decided*

CAROLINE: Eh bien, la leçon a bien marché°; il a écouté et il a compris et appris° beaucoup de choses.

---

a bien marché *went well* / **a compris et appris** *understood and learned*

AVEZ-VOUS COMPRIS?

1. Quand Julie arrive à la maison, comment va Caroline? Pourquoi?
2. Caroline est-elle contente de sa leçon?
3. Qu'est-ce que M. Tran a dit à la fin de la leçon?
4. Pourquoi Caroline a-t-elle besoin d'argent?
5. Julie dit: «Ne te fais pas de souci.» Pourquoi?
6. Que pensez-vous de Julie maintenant?

CAROLINE: Mais à la fin° de la leçon il a dit: «Désolé, je n'ai pas d'argent. J'ai oublié° mon portefeuille au bureau! Je vais vous payer° la semaine prochaine.» En attendant°, qu'est-ce que je vais faire? J'ai vraiment besoin d'acheter un livre pour mon cours de droit aujourd'hui!

à la fin *at the end* / ai oublié *forgot* / vous payer *pay you* / En attendant *In the meantime*

JULIE: Ne te fais pas de souci°. Regarde! Je viens de retrouver un billet de deux cents francs que j'ai oublié dans mon sac. Prends l'argent et achète ton livre. Et après, s'il reste quelques francs on va prendre un café ensemble.

CAROLINE: Tu es vraiment un ange!

Ne te fais pas de souci. *Don't worry.*

ET VOUS?

1. Travaillez-vous? Si oui, quel est votre travail? Êtes-vous bien payé(e) ou mal payé(e)?
2. Prenez-vous quelquefois des leçons particulières? Si oui, combien coûte la leçon? Est-ce cher ou raisonnable, à votre avis?
3. Oubliez-vous quelquefois votre portefeuille? votre sac? vos clés? Que faites-vous quand vous oubliez quelque chose?

VOUS ÊTES BRANCHÉS!

La vie universitaire

For French students, attending college is a full-time job. Most students do not have to work during their college years because their tuition is low. University registration fees, **les frais d'inscription,** are inexpensive by American standards because the French government heavily subsidizes higher education. Since there is also a time limit on how many years students may spend earning a degree (a total of three years is usually granted by the university to obtain a D.E.U.G. for example), they must apply themselves from the time they enter a university.

French students are required to take and pass a number of exams to demonstrate their knowledge of various subjects, and are usually graded on a scale from one to twenty, with **une note de dix sur vingt** *(a grade of 10/20)* being passing. For those students who fail to earn a passing grade, **un examen de rattrapage,** a kind of make-up exam, is sometimes given before the new term begins in the fall.

Résultats d'examen.

Most French students go directly to college after earning their **bac.** In French universities, it is therefore rather unusual to find older students who may have postponed obtaining a college education because they were working or raising a family. In the French system, students are expected to go to class, pass their exams, earn a degree, and finally, get a job.

VOTRE Q. I. CULTUREL

Est-ce vrai ou faux? Si ces phrases sont fausses, corrigez-les.

1. Beaucoup d'étudiants français sont obligés de travailler pour payer leurs cours.
2. Il n'y a pas d'examens dans les universités françaises.
3. Les frais d'inscription sont toujours très chers dans les universités françaises.

http://www.wiley.com/aventure.html

Review. You have already learned how to talk about the **passé immédiat (venir de** + infinitive) to tell about things that have just happened. See pp. 224–225.

■ POUR COMMUNIQUER

Talking about the past

IV LE PASSÉ COMPOSÉ AVEC *AVOIR*

Caroline **a donné** une leçon à M. Tran.
M. Tran **a dit:** «J'**ai oublié** mon portefeuille.»
Il **n'a pas payé** Caroline.
Julie et Caroline **ont parlé** de leur problème.

◆ To talk about specific events or actions that happened in the past, use the **passé composé.** The **passé composé** has three meanings in English.

j'ai mangé	*I ate* *I have eaten* *I did eat*

◆ For most verbs, the **passé composé** is formed by using the present tense of **avoir** (called the auxiliary verb) and a past participle.

manger	
j'**ai mangé**	nous **avons mangé**
tu **as mangé**	vous **avez mangé**
il / elle / on **a mangé**	ils / elles **ont mangé**

◆ The past participle of **-er** verbs is formed by dropping the **-er** of the infinitive and adding **-é.** It sounds exactly like the infinitive.

décide<s>r</s> ⟶ décid**é**   oublie<s>r</s> ⟶ oubli**é**
écoute<s>r</s> ⟶ écout**é**   trouve<s>r</s> ⟶ trouv**é**

◆ The past participle of irregular verbs is generally irregular.

Quelques participes passés irréguliers			
avoir	**eu**	faire	**fait**
boire	**bu**	lire	**lu**
dire	**dit**	mettre	**mis**
écrire	**écrit**	prendre	**pris**
être	**été**		

Elle **a dit**: «J'**ai écrit** deux lettres ce matin.»
Avez-vous **pris** mon livre?

◆ The negative of the **passé composé** is formed by putting a negative expression around the auxiliary verb **avoir.**

| Je **n'ai pas** lu le journal ce matin. | *I didn't read the paper this morning.* |
| Ils **n'ont rien** fait! | *They didn't do anything!* |

◆ Questions in the **passé composé** are formed the same way as questions in the present—with intonation, **n'est-ce pas, est-ce que,** or inversion. With inversion, questions that use a subject pronoun invert *only* the auxiliary verb and subject pronoun, which are then followed by the past participle.

| Tu **as fait** tes devoirs? | Est-ce que tu **as fait** tes devoirs? |
| Tu **as fait** tes devoirs, **n'est-ce pas?** | **As-tu** fait tes devoirs? |

Questions that use a noun as the subject of the sentence keep the noun in its original position and invert *only* the auxiliary verb and the subject pronoun, which are then followed by the past participle.

> **Les étudiants** ont pris le bus ce matin.
> Les étudiants **ont-ils** pris le bus ce matin?

POUR S'EXPRIMER

Quelques expressions de temps

hier	*yesterday*
hier soir	*last night*
hier matin	*yesterday morning*
avant hier	*the day before yesterday*
le mois dernier	*last month*
le week-end dernier / le week-end passé	*last weekend*
la semaine dernière / la semaine passée	*last week*
il y a deux jours, il y a cinq semaines	*two days ago; five weeks ago*
il y a trois mois	*three months ago*
il y a quatre ans	*four years ago*
il y a longtemps	*a long time ago*
déjà	*already*
tout à l'heure	*a little while ago*

ACTIVITÉS

Warm-up. Before doing activities for the **passé composé,** review the forms of the verb **avoir.** Some possible questions: **As-tu un chien?, As-tu un chat?, Vos parents ont-ils une maison?, Qu'est-ce que vous avez dans votre sac?, Quel âge as-tu?, Avez-vous des frères ou et des sœurs?, Tes amis ont-ils toujours raison?, Est-ce que nous avons un examen aujourd'hui?**

14. Les voisins. *The neighbors.* Dites ce que vous avez remarqué dans votre quartier hier.

MODÈLE: Mme Ripert / préparer / le déjeuner pour ses enfants
Mme Ripert a préparé le déjeuner pour ses enfants.

1. José / regarder / la télé toute la journée
2. M. Untel / lire / le journal avec son déjeuner
3. Michelle / écrire / une lettre
4. M. et Mme Filou / acheter / un nouveau sofa
5. Les Dupont / quitter / la maison à 7h00
6. Jean Lepetit / inviter / son amie à dîner
7. William / écouter / le compact d'Yves Duteil
8. Mme Enghien et sa sœur / boire / une bouteille de vin rouge
9. Mlle Samme / manger / un steak et des haricots verts
10. Max et moi / passer / la journée à lire

15. Travailler ou jouer? Vous aimez jouer, mais vos amis sont sérieux. Racontez ce que vous avez fait.

MODÈLE: Caroline / étudier / jouer au golf
>**Caroline a étudié, mais moi, je n'ai pas étudié. J'ai joué au golf.**

1. George et René / étudier / jouer au tennis
2. Simone / travailler / regarder la télé
3. Benoît / faire les devoirs / nager à la piscine
4. vous / écrire une dissertation / faire du sport
5. tu / lire un roman / lire des B.D.s
6. elles / répéter le vocabulaire / chanter
7. mes amis / écouter le professeur / écouter de la musique
8. Pierre et toi / faire une rédaction / faire la sieste

POUR S'EXPRIMER

Les dates

1000	mille
1515	mille cinq cent quinze
ou	mil cinq cent quinze (**Mil** spelled **M-i-l** is used for dates only.)
ou	quinze cent quinze
1789	mille sept cent quatre-vingt-neuf
	dix-sept cent quatre-vingt-neuf
2000	deux mille
2001	deux mille un
en 1997	en mille neuf cent quatre-vingt-dix-sept

---

16. Examen de civilisation. Julie a un examen de civilisation française. Aidez Julie à étudier.

MODÈLE: Stendhal / écrire / *Le rouge et le noir* / 1830
>**Stendhal a écrit *Le rouge et le noir* en 1830.**

1. Descartes / dire / «Je pense donc *(therefore)* je suis» / 1637
2. Louis XIV / mettre / Fouquet en prison / 1661
3. les Français / boire du champagne pour la première fois / 1715 grâce à Dom Pérignon
4. le docteur Paccard / faire / l'ascension du Mont Blanc / 1786
5. les révolutionnaires / prendre / la Bastille / 1789
6. Mirabeau et ses collègues / lire / la Déclaration des droits de l'homme / 1789
7. Rouget de Lisle / composer / La Marseillaise / 1792
8. Napoléon / être / emprisonné dans l'île Sainte Hélène / 1815
9. Saint-Exupéry / écrire *Le petit prince* / 1943

17. Nos activités. Qu'est-ce que votre famille et vous avez fait récemment?

MODÈLE: **La semaine dernière, ma grand-mère a fait la cuisine.**

hier	je	travailler
la semaine dernière	mes parents	manger au restaurant
pendant les vacances	ma mère	faire la cuisine
le week-end dernier	mon mari	regarder un film
lundi soir	ma petite amie	boire un kir
il y a longtemps	mes cousins	danser à la discothèque
tout à l'heure	ma tante	écrire des lettres
déjà	ma grand-mère	téléphoner aux amis
il y a deux jours	nous	prendre un pot au café
avant hier	mes frères	faire les courses

18. Je suis navré, mais... *I'm really sorry, but . . .* Le professeur vous demande votre devoir, mais où est votre devoir? Il faut inventer une bonne excuse!

MODÈLE: mon chien / manger
Mon devoir... euh... eh bien, mon chien a mangé mon devoir.

1. je / avoir le temps de faire mon devoir (négatif)
2. je / trouver mon devoir (négatif)
3. je / être malade
4. je / faire la cuisine et la vaisselle pour toute ma famille
5. mon frère / prendre mon devoir
6. je / oublier mon devoir dans ma chambre
7. ma sœur / mettre mon devoir dans son sac
8. Inventez une autre excuse.

 19. Quand avez-vous fait ça? Vous désirez savoir quand vos amis ont fait certaines choses. Posez des questions à votre partenaire.

■ MOTS À UTILISER: **pour la dernière fois** *for the last time* / **payer** *to pay*

MODÈLE: lire une histoire
—Quand as-tu lu une histoire pour la dernière fois?
—J'ai lu une histoire la semaine dernière.

1. faire la cuisine
2. écrire une carte postale
3. lire une pièce
4. payer un café à ton ami(e)

5. regarder la télé
6. jouer au basketball
7. écouter la radio
8. être en retard

 20. À vous! Ask your partner to tell you five things he or she has done in the last month. Write them down. Now tell a new partner about your first partner's activities and your own activities last month. Finally, ask your new partner what she or he did last month.

📖 LECTURE

LA PRINCESSE ET LE PÊCHEUR PAR PHAM DUY KHIÊM

Reading Strategy: Using cognates to help you understand a text

Pham duy Khiêm's story is a tale of unrequited love between the daughter of **un mandarin** (a high Asian official) and **un pêcheur** (a fisherman). In this scene, the fisherman, who has died of a broken heart, is being moved to his final resting place by his family years after his death.

La barque et le pêcheur.

1. Lisez rapidement les deux premières phrases de l'histoire et faites une liste de mots en français qui correspondent aux mots anglais suivants. Comparez votre liste à celle d'un(e) camarade de classe pour voir (see) si vous avez trouvé les mêmes mots et les mêmes significations.

    a. exhumed   **c.** sepulcher
    b. to transport   **d.** transluscent

2. Lisez le reste de l'histore en utilisant ce que vous venez d'apprendre au sujet des mots apparentés (cognates).

> Bien des années après, sa famille a exhumé ses restes pour les transporter à la sépulture définitive. Elle a trouvé dans le cercueil° une pierre° translucide. En guise d'ornement, elle l'a fixée à l'avant de la barque°. Un jour, le mandarin a passé, et a admiré la pierre; il l'a achetée, l'a remise à un tourneur° pour en tirer° une belle tasse à thé.
>
> Chaque fois qu'on y versait° du thé, on voyait° l'image d'un pêcheur dans sa barque faire lentement le tour de la tasse. La fille du mandarin a appris le prodige°, a voulu voir° elle-même. Elle a versé un peu de thé, l'image du pêcheur est apparue.
>
> Une larme est tombée° sur la tasse et celle-ci a fondu° en eau.

casket / stone

boat
l'a... *gave it to a stoneturner /* **pour...** *to make from it*
poured
saw

a... *heard about the wonder / to see*

une... *a tear fell*
celle-ci... *the latter melted*

—Adapted from Pham Duy Khiêm. «Le Cristal d'amour», *Légendes des terres sereines.* © Mercure de France 1951

3. Faites une liste des mots apparentés que vous avez remarqués. Puis résumez l'histoire pour votre partenaire.

R E N C O N T R E S

fidèle... faithful to his roots

M. Truong, un Vietnamien fidèle à ses racines°

Le VIÊT-NAM

POPULATION DU VIÊT-NAM: 72 millions d'habitants
SUPERFICIE: 329 566 km²
CAPITALE: Hanoi
LANGUES: vietnamien, chinois, anglais, français, russe

Parlez-moi un peu de vous.

Je m'appelle Pham Truong, et voici ma femme, Diep. J'ai 68 ans et nous sommes mariés depuis 42 ans. Nous avons cinq enfants tous mariés, et 13 petits enfants. Ma famille habite ici avec moi à Garden Grove en Californie, mais j'ai encore beaucoup de cousins et amis à Hô-Chi-Minh-Ville et à Hanoi.

Pourquoi parlez-vous si bien le français?

so much

Quand je suis né en 1928, les Français occupaient mon pays. J'ai fait mes études dans un lycée français à Saïgon. C'est pour ça que j'aime tant° cette langue.

Quand avez-vous quitté° le Viêt-nam? Pourquoi?

leave

war
est... *became*
à... *reluctantly*
return home

built / raised / hard
au... *at the beginning /*
prendre... *retire*

Oh, vous savez, la vie est tellement bizarre! En 1954, après la bataille de Diên Biên Phu, les Français ont quitté le Viêt-nam, mais les Américains sont arrivés, et la guerre° avec ses horreurs a continué. En 1976, au moment où le Viêt-nam est devenu° la République Socialiste du Viêt-nam, j'ai quitté mon pays à contrecœur° parce que j'aimais trop ma liberté. J'ai immigré aux États-Unis. J'espérais bien rentrer° chez moi un jour, mais voilà, cela n'a pas été possible. Alors, j'ai décidé de m'installer définitivement en Californie, près de Los Angeles. J'y ai bâti° une vie, et j'y ai élevé° mes enfants. J'ai travaillé très dur° et puis, au début° des années quatre-vingt-dix, j'ai décidé de prendre ma retraite°.

Que faites-vous maintenant?

Ma femme et moi, nous voyageons beaucoup, et on profite de la vie au maximum. Je passe beaucoup de temps avec ma famille et mes amis. Je médite et je lis. J'aime beaucoup les œuvres de l'écrivain Pham duy Khiêm. Et à la fin de chaque journée, je remercie le ciel de ses bienfaits°.

remercie... *count my blessings*

QUELQUES QUESTIONS

1. M. Truong parle un peu de l'histoire du Viêt-nam. Faites une liste de deux ou trois événements que M. Truong mentionne.
2. À votre avis, faut-il rétablir des relations politiques et diplomatiques avec un pays comme le Viêt-nam? Faites deux listes: une liste indiquant les raisons en faveur du rétablissement des relations politiques et diplomatiques et une autre liste indiquant les raisons contre *(against)*.

http://www.wiley.com/aventure.html

Talking about your activities (continued)   **Voir p. 215.**

>   Caroline **lit** son anglais et **écrit** une dissertation.

Avoiding repetition   **Voir p. 220.**

>   Avez-vous beaucoup de travail? Oui, j'**en** ai beaucoup.

Telling where you come from and what you have just done

Voir pp. 224 et 225.

>   Benjamin et Julie **viennent de** Californie.
>   Caroline **vient de** faire du café.

Talking about the past   **Voir p. 230.**

>   M. Tran **a compris** tout le vocabulaire.
>   Nous **avons mangé** au restaurant universitaire.

ÊTES-VOUS BRANCHÉS? ──────────

Mon journal. Comparez la vie universitaire américaine à la vie universitaire française. En quoi *(in what way)* sont-elles différentes? En quoi sont-elles similaires? Parlez des frais d'inscription, des examens, des notes et des diplômes en France et aux États-Unis.

Y ÊTES-VOUS ARRIVÉS? ──────────

A. Tout le monde en a pris! Tous vos amis voulaient *(wanted)* manger et boire de bonnes choses. Avec votre partenaire, indiquez ce qu'ils ont pris. À vous de décider!

MODÈLE: ta mère / prendre / du chocolat
>   —**Ta mère a pris du chocolat?**
>   —**Oui, ma mère en a pris.**
>   OU —**Non, ma mère n'en a pas pris.**

1. ton frère / manger / de la confiture
2. ton père / boire / trois tasses de thé
3. tes sœurs / prendre / trop de bonbons
4. toi, tu / manger / une tarte au citron
5. toi, tu / boire / une bière
6. Jean et toi, vous / prendre / deux Coca
7. Robert / manger / un kilo de cerises
8. nous / boire / un litre d'Orangina

B. Où est mon agenda *(datebook)?* Vous avez oublié votre agenda à la fac. Alors, quand est-ce que vos amis viennent dîner, étudier, ou jouer? Téléphonez chez eux pour confirmer les dates et les heures. Avec votre partenaire, recréez la conversation.

MODÈLE: tu / dîner / vendredi (samedi)
> —**Tu viens dîner vendredi?**
> —**Non, je ne viens pas dîner vendredi. Je viens samedi!**

1. vous / jouer au tennis / samedi matin (samedi après-midi)
2. Benoît, tu / étudier / cet après-midi (demain)
3. tu / regarder cette vidéo / à trois heures (à cinq heures)
4. Marie, tu / dîner / à 18h00 (à 20h00)
5. Caroline et Julie, vous / donner une leçon / vendredi (ce soir)
6. Maman, tu / déjeuner / dimanche (le week-end prochain)
7. M. et Mme de Martini, vous / prendre le thé / la semaine prochaine (dans deux semaines)
8. tu / écouter mon nouveau compact / tout à l'heure (demain soir)

Warm-up. Brainstorm a list of possible activities for **Activité C.** Write the infinitives on the board, being careful to avoid verbs conjugated with **être.** If you like, you may introduce **je suis allé(e)** as a lexical item, saying that it is an exception to the rules students have just learned.

C. Testez votre mémoire. Dites ce que vous avez fait, dit, mangé, bu, pris, écouté, regardé, écrit, lu.

1. Hier...
2. Avant hier...
3. La semaine passée...
4. Il y a trois semaines...
5. Il y a un mois...
6. Il y a deux ans...
7. Il y a dix ans...
8. Il y a longtemps...

 # PRONONCIATION

Le son [R]

One of the things that distinguishes native from non-native speakers is the pronunciation of certain sounds that are particular to individual languages. One French sound that falls into this category is [R]. Unlike an American **r,** which is pronounced partly with the lips, a French **r** is pronounced at the back of the mouth, nearly in the throat. If you know how to gargle, you know how to make a French **r.** You might even want to try gargling just to get the feel of how to make the French **r.** Do not round your lips or roll your tongue if you want to get the right sound.

1. Listen to your professor or lab tape and repeat the words ending in [R].

a. pa**r** **f.** mè**r**e
b. ca**r** **g.** pè**r**e
c. ga**r**e **h.** premiè**r**e
d. hie**r** **i.** derriè**r**e
e. frè**r**e **j.** derniè**r**e

2. Now try pronouncing words that have [R] in the middle.

a. ba**r**ré **f.** mo**r**tel
b. ca**r**ton **g.** no**r**mal
c. ga**r**age **h.** pa**r**ti
d. ma**r**i **i.** so**r**tie
e. ma**r**iage **j.** to**r**tue

3. Keep in mind the gargling sound of the French **r** and try to say words that begin with [R]. Remember not to round your lips or roll your tongue if you want to get the right sound.

a. **r**essembler **r**evenir **r**egarder
b. **r**éel **r**éaliste **r**évolution
c. **r**iz **r**iche **r**ythme
d. **r**ose **r**obe **r**oman
e. **r**are **r**at **r**adio

◆ V O C A B U L A I R E   A C T I F ◆

À dire, à écrire, à lire

dire *to say, to tell*
dire au revoir *to say goodbye*
dire bonjour (à) *to say hello (to)*
dire des bêtises *to say silly things*
dire des mensonges *to tell lies*
dire la vérité *to tell the truth*
dire merci *to say thank you*

écrire *to write*
écrire une carte postale *to write a postcard*
écrire un devoir *to write an assignment*
écrire une dissertation *to write a paper*
écrire une lettre *to write a letter*
écrire un livre *to write a book*
écrire un mot *to write a note*

lire *to read*
lire une bande dessinée (B.D.) *to read a comic book*
lire un livre *to read a book*
lire un magazine *to read a magazine*
lire une pièce de théâtre *to read a play*
lire un poème *to read a poem*
lire un roman *to read a novel*

Pronom Adverbial

en *some, any*

Quelques pays où l'on parle français

l'Algérie *Algeria*
la Belgique *Belgium*
le Cameroun *Cameroon*

la Côte d'Ivoire *Ivory Coast*
le Maroc *Morocco*
le Sénégal *Senegal*

la Tunisie *Tunisia*
le Viêt-nam *Vietnam*

Quelques adjectifs de nationalité

algérien(ne) *Algerian*	ivoirien(ne) *Ivorian*	tunisien(ne) *Tunisian*
belge *Belgian*	marocain(e) *Moroccan*	vietnamien(ne) *Vietnamese*
camerounais(e) *Cameroonian*	sénégalais(e) *Senegalese*	

Quelques expressions de temps

avant hier *the day before yesterday*	il y a cinq semaines *five weeks ago*	le mois dernier *last month*
déjà *already*	il y a trois mois *three months ago*	la semaine dernière *last week*
hier *yesterday*	il y a quatre ans *four years ago*	la semaine passée *last week*
hier soir *yesterday night*	il y a longtemps *a long time ago*	le week-end dernier *last-week-end*
hier matin *yesterday morning*		le week-end passé *last week-end*
il y a deux jours *two days ago*		

Les dates *(voir p. 233)*

Autres verbes

décrire *to describe*	revenir *to come back*	venir de (+ infinitive) *to have just done something*
devenir *to become*	venir *to come*	

Mots et expressions utiles

argent *(m)* *money*	une leçon *lesson*	pour la dernière fois *for the last time*
avoir le temps *to have the time*	des lunettes *(f)* *glasses*	la vie *life*
donner *to give*	oublier *to forget*	
gagner *to earn*	payer *to pay*	

Chapitre 8 ◆ # MALADE COMME UN CHIEN

PRÉSENTATION ÉCLAIR

POUR COMMUNIQUER

Talking about your activities (continued)
Giving more details
Talking about quantity (continued)
Talking about the past (continued)

POUR Y ARRIVER

Les verbes **partir, sortir, dormir, mentir, servir**

Les pronoms relatifs **qui** et **que**
L'adjectif indéfini **tout**
Le passé composé avec **être**

POUR S'ADAPTER À LA CULTURE

Comment se soigner en France
Les monuments et les musées de Paris

PREMIER ÉPISODE T 50

Julie habite à Rouen depuis quelques mois°, mais elle n'a pas encore° visité Paris. Julie demande à Caroline de l'accompagner°.

JULIE: Tu as déjà visité Paris, Caroline? J'aimerais bien voir° la tour Eiffel, l'Arc de Triomphe et le Louvre.

CAROLINE: Bien sûr! Et je connais° très bien les clubs de jazz, les discothèques, les bons petits restaurants dans le Quartier latin. Je peux te donner les adresses si tu veux°.

—————
depuis quelques mois *for a few months* / **encore** *yet* /
l'accompagner *to accompany her* / **J'aimerais bien voir**
I'd really like to see / **connais** *know, be familiar with* /
si tu veux *if you want*

JULIE: C'est sympa, mais tu n'as pas envie de m'accompagner? Imagine un peu, toi et moi, à Paris, on sort°, on mange au restaurant, on s'amuse°, on visite, ça va être génial!°

CAROLINE: Quand est-ce que tu penses partir?°

JULIE: Nous partons jeudi soir, et nous allons revenir tôt° lundi matin.

—————
on sort *we'll go out* / **on s'amuse** *we'll have fun* /
génial *great* / **partir** *to leave* / **tôt** *early*

AVEZ-VOUS COMPRIS?

1. Dans notre histoire, quelle ville est-ce que Julie n'a pas encore visitée?
2. Quels monuments / musées est-ce que Julie désire visiter à Paris? À votre avis, est-ce un bon choix *(choice)?* Pourquoi ou pourquoi pas?
3. Quel quartier est-ce que Caroline connaît bien?
4. Qu'est-ce que Julie demande à Caroline?
5. Qui va aussi accompagner Julie à Paris?
6. À votre avis, est-ce que Caroline a envie d'aller à Paris avec Benjamin et Julie? Pourquoi ou pourquoi pas?

CAROLINE: Nous?
JULIE: Oui, j'ai invité Benjamin aussi! Tu l'aimes bien, non?

CAROLINE: Oui, mais ce week-end, c'est difficile. J'ai un examen à préparer, j'ai besoin d'étudier...
JULIE: Allez! Viens avec nous...

Culture. The Latin Quarter is historically a student district. Situated close to the center of Paris, it is home to **la Sorbonne,** the university founded in 1253. It is named **le Quartier latin** because Latin was the language spoken at the **Sorbonne** from **le Moyen Age** *(the Middle Ages)* to the Revolution.

ET VOUS?

1. Quelle ville avez-vous envie de visiter?
2. Quand avez-vous l'intention d'y aller?
3. Qu'est-ce que vous préférez faire quand vous visitez une ville? faire une promenade? visiter les monuments? les musées? les églises? les magasins?
4. En général, est-ce que vous voyagez seul(e)? avec des amis? avec votre famille? Pourquoi?
5. Récemment quelle ville avez-vous visitée? Qu'est-ce que vous avez aimé? détesté?

Talking about your activities (continued)

I **LES VERBES *PARTIR, SORTIR, DORMIR, MENTIR, SERVIR***

Julie et Caroline **partent** pour Paris?
Benjamin **part-il** avec elles?
Le week-end, nous **sortons** quelquefois avec des amis.
Et vous, quel jour **sortez-vous?**

◆ **Partir** *(to leave)* and **sortir** *(to go out)* are irregular verbs.

partir	sortir
je **pars**	je **sors**
tu **pars**	tu **sors**
il / elle / on **part**	il / elle / on **sort**
nous **partons**	nous **sortons**
vous **partez**	vous **sortez**
ils / elles / **partent**	ils / elles **sortent**

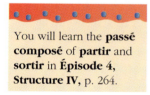

You will learn the **passé composé** of **partir** and **sortir** in **Épisode 4, Structure IV,** p. 264.

◆ **Partir** is the opposite of **arriver. Partir (de)** means *to leave (from),* and **partir pour** *to leave for.*

En général, je **pars** à sept heures.
Je **pars** de la maison tard.
Je **pars** pour la France en été.

◆ **Sortir** is the opposite of **entrer. Sortir de** means *to exit from* or *go out.*

Les étudiants **sortent** avec leurs amis le samedi soir.
Nous **sortons** du cours de français à dix heures.

◆ **Dormir** *(to sleep),* **mentir** *(to lie),* and **servir** *(to serve)* follow the same conjugation pattern as **sortir** and **partir** in the present tense.

dormir	mentir	servir
je **dors**	je **mens**	je **sers**
tu **dors**	tu **mens**	tu **sers**
il / elle / on **dort**	il / elle / on **ment**	il / elle / on **sert**
nous **dormons**	nous **mentons**	nous **servons**
vous **dormez**	vous **mentez**	vous **servez**
ils / elles **dorment**	ils / elles **mentent**	ils / elles **servent**
PASSÉ COMPOSÉ		
J'ai dormi	J'ai servi	J'ai menti

ACTIVITÉS

 1. À quelle heure partent-ils? Dites à votre partenaire à quelle heure les gens partent.

MODÈLE: M. Dupont / 7h45
—**À quelle heure est-ce que M. Dupont part?**
—**Il part à 7h45.**

1. Mme Duchesne / 8h30
2. M. et Mme Durand / 8h45
3. M. Valette / 10h
4. ma camarade de chambre et moi, nous / 7h45

5. vos amis et vous, vous / 12h
6. M. et Mme Jaudel / 13h
7. Et toi? Jeannette, tu / 12h15
8. Et moi, je / ?

2. Que font les Parisiens après le travail? Un statisticien décide d'examiner les loisirs *(leisure activities)* des Parisiens. Dites quand ils sortent de leur travail, et imaginez où ils vont après.

■ **POSSIBILITÉS:** la piscine, le stade, le cinéma, le théâtre, le restaurant, le concert, la cafétéria, chez des amis...

MODÈLE: M. Dupont / université / 6h
M. Dupont sort de l'université à 6 heures et il va à la piscine.

1. Mme Valette / fac / 17h30
2. M. et Mme Durand / université / 16h15
3. Paul et moi, nous / cours de français / 19h30
4. votre petit(e) ami(e) et vous, vous / travail / 18h00
5. M. Duchesne / boulangerie / 18h45
6. tu / librairie / 17h
7. M. et Mme Jaudel / bibliothèque / 16h30
8. et moi, je / boutique / 18h30

 3. Votre curiosité n'a pas de bornes. *(knows no bounds)*
Posez ces questions à deux partenaires. Inventez-en d'autres si vous en avez envie.

1. La nuit, combien d'heures dormez-vous en général? Est-ce suffisant?
2. Le matin, à quelle heure partez-vous de la maison? Et les autres membres de votre famille?
3. Quel(s) jour(s) sortez-vous le soir? En général, quand vous sortez, où allez-vous? Avec qui?
4. Mangez-vous souvent au restaurant? Qui sert le repas au restaurant? Et à la maison?
5. Quand vous sortez, comment êtes-vous le lendemain *(next day)*?
6. Dormez-vous dans certaines de vos classes? Pourquoi? Pourquoi pas?
7. Dites-vous toujours la vérité ou mentez-vous quelquefois à vos parents? À vos professeurs? À votre professeur de français? Pourquoi ou pourquoi pas?

Follow-up. If you wish students to practice the **tu** form, ask them to interview only one student and to modify all the questions to the **tu** form.

DEUXIÈME ÉPISODE

Caroline a travaillé très dur° pendant la semaine, et elle a terminé ses révisions° pour son examen de lundi prochain. Elle a bien mérité° un week-end de détente° et décide de partir avec Julie et Benjamin à Paris.

Voilà les trois amis qui arrivent à l'hôtel Le Latin. Ils sont maintenant dans leurs chambres.

BENJAMIN: Nous sommes enfin à Paris. Eh! les filles, vous aimez l'hôtel que j'ai déniché?°

CAROLINE: Euh...

JULIE: Mais oui, il n'est pas mal et pas trop cher non plus°.

---

dur *hard* / **révisions** *review* / **a mérité** *earned* / **un week-end de détente** *a relaxing weekend* / **que j'ai déniché** *that I dug up* / **non plus** *either*

BENJAMIN: Alors, Caroline, on commence la visite? On y va? Tu vas être notre guide, n'est-ce pas?

CAROLINE: Oh, tu sais, moi, je ne suis pas parisienne... Mais, au fait, Julie, je t'ai vu prendre un cachet d'aspirine° dans le train. Est-ce que tu as toujours mal à la tête?°

---

je t'ai vu prendre un cachet d'aspirine *I saw you take an aspirin tablet* / **tu as toujours mal à la tête?** *Do you still have a headache?*

AVEZ-VOUS COMPRIS?

1. Qu'est-ce que Caroline a fait avant de partir à Paris?
2. Est-ce que Caroline et Julie aiment l'hôtel? Expliquez.
3. Comment va Julie?
4. Quels sont les symptômes de Julie?
5. Quelle est la réaction de Benjamin? Est-il inquiet *(worried)*?
6. Quelle est la réaction de Caroline? À votre avis, qu'est-ce que Caroline pense de Benjamin? Expliquez.

JULIE: Oui, et puis, je suis fatiguée°, et maintenant j'ai chaud et je ne me sens° pas bien. J'ai un peu mal au cœur°, j'ai le nez qui coule° et j'ai la tête qui tourne°.

BENJAMIN: Qu'est-ce qui ne va pas? Tu as de la fièvre?°

JULIE: Oui, un peu.

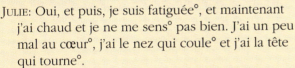

fatiguée *tired* / **je ne me sens pas bien** *I don't feel well* / **j'ai un peu mal au cœur** *I feel a little sick to my stomach* / **j'ai le nez qui coule** *I've got a runny nose* / **j'ai la tête qui tourne** *I'm dizzy* / **fièvre** *fever*

BENJAMIN: Ne t'en fais pas°, Julie, tu es en de bonnes mains°.

CAROLINE: Julie, ne t'inquiète pas! Benjamin est médecin maintenant! Il va te dire les médicaments° que tu dois° prendre. Allons, Benjamin, soyons sérieux!°

Ne t'en fais pas *don't worry* / **en de bonnes mains** *in good hands* / **médicaments** *medicine* / **dois** *must* / **Allons, Benjamin, soyons sérieux!** *Come on, Benjamin, let's be serious!*

ET VOUS?

1. Quand vous voyagez, est-ce que vous aimez descendre *(to stay)* dans un hôtel ou chez des amis? Expliquez.
2. Partez-vous souvent en week-end? Si oui, où?
3. Quand est-ce que vous avez été malade pour la dernière fois? Qu'est-ce que vous avez attrapé *(catch)*? Un rhume *(a cold)*? La grippe? *(the flu)*
4. Avez-vous pris de l'aspirine? un autre médicament?

MALADE COMME UN CHIEN

VOUS ÊTES BRANCHÉS!

Comment se soigner en France

Going to the **pharmacie** in France is quite different from stopping in an American drugstore. While you can buy wrapping paper and candy, as well as medicine in a drugstore, the primary purpose of a French **pharmacie** is to dispense **médicaments** (*drugs*).

An American pharmacist's role is different from that of a French pharmacist. In the United States, an American pharmacist is only legally allowed to fill prescriptions, while a French pharmacist is permitted to give limited medical advice for common ailments and provide certain medications without a prescription. If you are not feeling well, a French pharmacist is often the first professional you can seek help from.

If you suffer from a more serious condition, you need to consult a physician. Health care is readily available and very affordable by American standards. All full-time workers, children, and retirees are cov-

À la pharmacie.

ered by a national health plan, which allows an individual to choose his or her own personal doctor. As in the United States, physicians usually write **ordonnances** (*prescriptions*), that patients must fill at the pharmacy.

The process of getting a prescription filled is different in France and in the United States. You must often wait a long time in the United States for the pharmacist to count the number of pills you need; however, in a French pharmacy, medicine comes prepackaged. The pharmacist simply hands you the number of boxes you need, thus filling your prescription accurately and rapidly.

Whether you need advice, aspirin, or a prescription filled, look for the sign of the green cross that indicates **une pharmacie** in any French city, and you will most likely get the help you seek.

La pharmacienne vous sert.

VOTRE Q. I. CULTUREL

Qu'en pensez-vous? Choisissez la réponse appropriée.

1. Dans une pharmacie en France, on peut acheter
   a. une radio.
   b. des médicaments.
   c. des boissons fraîches.

http://www.wiley.com/aventure.html

2. Le pharmacien en France
   a. ne donne pas de conseils médicaux *(medical advice)* à un client.
   b. a le droit *(right)* de donner des conseils médicaux limités à un client.
   c. est capable de remplacer le médecin et d'écrire une ordonnance.
3. On indique la présence d'une pharmacie par
   a. une croix verte.
   b. une croix rouge.
   c. une croix bleue.

 Expliquez l'essentiel à votre partenaire. Choisissez un sujet et allez-y! Votre partenaire va accepter votre explication, la modifier, ou y ajouter *(add)* quelques détails.

1. Nommez deux différences entre une pharmacie en France et une pharmacie chez vous.
2. En France, on n'est pas autorisé à choisir des médicaments dans une pharmacie. Il faut toujours demander au pharmacien. Qu'en pensez-vous?

IL Y A UN PROBLÈME: QU'EN PENSEZ-VOUS?

Julie a le nez qui coule, elle a la tête qui tourne, et elle a mal à la tête. Benjamin a envie de faire quelque chose.
   Devrait-il

a. aller chercher un médecin?
b. aller à la pharmacie?
c. ramener *(take back)* Julie à Rouen?
d. laisser *(leave)* Julie à l'hôtel et visiter Paris?
e. Avez-vous une autre solution?

Justifiez votre réponse.

À VOUS DE JOUER

Vous êtes à la cafétéria sur le campus avec votre ami(e). Il / Elle ne se sent pas très bien et dit qu'il / elle est malade. Mais vous avez un examen important à passer. Que faites-vous?
   Moi, je

a. lui dis «Au revoir. Je vais passer mon examen.»
b. commence à crier «Au secours! *(Help!)*»
c. demande s'il y a un médecin à la cafétéria.
d. décide d'accompagner mon ami(e) à l'infirmerie et j'arrive en retard pour mon examen.
e. Avez-vous une autre solution?

Justifiez votre réponse.

Giving more details

II **LES PRONOMS RELATIFS** *QUI* **ET** *QUE*

> Julie a le nez **qui** coule. Elle a aussi la tête **qui** tourne.
> Benjamin donne à Julie les médicaments **qu'**elle prend.
> Benjamin, **que** Julie aime beaucoup, est vraiment gentil avec elle.

◆ A relative pronoun allows you to combine two simple sentences into a complex one. It is always preceded by the noun to which it refers.

Voilà l'aspirine *que* je cherche.   *There's the aspirin that I am looking for.*

Je connais un homme *qui* travaille à Lyon.   *I know a man who works in Lyon.*

◆ Unlike English, French never omits relative pronouns.

> *The man **who is** speaking English is from Vancouver.*
> OR   *The man speaking English is from Vancouver.*
> BUT   L'homme **qui** parle anglais est de Vancouver.

◆ **Qui** *(who, that, which)* can represent a person or a thing. It is used to replace a noun that is the *subject* of the relative clause. **Qui** is always followed by a verb and is never used in a contraction.

> C'est **Julie. Julie** est malade.
> C'est Julie **qui** est malade.

> Voilà **la pharmacie. La pharmacie** est près de l'hôtel.
> Voilà la pharmacie **qui** est près de l'hôtel.

> **Ma cousine Sylvie** habite à Neuilly. **Ma cousine Sylvie** est pharmacienne.
> **Ma cousine Sylvie, qui** habite à Neuilly, est pharmacienne.

FOR RECOGNITION ONLY Sometimes **qui** is introduced by a preposition. The most common prepositions that precede **qui** are **à, chez, avec,** and **pour.**

> **Julie** est malade. Caroline est allée à Paris avec **Julie.**
> L'amie **avec qui** Caroline est allée à Paris est malade.

◆ **Que** *(that, which, whom)* can also represent a person or a thing, but is used when the noun it replaces is the **direct object** of the relative clause. **Que** becomes **qu'** in front of a vowel or a silent **h.**

Voilà **les médicaments.** Julie va prendre **les médicaments.**
Voilà les médicaments **que** Julie va prendre.

Voilà **les fleurs.** Elle achète **les fleurs.**
Voilà les fleurs **qu'**elle achète.

Vous aimez **l'hôtel?** J'ai trouvé **l'hôtel.**
Vous aimez l'hôtel **que** j'ai trouvé?

Caroline est étudiante. Benjamin aime bien **Caroline.**
Caroline, **que** Benjamin aime bien, est étudiante.

The singular form of **les yeux** is **l'œil** *(m).* It is used in the expression **Mon œil,** which is what you say when you don't believe what someone has just told you. It is accompanied by the gesture of pulling down slightly on your lower eyelid.

POUR S'EXPRIMER

T 52

Les parties du corps

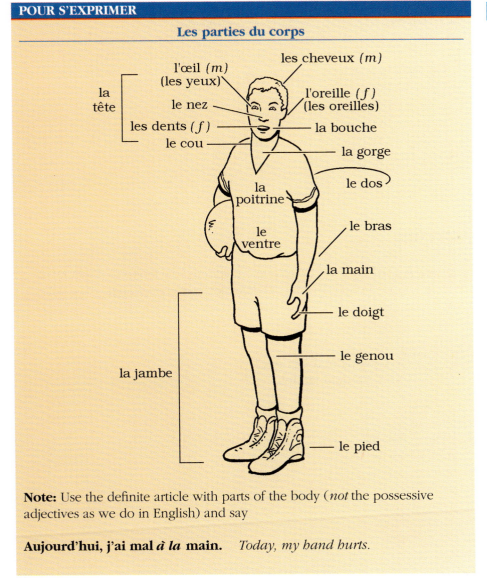

la tête
l'œil *(m)*
(les yeux)
le nez
les dents *(f)*
le cou
les cheveux *(m)*
l'oreille *(f)*
(les oreilles)
la bouche
la gorge
le dos
la poitrine
le ventre
le bras
la main
le doigt
le genou
la jambe
le pied

Note: Use the definite article with parts of the body (*not* the possessive adjectives as we do in English) and say

Aujourd'hui, j'ai mal *à la* main. *Today, my hand hurts.*

Se sentir is a pronominal verb (Chapter 10). It is conjugated like **dormir**.

Have students mime each of the sentences or have students mime in pairs: one complains about a body ache, the other student mimes where his/her partner hurts.

Culture. For fun, you may wish to give your students the expressions **avoir mal aux cheveux, avoir la gueule de bois,** *(to have a hang-over).* Young French people also use the expression **avoir le pivert.**

Petits problèmes de santé	
Qu'est-ce qui ne va pas?	*What's wrong?*
Je suis malade.	*I am sick.* ≠ Je vais (très) bien.
Je suis malade comme un chien.	≠ Je suis en (pleine) forme.
Je ne me sens pas bien.	*I don't feel well.*
Je suis fatigué(e).	*I'm tired.*
Je suis déprimé(e).	*I'm depressed.*
J'ai le nez qui coule.	*I have a runny nose.*
J'ai la gorge qui pique.	*My throat is irritated.*
J'ai de la fièvre.	*I have a fever.*
J'ai mal au cœur.	*I feel nauseated.*
J'ai un rhume.	*I have a cold.*
J'ai la grippe.	*I have the flu.*
J'ai mal partout.	*I hurt everywhere.*
avoir mal à	*to hurt (in a part of the body)*
J'ai mal **à la** tête.	*My head hurts; I have a headache.*
J'ai mal **à l'**œil.	*My eye hurts.*
J'ai mal **aux** yeux.	*My eyes hurt.*
J'ai mal **à la** main.	*My hand hurts.*
J'ai mal **au** ventre.	*My stomach hurts; I have a stomach ache.*
tousser	*to cough*

ACTIVITÉS

Grammar. Review **à** + the definite article before working on the expression **avoir mal à.**

 4. À l'infirmerie. Beaucoup d'étudiants sont malades. L'infirmière interroge chaque personne et demande ce qui ne va pas. Avec votre partenaire, recréez le dialogue.

MODÈLE: tête / dos
—**Avez-vous mal à la tête?**
—**Non, j'ai mal au dos.**

1. tête / nez
2. ventre / poitrine
3. yeux / bouche
4. oreilles / cou
5. pied / main
6. main / doigt
7. genou / jambe
8. dos / partout

5. Qu'est-ce qui arrive si... ? *What happens if . . . ?* Finissez les phrases en imaginant où on a mal.

Modèle: Si on passe la nuit par terre, on...
 Si on passe la nuit par terre *(on the ground),* **on a mal au dos.**

1. Si je regarde beaucoup la télé, je...
2. Si ma sœur mange trop de sucre, elle...
3. Si on reste trois heures au téléphone, on...
4. Si un étudiant écrit trop de compositions, il...
5. Si le professeur parle beaucoup, il...
6. Si mon amie fume un paquet de cigarettes par jour, elle...
7. Si je joue au tennis toute la journée, je...
8. Si on fait un marathon, on...

6. Julie est malade. Expliquez ce qui *(what)* ne va pas en choisissant une solution logique.

Modèle: Julie... est malade
 Julie, qui est loin de chez elle, est malade.

	Solutions possibles
1. Julie... a de la fièvre.	qui sont amis
2. Elle a le nez...	qui tourne
3. Elle a la tête...	qui est malade
4. Benjamin... est inquiet.	qui aime bien Julie
5. Julie et Benjamin... parlent du problème.	qui est loin de chez elle
6. Benjamin... cherche une solution.	qui coule
	qui désire aider Julie

 7. Qu'en pensez-vous? Vous cherchez quelqu'un pour sortir avec vous. Interrogez votre partenaire pour connaître ses goûts *(to find out what he or she likes)*.

Modèle: aime le cinéma
 Aimes-tu le cinéma?

Demandez-lui s'il ou si elle
1. aime les films qui sont en noir et blanc
2. préfère les films qui sont en couleur
3. aime ou déteste les héros romantiques, les héros tragiques
4. préfère les héroïnes qui sont actives, courageuses, énergiques ou les héroïnes qui sont passives
5. préfère les films qui ont un thème historique ou les films qui racontent une belle histoire d'amour *(love story)*

8. Comment en savoir plus? Interrogez votre partenaire et découvrez ses goûts.

MODÈLE: acteur / préférer
> —**Quel est l'acteur que tu préfères?**
> —**L'acteur que je préfère est Gérard Depardieu.**

1. actrice / préférer
2. le groupe musical / écouter beaucoup
3. les vêtements / porter souvent
4. le professeur / aimer bien
5. le professeur / détester
6. le cours / préférer
7. l'émission de télévision / regarder souvent

9. À vous de juger. *It's up to you to judge.* Dites ce que vous pensez de ces personnes en complétant les phrases de façon appropriée.

MODÈLE: Janet Jackson
> **Janet Jackson, qui est chanteuse, est super.**
> OU **Janet Jackson, que je regarde à la télé, est très sexy.**

Gilles Vigneault	qui est acteur / actrice	vieux / vieille
Julia Roberts	que j'adore	assez jeune
Bridget Fonda	que je déteste	(très) sexy
Halle Berry	que je regarde à la télé	beau / belle
Keanu Reeves	qui chante bien	terrible
Barbra Streisand	qui joue mal	formidable
Oprah Winfrey	que je (ne) respecte (pas)	abominable
Whitney Houston	qui est chanteur / chanteuse	super
Gloria Estéfan	qui est canadien	extra
Alanis Morissette	qui joue bien	génial(e)

10. Pas moyen de l'arrêter! *No way to stop him!* Complétez les phrases.

Follow-up. Ask students to add a clause beginning by **parce que** justifying their choice.

MODÈLE: Je déteste les classes qui...
> **Je déteste les classes qui sont très difficiles.**

Je déteste les professeurs que...
> **Je déteste les professeurs que je ne comprends pas.**

1. J'adore les professeurs qui...
2. Je préfère les filles que...
3. Je déteste les étudiants qui...
4. J'aime beaucoup les classes qui...
5. Je n'aime pas du tout les cours que...
6. Je préfère les professeurs qui...
7. J'aime assez les livres que...
8. Je déteste les examens que...

Alanis Morissette.

Benjamin revient de la pharmacie avec des cachets°, des pastilles° et un sirop.

BENJAMIN: Voilà Julie, j'ai tout ce qu'il te faut°. J'ai décrit tes symptômes à la pharmacienne, et elle m'a donné tous ces médicaments.

——————
des cachets *pills* / **des pastilles** *lozenges* / **tout ce qu'il te faut** *everything you need*

JULIE: Je vais prendre tout ça?°

BENJAMIN: Mais oui, si tu veux visiter Paris avec nous demain. Toutes les deux heures°, tu prends un cachet, toutes les quatre heures, deux cuillères à soupe° de sirop, et quand tu as mal à la gorge, une pastille. En plus, tu vas rester au lit aujourd'hui.

——————
tout ça *all of that* / **toutes les deux heures** *every two hours* / **deux cuillères à soupe** *two tablespoons*

AVEZ-VOUS COMPRIS?

1. De quel magasin est-ce que Benjamin revient?
2. Qu'est-ce que Benjamin y a acheté?
3. Quelle est la réaction de Julie quand Benjamin lui donne tous les médicaments?
4. Quels médicaments est-ce que Julie a besoin de prendre? Comment?
5. Qu'est-ce que Julie a envie de faire? À votre avis, est-ce raisonnable?
6. Qu'est-ce que Benjamin et Caroline décident de faire ensemble? Sont-ils maintenant de bons amis? Expliquez.

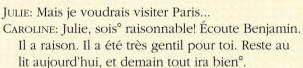

JULIE: Mais je voudrais visiter Paris...

CAROLINE: Julie, sois° raisonnable! Écoute Benjamin. Il a raison. Il a été très gentil pour toi. Reste au lit aujourd'hui, et demain tout ira bien°.

―――――
sois *be* / **tout ira bien** *everything will be fine*

Benjamin et Caroline disent au revoir à Julie et partent pour visiter Paris.

CAROLINE: C'est très sympa ce que tu as fait pour Julie.

BENJAMIN: Je fais l'impossible pour les gens que j'aime, Caroline.

ET VOUS?

1. Allez-vous souvent à la pharmacie?
2. Quand y allez-vous en général?
3. Êtes-vous souvent malade?
4. Quand vous êtes malade, que faites-vous?
5. Allez-vous chez le médecin immédiatement?
6. En général, prenez-vous des médicaments? Pourquoi ou pourquoi pas?

POUR COMMUNIQUER

Talking about quantity (continued)

III L'ADJECTIF INDÉFINI *TOUT*

> Je passe **tout** mon temps à la bibliothèque.
> **Toute** la classe étudie pour l'examen.
> La pharmacienne a donné **tous** les médicaments à Benjamin.
> Il est important de prendre ce sirop **toutes** les deux heures.

	(m)	*(f)*
SINGULIER	tout	toute
PLURIEL	tous	toutes

◆ The adjective **tout** expresses different aspects of totality. It may mean *all, the whole...,* or *every...* Since **tout** is an adjective, it must agree in number and gender with the noun(s) it modifies.

J'ai mangé **tout** le chocolat.	*I ate all the chocolate.*
J'ai passé **toute** la journée chez moi.	*I spent the whole day at my house.*
Nous travaillons **tous** les jours.	*We work every day.*
Caroline va au gymnase **toutes** les semaines.	*Caroline goes to the gym every week.*

◆ **Toute la matinée (journée, soirée, année)** means *the whole morning (day, evening, year)* or *all morning (day, evening, year) long.*

◆ **Tous les matins (jours, soirs, mois, ans, samedis, etc.)** means *every morning (day, evening, month, year, Saturday, etc.)*

◆ **Toutes les semaines (heures, nuits)** means *every week (hour, night).* Numbers may also be included to indicate frequency.

Prenez ce médicament **toutes les trois heures.**	*Take this medicine every three hours.*

◆ **Tout à l'heure** means *in a little while* or *a little while ago.* Say **À tout à l'heure** to someone you intend to see later that same day or evening. Note that it is *not* used like its English equivalent *See you later* to mean *Good-bye* in general.

Je vais faire mes devoirs **tout à l'heure.**	*I'm going to do my homework later.*
À tout à l'heure au Café de Flore, Julie! D'accord, vers dix-huit-heures!	*See you later at the Café de Flore, Julie! OK, around 6 p.m.!*

◆ **Tout le monde** means *everyone.* It is always followed by a verb in the third person singular in French.

Tout le monde est content en vacances.   *Everyone is happy on vacation.*

◆ **Tout à coup** and **tout d'un coup** mean *all of a sudden.*

Tout à coup, les étudiants ont compris la question.   *All of a sudden the students understood the question.*

ACTIVITÉS

11. Le monde idéal des professeurs. Les professeurs imaginent un monde idéal. Pouvez-vous *(can you)* l'imaginer aussi?

MODÈLE: _____ la classe comprend bien.
  Toute la classe comprend bien.

1. _____ les étudiants sont à l'heure.
2. _____ les étudiantes travaillent beaucoup.
3. _____ la classe participe bien.
4. _____ le monde parle bien le français.
5. _____ les compositions sont brillantes.
6. _____ les étudiants écoutent le professeur.
7. Les étudiants écoutent _____ le temps.

12. Le monde idéal des étudiants. Maintenant c'est votre tour *(it's your turn).* Imaginez le monde idéal des étudiants.

MODÈLE: les exercices / facile
  Tous les exercices sont faciles.

1. les réponses / amusant
2. les questions / facile
3. les professeurs / sympathique
4. les week-ends / libre
5. les examens / facile
6. la classe / sympathique
7. le travail / stimulant

 13. Tout le monde répond. Demandez à votre partenaire ce qu'il / elle en pense. Utilisez des expressions proposées pour répondre.

MODÈLE: —**Qui déteste les devoirs difficiles?**
  —**Tout le monde.**

1. Qui invites-tu chez toi?
2. Quand travailles-tu?
3. Quand désires-tu terminer cet exercice?
4. Quand prépares-tu ton déjeuner?
5. Quand vas-tu manger au restaurant?
6. Qui déteste les examens?
7. Qui adore faire la grasse matinée?
8. Quand vas-tu au cinéma?
9. Quand est-ce que vous avez compris la question?

Réponses possibles

toutes mes amies
tous mes amis
tout à l'heure
tous les jours
tous les mois
tout le monde
toutes les semaines
tout à coup
tout de suite
tout le temps
tous les week-ends

Caroline et Benjamin rentrent à l'hôtel et racontent° leur journée à Julie.

CAROLINE: Alors, Julie, ça va mieux?°

JULIE: Oui, beaucoup mieux. J'ai pris tous les médicaments, et j'ai bien dormi. Mais je suis tellement déçue°, je n'ai encore rien vu° à Paris!

—————

racontent *tell about* / **ça va mieux?** *feeling better?* / **tellement déçue** *so disappointed* / **je n'ai encore rien vu** *I haven't seen anything yet*

BENJAMIN: On va te raconter, n'est-ce pas Caroline? Benjamin et Caroline se regardent et se sourient°.

CAROLINE: D'abord, nous sommes allés à la tour Eiffel. Nous sommes montés dans le métro juste à côté de l'hôtel, et nous sommes descendus à Trocadéro. Quelle vue magnifique! Et il y avait° beaucoup de touristes qui prenaient° des photos.

BENJAMIN: Caroline et moi, nous aussi, on a pris une photo. J'espère° que la photo de nous deux devant la tour Eiffel va être bonne!

—————

se sourient *smile at each other* / **il y avait** *there were* / **prenaient** *were taking* / **J'espère** *I hope*

AVEZ-VOUS COMPRIS?

1. Est-ce que Julie va mieux? Pourquoi ou pourquoi pas?
2. Où est-ce que Caroline et Benjamin sont allés d'abord?
3. Ils ont pris le métro. À quelle station est-ce qu'ils sont descendus?
4. Qu'est-ce qu'ils ont fait devant la tour Eiffel?
5. Ensuite, où ont-ils fait une promenade?
6. Quel musée ont-ils visité?
7. Est-ce que Benjamin a aimé le Louvre? Qu'est-ce qu'il a beaucoup admiré?
8. Demain, qu'est-ce qu'ils vont faire tous les trois?
9. Qu'est-ce que Caroline pense de Benjamin maintenant?

CAROLINE: Après, nous sommes partis faire une longue promenade sur les Champs-Élysées. Nous avons beaucoup discuté et nous avons pris un café à la terrasse d'un café.

BENJAMIN: Enfin, nous sommes arrivés au musée du Louvre. C'est fantastique, Julie. Il y a des pyramides en verre° à l'extérieur. Nous sommes entrés dans l'aile Richelieu°, tu sais, la nouvelle partie du musée, et à côté de tout cet art extraordinaire, il y a un Virgin Megastore! Incroyable, non?

---

en verre *of glass* / **l'aile Richelieu** *the Richelieu wing*

JULIE: Benjamin, tu es allé au Louvre pour voir° le Virgin Megastore?!

CAROLINE: Mais non, Julie! On s'est bien amusés° et on a vu° beaucoup de choses intéressantes! Maintenant, repose-toi° encore un peu, et demain, on va continuer la visite ensemble.

---

voir *to see* / **On s'est bien amusés** *We had a great time* / **on a vu** *we saw* / **repose-toi** *rest up*

ET VOUS?

1. Quelle ville avez-vous visitée récemment?
2. Comment avez-vous visité cette ville? à pied? en voiture? en bus?
3. Quel(s) monument(s) avez-vous visité(s)? Quel monument avez-vous préféré?
4. Avez-vous pris une photo devant votre monument préféré? Avez-vous demandé à quelqu'un d'autre de prendre votre photo?
5. Avez-vous déjà visité Paris? Si oui, quand? Avez-vous aimé votre visite? Pourquoi ou pourquoi pas?
6. Quels monuments de Paris pouvez-vous nommer *(can you name)*?

Culture
• **Richelieu** (1585–1642), a famous minister under Louis XIII, ruled France for eighteen years. He strengthened the monarchy, encouraged colonial expansion, and pursued the construction of the Louvre Palace to which he had the **aile Richelieu** added.
• The **Virgin Megastore** store is part of a world-wide chain where you can buy compact discs, posters, headphones, concert tickets, and other music-related items.

VOUS ÊTES BRANCHÉS

Les monuments et les musées de Paris

1.

2.

3.

LOUVRE

ENTREE MUSEE

04-07-94 12:06
CAS002 635

40.00

04-07-94 CAS002 635

Attention :
A partir du 18 Novembre 1993, seule l'aile Richelieu
est ouverte en nocturne le Lundi

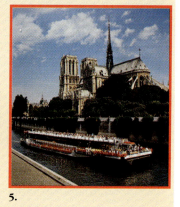
4.   5.

1. La pyramide. 2. Le Musée d'Orsay. 3. Le Centre
Pompidou. 4. L'Arc de Triomphe. 5. Notre-Dame.

Built in 1889 for the **Exposition Universelle** *(World's Fair),* **la tour Eiffel,** which looms over the city skyline, is the classic symbol of Paris. It is often a tourist's first stop in the French capital.

Two other monuments on every tourist's itinerary are **l'Arc de Triomphe,** commissioned by **Napoléon** in 1805 to celebrate his victories in battle, and the cathedral **Notre-Dame de Paris,** a world-famous example of Gothic architecture dating from the 12th century.

No visit to Paris would be complete without a stop at some of its extraordinary museums. **Le Louvre,** home to the Mona Lisa **(La Joconde),** has been one of the world's greatest museums since 1793. Nearly 200 years after its opening, I. M. Pei, an American architect, was commissioned to create a new main entrance and restore the Richelieu wing of the museum. His modernistic steel and glass pyramid rises 69 feet above the **Cour Napoléon,** in distinct counterpoint to the Renaissance architecture around it.

Another controversial structure in Paris is **le Centre Pompidou,** also known as **Beaubourg.** Totally futuristic, with glass walls, steel gridwork, and pipes visible everywhere, it seems as though the structure is inside out. Collections contain works from cubism, fauvism, the Dada movement, surrealism, Pop Art, and other movements of the twentieth century.

A third museum worth a visit is **le Musée d'Orsay.** Originally a train station, it now houses a vast collection of 19th century art, including many works by Monet, Manet, Pissaro, Degas, and Renoir, artists of the Impressionist School.

Whether making a short or extended visit to Paris, be sure to include its monuments and museums for a memorable trip.

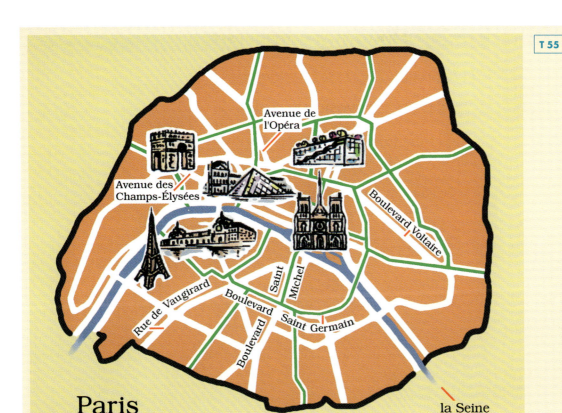

Paris

la Seine

VOTRE Q. I. CULTUREL

1. Trois musées à Paris sont
   a. la tour Eiffel, le Centre Pompidou, et le Louvre.
   b. le Louvre, le Centre Pompidou, et le musée d'Orsay.
   c. l'arc de Triomphe, le musée d'Orsay, et le Centre Pompidou.

2. L'arc de Triomphe et la tour Eiffel datent du
   a. dix-huitième siècle *(century)*.
   b. douzième siècle.
   c. dix-neuvième siècle.

3. Deux structures ou musées très modernes sont
   a. la Pyramide et Beaubourg.
   b. la tour Eiffel et le musée d'Orsay.
   c. Notre Dame et le Centre Pompidou.

 Expliquez l'essentiel à votre partenaire. Choisissez un sujet, résumez ce que vous savez *(what you know)* à votre partenaire qui vous pose des questions supplémentaires.

1. Il ne faut pas modifier les quartiers et les bâtiments (*buildings*) historiques. Êtes-vous d'accord? Pourquoi ou pourquoi pas?
2. Choisissez le monument ou le musée que vous préférez et dites pourquoi.

http://www.wiley.com/aventure.html

Review. You already know how to talk about things that happened in the past using the verb **avoir** and a past participle. (See Chapter 7, p. 230.)

■ POUR COMMUNIQUER

Talking about the past (continued)

IV LE PASSÉ COMPOSÉ AVEC *ÊTRE*

> Julie **est tombée** malade.
> Caroline et Julie **sont arrivées** à Paris.
> Caroline et Benjamin **sont allés** à la pharmacie.
> Benjamin **n'est pas sorti** avec Julie.

◆ Some verbs form their **passé composé** with the verb **être** and a past participle.

> Le professeur **est entré** dans la classe à huit heures.
> Mme Boileau et son fils **sont descendus** du bus à Notre-Dame.

◆ For these verbs, the past participle agrees in number and in gender with the subject of the verb.

> Benjamin est né en Californie.
> Caroline est né**e** en France.
> Les parents de Caroline sont né**s** en France aussi.
> Mais ses nièces sont né**es** en Angleterre.

◆ The negative form of these verbs follows the same pattern as verbs conjugated with **avoir,** with **ne** and **pas** surrounding **être.**

> Nous **ne** sommes **pas** allés au café.
> Elle **n'**est **pas** sortie.

◆ There are several ways to remember which verbs are conjugated with **être:**

1. You can think of things you might do in, around, or in relation to your home.
   aller, venir
   entrer, sortir
   arriver, partir
   descendre, monter
   tomber
   rester
   naître, mourir

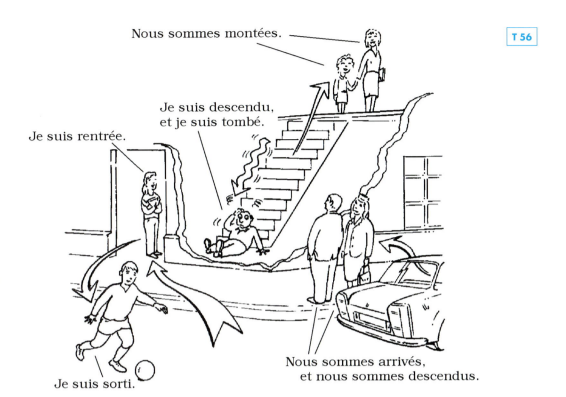

Nous sommes montées.

Je suis descendu,
et je suis tombé.

Je suis rentrée.

Je suis sorti.

Nous sommes arrivés,
et nous sommes descendus.

2. You can memorize the acronym *DR.* and *MRS. VANDERTRAMP.* Each letter
of the names represents one verb conjugated with **être.**

infinitif	*participe passé*	
Descendre	descendu(e)(s)	*to go down; to get off*
Rester	resté(e)(s)	*to stay*
Monter	monté(e)(s)	*to go up; to climb, to get in*
Rentrer	rentré(e)(s)	*to go home; to re-enter*
Sortir	sorti(e)(s)	*to go out; to exit*
Venir	venu(e)(s)	*to come*
Aller	allé(e)(s)	*to go*
Naître	né(e)(s)	*to be born*
Devenir	devenu(e)(s)	*to become*
Entrer	entré(e)(s)	*to enter; to go in*
Revenir	revenu(e)(s)	*to come back*
Tomber	tombé(e)(s)	*to fall*
Retourner	retourné(e)(s)	*to return*
Arriver	arrivé(e)(s)	*to arrive*
Mourir	mort(e)(s)	*to die*
Partir	parti(e)(s)	*to leave; to depart*

Extension. You might also explain to students that the verbs conjugated with **être** often indicate movement where the whole body is involved.

You will learn to conjugate **descendre** in Chapter 11. **Naître** and **mourir** are usually used in the past tense.

◆ Derived verbs like **revenir** and **devenir** or **remonter** are also conjugated with **être**.

Elle **est revenue** seule.

◆ The past participles for some of the verbs conjugated with **être** are irregular.

descendre	**descendu**
mourir	**mort**
naître	**né**
partir	**parti**
sortir	**sorti**
venir	**venu**

ACTIVITÉS

Warm-up. Before doing the activities using **être** in the **passé composé,** read off a list of verbs conjugated either with **être** or **avoir.** Have students clap every time they hear an **être** verb, then repeat the list, and ask students to raise their hand when they hear a verb conjugated with **avoir.** If you like, repeat the list a third time and have students clap or raise their hands while listening for both types of verb.

14. Une lettre de Paris. Julie écrit vite une lettre à son amie Rosie. Elle décrit le dernier jour du week-end qu'elle a passé à Paris avec Caroline et Benjamin. Aidez Rosie à lire les verbes que son amie a mal écrits.

Chère Rosie,

Bonjour de Paris! Nous (1. arriver) _____ vendredi soir, et nous (2. aller) _____ directement à notre hôtel. Quand je (3. entrer) _____ dans la chambre, j'ai trouvé un grand lit pour nous trois! Caroline et moi (4. descendre) _____ à la réception, et nous avons demandé une autre chambre pour Benjamin. Ce soir-là j'ai été malade, et je (5. rester) _____ au lit.

Samedi soir, tout allait bien (was fine). Benjamin et Caroline (6. sortir) _____ chercher un restaurant: Benjamin (7. rester) _____ à la terrasse, mais Caroline (8. revenir) _____ me chercher à l'hôtel. Alors, nous (9. sortir) _____ vers 8 heures pour dîner, mais nous (10. ne pas rentrer) _____ tout de suite après parce que nous n'étions pas (weren't) trop fatigués.

Nous (11. aller) _____ dans un club de jazz où nous avons écouté des musiciens formidables! Enfin, quand nous (12. monter) _____ dans nos chambres, il était (was) trois heures du matin! Je vais te raconter nos autres aventures très bientôt.

Je t'embrasse,
Julie

15. Cherchez le coupable *(the guilty one).* Madame Martin a été la victime d'un meurtre *(murder).* L'inspecteur Colombeau et son assistant Bêtepense cherchent le coupable. Malheureusement l'assistant est incapable de prendre des notes correctes! Avec votre partenaire, aidez-le à remettre les choses en place.

MODÈLE: Madame Martin / partir à huit heures? / arriver
   —**Mme Martin est partie à huit heures?**
   —**Pas du tout. Elle n'est pas partie à huit heures; elle est arrivée à huit heures.**

1. Mme Martin / entrer dans le restaurant avec son amie / sortir du restaurant
2. Mme Martin et son amie / arriver ensemble / partir ensemble
3. les autres amis de Mme Martin / aller au restaurant aussi / aller chez elle
4. Mme Martin et son mari / descendre de leur voiture vers six heures / monter dans la voiture
5. Mme Martin / rester seule hier soir / sortir avec son mari
6. son mari / rester à Paris après le dîner hier soir / rentrer à la maison
7. Mme Martin / naître à Marly-le-roi / mourir

 16. Qu'est-ce que vous avez fait hier? Imaginez ce que votre partenaire a fait hier. Votre partenaire va vous dire si vous avez raison ou tort.

MODÈLE: aller au cinéma
   —**Vous êtes allé(e) au cinéma.**
   —**Vous avez raison. Je suis allé(e) au cinéma.**
OU —**Vous avez tort. Je ne suis pas allé(e) au cinéma.**

   manger au restaurant universitaire
   —**Vous avez mangé au restaurant universitaire.**
   —**Vous avez raison. J'ai mangé au restaurant universitaire.**
OU —**Vous avez tort. Je n'ai pas mangé au restaurant universitaire.**

1. faire les devoirs
2. rester à la maison
3. sortir
4. regarder la télé
5. écrire une lettre
6. aller au gymnase
7. revenir à la résidence avant huit heures
8. aller à la bibliothèque

 17. Une enquête. Find out from your partner five things he or she has done recently. Don't forget to tell when he or she did them. Use expressions such as **hier, hier matin, récemment, la semaine dernière,** and **lundi passé** in your answers.

MODÈLE: —**Qu'as-tu fait hier?**
   —**Je suis allée au cinéma avec mes amis. Et toi?**
   —**Moi, j'ai mangé au restaurant.**

Warm-up. Have students brainstorm a list of at least ten verbs that they can use in **Activité 17.**

LECTURE

PARIS AT NIGHT PAR JACQUES PRÉVERT

Reading Strategy: Reading Poems

Reading a poem is often quite different from reading a passage in prose. What are some ways to best understand a poem?

First, notice the form of the poem. **Les vers** *(lines)* may be of varying length. The poet may choose to use **des rimes** *(rhymes)* or **des vers libres** *(free verse)*. He or she may group **les vers** into **strophes** *(stanzas)*.

Second, look at the vocabulary itself. Which words or phrases did the poet choose to express his or her thoughts? Are there any repetitive phrases in the poem? If so, what do they mean?

Finally, read the poem again to form a general impression of the poet's work.

Jacques Prévert (1900–1977), French poet born in Neuilly-sur-Seine, created a popular kind of poetry characterized by the use of very simple language. He became famous in 1946 with the publication of ***Paroles,*** from which **Paris at night** is taken. His work is still very popular today, and he is remembered both for his poetry and his contribution to French cinema. (He wrote several outstanding screenplays. Among them are the dialogues for ***Les visiteurs du soir*** and ***Les enfants du paradis***).

1.
a. Lisez le poème et analysez sa forme. Parlez du nombre de vers, de la rime (est-ce un poème en vers libres ou y a-t-il des rimes?) et des strophes.
b. Quel vocabulaire est-ce que Prévert utilise? Quelles parties du corps décrit-il? Y a-t-il des expressions répétées? Si oui, quelles sont ces expressions et pourquoi le poète les répète-t-il?
c. Relisez le poème. Quelle est votre impression générale? Expliquez.

first / face

pour... *to remind me of all that*

En... *holding you*

Paris at night

Trois allumettes une à une allumées dans la nuit
La première° pour voir ton visage° tout entier
La seconde pour voir tes yeux
La dernière pour voir ta bouche
Et l'obscurité tout entière pour me rappeler tout cela°
En te serrant° dans mes bras

Paroles by Jacques Prévert, Éditions Gallimard, 1946

2. Répondez aux questions suivantes.

a. Imaginez où cette scène se passe *(takes place)?*
b. Qui sont les personnages *(characters)?*
c. Décrivez ce qui se passe du vers 2 au vers 5.
d. À votre avis, quelle relation existe entre les deux personnages du poème? Justifiez.

Talking about your activities (continued) **Voir p. 244.**

> Nous **partons** après la classe.
> Caroline **sort** avec Benjamin.

Giving more details **Voir p. 250.**

> Julie est une fille **qui** comprend bien le français.
> Benjamin a donné le magazine **qu'**il a acheté à Caroline.
> Les livres **que** j'aime coûtent très cher.

Talking about quantity (continued) **Voir p. 258.**

> Je sors le samedi avec **toutes** mes amies.
> **Tout le monde** aime aller au cinéma.

Talking about the past (continued) **Voir p. 264.**

> Benjamin et Caroline **sont arrivés** au musée à midi.
> Julie **est restée** à l'hôtel.

ÊTES-VOUS BRANCHÉS?

Mon journal. Vous avez appris beaucoup de choses sur les médecins et les pharmaciens. Quelles différences et similarités y a-t-il entre le système médical en France et aux États-Unis? Quels sont les avantages et les inconvénients du système français et du système américain? Vous avez aussi découvert quelques monuments et musées de Paris. Si vous avez la possibilité d'aller à Paris, qu'est-ce que vous allez visiter? Pourquoi?

Y ÊTES-VOUS ARRIVÉS?

A. Écrivez une lettre à un(e) ami(e). Parlez de votre dernier voyage. Dites quand vous êtes parti(e)(s), où vous êtes allé(e)(s), quand vous êtes rentré(e)(s) et avec qui vous êtes sorti(e)(s). Donnez beaucoup de détails. Si vous n'avez pas fait de voyage, imaginez-en un.

B. Les goûts du professeur. Imaginez les goûts du professeur.

MODÈLE: **Le professeur adore les étudiants qui arrivent à l'heure.**
Le professeur déteste les étudiants qui ne font pas leurs devoirs.
Le professeur aime bien la pizza qu'il achète à Pizza World.

Possibilities

students that arrive late
sandwiches that the cafeteria makes
classes that are easy
students that do their homework

the book that the students have
the questions that the students ask
???

C. Tout va bien. Donnez la réponse appropriée.

1. PHILIPPE: Au revoir, Églantine! À plus tard!
    ÉGLANTINE: **a.** À tout à l'heure.
    b. Tout le monde.
    c. Tout le temps.

2. PAUL: Bonjour, monsieur le professeur!
    PROFESSEUR: **a.** À tout de suite!
    b. Bonjour tout le monde!
    c. Toutes les semaines!

3. ANNE: Vous travaillez constamment?
    EVELYNE: **a.** Oui, tout le temps.
    b. Oui, tous les mois.
    c. Oui, tous les ans.

4. IRVANA: Vous allez quelquefois en France?
    ABEL: **a.** Oui, tous les matins.
    b. Oui, tous les deux jours.
    c. Oui, tous les ans.

5. MICHEL: Votre femme et vous venez chez moi?
    JAIME: **a.** Oui, tous les deux.
    b. Oui, toutes les deux.
    c. Oui, tout le monde.

6. BRUNO: Il est midi. Vous allez déjeuner à la cafétéria?
    FARBOU: **a.** Oui, mais pas toutes les semaines.
    b. Oui, tout le temps.
    c. Oui, mais pas tout de suite.

 PRONONCIATION

L'ÉLISION

You have certainly noticed by now that the final vowel in certain words is dropped when it comes in contact with a following word that begins with a vowel sound. Written French shows that a vowel has been dropped by replacing it with an apostrophe. This happens with three vowels in particular:

e

je + habite ⟶ j'habite
le + appartement ⟶ l'appartement
le + hôtel ⟶ l'hôtel
ce + est ⟶ c'est
que + il ⟶ qu'il
entre + acte ⟶ entr'acte

a

la + amie ⟶ l'amie
la + herbe ⟶ l'herbe

i

si + il ⟶ s'il

Note: Elision does not occur *every* time two vowels come in contact. For example, the **i** in **qui** is never elided, the silent **e** at the end of **elle, notre,** and **votre** is kept, and the possessive adjectives **ma, ta,** and **sa** are changed to the masculine forms to avoid vowel-to-vowel contact.

Le professeur **qui e**st dans la classe est sympathique.
La classe est grande. **Elle e**st blanche.
Mon assistante est fantastique.
Ton erreur est normale.
Son ambition est immense.

When elision has occurred, the two words are pronounced as a single word. There is no pause where the apostrophe has been inserted.

Listen to your professor or lab tape and pronounce the words below.

l'enfant	d'Orsay	j'aime
l'aéroport	d'argent	j'adore
l'héroïne	qu'elle	j'habite
l'arc	qu'ils	j'écris
l'arche	c'est	j'ai

◆ V O C A B U L A I R E ◆

Les parties du corps

la bouche *mouth*	le genou *knee*	l'oreille *(f) ear*
le bras *arm*	la gorge *throat*	le pied *foot*
les cheveux *(m) hair*	la jambe *leg*	la poitrine *chest*
le cou *neck*	la main *hand*	la tête *head*
les dents *(f) teeth*	le nez *nose*	le ventre *belly*
le doigt *finger*	l'œil *(m) eye*	les yeux *(m) eyes*
le dos *back*		

Problèmes de santé

Qu'est-ce qui ne va pas? *What's wrong?*

Je ne me sens pas bien. *I don't feel well.*

Je suis déprimé(e). *I am depressed.*

Je suis en (pleine) forme. *I am feeling great.*

Je suis fatigué(e). *I am tired.*

Je suis malade (comme un chien). *I am sick (as a dog).*

Je vais très bien. *I am fine.*

J'ai de la fièvre. *I have a fever.*

J'ai la gorge qui pique. *My throat is irritated.*

J'ai la grippe. *I have the flu.*

J'ai le nez qui coule. *My nose is running.*

J'ai un rhume. *I have a cold.*

avoir mal à... *to hurt*

J'ai mal partout. *I hurt everywhere.*

J'ai mal au cœur. *I feel nauseated.*

J'ai mal à la main. *My hand hurts.*

J'ai mal à la tête. *My head hurts; I have a headache.*

J'ai mal au ventre. *My stomach hurts; I have a stomach ache.*

J'ai mal aux yeux. *My eyes hurt.*

tousser *to cough*

Quelques expressions avec tout

tout, toute, tous, toutes *every, all*

toute l'année *all year long*

tout à coup / tout d'un coup *all of a sudden*

À tout à l'heure. *See you later.*

toute la journée *all day long*

tous les jours *every day*

tous les matins *every morning*

toute la matinée *all morning long*

tous les mois *every month*

tout le monde *everyone*

toutes les semaines *every week*

tous les soirs *every night*

toute la soirée *all evening long*

tout le temps *all the time*

Verbes conjugués avec être

aller *to go*

arriver *to arrive*

descendre *to go down; to get off*

devenir *to become*

entrer *to enter; to go in*

monter *to go up; to climb, to get in*

mourir *to die*

naître *to be born*

partir *to leave; to depart*

rentrer *to go home; to re-enter*

rester *to stay*

retourner *to return*

revenir *to come back*

sortir *to go out; to exit*

tomber *to fall*

venir *to come*

Quelques autres verbes utiles

dormir *to sleep*

mentir *to lie*

servir *to serve*

Pronoms relatifs

que *whom; which; that*

qui *who; which; that*

Chapitre 9 • LA SOIRÉE INTERNATIONALE

PRÉSENTATION ÉCLAIR

POUR COMMUNIQUER

Making, accepting, and refusing requests
Giving orders
Talking about your activities (continued)
Avoiding repetition (continued)
Giving precise orders

POUR Y ARRIVER

Les verbes **pouvoir** et **vouloir**
L'impératif

Jouer à et jouer de

Les pronoms objets directs
L'impératif avec les pronoms

POUR S'ADAPTER À LA CULTURE

Les loisirs
Les vacances et les sports

1

Il est huit heures du soir, et Benjamin est dans sa chambre. Il a passé° une excellente journée à l'université aujourd'hui. Il a bien travaillé dans tous ses cours, il a bien compris ses professeurs, et il a eu une bonne note à son premier examen d'économie.

——————
a passé *spent*

2

Benjamin est assis sur son lit. Il regarde les photos du week-end à Paris. Tout à coup, le téléphone sonne°. Mme Bouverot appelle Benjamin.

MME BOUVEROT: Benjamin, Benjamin, téléphone, c'est pour toi...
BENJAMIN: Oui, j'arrive!

——————
sonne *rings*

AVEZ-VOUS COMPRIS?

1. Quelle heure est-il? Comment Benjamin va-t-il?
2. Qu'est-ce que Benjamin a fait aujourd'hui?
3. Qui téléphone? Pourquoi?
4. Quand est-ce que Jean-Loup va venir chercher Benjamin?

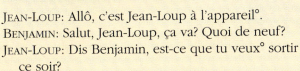

JEAN-LOUP: Allô, c'est Jean-Loup à l'appareil°.

BENJAMIN: Salut, Jean-Loup, ça va? Quoi de neuf?

JEAN-LOUP: Dis Benjamin, est-ce que tu veux° sortir ce soir?

BENJAMIN: Oui, pourquoi pas?

JEAN-LOUP: La soirée° internationale, ça t'intéresse?

BENJAMIN: Oui, je voudrais bien y aller.

_____

à l'appareil *on the phone* / **tu veux** *do you want* / **soirée** *party*

JEAN-LOUP: Je peux° passer te prendre en voiture si tu veux.

BENJAMIN: Ça, c'est vraiment sympathique. À quelle heure penses-tu venir?

JEAN-LOUP: Dans une petite demi-heure°.

BENJAMIN: D'accord. À tout de suite!

_____

peux *can* / **une petite demi-heure** *about half an hour*

ET VOUS?

1. Comment allez-vous aujourd'hui? Êtes-vous content(e)? triste?
2. Hier, avez-vous passé une bonne journée à l'université?
3. Dans quel(s) cours avez-vous bien compris le professeur à la fac hier? Dans quels cours avez-vous mal compris le professeur?
4. Y a-t-il des soirées sur votre campus? Y allez-vous seul(e)? avec des amis?
5. Est-ce que vous allez souvent au cinéma ou au restaurant avec vos amis? Pourquoi ou pourquoi pas?

VOUS ÊTES BRANCHÉS!

Les loisirs

Les loisirs en France.

With an average work week 39 hours long, the French enjoy a fair amount of free time. What do they do for **les loisirs** *(leisure activities)*? They watch television, listen to music, read, or go to the movies.

Although watching TV is very popular, listening to music is the leisure activity that has grown the most in the last ten to twenty years. One person out of four listens to a CD or a cassette daily. Most people enjoy listening to **chansons** *(popular songs)*, and many enjoy **la musique classique, le jazz,** and **le rock.**

Among teenagers, **le rock** is the most popular kind of music, and people in the 20–30 year-old group listen to **le jazz** most often. Music from other countries, in particular from the United States, is quite popular.

When they aren't listening to music, the French read. Books and magazines are favorites, while daily newspapers lag behind. Home delivery of newspapers is not available everywhere in France, and the rising cost of a newspaper, about eight francs ($1.50) a day, has added to the decline in daily newspaper readership.

Another popular leisure activity in France is **le cinéma** *(the movies)*. The French love movies, particularly comedies and adventure movies. They see a lot of American films, usually **doublés** *(dubbed)* for the French market, but there are also many French films. In fact, popular French films are often remade by American studios for audiences in the United States.

VOTRE Q. I. CULTUREL

Qu'en pensez-vous? Choisissez les réponses appropriées.

1. Les Français travaillent
   a. trente heures par semaine.
   b. quarante-cinq heures par semaine.
   c. trente-neuf heures par semaine.

2. Dans les vingt dernières années la musique, comme loisir,
   a. est restée stable.
   b. a beaucoup progressé.
   c. a régressé.

3. Les Français préfèrent lire
   a. des poèmes.
   b. des journaux.
   c. des livres et des magazines.

 Expliquez l'essentiel à votre partenaire. Choisissez un sujet et allez-y!

1. Résumez les types de musique que les Français préfèrent.
2. Expliquez pourquoi la majorité des Français ne lit pas un journal tous les jours.

http://www.wiley.com/aventure.html

■ POUR COMMUNIQUER

Making, accepting, and refusing requests

I   LES VERBES *POUVOIR* ET *VOULOIR*

Jean-Loup **peut** passer prendre Benjamin ce soir.
Ils **peuvent** aller à la soirée internationale parce qu'ils n'ont pas d'examen demain.
Pouvez-vous m'aider?
«Est-ce que tu **veux** aller à cette soirée?» demande Jean-Loup.
   Et vous, **voulez**-vous sortir ce week-end?

◆ **Pouvoir** *(to be able to, can, may)* and **vouloir** *(to want, to wish)* are both irregular verbs, but they have similar conjugations. Note that there are two stems for these verbs: one stem for the **nous** and **vous** forms, and one stem for all the other forms. This is true for many irregular verbs.

pouvoir	vouloir
je **peux**	je **veux**
tu **peux**	tu **veux**
il / elle / on **peut**	il / elle / on **veut**
nous **pouvons**	nous **voulons**
vous **pouvez**	vous **voulez**
ils / elles **peuvent**	ils / elles **veulent**

◆ **Pouvoir** is usually followed by an infinitive. **Vouloir** may be followed by an infinitive or a noun.

> Nous **pouvons aller** au cinéma ce week-end.
> **Voulez**-vous **manger** au restaurant?
> Elle **veut** ce dessert au chocolat.

◆ In the past tense, both **pouvoir** and **vouloir** have irregular past participles.

> Je n'ai pas **pu** aller à l'université hier.
>
> Sébastien n'a pas **voulu** y aller.

> *I wasn't able to go to the university yesterday.*
>
> *Sébastien didn't want (was unwilling) to go there.*

POUR S'EXPRIMER

Comment demander, offrir, accepter, et refuser poliment

DEMANDER QUELQUE CHOSE POLIMENT

Pourrais-tu... / Pourriez-vous... (me, nous + infinitive)	*Could you . . . ([for] me, us)*
Pourrais-tu me passer le sel?	*Could you pass me the salt?*
Je voudrais...	*I would like . . .*
Je voudrais du chocolat.	*I would like some chocolate.*
Je voudrais partir maintenant.	*I would like to leave now.*

OFFRIR QUELQUE CHOSE POLIMENT

Voudrais-tu... / Voudriez-vous... (me, nous + infinitive),	*Would you . . . ([for] me, us)*
Voudriez-vous nous téléphoner?	*Would you like to call us?*
Je pourrais...	*I could . . .*
Je pourrais aider votre mère.	*I could help your mother.*

ACCEPTER POLIMENT

Je veux bien.	*Yes, I would.; I gladly accept.*
Volontiers.	*Gladly.*
Avec plaisir.	*With pleasure.*
Mais, bien sûr.	*Certainly, of course.*
Mais, certainement.	*Certainly.*

REFUSER POLIMENT

(Je suis) désolé(e), je ne peux pas.	*(I'm) sorry, I can't.*
Ça m'est impossible pour l'instant.	*It's impossible for me right now.*

ACTIVITÉS

1. Qu'est-ce que tu peux faire? Marie, Pierre, Stéphanie et Sébastien vont faire du camping. Les deux filles organisent les activités. Imaginez ce qu'elles disent.

MODÈLE: moi, je / faire les courses
—**Moi, je peux faire les courses.**

1. moi, je / aller au supermarché
2. toi, tu / préparer le pique-nique
3. Pierre / téléphoner au camping
4. Sébastien / mettre la tente dans la voiture
5. Sébastien et Pierre / trouver un plan *(map)* de Vienne
6. et Stéphanie et toi, vous / préparer l'itinéraire
7. nous / passer un week-end super!

2. Vous voulez ou vous ne voulez pas? Imaginez les désirs de différentes personnes.

MODÈLE: je / étudier (seul(e) / avec un ami)
Je veux étudier seul(e). Je ne veux pas étudier avec un ami.
OU **Je ne veux pas étudier seul(e). Je veux étudier avec un ami.**

■ MOTS À UTILISER: **rencontrer** *to meet* / **voir** *to see*

1. je / aller à McDonalds (aller à Burger King)
2. nous / aller au cinéma (faire nos devoirs)
3. les étudiants / dîner au restaurant (rester à la maison)
4. vous / étudier à la bibliothèque (étudier dans votre chambre)
5. tu / sortir avec tes amis (sortir avec tes parents)
6. ton ami(e) / passer un examen (passer le week-end à Nice)
7. le professeur / écrire un examen (voir un film)
8. les étudiantes / faire leurs devoirs (rencontrer leurs amis au café)

 3. Soyons polis! *Let's be polite!* À un dîner très chic, vous demandez poliment ce que vous désirez. Jouez la scène avec votre partenaire et inventez beaucoup de phrases.

MODÈLE: —**Pourriez-vous me passer l'eau, Madame?**
—**Avec plaisir.**
OU —**Je suis désolée, il n'y en a plus.**

Pourrais-tu	me		le sel	Volontiers.
Pourriez-vous	nous	passer	l'eau	Avec plaisir.
			le vin	Mais certainement.
			le pain	Désolé(e), il n'y en a pas.
			le poivre	Désolé(e), il n'y en a plus.

> The conjugation of the verb **voir** will be taught in Chapter 15.

> **Follow-up.** As a follow-up to **Activité 2,** have students choose five of their answers and justify them. For example, **Je veux aller à Burger King parce que je préfère leurs hamburgers.**

> **Warm-up.** Before **Activité 3,** have students brainstorm what people usually ask for when sitting down to dinner. Remind them of vocabulary like **sel, poivre,** and **eau.**

DEUXIÈME ÉPISODE T 58

Voilà Benjamin!

Enchanté!

1

Tu veux boire?

Non, merci!

2

Jean-Loup et Benjamin arrivent à la soirée. Là, ils rencontrent d'abord Sébastien, le président du club international.

JEAN-LOUP: Bonsoir, Sébastien, je voudrais te présenter un ami. Voilà Benjamin Wilson. Il est américain et fait ses études° de commerce international ici cette année.

SÉBASTIEN: Enchanté, Benjamin! Il y a des amuse-gueule° et du vin sur la table. Prends un verre et viens discuter avec nous.

BENJAMIN: Volontiers!

---

fait ses études *is studying* / **amuse-gueule** *finger food; appetizers*

Benjamin commence à parler avec un groupe d'étudiants. Ils viennent de partout. Léopold vient du Sénégal, son copain° Stéphane vient de Louisiane, et Mahomed de Tunisie.

BENJAMIN: Tu veux boire quelque chose d'autre? Tu veux encore du vin, Léopold?

LÉOPOLD: Non, merci. Je vais rentrer en voiture et, tu connais° bien cette vieille publicité: Boire ou conduire, il faut choisir!° Apporte-moi plutôt° un verre de jus de pomme, s'il te plaît!

---

copain *buddy; pal* / **connais** *know* / **Boire ou conduire, il faut choisir!** *Drinking or driving, one has to choose!* / **Apporte-moi plutôt** *Bring me instead*

Culture. You may wish to tell your students about a more recent ad on the same subject: **Après deux verres, tout s'accélère.**

AVEZ-VOUS COMPRIS?

1. Qui est-ce que Benjamin et Jean-Loup rencontrent quand ils arrivent?
2. D'où viennent Mahomed, Léopold et Stéphane?
3. Qu'est-ce que Léopold veut boire? Pourquoi?
4. Qui tombe? À votre avis, pourquoi est-ce qu'il tombe?
5. Qu'est-ce que Benjamin recommande à l'étudiant? À votre avis, est-ce que c'est une bonne idée?

Benjamin va chercher les boissons. Tout le monde s'amuse bien°. Tout d'un coup, un étudiant avec un verre de vin rouge à la main arrive pour participer à leur discussion, mais il glisse° et... patatras°, le voilà par terre!°

L'ÉTUDIANT: Zut!° Aïe!° mon derrière, que je suis bête! et j'ai mal au dos! Et puis mon pantalon! Oh! Il y a des taches° de vin partout!

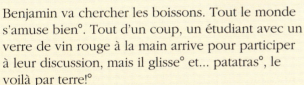

s'amuse bien *is having a good time* / **glisse** *slips* / **patatras** *crash* / **le voilà par terre** *there he is on the ground* / **zut** *shoot* / **aïe** *ouch* / **taches** *stains*

Benjamin vient l'aider.

BENJAMIN: Ça va? Et ton pantalon? Pas de problèmes! Mets du sel sur les taches et puis surtout fais attention où tu mets les pieds. Et puis, prends un café, c'est peut-être° plus prudent!

peut-être *maybe*

Culture. You may want to share with your students some very colloquial and *not* very polite French. **Merde,** although quite vulgar in English, is widely used in France to wish people good luck. It is also used to express a variety of emotions as might happen when you slip and fall.
Mercredi is used in the same way that *shoot* is used to disguise a desire to use a vulgar term.

ET VOUS?

1. Est-ce que vous allez souvent à des soirées sur votre campus? Pourquoi ou pourquoi pas?
2. Y a-t-il des étudiants de pays différents sur votre campus? D'où viennent-ils?
3. Quand vous sortez, qu'est-ce que vous buvez en général? un jus de fruit? un coca?
4. Quand il y une soirée chez vos amis, qu'est-ce qu'ils servent à manger? à boire?
5. Et vous, qu'est-ce que vous aimez servir? Pourquoi?

■ POUR COMMUNIQUER

Giving orders

▐ L'IMPÉRATIF

> **Apporte**-moi un verre de jus de pomme, s'il te plaît.
> **Allons** à la soirée.
> **Ne buvez pas** trop.
> **Faites** attention.

◆ Use the imperative form of a verb when you need to give orders, directions, advice, or suggestions.

◆ Each verb has three imperative forms:

Parle au professeur.	*Speak to your teacher.*
Parlons à nos amis.	*Let's speak to our friends.*
Parlez à votre médécin, M. Petit.	*Speak to your doctor, Mr. Petit.*

◆ The imperative forms are based on the present tense, but they do not include a subject pronoun.

prendre	boire	faire
prends	bois	fais
prenons	buvons	faisons
prenez	buvez	faites

◆ The **tu** form of **-er** verbs and **aller** drops its **-s.** All other verbs use the complete present tense **tu** form for the imperative. **Nous** and **vous** forms of the imperative are the same as their present tense forms.

Present Tense	Imperative	Present Tense	Imperative
~~Tu~~ parl**es**	*Parle*	~~Tu~~ *vas*	**Va**
~~Nous~~ parl**ons**	*Parlons*	~~Nous~~ *all**ons***	*Allons*
~~Vous~~ parl**ez**	*Parlez*	~~Vous~~ *all**ez***	*Allez*

◆ **Avoir** and **être** have irregular imperative forms.

avoir	être
aie	sois
ayons	soyons
ayez	soyez

◆ To form the negative imperative, place **ne** before the verb and **pas** after it.

> **Travaille** beaucoup aujourd'hui.   **Ne travaille pas** trop demain.

4. Ce qu'il dit, ce qu'il veut dire. Votre professeur est toujours très poli. Expliquez aux autres étudiants ce qu'il veut dire. Avec un(e) partenaire, jouez les deux rôles.

MODÈLE: fermer la porte
    PROF: Voulez-vous fermer la porte s'il vous plaît?
    VOUS: Fermez la porte, s'il vous plaît.

1. écouter votre partenaire   **3.** aller au tableau   **5.** lire le chapitre
2. écrire la réponse   **4.** avoir un peu de patience   **6.** être attentifs

 5. Eh bien... euh, ne travaille pas. Votre ami(e) n'a envie de rien faire. Vous êtes d'accord avec ce qu'il / elle dit. Jouez les deux rôles.

MODÈLE: aller au cinéma
    —Je ne veux pas aller au cinéma.
  OU **—Je n'ai pas envie d'aller au cinéma.**
  OU **—Je n'aime pas (du tout) aller au cinéma.**
    —Eh bien..., ne va pas au cinéma.

1. aller au centre commercial   **4.** boire du café   **7.** étudier
2. faire les courses   **5.** faire mes devoirs
3. manger de la pizza   **6.** écouter de la musique

 6. Alors qu'est-ce qu'on fait? Sébastien demande toujours l'avis de sa petite amie, Sophie, avant de faire quelque chose. Avec votre partenaire, jouez les deux rôles.

■ **MOT À UTILISER: plutôt** *instead*

MODÈLES: acheter / ce compact / oui
    SÉBASTIEN: **Tu veux acheter ce compact?**
      SOPHIE: **D'accord! Achetons ce compact!**

    acheter / cet ordinateur / non / acheter cette stéréo
    SÉBASTIEN: **Tu veux acheter cet ordinateur?**
      SOPHIE: **Non, n'achetons pas cet ordinateur; achetons plutôt**
          cette stéréo.

1. aller au cinéma ce soir (oui)   **5.** écouter la radio (non / inviter nos amis)
2. prendre un café avant le film (oui)   **6.** bavarder avec nos amis demain soir (oui)
3. dîner à la cafétéria (non / dîner au restaurant)   **7.** inviter Robert à dîner (oui)
4. regarder la télévision demain
(non / aller au concert)   **8.** sortir avec Marie-T et Joseph
(non / sortir avec Anne et Luc)

7. Voilà des suggestions. Vous avez étudié la psychologie le semestre dernier, et maintenant vous avez des suggestions pour tout le monde. Donnez trois suggestions à vos parents, trois à votre professeur, et trois à votre meilleur(e) ami(e). Ensuite, proposez trois choses que vous et votre meilleur(e) ami(e) pouvez faire ensemble.

TROISIÈME ÉPISODE

Jean-Loup et Benjamin sont encore à la soirée internationale. Ils écoutent un groupe de musiciens fantastiques qui jouent de la guitare et du saxophone. Jean-Loup connaît° bien Benjamin et il sait° que Benjamin s'intéresse toujours aux jeunes filles.

connaît *(he) knows* / **sait** *knows*

JEAN-LOUP: Dis Benjamin, tu connais la fille en rouge là-bas?
BENJAMIN: Non. Qui est-ce?
JEAN-LOUP: C'est Madeleine. Elle est très intelligente et je la° trouve très gentille aussi. Et sa meilleure amie, Brigitte, est très sportive comme toi. Est-ce que tu veux que je les° invite à jouer au tennis avec nous le week-end prochain?

la *her* / **les** *them*

AVEZ-VOUS COMPRIS?

1. À qui est-ce que Benjamin s'intéresse?
2. Comment s'appellent les filles que Jean-Loup regarde?
3. Qu'est-ce qu'il a envie de faire?
4. Benjamin est-il d'accord? Pourquoi ou pourquoi pas?
5. Benjamin rougit comme une tomate. Pourquoi?
6. À votre avis, est-ce que Benjamin est amoureux? Pourquoi?

BENJAMIN: Non, je vais faire de l'escalade° avec Caroline et Julie.

JEAN-LOUP: Julie, c'est ton amie américaine, n'est-ce pas? Mais Caroline? Tu sors avec Caroline? Elle est comment? Allez, raconte...

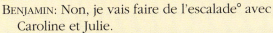

faire de l'escalade *to go rock climbing* / **Allez, raconte...** *Come on, tell (me) . . .*

Jean-Loup regarde bien Benjamin qui rougit comme une tomate.

BENJAMIN: Eh bien, euh... euh... euh...

JEAN-LOUP: Benjamin, non, ce n'est pas possible! Tu es amoureux?°

BENJAMIN: Tu en as des idées°... Bien sûr que non! Je la trouve simplement très sympathique et... très jolie aussi. Voilà tout.

amoureux *in love* / **Tu en as des idées** *You've got some weird ideas*

ET VOUS?

1. Sortez-vous souvent? Quand? Avec qui?
2. Comment s'appellent vos amis?
3. Qu'avez-vous envie de faire le week-end en général? et ce week-end?
4. Restez-vous dans votre ville ou partez-vous en week-end?
5. En général, où rencontrez-vous vos amis? dans votre ville? dans une autre ville?

Culture. People often use the phrase **allez** as linguistic "filler," much as Americans say "Come on" or "OK" even when they don't expect the listener to come somewhere or agree with them.

VOUS ÊTES BRANCHÉS

Les vacances et les sports

When the French go on vacation, they usually head for **la plage** *(the beach)* or the **la campagne** *(country)*, where they participate in two of their favorite activities: reading and sports.

Since 1982, every working adult has been entitled by law to five weeks of **congés payés** *(paid vacation)* per year. Most people take three or four weeks in one block, and use their remaining days to take several long weekends. One of the preferred vacation destinations is the south of France, known for its sunny climate, beautiful rivers and forests, and the Mediterranean Sea. In July and August, highways are jammed with vacationers headed for their ideal vacation spot.

Some of the

Les grand départs.

Escalade.

most popular vacation activities are sports. The French take their sports seriously, and often choose to deepen their knowledge and improve their athletic skills by participating in classes and/or **stages** *(clinics, camps)* to achieve their goals. Among the favorite sports are **le golf, le tennis, la natation** *(swimming)*, **la planche à voile** *(windsurfing)*, **le deltaplane** *(hang-gliding)*, **l'escalade** *(rock climbing)*, and **le VTT** *(off-road* or *mountain biking)*.

Why are sports so important to French people? For almost everyone, the answers are the same: to feel better physically, and to escape from their daily routine.

VOTRE Q. I. CULTUREL

 Expliquez l'essentiel à votre partenaire. Choisissez une question et allez-y.

1. Nommez deux destinations favorites des Français pour leurs vacances d'été et deux de leurs activités favorites. Comparez-les à vos vacances.
2. Quelle est l'attitude des Américains vis-à-vis du sport? Y a-t-il une seule *(single)* attitude? Comparez votre attitude à l'attitude des Français.
3. Expliquez pourquoi on devrait faire du sport.

http://www.wiley.com/aventure.html

Talking about your activities (continued)

IIIA *JOUER À ET JOUER DE*

Benjamin **joue au baseball.**
Nous apprenons à **jouer du piano.**

◆ The verb **jouer** *(to play)* is sometimes followed by either **à** or **de. Jouer à** is used with games and sports while **jouer de** is used with musical instruments. In each case, the definite article is used with the noun.

Sébastien et ses amis **jouent aux cartes.**	*Sébastien and his friends are playing cards.*
Qui **joue de la trompette?**	*Who plays trumpet?*

POUR S'EXPRIMER

Les loisirs

QUELQUES SPORTS ET JEUX *Some sports and games*

le baseball	*baseball*
le basket-ball (le basket)	*basketball*
les boules *(f)*	*bocce ball; lawn bowling*
les cartes *(f)*	*cards*
les dames *(f)*	*checkers*
les échecs *(m)*	*chess*
le football	*soccer*
le football américain	*football*
le golf	*golf*
le hockey	*hockey*
la natation	*swimming*
le tennis	*tennis*
le volley-ball (le volley)	*volleyball*

AUTRES ACTIVITÉS *Other activities*

faire du deltaplane	*to go hang-gliding*
faire de l'escalade	*to go rock climbing*
faire de la planche à voile	*to go windsurfing*
faire du rafting	*to go river rafting*
faire de la randonnée	*to go hiking*
faire du ski de fond	*to go cross-country skiing*
faire du ski nautique	*to go water skiing*
faire du VTT	*to go mountain (off-road) biking*
faire de la voile	*to go sailing*

QUELQUES INSTRUMENTS DE MUSIQUE	*Some musical instruments*
la batterie	*drums*
la guitare	*guitar*
le piano	*piano*
le saxophone	*saxophone*
la trompette	*trumpet*
le violon	*violin*

QUELQUES LIEUX DE VACANCES	*Some vacation spots*
la campagne	*the country(side)*
la mer	*the seashore*
la montagne	*the mountains*
la plage	*the beach*

ACTIVITÉS

 8. Où est-ce qu'on fait ça? Votre partenaire veut savoir *(know)* où aller pour pratiquer ses sports favoris. Répondez-lui.

MODÈLE: —**Où vas-tu pour faire de la voile?**
—**Quand je fais de la voile, je vais à la mer.**

—**Où vas-tu pour jouer au volley-ball?**
—**Quand je joue au volley-ball, je vais à la plage.**

	voile	
	planche à voile	
	ski de fond	
	escalade	
	randonnée	la montagne
faire	tennis	la mer
jouer	VTT	la campagne
	rafting	la plage
	volley-ball	
	boules	
	football	
	basket-ball	

9. Pouvez-vous nommer quelqu'un qui... ? Aimez-vous les sports et la musique? Demander à votre partenaire de nommer quelqu'un qui fait les activités suivantes. Attention au choix entre **à** et **de.**

T 60

MODÈLE: —**Qui joue de la batterie?**
—**Phil Collins joue de la batterie.**

—**Qui joue aux dames?**
—**Mes cousins Gustave et Gilbert jouent aux dames.**

1   2   3   4

5   6   7   8

■ POUR COMMUNIQUER

Avoiding repetition (continued)

IIIB LES PRONOMS OBJETS DIRECTS

Où mettez-vous **mon livre?** Je **le** mets sur la table.
Est-ce qu'elle déteste **la classe?** Oui, elle **la** déteste.
Est-ce que vous **m'**aimez? Non, je ne **vous** aime pas.
Aimez-vous **les films italiens?** Non, je ne **les** aime pas.

> **Review.** You already know that you can avoid repeating words for certain places by using the pronoun **y**, and that **en** expresses the idea of *some, any,* or other amounts that have already been mentioned once. (See Chapters 5 and 7.)

◆ Direct objects answer the questions *what?* or *whom?* The direct object is the thing or person directly affected by the verb.

Je regarde **la télévision.**
Nous écoutons **nos parents.**

◆ The direct object of a verb can be represented by a pronoun. Four direct object pronouns refer specifically to people, and three refer to either people or things.

Les pronoms objets directs		
PEOPLE		
me (m')	nous	
te (t')	vous	
PEOPLE OR THINGS		
le (l')	la (l')	les

Est-ce que tu écoutes **tes professeurs?**—Oui, je **les** écoute.
Est-ce que tu écoutes **tes compacts?**—Oui, je **les** écoute.

◆ Direct object pronouns are placed immediately before the verb. See p. 169 for a review of pronoun placement.

Quand regardes-tu la télévision?—Je **la** regarde le week-end.
Est-ce que Jean-Loup regarde la jeune fille?—Oui, il **la** regarde.
Est-ce que Stéphane vous invite?—Oui, il **nous** invite.

◆ To use a direct object pronoun in the **passé composé,** place the pronoun in front of the conjugated form of **avoir.** The past participle must agree with the direct object pronoun.

L'accord du participe passé	
SINGULIER (*m*)	Est-ce qu'il a écouté **le professeur?** —Oui, il **l'**a écouté.
SINGULIER (*f*)	Est-ce qu'il a regardé **la jeune fille?** —Oui, il **l'**a regardé**e.**
PLURIEL (*m*)	Est-ce que tu **nous** as écoutés? —Oui, je **vous** ai écoutés.
PLURIEL (*f*)	Est-ce que les garçons ont invité **les filles?** —Oui, ils **les** ont invité**es.**

Note: When **y** and **en** are used with the **passé composé,** no past participle agreement is made because they are not *direct object* pronouns.

> À quelle heure est-ce que Jean-Loup est arrivé **à la fête?**—Il **y** est arrivé à sept heures.
> Qui a pris **du jus de pomme?**—Stéphane **en** a pris.

◆ With two or more verbs, the pronoun precedes the verb that directly affects it.

> Qui va boire ce vin?—Nous allons **le** boire.
> Est-ce qu'elle veut nous inviter, Sébastien et moi?—Oui, elle veut **vous** inviter.

◆ For negative forms of the present and **passé composé,** remember to place the negation around *both* the pronoun and verb.

> Elles **ne** nous invitent **pas** à la soirée.
> Vous **ne** m'avez **pas** écouté.

◆ When there is more than one verb, the negation goes around the conjugated verb.

> Benjamin **ne** va **jamais** les manger.
> Elle **ne** peut **plus** t'écrire.

ACTIVITÉS

10. Mes préférences. Répondez aux questions en utilisant un pronom objet direct.

MODÈLE: Aimez-vous la musique classique?
　　　　—Oui, je l'aime.
　OU　**—Non, je ne l'aime pas.**

1. Aimez-vous la musique punk?
2. Aimez-vous la cuisine de votre mère? La cuisine de votre sœur?
3. Adorez-vous Mariah Carey?
4. Détestez-vous les devoirs et les examens?
5. Aimez-vous le dernier film de Tom Hanks?
6. Aimez-vous les films de Kevin Costner et les films de Mel Gibson?
7. Adorez-vous Julia Roberts?

11. Je vais le faire demain. Vous invitez votre ami(e) à faire beaucoup de choses, mais il / elle n'est pas libre.

MODÈLE: regarder la télévision (ce soir / demain)
  —**Veux-tu regarder la télé ce soir?**
  —**Je ne peux pas la regarder ce soir. Je vais la regarder demain.**

1. écouter mon nouveau compact (maintenant / tout à l'heure)
2. étudier ton français (aujourd'hui / demain matin)
3. préparer le dîner (ce soir / après demain)
4. mettre la cassette de Phil Collins (cet après-midi / demain)
5. regarder la vidéo de mes vacances (maintenant / un autre jour)
6. manger cette salade (ce soir / demain soir)
7. acheter les compacts de House Party (ce matin / demain)

Warm-up. Before doing **Activité 13,** you may want to explain some terms of endearment to your students: **mon (ma) chéri(e), mon trésor, mon chou, mon amour, ma puce.**

 12. Rassure-moi! Rassurez votre copain (copine) ou votre mari (femme). Jouez les rôles avec un(e) partenaire.

MODÈLE: —**Est-ce que tu me trouves jolie?**
  —**Oui, mon amour, je te trouve jolie.**

  —**Est-ce que tu m'aimes?**
  —**Bien sûr, ma puce! Je t'aime!**

1. Est-ce que tu m'adores?
2. Est-ce que tu m'admires?
3. Est-ce que tu me trouves intelligent(e)?
4. Est-ce que tu vas m'aimer demain?
5. Est-ce que tu vas me trouver sexy dans dix ans?
6. Est-ce que tu vas toujours m'adorer?

Writing activity. You may wish to have students do **Activité 14** as a written assignment to verify agreement of the past participle.

 13. Alors, racontez! À la soirée, Benjamin et Jean-Loup retrouvent leur ami Philippe qui est arrivé en retard. Il pose beaucoup de questions. Jouez les rôles avec deux partenaires. Utilisez les pronoms objets directs pour répondre aux questions.

■ MOTS À UTILISER: **demander (quelqu'un)** *to ask for (someone)* / **remarquer** *to notice* / **goûter** *to taste*

MODÈLE: PHILIPPE: **As-tu remarqué Anne?**
BENJAMIN: **Oui, je l'ai remarquée.**
OU BENJAMIN: **Non, je ne l'ai pas remarquée.**

PHILIPPE: **Avez-vous regardé les décorations?**
JEAN-LOUP: **Oui, nous les avons regardées.**
OU JEAN-LOUP: **Non, nous ne les avons pas regardées.**

1. Avez-vous mangé ce pâté?
2. As-tu remarqué les filles là-bas, Benjamin?
3. Avez-vous goûté les hors-d'œuvre?
4. Est-ce que quelqu'un m'a demandé?
5. Est-ce que Florence vous a invités à danser?
6. Avez-vous invité Florence à danser?

14. Recommençons! Un autre copain, Jean-Paul, est arrivé après Philippe et lui aussi, il pose beaucoup de questions. Utilisez les pronoms objets directs, **y,** ou **en** pour répondre aux questions.

Writing activity. You may wish to have students do **Activité 15** as a written assignment to verify agreement of the past participle.

■ MOTS À UTILISER: **copain** *pal; boyfriend* / **copine** *pal; girlfriend*

1. Est-ce que Jeannette vous a invités?
2. Est-ce que nos copains sont allés dans la cuisine?
3. Est-ce qu'ils ont préparé des gâteaux?
4. Est-ce que Marie-Pierre m'a demandé?
5. Est-ce qu'elle a parlé de son petit problème?
6. Est-ce que nos copines nous ont demandés?

15. Interview. Posez les questions suivantes à votre partenaire. Il / elle va répondre en utilisant un pronom. Demandez-lui s'il / si elle

1. va regarder la télé ce soir.
2. a regardé la télé hier soir.
3. a fait ses devoirs hier.
4. va étudier le français pendant les vacances.
5. va aller en France pendant les vacances.
6. aime vos amis et vous.
7. va vous inviter chez lui / elle.
8. va manger une pizza ce soir.
9. est allé(e) au cinéma le week-end dernier.
10. va aller au cinéma le week-end prochain.
11. Avez-vous d'autres questions?

Benjamin passe une soirée fantastique. Il parle avec ses amis; il rencontre beaucoup d'autres personnes. Son ami Jean-Loup est parti il y a une heure déjà, et Benjamin, qui n'a pas d'examen demain, continue à bavarder° tranquillement. Il ne fait pas attention à l'heure. Tout à coup il regarde l'horloge°.

bavarder *to chat* / **l'horloge** *the clock*

BENJAMIN: Non, ce n'est pas vrai! Il est deux heures du matin! Zut alors, j'ai raté° le dernier tram! Qu'est-ce que je vais faire?
STÉPHANE: Rentre chez toi à pied.
BENJAMIN: Oui, j'imagine que je n'ai pas le choix.

raté *missed*

AVEZ-VOUS COMPRIS?

1. Comment est la soirée de Benjamin?
2. Quelle heure est-il?
3. Qu'est-ce que Benjamin a raté?
4. Quelle solution Stéphane propose-t-il?
5. Benjamin a un autre problème. Qu'est-ce qu'il ne trouve pas?
6. Quelle autre solution est-ce que Faridé propose? À votre avis, est-ce une bonne idée?

Benjamin met sa veste. Il est prêt à° partir. Il met la main dans sa poche°, et il découvre° que ses clés° n'y sont pas.

BENJAMIN: Ça alors, je n'ai pas mes clés. Je les ai perdues° ou laissées° à la maison? Aïe, Aïe, Aïe! Comment est-ce que je vais rentrer chez les Bouverot à deux heures du matin sans° clés?

———
prêt à *ready to* / **poche** *pocket* / **découvre** *discovers* / **clés** *keys* / **Je les ai perdues** *I lost them* / **laissées** *left* / **sans** *without*

STÉPHANE: Tes clés, tu es sûr qu'elles ne sont pas dans tes poches? Cherche-les bien.
BENJAMIN: Rien.
FARIDÉ: Téléphone donc aux Bouverot.
MAHOMED: Oui, appelle-les.
BENJAMIN: À deux heures du matin? Vous êtes fous!° Il est trop tard pour téléphoner. Je suis vraiment dans le pétrin!°

———
fous *crazy* / **dans le pétrin** *in a fix*

ET VOUS?

1. Aimez-vous aller à des soirées?
2. Généralement à quelle heure partez-vous d'une soirée?
3. Comment rentrez-vous chez vous? à pied? en bus? en voiture?
4. Est-ce que vous prenez le bus quelquefois?
5. Si oui, que faites-vous quand vous ratez le bus?
6. À qui téléphonez-vous si vous ratez le bus? Pourquoi?
7. À quelle heure est-ce qu'il est trop tard pour téléphoner chez vous?
8. À quelle heure est-ce qu'il est trop tard pour téléphoner à vos parents? à vos amis?

IL Y A UN PROBLÈME: QU'EN PENSEZ-VOUS?

Benjamin a raté le dernier tram, et il n'a pas les clés de la maison. Que va-t-il faire?

Devrait-il

a. téléphoner chez les Bouverot?

b. passer la nuit chez un ami?

c. aller à l'hôtel?

d. rentrer à pied et frapper *(knock)* à la porte des Bouverot?

e. Avez-vous une autre solution?

Justifiez votre réponse.

À VOUS DE JOUER

Vous êtes au centre commercial avec des amis. Quand vous retournez au parking, vous ne trouvez pas les clés de votre voiture. Que faites-vous?

Moi, je

a. cherche les clés dans tous les magasins où j'ai fait mes courses.

b. dis à mes amis de rentrer en bus.

c. téléphone à ma famille, et je demande à quelqu'un de venir nous chercher.

d. téléphone au garage qui se trouve à côté du centre commercial.

e. Avez-vous une autre solution?

Justifiez votre réponse.

■ POUR COMMUNIQUER

Giving precise orders

IV **L'IMPÉRATIF AVEC LES PRONOMS**

Fais tes exercices, Benjamin. **Fais-les** tout de suite!
Allons au café. D'accord. **Allons-y!**
Ne mettez pas de sel sur vos légumes. N'**en mettez** pas.

Review. You already know how to give orders, advice, and suggestions. (See p. 282.) You also know how to use pronouns to avoid repeating words for people, places, and things. (See p. 289.)

◆ It is a simple process to combine the imperative with object pronouns.

Regarde les jeunes filles. ⟶ Regarde-**les.**
Achetons ces fleurs pour elles. ⟶ Achetons-**les** pour elles.
Écoutez Jean-Loup et moi. ⟶ Écoutez-**nous.**

Review. Remember the "triple A" rule: **A**ttachez **A**ffirmatif **A**près. *(Attach Affirmative After.).*

◆ When the order or advice you give is in the affirmative, place the pronoun directly after the verb and attach it to the verb with a hyphen. This rule applies to all the pronouns you have studied so far.

Allez au café. ⟶ Allez-**y.**
Prends du camembert. ⟶ Prends-**en.**
Faisons nos devoirs. ⟶ Faisons-**les.**

◆ Some small changes must be made to help in the pronunciation of certain forms.

When **me** is attached after an imperative, change it to **moi.**

Regardez-**moi.** *Look at me.*

Note: When **y** and **en** are attached to the familiar form of the imperative of regular **-er** verbs and **aller,** add **s** to the end of the verb.

Donne du chocolat à Kristina. ———→ Donne**s-en** à Kristina.
Achète des fleurs. ———→ Achète**s-en.**
Va au restaurant. ———→ Va**s-y.**

◆ If your order or advice is negative, place the pronouns in the usual position before the verb.

Ne fume pas de cigarettes. ———→ N'**en** fume pas.
N'allons pas au bar. ———→ N'**y** allons pas.
Ne regardez pas Jean. ———→ Ne **le** regardez pas.

ACTIVITÉS

 16. Non! Je refuse! Cathy, qui a dix ans, refuse d'obéir à sa mère. Elle préfère donner des ordres à sa sœur! Que dit-elle? Jouez les rôles avec un(e) partenaire.

MODÈLE: LA MÈRE: **Range tes affaires!**
CATHY: **Range-les!**

LA MÈRE: **N'écoute pas tes cassettes!**
CATHY: **Ne les écoute pas!**

1. Range ta chambre!
2. Écoute ton père!
3. N'écoute pas les conseils de tes amis!
4. Fais tes devoirs!
5. Écris tes dissertations à l'avance!
6. Ne prends pas ton petit déjeuner dans ta chambre!

17. Répétez, s'il vous plaît! Les étudiants n'écoutent pas le professeur. Répétez ce qu'il dit en utilisant un pronom: **y, en, le, la,** ou **les.**

MODÈLE: Allez au tableau.
—**Allez-y!**

1. Rendez les devoirs.
2. Écoutez cette phrase.
3. Répondez à la question.
4. Restez dans la salle de classe.
5. Prenez de la craie.
6. Ne mangez pas de chewing-gum ici.
7. Ne faites pas cet exercice.

18. Je veux faire des choses amusantes! Vous êtes obligé(e) de faire certaines choses, mais votre partenaire va vous proposer une activité qui est plus amusante. Acceptez-vous ou refusez-vous sa proposition?

MODÈLE: Va à la librairie.
>—**N'y va pas! Va à la plage!**
>—**D'accord! J'y vais!**
>OU —**Mais non! Je n'y vais pas!**

1. Fais tes devoirs.
2. Mange des légumes.
3. Écris ta dissertation.

4. Va au laboratoire.
5. Écoute le professeur.
6. Étudie ta leçon.

 19. Voilà ce que je propose... Vous proposez des activités à deux partenaires. Acceptent-ils vos suggestions?

MODÈLE: regarder la télé
>—**Regardons la télé.**
>—**Oui, regardons-la!**
>OU —**Non, ne la regardons pas!**

1. étudier le vocabulaire
2. aller au cinéma
3. manger des escargots

4. écrire des lettres à la femme du président
5. faire nos exercices
6–10. Proposez 5 activités de plus à vos partenaires.

 **LECTURE**

LE CINÉMA

Reading strategy: Using cognates to help you understand a text

1. Lisez rapidement les deux premières lignes du passage à la p. 299 et faites une liste de mots en français qui correspondent aux mots anglais. Comparez votre liste à celle d'un(e) camarade de classe pour voir si vous avez trouvé les mêmes mots et les mêmes significations.

a. video
b. access
c. equipped

d. techniques
e. modern

2. Lisez le reste du passage en utilisant ce que vous avez appris au sujet des mots apparentés pour répondre aux questions.

a. Est-ce que les Français vont au cinéma plus ou moins souvent depuis le développement des magnétoscopes?

Le cinéma

Cinéphiles, les Français fréquentent pourtant moins les salles depuis le développement de la vidéo à domicile, et l'accès aux chaînes câblées. Quelques salles sont équipées de techniques modernes (son dolby stéréo, effets spéciaux, écran géant) afin de séduire le spectateur.

Les films nouveaux sortent le mercredi. Le cinéma français produit une grande diversité de films et révèle régulièrement des jeunes talents.

Les programmations étrangères sont visibles au choix en VO (version originale) sous-titrées en français, ou en version française. Le mercredi est le jour de tarif réduit pour tous.

b. Quels sont deux développements qui encouragent les Français à rester plus souvent à la maison?

c. En général les nouveaux films sortent quel jour en France? Et chez vous? Y a-t-il un prix spécial ce jour-là? Si oui, pour qui?

d. Chez vous, est-il possible de voir des films étrangers *(foreign)* en langue originale? Quelle est l'abbréviation pour ce type de film en France?

e. Comment dit-on *subtitled* en français?

DES FESTIVALS DE CINÉMA

- Le festival de Cannes, créé en 1946, il décerne une palme d'or (Alpes maritimes).
- Le festival du film américain à Deauville (Calvados).
- Le festival du film fantastique à Avoriaz (Haute-Savoie).
- Le festival du western en plein air à Paris.
- Le festival du film d'humour à Chamrousse (Isère).
- À Paris, chaque année, les professionnels du cinéma priment les plus grands talents et les meilleures réalisations qui reçoivent un "César", distinction honorifique symbolisée par une statuette créée par le sculpteur César.

---

3. Regardez la liste de festivals de cinéma. Trouvez les festivals qui correspondent aux films, puis mettez les titres avec leurs équivalents français,

_____ **1.** *The Good, the Bad and the Ugly*

_____ **2.** *Star Wars*

_____ **3.** *Four Weddings and a Funeral*

a. *La Guerre des étoiles*

b. *Quatre mariages et un enterrement*

c. *Le Bon, la brute et le méchant*

4. Cherchez les festivals sur la petite carte *(map)*.

Writing Strategy: Summarizing, giving your opinion, and justifying it

If you are going to write a review of a book, article, or movie, one of the first steps you should take is to summarize. This means that you must find the main ideas or themes of the work you are reviewing and restate them in a more concise way, leaving out all but the most important information.

Next, you need to explain what you think of the article or movie. Did you like it or dislike it? Would you recommend it to a friend? Would you read it or see it again?

Finally, you must justify your opinion. Was it a good or bad book, article, or movie because of the style, the plot, the characters, or some other element?

1. Faridé est allée au cinéma la semaine dernière et elle a vu *(saw)* le film *Mr. Holland's Opus*, qu'elle a adoré. Elle écrit à son ami Mamoud pour lui raconter ses impressions.

Lisez la lettre. Montrez *(show)* à votre partenaire la partie de la lettre qui résume le film. Ensuite, trouvez les phrases qui indiquent ce que Faridé pense de *Mr. Holland's Opus.* Pourquoi est-ce que Faridé a aimé le film?

Cher Mamoud,

Samedi soir j'ai vu° un film absolument superbe. <u>Mr. Holland's Opus</u> est l'histoire d'un musicien qui, pour gagner sa vie°, devient prof de musique dans une école secondaire. Il veut partager° son amour de la musique avec ses élèves mais, au début, ils ne s'intéressent pas à la musique traditionnelle. Pour M. Holland, il s'agit alors d'un défi°. Il doit trouver le moyen° d'intéresser ses élèves. À la fin du film, (je ne veux pas tout te raconter°) il y arrive°, et tout est bien qui finit bien.

L'histoire est très touchante (j'ai pleuré!), et les personnages° sont très réels. J'ai beaucoup pensé à notre prof de musique, M. Bensimon.

Ce film est un chef-d'œuvre° à ne pas manquer°. Va le voir, et dis-moi si toi aussi, tu adores ce film.

Je t'embrasse,

Faridé

saw

gagner... *to earn a living*
to share

challenge / way

to tell / il... he does it

characters

masterpiece / à... not to be missed

2. Maintenant à vous d'écrire une lettre à votre ami(e). Résumez le dernier film / livre que vous avez vu / lu. Dites ce que vous en pensez et pourquoi. Pour vous aider, voici quelques expressions utiles.

POUR RÉSUMER

Ce film raconte l'histoire de...	*This film tells the story of . . .*
... est l'histoire de...	*. . . is the story of . . .*
Dans ce film, il s'agit de...	*This film is about . . .*

Il s'agit de is an impersonal expression. No subject other than **il** can be used with this expression. To say, *This book (film, article) is about,* say **Dans ce livre (film, article), il s'agit de...**

POUR DONNER VOTRE OPINION

Positive

Ce film est superbe!	*This movie is great!*
J'adore ce film!	*I love this movie!*
Ce film est un chef-d'œuvre!	*This movie is a masterpiece!*
C'est un film à ne pas manquer!	*This is a must-see movie!*

Négative

C'est un film idiot!	*This movie is dumb!*
C'est un navet!	*This is a really bad movie; it's a lemon (literally, a turnip)*

POUR JUSTIFIER

J'adore ce film parce que la photographie est superbe!	*I love this movie because the photography is superb!*
J'aime bien ce film parce que les acteurs jouent vraiment bien.	*I like this movie because the actors act really well.*
Ce film est spectaculaire parce que les costumes sont d'époque.	*This movie is spectacular because the costumes are authentic period costumes.*
L'histoire est touchante.	*The story is touching.*
Les personnages sont très réels.	*The characters are very believable.*

Et maintenant, à vos stylos!

R E N C O N T R E S

stylish ## Une jeune Tunisienne dans le vent°

En général, chez moi, on se marie jeune.

POPULATION: 8 726 562
SUPERFICIE: 163 612 km²
CAPITALE: Tunis
LANGUES: arabe et français

Décrivez-vous.

Je m'appelle Saïda Masmoudi, et j'ai 19 ans. J'habite à La Goulette, une ville tout près de Tunis, la capitale tunisienne. Je suis célibataire, mais je pense me marier après avoir fini mes études. Beaucoup de mes amies sont déjà mariées, et je ne veux pas rester *old maid* vieille fille!°

Vieille fille à dix-neuf ans?!

Mais oui! En Tunisie, on se marie assez jeune en général. Mes deux sœurs *for* Fahtia et Wassila sont mariées depuis° trois ans, et elles sont plus jeunes que moi! Mon frère Mahomed est célibataire comme moi, mais il est parti faire des études à l'Université de Grenoble, en France. Il va probablement trouver une femme l'année prochaine.

Quelle sorte d'études faites-vous?

l' École... teacher's college Je suis étudiante à l'École normale supérieure° parce que je voudrais être professeur comme ma voisine, Layla Abidi. J'ai passé mon bac, mais j'ai encore *to teach* quatre ans d'études avant d'avoir un travail. Je voudrais enseigner° l'histoire.

Pourquoi l'histoire?

Did you know Parce qu'on apprend tant de choses quand on étudie son passé. Saviez-vous° que le grand général Hannibal, qui a traversé les Alpes avec une armée *B.C.* d'éléphants en 218 av. J.-C.°, était de Carthage, une ancienne ville tunisienne? Et je voudrais aussi que mes étudiants apprennent qu'ils ont un rôle à jouer dans l'histoire. Par exemple, en 1956, ma grand-mère a été une des premières femmes tunisiennes à voter et à faire partie de l'Union Nationale des Femmes Tunisiennes.

Que faites-vous quand vous avez du temps libre?

J'aime lire *Jeune Afrique,* un journal rédigé° par de jeunes Tunisiens qui habitent maintenant à Paris.   *written*

Pouvez-vous nous résumer votre philosophie personnelle en quelques mots?

Tous les jours, faites ce que vous pouvez pour améliorer° votre monde.   *to improve*

QUELQUES QUESTIONS

1. Qu'avez-vous appris sur la Tunisie?
2. Quand les filles se marient-elles en Tunisie? À votre avis, quel est l'âge idéal pour le mariage? Pourquoi?
3. Résumez la philosophie de Saïda. Quelle est votre philosophie personnelle? Justifiez-la.

RÉVISION ÉCLAIR

Making, accepting, and refusing requests   **Voir p. 277.**

> **Voulez**-vous partir maintenant?
> Je ne **peux** pas faire la cuisine ce soir.

Giving orders   **Voir p. 282.**

> **Téléphonez** à vos parents.
> **Allons** à la soirée de Benjamin.
> N'**écris** pas dans tes livres.

Talking about your activities (continued)   **Voir p. 287.**

> Je **joue** souvent **au tennis.**
> Nous **jouons de la guitare** avec nos amis.
> Elles **font du deltaplane** le week-end.

Avoiding repetition (continued)   **Voir p. 289.**

> Elle invite ses amis. Elle **les** invite.
> Tu as regardé la télé. Tu **l'**as regardée.

Giving precise orders   **Voir p. 296.**

> Fais tes devoirs. **Fais-les.**
> Mangeons cette glace. **Mangeons-la.**

ÊTES-VOUS BRANCHÉS?

 Mon journal. Est-ce que les Français aiment le sport? la musique? le cinéma? Où vont-ils passer leurs vacances? Quand et où partent-ils? Dans votre journal, écrivez vos idées et impressions sur les loisirs en France, et comparez-les à vos activités et à vos vacances.

Y ÊTES-VOUS ARRIVÉS?

 A. Je peux si je veux. Dites à votre partenaire

1. trois choses que vous voulez, et dites pourquoi.
2. trois choses que vous voulez faire, et dites pourquoi.
3. trois choses que vous ne pouvez pas faire à la maison, et dites pourquoi.

B. Faites ça pour moi! Vous voulez obliger votre professeur à faire (ou ne pas faire) au moins cinq choses. Que dites-vous à votre professeur? Si vous manquez d'inspiration, utilisez la liste de verbes.

manger   préparer   aller   écouter   regarder   prendre   boire
donner   sortir   dormir   acheter   faire   mettre   être   avoir

MODÈLE: donner
> **Donnez moins d'examens, madame (monsieur)!**
> OU **Ne donnez pas d'examens, madame (monsieur)!**

 C. Ils sont très rapides! Demandez ce que les gens vont faire. Votre partenaire va répondre que c'est déjà fait. Utilisez un objet direct dans la question et un pronom objet direct dans la réponse.

MODÈLE: vous / manger
> —**Allez-vous manger ce gâteau?**
> —**Non, nous n'allons pas le manger. Nous l'avons déjà mangé!**

1. tu / regarder
2. elle / écouter
3. ils / préparer
4. nous / faire
5. vous / acheter
6. on / prendre
7. il / inviter

PRONONCIATION

LE «h» FRANÇAIS

You have already learned that certain letters in French are silent. The letter **h** is such a letter. However, there are actually two kinds of **h**'s that occur at the beginning of a word, and each is treated differently.

H muet

In French, a word beginning with **h** is usually treated as if it begins with a vowel. This is similar to English words like *honor* or *hour*. Use **liaison** (see Chapter 1, p. 42) or **élision** (see Chapter 8, p. 270) to link articles, adjectives, and numbers to words beginning with mute **h.** For example, you *must* pronounce **un homme** [œnɔm], and **l'homme** [lɔm].

1. Listen to your professor or lab tape and repeat the words below. Be sure to pronounce the articles, adjectives, numbers (**l'**, **un**, **une**, **cet**, **cette**, **mon**, **six**) to show the **h** is mute, and the word begins with a vowel sound.

un hôtel	l'hôtel	cet hôtel	mon hôtel
un hôpital	l'hôpital	cet hôpital	ton hôpital
un homme	l'homme	cet homme	vos hommes
une histoire	l'histoire	cette histoire	mes histoires
une heure	l'heure	cette heure	six heures

Pronunciation. Be sure to emphasize that **liaison** is required when the article **un** is followed by a noun beginning with a vowel sound.

H aspiré

Some words beginning with **h** are treated as though they begin with a consonant. Even though the **h** is still silent, articles, adjectives, and numbers used with the noun are pronounced as if a consonant were present.

2. Listen to your professor or lab tape and repeat the words below. Be sure to *avoid* linking these words with the consonants that precede them or dropping the vowel of the article.

la harpe	le hasard *(chance; luck)*	les haricots
la haine *(hate)*	le héros *(the hero)*	les handicapés
la Hollande	le hockey	les hors-d'œuvre

Note: In the combination **th, h** is also silent. In the words below, all **th** spellings are pronounced [t], as though **h** were not present at all.

3. Pronounce these words.

   thé   Thierry   mathématiques   bibliothèque

4. Copy the following words and fill in the missing definite article (**le, la, l'**, **les**), being careful to determine whether the word begins with **h muet** or **h aspiré.** Then say the words and their appropriate articles aloud. Listen to your professor or lab tape when you have finished to check your answers.

a. _____ hôtel   **d.** _____ hôpital   **g.** _____ héros
b. _____ hasard   **e.** _____ Hollande   **h.** _____ heure
c. _____ haricots   **f.** _____ homme   **i.** _____ hors-d'œuvre

Quelques sports et jeux *Some sports and games*

le baseball *baseball*
le basket-ball (le basket)
  basketball
les boules (f) *bocce ball; lawn*
  bowling
les cartes (f) *cards*

les dames (f) *checkers*
les échecs (m) *chess*
le football *soccer*
le football américain *football*
le golf *golf*

le hockey *hockey*
la natation *swimming*
le tennis *tennis*
le volley-ball (le volley)
  volleyball

Quelques instruments de musique *Some musical instruments*

la batterie *drums*
la guitare *guitar*

le piano *piano*
le saxophone *saxophone*

la trompette *trumpet*
le violon *violin*

Quelques lieux de vacances *Some vacation spots*

la campagne *the country(side)*
la mer *the seashore*

la montagne *the mountains*

la plage *the beach*

Pronoms objets directs

me (m') *me*
te (t') *you*
le (l') *him; it*

la (l') *her; it*
nous *us*

vous *you*
les *them*

Verbes

bavarder *to chat*
demander *to ask for*
goûter *to taste*
pouvoir *can; be able to*
remarquer *to notice*
rencontrer *to meet*
voir *to see*
vouloir *to want*
faire du deltaplane *to go hang-gliding*

faire de l'escalade *to go rock climbing*
faire de la planche à voile *to go windsurfing*
faire du rafting *to go river rafting*
faire de la randonnée *to go hiking*

faire du ski de fond *to go cross-country skiing*
faire du ski nautique *to go water skiing*
faire du VTT *to go mountain (off-road) biking*
faire de la voile *to go sailing*

Expressions de politesse

Pourrais-tu... / Pourriez-vous...
  Could you . . .
Je pourrais... *I could . . .*
(Je suis) désolé(e). *(I am) sorry.*
Je ne peux pas. *I can't.*

Ça m'est impossible pour
  l'instant. *It's impossible for me right now.*
Voudrais-tu... / Voudriez-vous...
  Would you . . .
Je voudrais... *I would like . . .*

Avec plaisir. *With pleasure.*
Je veux bien. *Yes, I would.; I gladly accept.*
Mais bien sûr. *Certainly.*
Mais certainement. *Certainly.*
Volontiers. *Gladly.*

Autres mots et expressions utiles

aïe *ouch*
un copain *pal; boyfriend*

une copine *pal; girlfriend*
peut-être *perhaps; maybe*

plutôt *instead*
zut *darn; shoot*

Chapitre 10 • UNE JOURNÉE DIFFICILE

PRÉSENTATION ÉCLAIR

POUR COMMUNIQUER

Talking about knowledge and abilities
Talking about daily activities
Giving orders (continued)
Talking about the past (continued)

POUR Y ARRIVER

Les verbes **savoir** et **connaître**
Les verbes pronominaux

Les verbes pronominaux à l'impératif
Les verbes pronominaux au passé composé

POUR S'ADAPTER À LA CULTURE

S'acheter des vêtements et des chaussures en
  France
Se faire couper les cheveux

🎧 PREMIER ÉPISODE T62

Julie sort de son cours de civilisation française. Elle rencontre son amie Florence.

JULIE: Hé, salut Florence, ça va?

FLORENCE: Pas mal, et toi?

JULIE: Moi, comme-ci, comme ça, tu sais. J'ai un partiel° avec Madame Villette la semaine prochaine. Dis, tu la connais°, toi, Madame Villette? Qu'est-ce qu'il faut savoir° pour avoir une bonne note à son examen? Franchement°, je m'inquiète° un peu, je ne sais pas trop comment me préparer à cet examen...

FLORENCE: Ne t'en fais pas!° Je la connais bien. Elle est vraiment sympa, et ses examens sont assez faciles en général.

---

partiel *midterm* / **tu la connais** *you know her* / **savoir** *to know* / **Franchement** *Frankly* / **je m'inquiète** *I worry* / **Ne t'en fais pas** *Don't worry*

AVEZ-VOUS COMPRIS?

1. Quand Julie sort de son cours, qui est-ce qu'elle rencontre?
2. Quand Julie a-t-elle un partiel? Avec quel professeur?
3. Qu'est-ce que Julie demande à Florence? Pourquoi?
4. Décrivez les examens de Madame Villette.
5. Quel exercice est-ce que Julie sait faire maintenant?
6. Faites une liste des conseils *(advice)* que Florence donne à Julie.

FLORENCE: Est-ce que tu sais par cœur° les dates qu'elle a données en cours?

JULIE: Euh, euh, un peu, je...

FLORENCE: Apprends-les bien, elle va certainement les demander. Est-ce que tu connais bien les auteurs° de la période que vous étudiez?

JULIE: J'ai lu tous les livres au programme et je pense que ça va.

FLORENCE: Est-ce que tu sais faire une explication de texte?° Elle en met toujours une à ses partiels!

JULIE: Oui, ça va beaucoup mieux; je crois que j'ai compris.

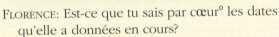

tu sais par cœur *do you know by heart* / **auteurs** *authors* / **explication de texte** *close textual analysis*

FLORENCE: Bon, alors, tout va bien, ne te fais pas de souci°. Révise° et dors bien la veille°.

JULIE: Salut, Florence, et merci pour tout!

FLORENCE: À la prochaine°. Salut!

ne te fais pas de souci *don't worry* / **Révise** *Review* / **la veille** *the night before* / **À la prochaine.** *See you later.*

Culture. French students are trained, from about age twelve on, in **explication de texte,** an exercise that requires line by line, sometimes word by word, analysis of a given literary text. It is the base necessary for students to be able to perform more complicated exercises, such as a **commentaire de textes,** often required when taking the **baccalauréat** (see. Ch 7.).

ET VOUS?

1. Indiquez trois endroits *(places)* où vous rencontrez vos amis.
2. Faites une liste des partiels ou des examens importants que vous allez passer dans les deux semaines qui viennent.
3. D'habitude, comment êtes-vous avant un examen?
4. Pour votre examen de français, qu'est-ce qu'il faut savoir? Qu'est-ce qu'il faut faire pour réussir *(to succeed)*?
5. Est-ce que vous apprenez beaucoup de choses par cœur? Pourquoi? Pourquoi pas?
6. Pour vos examens, avez-vous beaucoup de choses à lire? Est-ce que vous lisez tout ce que le professeur demande? Pourquoi ou pourquoi pas?

■ POUR COMMUNIQUER

Talking about knowledge and abilities

I   LES VERBES *SAVOIR* ET *CONNAÎTRE*

> Pour son examen, Julie **sait** beaucoup de dates par cœur.
> En général, les étudiants français **savent** faire une explication de texte.
> Tu **connais** Rouen?
> Florence **connaît** bien Mme Villette.
> Et vous, **connaissez-vous** bien vos professeurs?

◆ The verbs **savoir** (*to know a fact* or *how to do something*) and **connaître** (*to know; to be familiar with,* or *be acquainted with a person or place*) are both irregular verbs. As their translations above show, they are <u>not</u> equivalent in meaning or use.

savoir	connaître
je **sais**	je **connais**
tu **sais**	tu **connais**
il / elle / on **sait**	il / elle / on **connaît**
nous **savons**	nous **connaissons**
vous **savez**	vous **connaissez**
ils / elles **savent**	ils / elles / **connaissent**
PASSÉ COMPOSÉ	
J'ai **su**	J'ai **connu**

The **imparfait**, a past tense you will study in Chapter 11, is usually used to express past time with **savoir** and **connaître**. In the **passé composé, savoir** and **connaître** have particular meanings.

Je **savais** que Julie avait des problèmes. *I knew that Julie had some problems last year.*

J'**ai su** que Julie avait des problèmes. *I found out that Julie had some problems.*

Caroline **a connu** Benjamin en France. *Caroline met Benjamin in France.*

◆ **Savoir** is used to talk about something you know because you have learned it, something you know how to do, or a fact that you know. It is usually followed by another verb in the infinitive form, a noun designating a thing or a fact, or the word **que.**

Je **sais** nager.	*I know how to swim.; I can swim.*
Savez-vous votre numéro de sécurité sociale par cœur?	*Do you know your social security number by heart?*
Florence **sait** l'espagnol.	*Florence knows Spanish.*
Les étudiants **savent** que l'examen va être facile.	*Students know that the exam will be easy.*

◆ **Connaître** is normally used to say that you know people and places.

> **Connaissez**-vous bien la personne à côté de vous? Julie et Florence **connaissent** bien Rouen.

ACTIVITÉS

1. Qu'est-ce qu'ils savent? Dites ce que ces personnes savent ou ne savent pas.

■ MOTS À UTILISER: **dur** *hard* / **presque** *almost* / **par cœur** *by heart*

1. Est-ce que vos parents savent faire du ski?
2. Votre père sait-il parler espagnol?
3. Est-ce que votre frère / sœur sait jouer au football? au tennis? au golf?
4. Qu'est-ce que vos amis savent faire? nager? danser? parler chinois?
5. Est-ce que vos amis savent que vous travaillez dur ce semestre?
6. Savez-vous quand nous allons avoir le prochain examen de français?
7. Savez-vous presque tous vos verbes irréguliers par cœur?

 2. Et vous, quels endroits / personnes connaissez-vous? Avec votre partenaire, posez et répondez à ces questions à tour de rôle.

1. Quelle ville est-ce que tu connais bien? Quels monuments?
2. Connais-tu très bien le campus?
3. Et sur le campus, quels professeurs connais-tu bien?
4. Est-ce que tous tes professeurs te connaissent bien?
5. Est-ce que le professeur connaît tes amis? Pourquoi ou pourquoi pas?

3. Le petit futé! *The smart one!* Est-ce *savoir* ou *connaître?* À vous de faire le plus de phrases possibles. Soyez futés!

MODÈLE: **Je (ne) sais (pas) le numéro de mes amis par cœur.**
  OU **Je (ne) connais (pas) bien tes parents.**

je		l'adresse d'un bon restaurant
tu		parler bien l'espagnol
mes parents	savoir	la ville de Paris
mes amis et moi	connaître	danser
vous		que l'examen final est bientôt
le professeur		beaucoup de verbes français par cœur
		ces gens

 4. À vous! Maintenant, c'est à vous de poser quelques questions à votre partenaire.

Find out if your partner knows
1. five people in the class very well.
2. how old they are.
3. the city of Paris.
4. monuments in his/her own city. If so, which monuments?
5. what time the bookstore closes on campus.
6. the address of a good restaurant close to campus.

DEUXIÈME ÉPISODE

Aujourd'hui, Julie a une journée bien chargée°. Elle a un partiel demain et l'anniversaire de sa mère dans deux semaines. Il faut trouver un cadeau!° Il n'y pas de temps à perdre°. Voilà comment elle organise sa journée.

Il est cinq heures du matin, et Julie se réveille° avec difficulté. Elle se lève°. Il fait encore noir. Alors, elle prend ses notes et commence à étudier au lit.

Vers sept heures, elle entend Caroline qui se prépare pour aller à l'université.

---

bien chargée *very busy* / **cadeau** *present* / **perdre** *to lose* / **se réveille** *wakes up* / **se lève** *gets up*

Alors, Julie se lève, elle se lave°, elle s'habille°, elle se brosse° les dents et les cheveux, et puis elle se maquille°. Caroline et Julie prennent le petit déjeuner ensemble. Elles mangent et parlent de leur emploi du temps°.

Caroline suggère une nouvelle boutique près de la maison qui a de beaux vêtements pour la mère de Julie.

Maintenant, Julie se dépêche° d'arriver en cours à l'heure. À l'université, tout va bien. Elle finit son dernier cours à cinq heures.

---

se lave *washes (up)* / **s'habille** *gets dressed* / **se brosse** *brushes* / **se maquille** *puts on her make-up* / **emploi du temps** *schedule* / **se dépêche** *hurries*

AVEZ-VOUS COMPRIS?

1. Expliquez pourquoi la journée de Julie est chargée.
2. À quelle heure est-ce qu'elle se réveille? Où étudie-t-elle?
3. Citez trois choses que Julie fait avant d'aller à l'université.
4. À quelle heure Julie sort-elle de l'université? Où va-t-elle? Pourquoi?
5. Quelle sorte de vêtement est-ce que Julie achète pour sa mère?
6. Faites une liste des choses que Julie fait quand elle rentre chez elle.

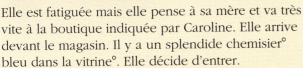

Elle est fatiguée mais elle pense à sa mère et va très vite à la boutique indiquée par Caroline. Elle arrive devant le magasin. Il y a un splendide chemisier° bleu dans la vitrine°. Elle décide d'entrer.

JULIE: Bonjour Madame, je voudrais voir le chemisier bleu qui est dans la vitrine.

LA VENDEUSE°: Mais, bien sûr Mademoiselle, en quelle taille?°

JULIE: Je ne sais pas exactement, c'est pour ma mère. Nous portons la même taille.

LA VENDEUSE: Eh bien, un 42, je pense. Voulez-vous l'essayer?°

JULIE: Volontiers! (pendant l'essayage) Ah oui, ma mère va l'adorer! Je le prends!

---

chemisier *blouse* / **vitrine** *store window* / **vendeuse** *saleswoman* / **taille** *size* / **essayer** *to try on*

Encore cinq minutes, et la voilà rentrée à la maison! Ouf, la journée est finie, enfin presque... Il faut encore étudier pour demain. Julie et Caroline dînent; elles se parlent un petit moment, puis chacune° s'enferme° dans sa chambre pour étudier. Vers minuit, Julie se couche° et s'endort°. Quelle journée!

---

chacune *each of them* / **s'enferme** *shuts herself* / **se couche** *gets into bed* / **s'endort** *falls asleep*

ET VOUS?

1. Le professeur se lève à sept heures. Et vous? À quelle heure vous levez-vous? Je me lève...

2. Est-ce que vous étudiez au lit quelquefois? Pourquoi ou pourquoi pas?

3. À l'université, quels sont vos jours chargés? Arrivez-vous toujours en classe à l'heure? Pour quel(s) cours êtes-vous quelquefois en retard?

4. Où allez-vous dîner ce soir? À quelle heure?

5. Après le dîner, qu'est-ce que vous allez faire?

313

VOUS ÊTES BRANCHÉS!

S'acheter des vêtements et des chaussures en France

When traveling or living in France, you may want to purchase some new clothes and shoes. The French use a different system of sizes for both items. Whether you are being asked what your clothing size is **(Quelle est votre taille?)**, or what your shoe size is **(Quelle est votre pointure?)**, you need to be somewhat familiar with European sizing. Look at the following charts and figure out your French size.

Femmes: robes, jupes, et chemisiers

France	36	38	40	42	44	46
USA	⁵⁄₆	⁷⁄₈	⁹⁄₁₀	¹¹⁄₁₂	¹³⁄₁₄	¹⁵⁄₁₆

Femmes: chaussures

France	36½	37	37½	38	39	40	41	42
USA	5	5½	6	6½	7½	8½	9	10

Hommes: costumes *(suits)*

France	36	38	40	42	44	46
USA	35	36	37	38	39	40

Hommes: chemises

France	37	38	39	40	41	42
USA	14½	15	15½	16	16½	17

Hommes: chaussures

France	41	42	43	44	45
USA	7½	8½	9	10	11

Les soldes.

Young French people like casual American-style clothes very much, whereas the older generation still prefers more formal and classic attire. Like American consumers, the French look for value and often for **soldes** *(sales)*. For those interested in **la haute couture** *(high fashion)*, Paris is home to many famous **couturiers** *(fashion designers)*.

Whether you are looking for bargains or a particular style, you are now ready for shopping for shoes and clothes in France.

VOTRE Q. I. CULTUREL

Qu'en pensez-vous? Choisissez les réponses appropriées.

1. Vous voulez acheter une paire de chaussures. Quelle est la question que la vendeuse va vous poser?
   a. Comment vous appelez-vous?
   b. Quelle est votre taille?
   c. Quelle est votre pointure?

2. Aux États-Unis, quand vous achetez des chaussures (homme 8½, femme 10), quelle est votre pointure en France?
   a. 40   b. 41   c. 42

http://www.wiley.com/aventure.html

3. Si vous n'êtes pas riche et si vous avez besoin de vêtements, que cherchez-vous?
   a. des soldes?
   b. de la haute couture?
   c. une boutique chic?

 Expliquez l'essentiel à votre partenaire. Choisissez un sujet et allez-y! Votre partenaire va accepter votre explication, la modifier ou y ajouter quelques détails.

1. Un client entre dans votre boutique et regarde les vêtements. Quelle question lui posez-vous pour savoir sa taille?
2. Décrivez le type de vêtements que les jeunes Français aiment porter. Comparez-les aux vêtements que vous aimez porter.

■ POUR COMMUNIQUER

Talking about daily activities

II   LES VERBES PRONOMINAUX

Julie **se lève** à cinq heures du matin pour étudier.
Quand ils ont des examens, les étudiants ne **se parlent** pas.
Est-ce que **vous vous dépêchez d'**arriver à l'heure?
Vous préférez **vous habiller** en jean ou en robe?

◆ When you learned how to introduce yourself, you mastered your first **verbe pronominal. Je m'appelle...** is a form of the verb **s'appeler.** All **verbes pronominaux** include the pronoun **se (s')** in the infinitive.

   s'appeler   se parler   se laver

◆ When **verbes pronominaux** are conjugated, pronouns that agree with the subject pronoun are used. These are called *reflexive pronouns.*

se laver	s'habiller
je **me lave**	je **m'habille**
tu **te laves**	tu **t'habilles**
il / elle / on **se lave**	il / elle / on **s'habille**
nous **nous lavons**	nous nous **habillons**
vous **vous lavez**	vous vous **habillez**
ils / elles **se lavent**	ils / elles **s'habillent**

Note: When the verb starts with a vowel sound, the pronouns **me, te, se** become **m', t', s'.**

◆ There are three kinds of **verbes pronominaux: réfléchi, réciproque,** and **idiomatique.**

1. If you do something *to* or *for yourself,* use a **verbe pronominal réfléchi.**

Je **me lève** tous les jours à six heures.	*I get up every day at six.*
Tu **te laves** et tu **te brosses** les dents.	*You wash (yourself) and you brush your teeth.*
Nous **nous maquillons** tous les jours.	*We put on make-up every day.*

Note: Verbs like **se lever** have accent changes when conjugated (see Chapter 5, p. 163): Elle se lève.

2. When two or more people do something *to* or *for each other,* a **verbe pronominal réciproque** is used.

Nous **nous parlons** français.	*We speak French to each other.*
Ils **se retrouvent** à la cafétéria.	*They meet (each other) in the cafeteria.*

3. You may also use **verbes pronominaux idiomatiques.** These verbs do not fit in either of the categories above. Some of the common ones are **s'amuser** *(to have fun),* **s'appeler** *(to be called),* **se dépêcher (de)** *(to hurry),* **s'inquiéter** *(to worry),* **se trouver** *(to be located).*

Nous **nous inquiétons** quand nos amis sont en retard.
Dans la classe, on **s'amuse** bien.

◆ To ask a question using a **verbe pronominal,** most people place **est-ce que** in front of it or use intonation. With inversion, the reflexive pronoun still precedes the verb, but the subject follows it.

Est-ce que **vous vous dépêchez** souvent?
Vous vous dépêchez souvent?
Quand **vous dépêchez-vous?**

◆ If you want to make a sentence negative in the present tense, place **ne** just before the reflexive pronoun and **pas** after the verb. Follow the rule you learned with direct object pronouns, p. 291.

Je **ne** me lève **pas** à cinq heures du matin!
Vous **ne** vous amusez **pas** pendant les examens.

◆ When you use a **verbe pronominal** in the infinitive form with another verb, make sure that the reflexive pronoun agrees with the subject of the sentence.

Lundi prochain, **je** vais **me** lever à 6 heures.
Le professeur n'aime pas **se** coucher à minuit!
Après une semaine difficile, **nous** avons besoin de **nous** amuser.

◆ When you use a **verbe pronominal** with part of the body, use the definite article, not the possessive adjective as in English.

Je me lave **les** mains.	*I wash <u>my</u> hands.*
Elle se brosse **les** dents.	*She brushes <u>her</u> teeth.*

Comment parler de ses actions

s'amuser	*to have fun*	se laver	*to wash (up)*
se brosser les dents / les cheveux	*to brush one's teeth/hair*	se lever	*to get up*
se coiffer	*to comb; to set one's hair*	se maquiller	*to put make-up on*
se coucher	*to go to bed*	se parfumer	*to put perfume on*
se dépêcher (de)	*to hurry*	se parler	*to speak to each other*
se déshabiller	*to get undressed*	se préparer	*to get ready*
se disputer (avec)	*to argue*	se promener	*to take a walk*
s'embrasser	*to kiss*	se raser	*to shave*
s'habiller	*to get dressed*	se réveiller	*to wake up*
s'inquiéter	*to worry*	se téléphoner	*to call each other*

ACTIVITÉS ─────────────────────────────── `T64`

5. Qu'est-ce qu'ils font? Décrivez les actions des personnes suivantes.

MODÈLE: **Elle se réveille.**

elle

1. ils

2. je

3. nous

4. elles

5. vous

6. elle

7. tu

8. nous

9. il

10. elles

Preparation. To make students more comfortable with **Activité 6,** remind them that they may tell the truth or invent their answers as they see fit.

6. Mais ils ne font pas ça! Votre amie décrit ce que ses parents et ses amis font. Comparez leurs habitudes avec les habitudes de votre famille et de vos amis.

MODÈLE: Mon père se lève à cinq heures du matin.
Pas chez moi, mon père ne se lève pas à cinq heures. Il se lève à...
OU **Chez moi aussi, mon père se lève à cinq heures du matin.**

1. Ma mère se coiffe souvent.
2. Mon père se promène le week-end.
3. Moi, je m'amuse dans ma chambre.
4. Le matin, je m'habille en trente minutes et, le soir, je me déshabille en trente secondes.
5. Je me prépare un sandwich au jambon tous les jours.
6. Ma sœur (mon amie) et moi, nous nous disputons constamment.

7. Et ce week-end, qu'est-ce que vous allez faire? Vous parlez à votre meilleur(e) ami(e). Dites-lui ce que les gens que vous connaissez vont faire ce week-end.

MODÈLE: **Je vais me lever à midi!**
OU **Je ne vais pas m'habiller élégamment.**

je		se réveiller à midi
ma mère		s'embrasser gentiment
mon / ma petit(e) ami(e)		s'habiller élégamment
et moi, nous		se parler pendant une heure
mon mari / ma femme	aller	s'amuser
mes parents		se disputer
mon professeur de français		se téléphoner
papa et moi		se coucher tard
ma fille / mon fils		s'inquiéter comme toujours
		se promener
		se parfumer
		se dépêcher pour aller au cinéma

 8. Et votre routine? Demandez à votre partenaire de répondre à quelques questions.

1. À quelle heure te lèves-tu pendant la semaine? et pendant le week-end?
2. Est-ce que tu te maquilles / te rases tous les jours?
3. Aimes-tu te maquiller? te raser? te parfumer?
4. À quelle heure préfères-tu te coucher?
5. Aimes-tu t'amuser ou préfères-tu travailler?
6. Ce week-end, vas-tu sortir? Où? Avec qui?
7. Vas-tu t'habiller élégamment? Si oui, que vas-tu porter?

Follow-up. After students complete **Activité 8,** have them repeat or comment on the information their partner gives.

 9. De vrais jumeaux. *True twins.* Find two people in the class that . . .

1. get up the same time you do.
2. brush their teeth the same number of times you brush your teeth a day.
3. go to bed at the same time you go to bed at night.
4. love to have fun.

Tout est calme, tranquille dans l'appartement. Caroline dort bien dans sa chambre et Julie ronfle° dans la sienne°. Le radio-réveil° de Julie se met en marche°: «...Bonjour, il est huit heures et voilà les dernières nouvelles...»

———

ronfle *is snoring* / **la sienne** *hers* / **radio-reveil** *clock-radio* / **se met en marche** *starts up*

Caroline se réveille. Elle se lève et se met à° faire du café. Elle se prépare une tartine° et commence à la manger quand, tout à coup, elle se met à réfléchir°:

CAROLINE: Mais, c'est mercredi aujourd'hui. C'est bizarre... je n'ai pas entendu° Julie ce matin, et elle a son partiel à neuf heures... Non, ce n'est pas possible. Elle ne s'est pas...

———

se met à *begins to* / **une tartine** *bread and butter* / **réfléchir** *think* / **je n'ai pas entendu** *I didn't hear*

AVEZ-VOUS COMPRIS?

1. Où se trouvent Caroline et Julie au début de l'épisode? Que font-elles?
2. Qu'est-ce que Caroline fait quand elle se réveille?
3. Caroline remarque que Julie est encore au lit. Quelle est sa réaction? Que fait-elle?
4. Quelle est la première réaction de Julie? Et après quelques minutes?
5. Pourquoi est-ce que Julie a besoin de se dépêcher?
6. À votre avis, va-t-elle pouvoir arriver à l'heure pour son examen? Pourquoi ou pourquoi pas?

◆ To form the future tense, you usually only need to add the future endings **(ai, as, a, ons, ez, ont)** to the infinitive. **Note:** all future stems end in **-r;** if the verb in the infinitive ends in **-re,** drop the **e.**

Le futur	
INVITER	ATTENDRE
j'inviter**ai**	j'attendr**ai**
tu inviter**as**	tu attendr**as**
il / elle / on inviter**a**	il / elle / on attendr**a**
nous inviter**ons**	nous attendr**ons**
vous inviter**ez**	vous attendr**ez**
ils / elles inviter**ont**	ils / elles attendr**ont**

◆ Some future stems are irregular. Here are the most common ones:

Irregular future stems					
infinitive	*future stem*	*future tense*	*infinitive*	*future stem*	*future tense*
aller	**ir-**	j'**irai**	pouvoir	**pourr-**	je **pourrai**
avoir	**aur-**	j'**aurai**	savoir	**saur-**	je **saurai**
être	**ser-**	je **serai**	venir	**viendr-**	je **viendrai**
faire	**fer-**	je **ferai**	vouloir	**voudr-**	je **voudrai**
pleuvoir	**pleuvr-**	il **pleuvra**			

Note: The future of the expression **il faut** is **il faudra;** the infinitive of the verb is **falloir.**

◆ To express a hypothesis, use a **si** *(if)* construction. When the main clause contains the future tense, the verb in the **si** clause is generally in the *present* tense. As in English, the **si** clause can either begin or end the sentence.

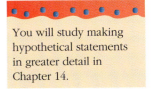
You will study making hypothetical statements in greater detail in Chapter 14.

Si nous **allons** au laboratoire, nous **aurons** une bonne note.
Tu **comprendras** le professeur **si** tu **fais** attention.

◆ In contrast to English, which often uses the present tense to express a future action, French uses the *future* tense to express future actions after the following words.

quand	*when*
lorsque	*when*
aussitôt que	*as soon as*
dès que	*as soon as*

Quand and **lorsque** are used interchangeably to mean *when,* and **dès que** and **aussitôt que** are used interchangeably to mean *as soon as.*

Quand nos parents **arriveront,** nous mangerons.

When *our parents* **arrive,** *we will eat.*

Les étudiants seront contents **lorsqu**'ils **auront** un «A».	*The students will be happy **when** they **get** an "A".*
Aussitôt qu'elle **saura** sa leçon, elle ira jouer.	***As soon as** she **knows** her lesson, she'll go play.*
Vous regarderez la télévision **dès que** vous **terminerez** la vaisselle.	*You'll watch TV **as soon as** you **finish** the dishes.*

POUR S'EXPRIMER

Quelques expressions qui indique ce que l'on va faire plus tard

après demain	*(the) day after tomorrow*
dans... jours / ans	*in . . . days/years*
le jour prochain	*the next day*
le lendemain	*the next day*
l'année prochaine	*next year/the following year*

ACTIVITÉS

1. Que vont-ils faire et quand? Racontez les activités des personnes mentionnées et décidez du moment où elles vont les accomplir.

MODÈLE: **Nous partirons en vacances dans quatre jours.**

je	partir en vacances	demain
ma mère	faire les courses	dans... mois
mes amis	passer un examen	le mois prochain
tu	voyager en France	dans... an(s) / mois
nous	prendre l'avion	après-demain
vous	rendre les compositions	la semaine prochaine
	aller au concert	le lendemain

 2. Si je peux, je le ferai. Pendant le week-end, vos ami(e)s vous demandent de faire beaucoup de choses, mais vous êtes réaliste, vous n'avez pas beaucoup de temps. Avec un(e) partenaire, jouez les rôles.

MODÈLE: Si tu as le temps, (aller) _____-tu au cinéma avec nous?
   —**Si tu as le temps, iras-tu au cinéma avec nous?**
   —**Oui, si j'ai le temps, j'irai au cinéma avec vous.**

1. Si tu n'as pas d'examen, (venir) _____-tu passer le week-end?
2. Si tes parents te donnent la voiture pour le week-end, (faire) _____-nous un petit voyage ensemble?
3. Si tu peux, (aller) _____-nous en Ardèche?
4. Si ton meilleur ami veut venir, tu (être) _____ content(e), non?
5. Si tes autres copains sont libres, est-ce qu'ils (vouloir) _____ venir avec nous?

406   quatre cent six   **Chapitre 13**

6. Si les guides sont là, est-ce qu'ils (savoir) _____ quoi faire en cas de problème?

7. S'il fait beau, nous (passer) _____ un week-end superbe, n'est-ce pas?

3. Dans la mesure du possible. Tout le monde fait ce qu'il peut dans la mesure de ses possibilités. Soyez logique et dites ce qu'ils font.

■ MOT À UTILISER: **besoins** *needs*

MODÈLE: je / avoir le temps / aller au cinéma.
> **Si j'ai le temps, j'irai au cinéma.**

tu / acheter un billet / prendre le train
> **Si tu achètes un billet, tu prendras le train.**

1. nous / avoir de l'argent / aller au théâtre.
2. vous / gagner à la loterie / partir au Sénégal
3. tu / faire vite tes bagages / pouvoir prendre l'avion
4. tes amis / avoir le temps / venir à la maison
5. Benjamin / aimer Caroline / lui téléphoner
6. vos parents / comprendre vos besoins / vous donner de l'argent
7. je / arriver à l'heure / partir tôt
8. ton / ta meilleur(e) ami(e) / avoir une bonne note / t'inviter au restaurant

4. Chez la voyante. *At the fortune teller.* Vous êtes voyante. Dites ce que vous voyez dans votre boule de cristal à votre partenaire, et il / elle vous dira s'il / si elle pense vous avez raison ou tort.

■ MOTS À UTILISER: **prendre sa retraite** *to retire*

MODÈLE: Quand vous (passer) le prochain examen de français, vous...
> —**Quand vous passerez le prochain examen de français, vous aurez une bonne note.**
> —**Je pense que vous avez raison. J'aurai une très bonne note.**

Lorsque vous (avoir) un peu plus d'argent...
> —**Lorsque vous aurez un peu plus d'argent, vous me le donnerez.**
> —**Je pense que vous avez tort. Je ferai un long voyage.**

1. Quand il (pleuvoir), vous...
2. Lorsque vous (avoir) quarante-cinq ans, vous...
3. Dès que vous (parler), votre fiancé(e), vous...
4. Aussitôt que vous (se marier), vous...
5. Quand vous (avoir) des triplés, vous...
6. Lorsque vous (aller) au mariage de vos enfants, vous...
7. Dès que vous (prendre) votre retraite, vous...
8. Quand vous (être) vieux / vieille, vous...
9. Lorsqu'il (falloir) partir, nous...

Grammar. Before doing **Activité 4,** remind students of the meanings of **quand, aussitôt que, dès que,** and **lorsque** and of the need to use the future tense with them when you describe an action taking place in the future.

DEUXIÈME ÉPISODE [T 76]

Tout le groupe est arrivé. Les guides et les membres du groupe font connaissance°. Benjamin parle aux deux guides du groupe, Georges et Christiane. Pendant ce temps Caroline est en grande conversation avec Marie-Paule, une Guadeloupéenne qui fait des études de sciences-politiques à Paris.

font connaissance *meet*

CAROLINE: Tu sais, j'aime beaucoup ton maillot de bain°. Il est vraiment super et on risque de tomber à l'eau. Alors, mieux vaut être à l'aise!°

MARIE-PAULE: Je vais te dire un petit secret... Je fais toujours très attention quand je choisis° mes maillots de bain. Je les achète dans une petite boutique près de la fac. Ils ont toujours des modèles extras!

CAROLINE: Il faut que tu me donnes l'adresse. J'ai besoin d'un nouveau maillot. Je viens de finir un régime°; j'ai maigri° un peu, un petit kilo, mais je ne sais pas si je réussirai° à résister aux tentations ce week-end! Au fait°, est-ce que tu es contente à Paris... de la fac? de tes profs?

maillot de bain *bathing suit* / **mieux vaut être à l'aise** *it's better to be comfortable* / **choisis** *choose* / **régime** *diet* / **j'ai maigri** *I lost weight* / **réussirai** *will succeed* / **au fait** *by the way*

AVEZ-VOUS COMPRIS?

1. Faites une liste des personnages de cet épisode. Résumez ce que vous savez sur chaque personne.
2. Décrivez la réaction de Caroline vis à vis du maillot de bain de Marie-Paule. Que veut-elle savoir?
3. Qu'est-ce que Caroline vient de finir? De quoi a-t-elle besoin? De quoi a-t-elle peur ce week-end?
4. Décrivez Caroline et Benjamin quand les bateaux partent.

Benjamin est maintenant en train de charger° les bateaux... Christiane finit d'y attacher les tentes.

CHRISTIANE: Tu sais, elle est vraiment sympa ta copine. Vous sortez ensemble depuis longtemps?°

Benjamin rougit° comme une tomate.

BENJAMIN: Euh, eh bien euh... *(Il ne sait pas quoi dire.)* Je l'aime... beaucoup... Je la connais depuis le début de l'année scolaire.

CHRISTIANE: Vous avez beaucoup de chance! Allez les enfants, on monte, on va y aller!

---

charger *to load* / **depuis lontemps** *for a long time* / **rougit** *turns red; blushes*

Les deux bateaux commencent à descendre la rivière. Benjamin et Caroline sont assis l'un à côté de l'autre. Ils se sourient°.

---

se sourient *are smiling at each other*

ET VOUS?

1. Quels vêtements portez-vous pour faire du rafting ou pour faire du canoë?
2. Faites-vous du régime quelquefois? En général, quand et pourquoi?
3. Connaissez-vous beaucoup de gens qui font du régime? À votre avis, pourquoi en font-ils? Est-ce toujours justifié?
4. Quels types de questions posez-vous à quelqu'un que vous ne connaissez pas bien?

POUR COMMUNIQUER

Talking about your activities (continued)

II **LES VERBES EN -*IR***

> Je **choisis** de faire un voyage en bateau.
> Benjamin **rougit** comme une tomate.
> Ils **finissent** de préparer les bateaux.
> J'**ai maigri** mais je ne sais pas si je **réussirai** à résister aux tentations ce week-end.

You have already learned two groups of regular verbs in French **-er** and **-re** verbs. The third and final group of regular verbs you will study are **-ir** verbs.

◆ To form the present tense of regular **-ir** verbs, drop the **-ir** from the infinitive and add the following endings: **is, is, it, issons, issez, issent.**

choisir (to choose)	
je chois**is**	nous chois**issons**
tu chois**is**	vous chois**issez**
il / elle / on chois**it**	ils / elles chois**issent**

> **Review.** Remember that verbs like **partir, sortir, dormir, servir,** and **se sentir** are *not* regular **-ir** verbs.

◆ In the **passé composé,** conjugate **-ir** verbs with **avoir** and make their past participle by dropping **-ir** from the infinitive and adding **-i.**

> J'**ai** chois**i** un maillot de bain rouge.
> La semaine dernière, nous **avons** réuss**i** à l'examen.

◆ In the **imparfait,** use the **nous** form of the present tense, drop **-ons,** and add the **imparfait** endings.

> Nous obéiss**ions** *(obeyed)* à nos parents quand nous étions enfants.
> Pendant le cours, les étudiants réféchiss**aient** *(thought)* beaucoup.

POUR S'EXPRIMER	
Quelques verbes utiles	
choisir (de + infinitif)	*to choose*
désobéir (à quelqu'un / quelque chose)	*to disobey (someone/something)*
finir (de + infinitif)	*to finish*
grandir	*to grow up*
grossir	*to put on weight*
maigrir	*to lose weight*

Tell students that many **-ir** verbs indicate a state of "becoming" and give examples such as **noircir, vieillir, blanchir,** and **verdir.**

Quelques verbes utiles	
obéir (à quelqu'un / quelque chose)	*to obey (someone/something)*
punir	*to punish*
réfléchir (à quelque chose)	*to think about (something); to ponder*
réussir (à un examen, à + infinitif)	*to succeed*
rougir	*to blush; to turn red*

ACTIVITÉS

5. Que font-ils? Décrivez les actions des personnes suivantes et faites les changements nécessaires.

MODÈLE: **Je choisis des livres intéressants.**

je	obéir	les devoirs de français
ma mère / mon père	grossir	pendant les vacances
mon / ma meilleur(e) ami(e)	choisir	à la question
un étudiant timide	grandir	quand c'est nécessaire
mes parents	réfléchir	des livres intéressants
tu	rougir	en classe
ma sœur et moi, nous	punir	à ses parents
vous	finir	après les vacances
un enfant	maigrir	tout le temps
mes enfants	désobéir	à l'examen
mon mari / ma femme	réussir	quelquefois

6. Interview. Posez quelques questions à votre partenaire et soyez prêt à raconter ce que vous savez aux autres membres de la classe.

1. Quels cours choisis-tu en général? Pourquoi?
2. As-tu beaucoup de devoirs? Est-ce que tu les finis toujours?
3. Dans quel(s) cours réfléchis-tu beaucoup ce semestre?
4. Quand ton chien mange le steak de tes parents, est-ce qu'ils le punissent?
5. À la maison, est-ce que tes parents te punissaient quand tu étais petit(e)? Comment?
6. Pendant les vacances, est-ce que tu maigris ou grossis? Pourquoi?
7. Dans ta famille, est-ce qu'il y a une personne qui maigrit ou grossit souvent? À ton avis, pourquoi?
8–9. Posez deux autres questions.

TROISIÈME ÉPISODE T 77

Les bateaux glissent lentement° sur la rivière. Il fait un temps splendide. Caroline et Benjamin se sourient gentiment. Benjamin a envie de prendre la main de Caroline mais il n'ose pas°. Soudain, ses pensées° sont vite interrompues.

———

glissent lentement *glide slowly along* / **il n'ose pas** *he doesn't dare* / **pensées** *thoughts*

CHRISTIANE: Attention tout le monde, on arrive aux rapides! Devant eux, l'eau qui était si calme il y a dix minutes bouillonne°, le courant s'accélère... Caroline prend le bras de Benjamin. Elle n'a pas vraiment peur, mais elle n'est pas vraiment tranquille non plus...

CAROLINE: C'est incroyable! Aïe, aïe, aïe, ça va vite...

———

bouillonne *is swirling and bubbling*

AVEZ-VOUS COMPRIS?

1. Décrivez la rivière quand le voyage commence.
2. À votre avis, pourquoi est-ce que Benjamin n'ose pas prendre la main de Caroline?
3. Quelle est la réaction de Caroline quand elle voit les rapides?
4. Expliquez pourquoi les sacs tombent à l'eau.
5. Pourquoi Christiane dit-elle à Benjamin d'attendre?
6. Après l'accident, est-ce que tout va bien? Expliquez.

Les bagages mal attachés commencent à bouger°
dangeureusement.

CAROLINE: Oh, mon Dieu, Benjamin. Regarde la
corde qui retient° nos affaires, elle va casser!°
Au moment où Caroline finit sa phrase, la corde
casse. Voilà le sac de couchage de Caroline, une
tente, et le sac à dos de Benjamin à l'eau! Benjamin
essaie de les attraper.

---

bouger *move around* / **la corde qui retient** *the rope that
is holding* / **casser** *break*

CHRISTIANE: Benjamin, attends deux minutes, on
retrouvera tout ça plus bas°. C'est trop
dangereux ici...

Quelques instants plus tard, ils retrouvent une
rivière calme et tranquille et... deux sacs qui flottent
devant eux. Benjamin saute° du bateau. À la nage,
il ramène° son sac à dos et la tente vers le bateau.

BENJAMIN: Georges, où est le troisième sac?
GEORGES: Il n'est pas là. Ça, ce n'est pas bon signe!
Il a dû couler°. Qu'est-ce qu'il y avait dedans?°
CAROLINE: Je pense que c'était mon sac de
couchage! Zut! Je vais dormir dans quoi ce soir?

---

plus bas *lower down* / **saute** *jumps* / **ramène** *brings
back* / **couler** *sunk* / **dedans** *inside*

ET VOUS?

1. Quand vous partez en vacances, cherchez-vous l'aventure ou le calme? Pourquoi?
2. Comment allez-vous passer vos prochaines vacances?
3. Préférez-vous passer vos vacances seul(e)? Avec un ou quelques amis? Avec un groupe? Quels sont les
   avantages, les inconvénients de chaque option?
4. Avez-vous eu des difficultés la dernière fois que vous êtes parti(e) en vacances? Si oui, décrivez-les. Si
   non, imaginez quelques problèmes possibles.

Le sac de couchage de Caroline est tombé à l'eau. Comment va-t-elle faire pour dormir ce soir?
    Elle devrait

a. dire au guide de trouver un autre sac pour elle.
b. partager *(share)* un sac avec Marie-Paule.
c. se coucher sans *(without)* sac de couchage.
d. Avez-vous une autre solution?

Justifiez votre réponse.

À VOUS DE JOUER

Vous venez de faire un voyage en avion. Quand vous arrivez à l'aéroport, votre valise n'est pas là. Que faites-vous?
    Moi, je (j')

a. attends un peu pour voir si elle arrive.
b. vais à ma destination sans bagages.
c. demande aux employés de la ligne aérienne de m'aider à chercher ma valise.
d. Avez-vous une autre solution?

Justifiez votre réponse.

VOUS ÊTES BRANCHÉS!

Un rendez-vous avec la préhistoire

For a history buff interested in prehistoric paintings, the Chauvet Cave in the Ardèche is a dream come true. This recent discovery holds one of the most exciting prehistoric finds to date.

In early 1995, Jean-Marie Chauvet, a Culture Ministry official monitoring prehistoric remains, walked into a cave and found some three hundred animal paintings and other artifacts. Left undiscovered for nearly 15,000 years, the **grotte** contains works that are still in excellent condition and that challenge our former conception of prehistoric art. In comparable sites, like Lascaux in France or Altamira in Spain, specialists have discovered paintings that generally depict animals hunted by prehistoric peoples—animals

Peinture préhistorique dans la grotte Chauvet.

such as **des bisons** *(bison)* and **des chevaux** *(horses)*. Here, in the Chauvet Cave, art experts are able to admire and study depictions of **des ours** *(bears)*, **des félins** *(felines)*, and **des rhinocéros** *(rhinoceroses)*, which were not part of the sustenance of early peoples and which were very rarely drawn on cave walls.

Although the significance of this find will take years to establish, and the public will be kept out of the site to preserve it, this discovery may eventually allow us to gain valuable insight into the culture, belief systems, and lives of our ancestors.

VOTRE Q. I. CULTUREL

Qu'en pensez-vous? Choisissez les réponses appropriées.

1. Qu'est-ce que Jean-Marie Chauvet a découvert?
2. Quelles sortes d'animaux est-ce que les peintures représentent?
3. Qui sera autorisé à entrer dans la grotte? le public? les scientifiques? Pourquoi?

 Expliquez l'essentiel à votre partenaire. Choisissez un sujet et allez-y! Votre partenaire va accepter votre explication, la modifier ou y ajouter quelques détails.

1. Citez d'autres grottes qui renferment *(hold)* des peintures préhistoriques.
2. Expliquez en quoi cette grotte et les peintures qu'elle contient sont différentes des autres.
3. À votre avis, quel est l'intêret de cette découverte?

Un bison

http://www.wiley.com/aventure.html

◼ POUR COMMUNIQUER

Describing your actions

III LES ADVERBES

> Caroline et Benjamin se sourient **gentiment.**
> Les bagages commencent à bouger **dangereusement.**
> **Aujourd'hui** nous allons visiter les gorges de l'Ardèche.

◆ Sometimes you want to give a little more information about how someone does something, or how often, when, or where an action is done. To express yourself more precisely, use an adverb to tell more about the verb.

Caroline n'a pas **vraiment** peur.	*Caroline isn't really afraid.*
J'ai mis votre sac **là-bas** près des autres.	*I put your bag over there by the others.*

◆ You may use adverbs such as **très, vraiment,** and **assez** to modify verbs, adjectives, and other adverbs.

Le guide explique **très gentiment** ce qu'il faut faire.	*The guide very nicely explains what needs to be done.*
Cette jeune femme est **vraiment** belle.	*That young woman is really pretty.*
Benjamin nage **assez bien.**	*Benjamin swims fairly well.*

◆ Regular adverbs may be formed by taking the feminine form of the adjective and adding **-ment.**

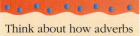

lent	lente + ment	⟶ **lentement**
sérieux	sérieuse + ment	⟶ **sérieusement**
actif	active + ment	⟶ **activement**
tranquille	tranquille + ment	⟶ **tranquillement**
Exception:	**gentil** + ment	⟶ **gentiment**

◆ For adjectives that end in a vowel, add **-ment** directly to the adjective without changing it to its feminine form.

tendre + ment	⟶ **tendrement**
absolu + ment	⟶ **absolument**
vrai + ment	⟶ **vraiment**
Exception: fou + ment	⟶ **follement**

◆ To form an adverb from an adjective ending in **-ant** or **-ent,** drop the **-nt,** then add **-mment.**

constant	constant + -mment	⟶ **constamment**
intelligent	intelligent + -mment	⟶ **intelligemment**

◆ Some adverbs are not formed directly from an adjective.

bon	**bien**
mauvais	**mal**
petit	**peu**

Caroline parle **bien** l'anglais.	*Caroline speaks English well.*
Le voyage a **mal** commencé.	*The trip started out badly.*
Benjamin a très **peu** mangé parce qu'il n'avait pas faim.	*Benjamin ate very little because he wasn't hungry.*

◆ Other adverbs have no relation to adjectives at all. Some of them are

assez	déjà	hier	souvent
aujourd'hui	demain	là-bas	très

◆ Adverbs that modify verbs are typically placed after the conjugated verb. In the **passé composé,** this is true of the short common adverbs (**déjà, mal, souvent**) which come between **être** or **avoir** and the past participle, but adverbs that end in **-ment** often follow the past participle.

Benjamin pense **constamment** à Caroline.
Elle a **déjà** accepté son invitation.
Caroline a répondu **lentement.**

◆ Adverbs of time often come at the beginning or end of a sentence.

Aujourd'hui nous descendons les rapides.
Elles ont fait les valises **hier.**

POUR S'EXPRIMER			
Quelques adverbes de manière et de lieu			
MANIÈRE			
absolument	*absolutely*	lentement	*slowly*
confortablement	*comfortably*	poliment	*politely*
constamment	*constantly*	rapidement	*rapidly*
difficilement	*with difficulty*	régulièrement	*regularly*
facilement	*easily*	sérieusement	*seriously*
follement	*madly*	tendrement	*tenderly*
fréquemment	*frequently*	tranquillement	*calmly*
gentiment	*nicely*	vraiment	*really, truly*
intelligemment	*intelligently*		
LIEU			
dehors	*outside*	ici	*here*
derrière	*behind; out back*	là-bas	*over there*
devant	*in front*		

ACTIVITÉS

7. Mon entourage. Répondez aux questions de votre partenaire pour décrire les membres de votre famille et / ou vos ami(e)s.

MODÈLE: travailler / sérieux
—**Qui travaille sérieusement?**
—**Mon ami Fred travaille sérieusement.**

1. fumer / fréquent
2. manger / bon
3. parler / gentil
4. danser / mauvais
5. parler / facile / le français
6. comprendre / rapide
7. rougir / régulier
8. maigrir / facile

8. Comment répondez-vous? Posez des questions à votre partenaire pour apprendre où, comment, et quand il / elle fait certaines activités, et répondez à votre tour. Utilisez un adverbe dans les réponses.

MODÈLE: —**Comment danses-tu?**
—**Moi, je danse assez bien. Et toi?**
—**Moi, je danse vraiment mal.**

1. Quand réponds-tu à mes questions?
2. Où as-tu mis tes livres?
3. Comment ton père parle-t-il anglais? espagnol? français?
4. Quand...
5. Comment...
6. Où...
7. Quand...
8. Combien de fois...

Follow-up. Have students tell classmates what they have learned.

QUATRIÈME ÉPISODE T 78

Le soir tombe. Tous nos sportifs sont réunis° autour d° 'un grand feu°. Ils chantent, mangent, et rient°. Ils ont passé une belle journée riche en émotions et ils sont tous un peu fatigués.

_____
réunis *gathered* / **autour de** *around* / **feu** *fire* / **rient** *laugh*

La soirée avance, et petit à petit, tout le monde va se coucher. Benjamin et Caroline, seuls, sont assis l'un à côté de l'autre.

CAROLINE: Tu sais, pendant quelques minutes, j'ai vraiment eu peur...

BENJAMIN: Quand on était dans les rapides?

CAROLINE: Oui, mais surtout quand tu es presque tombé du bateau au milieu de° tout ce courant. Ça, c'était fou!°

BENJAMIN: Oui, mais je savais que ton sac de couchage était dans l'eau et tu vois, malgré tout°, je n'ai pas réussi à le repêcher°. Je suis vraiment désolé.

_____
au milieu de *in the middle of* / **fou** *crazy* / **malgré tout** *in spite of everything* / **repêcher** *to recover*

AVEZ-VOUS COMPRIS?

1. Décrivez la scène autour du feu.
2. Quelle est la réaction de Caroline quand elle apprend que Benjamin est amoureux d'elle *(in love with her)*?
3. Quand c'est l'heure de se coucher, qu'est-ce que Benjamin propose à Caroline? Accepte-t-elle sa proposition? Si oui, pourquoi? Si non, pourquoi pas?

CAROLINE: Benjamin, ne sois pas bête. Il y a longtemps qu'on se connaît et je sais que tu as fait le maximum pour le repêcher. Tu crois qu'on parlera encore de cette aventure dans dix ans?

BENJAMIN: J'en suis sûr. Écoute, Caroline, je voulais te le dire depuis longtemps mais je n'ai jamais osé°. Tu occupes une place bien spéciale dans ma vie. Je veux dire que... je,... C'est-à-dire° que je suis... je suis...

CAROLINE: Amoureux?°

BENJAMIN: Oui.

CAROLINE: Moi aussi, Benjamin.

Ils s'embrassent tendrement, se lèvent, et marchent ensemble sous le ciel étoilé°, la main dans la main.

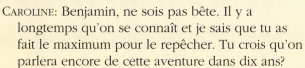

osé *dared* / **c'est-à-dire** *that is* / **amoureux** *in love* / **étoilé** *starry*

BENJAMIN: Tu sais, il est tard. Tu devrais aller dormir. J'ai mis mon sac dans ta tente. Tu seras bien...

CAROLINE: Et toi?

BENJAMIN: Ne t'inquiète pas. Georges m'a trouvé une couverture°. Ce soir, je dormirai bien à la belle étoile° et tu seras dans mes rêves°.

couverture *blanket* / **à la belle étoile** *under the stars* / **rêves** *dreams*

Remind students that they may make up a new persona or modify the truth in answering personal questions.

ET VOUS?

1. Avez-vous déjà fait du camping ou du rafting? Si oui, comment avez-vous trouvé cette expérience? Si non, voudriez-vous en faire?
2. En général, avec qui passez-vous vos vacances? Pourquoi?
3. Où aimez-vous passer vos vacances? dans la nature? dans un hôtel? loin ou près de chez vous? Expliquez.
4. Avez-vous déjà été amoureux (amoureuse)? Si oui, avez-vous déclaré votre amour? Si oui, comment? Êtes-vous encore amoureux(se) de cette personne? Pourquoi ou pourquoi pas?

Situating yourself using expressions of time

IV QUELQUES EXPRESSIONS DE TEMPS

Dans une semaine, ils auront de bons souvenirs du voyage.
Ils finiront la descente **en** trois jours.
Benjamin et Caroline feront du rafting **pendant** quelques jours.
Ils sont sur la rivière **depuis** vendredi après-midi.

◆ Occasionally you want to explain how long you have been doing something or how long it will take to get a job done. There are several different expressions of time to describe these situations.

1. **Dans** is used to express the time at which an action will be completed.

Je finirai mes devoirs **dans** deux heures. | *I will finish my homework **in** two hours.*

Dans can also express how far into the future an event will occur.

Je vous téléphonerai **dans** deux jours. | *I will call you **in** two days.*

2. **En** expresses how long it takes to do something.

Je finis toujours mes devoirs **en** vingt minutes. | *I always finish my homework **in** (within) twenty minutes.*

3. **Pendant** indicates the duration of a particular activity. Often used for actions that are habitual, **pendant** indicates a clear beginning and end for the activity.

Je joue au tennis **pendant** une heure tous les jours. | *I play tennis **for** an hour every day.*
Hier elles ont regardé la télé **pendant** deux heures. | *Yesterday they watched TV **for** two hours.*

◆ **Depuis** tells you that an action had a specific starting point in the past and has been continuous since it was begun. It is most often used with the present tense.

Depuis quand habites-tu ici? | *How long (Since when) have you lived here?*
J'habite ici **depuis** 1994. | *I have been living here **since** 1994.*
Depuis combien de temps habites-tu ici? | *How long have you lived here?*
J'habite ici **depuis** trois ans. | *I have been living here **for** three years.*

ACTIVITÉS

 9. Est-ce *en* ou *dans*? Posez les questions suivantes à votre partenaire, qui vous répondra.

■ **MOTS À UTILISER: être amoureux de** *to be in love with*

MODÈLES: Serez-vous encore étudiant(e) _____ dix ans?
> **—Serez-vous encore étudiant(e) dans dix ans?**
> **—Oui, je serai encore étudiant(e) dans dix ans.**
OU **—Non, je serai professeur dans dix ans.**

Allons-nous finir l'examen _____ quinze minutes?
> **—Allons-nous finir l'examen en quinze minutes?**
> **—Non, nous allons finir l'examen en cinquante minutes.**

1. Serons-nous en vacances _____ quinze jours?
2. Vos amis font-ils leurs devoirs _____ moins d'une heure?
3. Aurez-vous votre diplôme _____ deux ans?
4. Est-il possible de choisir ses vêtements _____ cinq secondes?
5. Serez-vous marié(e) _____ deux semaines?
6. Pouvez-vous manger une pizza _____ trois minutes?
7. Aimez-vous dîner _____ une demi-heure?
8. Votre grand-père sera-t-il toujours amoureux de votre grand-mère _____ dix ans?

10. Est-ce *depuis* ou *pendant*? Complétez les paragraphes suivants en utilisant **pendant** ou **depuis.**

Je joue du piano (1.) _____ l'âge de sept ans. Je suis obligé de répéter *(practice)* (2.) _____ deux heures tous les jours. Je prends des leçons avec mon professeur de piano (3.) _____ 1991. Il est professeur dans notre ville (4.) _____ dix ans. Avant ça, il a été au conservatoire de Strasbourg (5.) _____ quinze ans.

Il me dit que je dois continuer à répéter (6.) _____ les vacances si je veux être prêt pour le grand concert au début du mois. Alors (7.) _____ quelques semaines je suis très anxieux parce que je ne sais pas si je serai bien préparé. Nous saurons bientôt si j'ai assez travaillé!

 11. Interview. Ask your partner

1. if he or she will have his or her diploma in one year.
2. if he or she can do a homework assignment in 30 minutes.
3. how long he or she has been living here.
4. if he or she plays a musical instrument or sport, and if so, how long he or she has been playing.
5. how long he or she studies every day.
6. how long he or she watches TV or listens to music every day.
7. how long (since what year/month) he or she has been a student at your school.
8. how long he or she went to his or her last school.

Follow-up. After completing **Activité 10,** ask students questions such as **Depuis combien de temps habitez-vous ici?, Depuis quand étudiez-vous à cette université?,** and **Depuis combien de temps savez-vous parler français?** to reinforce the point that the present tense is used in sentences with **depuis.**

LES GORGES DE L'ARDÈCHE

Reading Strategy: Finding topic sentences and supporting details

Topic sentences give a reader the main idea of a paragraph and are often followed by detailed information that supports the main idea. You will use this strategy for the reading that follows.

 1. Lisez rapidement la brochure. Notez avec vos propres mots les trois idées les plus importantes de la lecture. Comparez votre liste aux listes des autres étudiants pour voir si vous avez trouvé les mêmes idées. Avec un(e) partenaire, choisissez les trois idées essentielles du texte.

You may want to have students read their ideas while you make a master list on the board. Then have students vote on the three main ideas.

L'Ardèche à la carte

A condition de savoir nager, la descente des Gorges de l'Ardèche ne présente pas de difficultés en été. Les amateurs de sensations fortes préfèrent venir dès le printemps pour profiter de courants plus rapides. Ce n'est pas votre cas ? Alors prenez le temps de vous arrêter. De nombreuses plages jalonnent le parcours. C'est l'occasion de vous baigner, de pêcher, d'escalader, de découvrir le milieu environnant, de faire, loin de tout, du naturisme…

MINI-DESCENTE - 6 KM
Un parcours d'initiation à la découverte de l'Ardèche et du canoë-kayak : prévoir une 1/2 journée.

DESCENTE DES GORGES DE L'ARDECHE
Un parcours de 24 km dans un site naturel, préservé, uniquement accessible en bateau ou à pied : prévoir une journée.

GRANDE DESCENTE DE L'ARDECHE
● Un parcours de 30 km, possible en 1 jour, enchaînant la mini-descente avec passage sous l'arche majestueuse du Pont d'Arc, puis les 24 km de la réserve naturelle des Gorges : en 2 jours avec bivouac.
● Maxi-descente un parcours de 60 km avec passage de barrages par les toboggans à canoë, un itinéraire très technique : en 3 jours

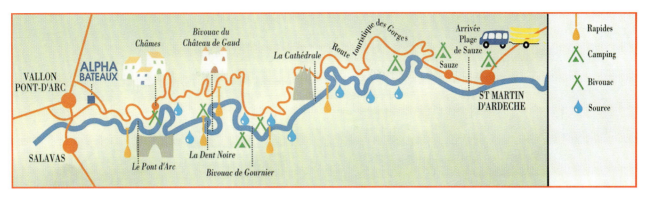

2. Relisez la brochure et répondez aux questions.

a. Qu'est-ce qu'il faut savoir avant de faire la descente de l'Ardèche?

b. Normalement, en quelle(s) saison(s) descend-on l'Ardèche?

c. En quelle saison les courants sont-ils les plus rapides?

d. Quelles autres activités sont possibles quand on descend la rivière? Auxquelles voudriez-vous participer?

e. Peut-on choisir des descentes différentes? Si oui, quelles sont les différences principales entre les parcours *(trips)?*

f. Si vous choisissez la descente des gorges de l'Ardèche, finirez-vous le parcours en une demi-journée, en une journée, ou en trois jours?

g. À votre avis, quelle descente les touristes typiques préfèrent-ils? Justifiez votre réponse.

Baignade au Pont d'Arc.

Une vie dans les îles

Une Guadeloupéenne.

POPULATION: 387 034 habitants
SUPERFICIE: 1780 km²
CHEF-LIEU: Basse-Terre
LANGUES: français et créole

Décrivez-vous.

Je m'appelle Amadée Leclerc, j'ai 58 ans et je suis mariée. J'ai trois enfants et deux petits-enfants, mais ils habitent loin, à Basse-Terre. Moi, j'habite depuis toujours près de Pointe-à-Pitre. J'y suis née et j'y mourrai un jour.

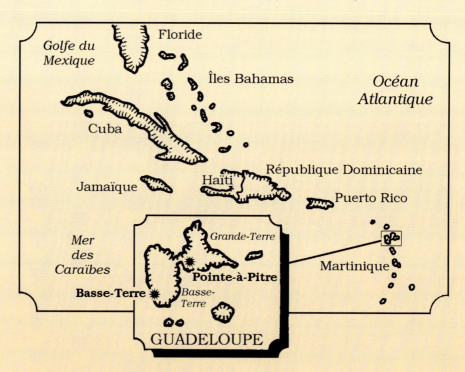

Culture. Point out that French speakers often use the negation to state an affirmative. For example, **Il ne fait pas chaud** means that it is *cold* weather.

sugar mill / **dans...** *all in all*

Que faites-vous dans la vie?

Je suis cuisinière dans un hôtel touristique. Ma mère m'a appris à faire la cuisine quand j'étais toute petite, et je me suis mise à travailler à l'âge de quatorze ans. J'aime bien mon travail; c'est quand même moins dur que le travail de mon mari qui travaille dans une sucrerie°. Dans l'ensemble° on n'est pas trop malheureux.

Quels sont vos passe-temps préférés?

J'aime bien la lecture, surtout les histoires d'amour. Et j'adore la musique! Je suis grand amateur° de notre musique antillaise, vous savez, les valses° et surtout les biguines!

(music) lover / waltzes

Qu'est-ce qu'une *biguine*?

Eh bien, c'est une danse où il faut balancer les hanches° tout en gardant les épaules immobiles. Tiens, écoutez celle-ci, ça s'appelle «La Guadeloupéenne.» C'était un grand succès d'Abel Beauregard et de son orchestre antillais dans les années cinquante, quand j'étais jeune. C'est un joli morceau, n'est-ce pas?

balancer... swing your hips

Que pensez-vous de l'avenir?

Tant que° j'ai ma santé et ma famille, tout va bien. Moi, j'ai toujours été optimiste, et je continue à l'être. Il faut croquer la vie à pleines dents°!

Tant... As long as
Il... You have to enjoy life to the fullest!

QUELQUES QUESTIONS

1. Décrivez brièvement Amadée Leclerc. Connaissez-vous d'autres personnes comme elle? Si oui, décrivez-les.
2. Que fait-elle dans la vie? Que pense-t-elle de son travail? Qu'est-ce qu'elle nous dit sur son mari?
3. Comment est-ce que Mme Leclerc s'amuse quand elle a du temps libre?
4. En quoi la musique qu'elle écoute est-elle spéciale?
5. Mme Leclerc est-elle jeune d'esprit? Justifiez votre réponse.

http://www.wiley.com/aventure.html

RÉVISION ÉCLAIR

Making plans (continued)   **Voir p. 404.**

> Quand tu **arriveras** chez moi, tu **seras** content.
> Nous **irons** à ce nouveau restaurant.
> Si elle a le temps, Julie **téléphonera** à sa mère.

Talking about your activities (continued)   **Voir p. 410.**

> Caroline et ses amis **choisissent** un bon bateau.
> Benjamin **rougit** comme une tomate.

Describing your actions   **Voir p. 415.**

> Marie est bavarde. Elle parle **constamment**.
> Benjamin et Caroline se sourient **gentiment**.
> Hier soir, les deux amis ont **bien** dormi.

Situating yourself using expressions of time **Voir p. 420.**

Dans deux jours nous serons de retour à Rouen.
Nous pouvons descendre la rivière **en** trois jours.
Benjamin connaît Caroline **depuis** le début de l'année.
Hier nous avons chanté **pendant** une heure.

ÊTES-VOUS BRANCHÉS?

 Une lettre à un(e) ami(e). Maintenant vous connaissez bien les richesses naturelles et artistiques de la région qui s'appelle l'Ardèche. Dans une lettre à un(e) ami(e), décrivez les activités et les visites que vous pouvez faire quand vous irez en Ardèche. Si possible, faites la comparaison entre l'Ardèche et une région que vous connaissez bien chez vous.

Y ÊTES-VOUS ARRIVÉS?

 A. Parlez-moi de votre vie... Demandez à votre partenaire

1. trois choses qu'il / elle fera l'été prochain.
2. une chose qu'il / elle fera pendant une heure ce soir.
3. un voyage qu'il / elle fera dans un an.
4. ce qu'il / elle peut finir comme travail en une heure.
5. où il / elle habite depuis 1995 (ou une autre année).

 B. Il est comment, votre ami? Décrivez votre meilleur(e) ami(e) ou une autre personne que vous connaissez bien à un(e) partenaire. Demandez-lui s'il / si elle connaît quelqu'un qui ressemble à votre ami(e). Utilisez au moins six adverbes et deux verbes en **-ir.**

MODÈLE: —**Bill rougit souvent, et il mange constamment. Connais-tu quelqu'un comme ça?**
—**Ma sœur est comme ça. Elle rougit quelquefois, et elle mange fréquemment.**

Follow-up. If you like, have students work in pairs for this assignment. After they write their letters, students will give their letter to another student who will write an answer based on the letter he or she has received.

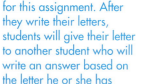 **C. Voilà ce que nous ferons ensemble.** Dans une lettre à un(e) ami(e), décrivez vos projets pour le week-end prochain. Mentionnez un minimum de cinq choses que vous ferez ensemble. Demandez-lui de vous répondre avec ses opinions et ses idées.

PRONONCIATION

Les sons [l] et [j]

Many words in both English and French are spelled with the letter **l**. Although some words may *look* exactly alike in the two languages, the pronunciation of **l** in French is quite different from its counterpart in English. Look over the list of French words you have already learned. When you say them, put the tip of your tongue against the back of your upper front teeth to get just the right sound for French [l].

1. Listen to your professor or lab tape and repeat the following words.

allemand	dollar	naturel
allez	lecture	politique
belle	lettre	seul
collant	livre	solution

Sometimes **-l** or **-ll** is not pronounced like [l] at all. As a rule, when the vowel **i** is followed by **-ll** or **-l**, and appears alone or with another vowel *in the same syllable,* the sound is [j], as in English <u>yesterday</u>.

2. Now listen to the your professor or lab tape as the following words are read.

trava *ille*	vi *eille*	j *uill*et
m *eill*eur	f *ille*	œil

Note: Some exceptions are **mille, million, tranquille, village,** and **ville,** which are all pronounced with the [l] sound rather than [j]. Two words in which the letter **l** is silent are **fils** and **gentil.**

3. Now using what you have learned, read the following phrases aloud. Then copy them on a sheet of paper and circle all the **l**s that sound like [j] and underline all the **l**s that sound like [l].

   a. Marseille est une belle ville.
   b. Il a gagné mille dollars à la loterie.
   c. Mes filles sont très gentilles.
   d. Elles habitent dans un petit village tranquille.

VOCABULAIRE ACTIF

Quelques expressions de temps

après demain   *(the) day after tomorrow*

aussitôt que   *as soon as*

depuis   *for; since*

dès que   *as soon as*

le lendemain   *the next day*

lorsque   *when*

la semaine / l'année prochaine   *next week/year*

Quelques verbes en -ir

choisir   *to choose*

désobéir   *to disobey*

finir   *to finish*

grandir   *to grow up*

grossir   *to gain weight*

maigrir   *to lose weight*

obéir   *to obey*

punir   *to punish*

réfléchir   *to think about; to ponder*

réussir   *to succeed*

rougir   *to turn red; to blush*

Quelques adverbes de lieu

dehors   *outside*

derrière   *behind; out back*

devant   *in front*

ici   *here*

là-bas   *over there*

Quelques adverbes de manière

absolument   *absolutely*

confortablement   *comfortably*

constamment   *constantly*

difficilement   *with difficulty*

facilement   *easily*

follement   *madly; crazily*

fréquemment   *frequently*

gentiment   *nicely*

intelligemment   *intelligently*

lentement   *slowly*

poliment   *politely*

rapidement   *rapidly*

régulièrement   *regularly*

sérieusement   *seriously*

tendrement   *tenderly*

tranquillement   *calmly*

Autres mots utiles

un besoin   *a need*

être amoureux amoureuse de   *to be in love with*

prendre sa retraite   *to retire*

si   *if*

Chapitre 14 ◆ **LA DISPUTE**

PRÉSENTATION ÉCLAIR

POUR COMMUNIQUER

Expressing wishes, making polite requests,
 and giving advice
Expressing hypotheses
Making comparisons
Making comparisons (continued)

POUR Y ARRIVER

Le conditionnel
Les propositions avec **si**
Le comparatif
Le superlatif

POUR S'ADAPTER À LA CULTURE

Albert Camus et Jean-Paul Sartre: deux
 écrivains français
Louis Pasteur et Marie Curie: deux
 scientifiques exceptionnels

Benjamin est rentré à Grenoble après un week-end extraordinaire avec Caroline. Il ne peut pas s'arrêter° de penser à elle. Le matin, il se lève, et Caroline est déjà dans ses pensées°. Pendant la journée quand il voit° quelque chose, il se dit: «Tiens, Caroline aimerait° ça», ou bien «Quelle horreur, je suis sûr que ça, ça ne lui plairait pas°». Le soir, il se couche et rêve d'elle. Bref, il est follement amoureux! Tout à coup, il se décide. Un amour° comme ça, c'est pour la vie. Alors, feuille de papier en main, voilà ce qu'il écrit à Caroline.

---

s'arrêter *to stop* / **pensées** *thoughts* / **voit** *sees* / **aimerait** *would like* / **ça ne lui plairait pas** *she wouldn't like that* / **amour** *love*

Grenoble, le 3 mai

Ma chérie°,

Je pense à toi constamment. Depuis dimanche, tu es dans mes pensées à chaque instant. Je n'arrête pas d'imaginer notre vie ensemble. Nous pourrions° habiter aux États-Unis ou en France, si tu préfères. Nous louerions° un joli petit appartement. Tu pourrais rester à la maison et me préparer de bons petits plats°.

---

chérie *darling* / **pourrions** *could* / **louerions** *would rent* / **de bons petits plats** *wonderful things to eat*

AVEZ-VOUS COMPRIS?

1. À qui Benjamin pense-t-il constamment?
2. Quels sont les sentiments de Benjamin vis-à-vis de Caroline?
3. Que décide-t-il de faire tout à coup? À votre avis, est-ce une bonne idée?
4. Décrivez comment Benjamin imagine leur vie de couple.
5. Que pensez-vous de son plan? Justifiez votre réponse.

3 Moi, je travaillerais dur pour subvenir à° nos besoins. Et puis, dans quelques années, nous aurions° deux ou trois enfants et nous serions les parents les plus heureux du monde°.

---
pour subvenir à *to take care of* / **aurions** *would have* / **serions les parents les plus heureux du monde** *would be the happiest parents in the world*

4 Je sais que mes parents feraient des grands-parents gâteaux° et qu'ils seraient tellement heureux pour nous. Ma mère adorerait venir nous voir, et je suis sûr que mon père passerait des heures à jouer avec la petite famille.

Caroline, réponds-moi vite,
Je t'envoie mille baisers°.
Benjamin

---
gâteaux *indulgent* / **Je t'envoie mille baisers.** *I'm sending you a thousand kisses.*

Presentation. Because of the very personal nature of this **Et Vous?,** you may wish to remind students that they may discuss their own experience or make up a persona. You may also want to do this section as a paired activity.

ET VOUS?

1. Avez-vous un(e) petit(e) ami(e)? une personne spéciale dans votre vie? Si non, imaginez votre homme / femme idéale pour répondre aux questions suivantes.
2. Quand pensez-vous à lui / à elle? Lui téléphonez-vous? Lui écrivez-vous souvent?
3. Imaginez-vous votre avenir *(future)* avec cette personne? Si oui, comment l'imaginez-vous?
4. Lui parlez-vous de votre avenir? Est-ce que cette personne vous en parle?
5. Est-ce que vous pensez à votre avenir de la même manière? Sur quoi êtes-vous d'accord? Sur quoi n'êtes-vous pas d'accord?

Expressing wishes, making polite requests, and giving advice

I **LE CONDITIONNEL**

Tiens, Caroline **aimerait** ça!
Nous **pourrions** habiter aux États-Unis.
Tu **resterais** à la maison, et tu me **préparerais** de bons petits plats.
Mes parents **seraient** tellement heureux pour nous.

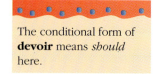

Review. You already know some expressions that use the conditional: **je voudrais, pourriez-vous?, pourrais-tu?** (Chapter 9, Épisode 1).

◆ To form the conditional, use the **futur** stems and the **imparfait** endings.

aimer	répondre
j'aimer**ais**	je répondr**ais**
tu aimer**ais**	tu répondr**ais**
il / elle / on aimer**ait**	il / elle / on répondr**ait**
nous aimer**ions**	nous répondr**ions**
vous aimer**iez**	vous répondr**iez**
ils / elles aimer**aient**	ils / elles répondr**aient**
finir	**pouvoir**
je finir**ais**	je pourr**ais**
tu finir**ais**	tu pourr**ais**
il / elle / on finir**ait**	il / elle / on pourr**ait**
nous finir**ions**	nous pourr**ions**
vous finir**iez**	vous pourr**iez**
ils / elles finir**aient**	ils / elles pourr**aient**

◆ Use the conditional for the following purposes:

1. to express a wish or desire

   Je **voudrais** partir en vacances.
   Nous **aimerions** sortir ce soir.

2. to make a request or a suggestion politely

   Pourriez-vous me prêter votre voiture?
   Voudrais-tu danser maintenant?

3. to give advice

   Ce **serait** gentil de l'inviter au restaurant.
   Ensuite, tu **devrais** l'emmener au cinéma.

The conditional form of **devoir** means *should* here.

4. to express the result of a condition that is contrary to fact

> Si j'avais plus de temps libre, je **voyagerais** beaucoup.
> Nous **irions** à Paris immédiatement si nous étions riches.

ACTIVITÉS

Some of the following expressions were introduced in Chapter 9, Épisode 1.

POUR S'EXPRIMER

Comment exprimer un désir et demander ou suggérer poliment

Aimerais-tu... / Aimeriez-vous...	*Would you like to . . .*
Ça / cela m'arrangerait de...	*It would help me to . . .*
Ça / cela vous arrangerait de...	*It would help you to . . .*
Ça / cela me dérangerait de...	*It would be a problem for me to . . .*
Ça me ferait plaisir de...	*It would make me happy to . . .*
Ce serait gentil de...	*It would be nice to . . .*
Serait-il possible de...	*Would it be possible to . . .*
Il serait possible de...	*It would be possible to . . .*
Je serais content(e) de...	*I would be happy to . . .*
Je serais heureux / heureuse de...	
Je serais ravi(e) de...	*I would be delighted to . . .*
Pourrais-tu... / Pourriez-vous...	*Could you . . .*
Voudrais-tu... / Voudriez-vous...	*Would you . . .*

1. On est poli! Dites poliment ce que vous pensez. Choisissez l'expression que vous préférez.

MODÈLE: **Ça me ferait plaisir d'inviter Julie au restaurant.**
OU **Je serais contente d'inviter Julie au restaurant.**

ça m'arrangerait de	inviter mon ami au cinéma
ça serait gentil de	sortir tôt ce soir
ça me ferait plaisir de	partir en week-end à Paris
je serais ravi(e) de	finir ce travail
je serais content(e) de	aller à la discothèque avec toi
je serais heureux / heureuse de	inviter Julie au restaurant
j'aimerais...	ne pas aller au travail demain

Culture. You may wish to give your students this proverb: **On attrape plus de mouches avec du miel qu'avec du vinaigre,** stressing that a polite expression may get the job done better than a mere order. It is a good lead-in to this activity.

2. À ta place... Vous aimez bien donner votre avis. Alors n'hésitez pas et allez-y!

MODÈLE: Mon frère regarde la télé. (je)
À sa place, j'irais au cinéma.

Mes parents mangent du pop-corn. (tu)
À leur place, tu mangerais du chocolat.

1. Mon père lit le journal. (mes amis et moi, nous)
2. Ma meilleure amie achète une cassette. (je)
3. Mes parents achètent un appartement. (tu)
4. Ma mère a acheté un maillot de bain rose. (mes ami(e)s)
5. Mon frère et moi, nous partons pour le Sénégal. (vous)
6. Mon professeur donne souvent des examens. (les étudiants)
7. Quand nous serons riches, nous visiterons le Togo. (mon / ma meilleur(e) ami(e))

3. Que de désirs! Imaginez ce que tout le monde voudrait faire. Faites tous les changements nécessaires.

MODÈLE: **Je serais content de partir en vacances.**

je		partir en week-end
mes parents	vouloir	faire la grasse matinée
vous	être content(e) de	acheter une belle voiture
le professeur	aimer	faire un voyage au Maroc
les étudiants	être ravi(e) de	avoir des étudiants énergiques
tu	être heureux / heureuse de	aller au cinéma ce soir
nous		gagner à la loterie

Qui va gagner.

4. Imaginez le résultat! Votre partenaire et vous, vous parlez des situations qui font rêver *(your fantasies)*. Qu'en dites-vous?

MODÈLE: Si j'avais un million, je...

    —**Si j'avais cinq millions de francs, je ferais une grande fête, n'est-ce pas?**

    —**Oui, si tu avais cinq millions de francs, tu ferais une grande fête.**

OU   —**Non, si tu avais cinq millions de francs, tu ferais un long voyage.**

1. Si je gagnais à la loterie, je...
2. Si mes parents étaient riches, ils...
3. Si ma sœur était très sympathique, elle...
4. Si mon professeur adorait ses étudiants, il...
5. Si nous pouvions partir en voyage, nous...
6. Si votre meilleur(e) ami(e) et vous aviez beaucoup de temps libre, vous...
7. Si tu étais libre, tu...

Follow-up. You can conclude this section by setting up situations for students. Some examples are **si j'étais riche..., si je gagnais à la loterie..., si j'étais le président de l'université...** Do a chain drill where students follow one another with their own ideas: **Si j'étais riche, j'irais à Paris. Si j'allais à Paris, je visiterais le Louvre. Si je visitais le Louvre, j'achèterais un poster de la Joconde...**

Des vacances de rêve en Côte d'Ivoire.

🎧 DEUXIÈME ÉPISODE T 80

Caroline est rentrée à Rouen, et elle a confié° avec émotion son week-end à Julie.

JULIE: Mais, c'est merveilleux! Benjamin est un garçon très sensible°, et depuis que je le connais, je ne l'ai jamais vu aussi sérieux. Il doit être très amoureux de toi, et, si tu veux mon avis, depuis assez longtemps.

CAROLINE: Tu crois?° Parce que moi, c'est sérieux. J'ai bien peur d'être vraiment amoureuse de lui.

JULIE: Caroline, j'en suis sûre...

---

a confié *confided* / **sensible** *sensitive* / **Tu crois?** *Do you think so?*

Julie entend un coup de sonnette° à la porte. Caroline va répondre. C'est le facteur° qui lui apporte un carnet de chèques et... une lettre de Benjamin.

---

un coup de sonnette *the door bell* / **facteur** *mailman*

AVEZ-VOUS COMPRIS?

1. Qu'est-ce que Caroline confie à Julie?
2. Qui est à la porte? Qu'est-ce qu'il apporte à Caroline?
3. Décrivez la réaction de Caroline quand elle lit la lettre de Benjamin? Pourquoi? Que feriez-vous à sa place?
4. Résumez la réaction de Julie et les conseils qu'elle donne à Caroline. A-t-elle raison ou tort, à votre avis?

Elle s'assied, commence à la lire. Le rouge lui monte aux joues. Furieuse, elle tend° sa lettre à Julie.

CAROLINE: Mais, il est malade... complètement malade.

JULIE: Non, il est amoureux et un peu rapide.

CAROLINE: Mais, de quel droit° planifie-t-il ma vie? S'il était sensible, il comprendrait que j'ai besoin de créer° ma propre vie, il ne m'enverrait° pas un plan quinquennal!°

JULIE: Euh, euh... s'il réfléchissait beaucoup, il ne serait pas amoureux. Et toi, Caroline, si tu étais dans ton état normal, tu ne t'arracherais pas les cheveux° pour si peu, c'est un simple malentendu°.

---

tend *holds out* / **droit** *right* / **créer** *create* / **enverrait** *would send* / **plan quinquennal** *five-year plan* / **tu ne t'arracherais pas les cheveux** *you wouldn't tear your hair out* / **malentendu** *misunderstanding*

CAROLINE: Un malentendu... Moi, rester à la maison à lui faire des petits plats! Un joli appartement et trois enfants... Un malentendu? Heureusement qu'il ne me donne pas la couleur de la tapisserie° du salon et le nom de tous les enfants! En ce moment, si je pouvais, je l'étranglerais...

JULIE: Moi, si j'étais à ta place, je lui téléphonerais, et je lui demanderais de s'expliquer...

CAROLINE: Jamais de la vie!°

---

tapisserie *wallpaper* / **Jamais de la vie!** *Never! Not on your life!*

ET VOUS?

1. Est-ce que vos parents / amis vous envoient souvent des lettres ou des cartes postales? À quelle occasion?
2. Est-ce que vous comprenez toujours bien la personne qui vous écrit?
3. Êtes-vous toujours d'accord avec elle?
4. En général, quand vous n'êtes pas d'accord avec votre meilleur(e) ami(e) ou votre petit(e) ami(e), que faites-vous?

437

VOUS ÊTES BRANCHÉS!

Albert Camus et Jean-Paul Sartre: deux écrivains français

Even though France is a relatively small country (it would fit within the state of Texas), French writers have earned twelve Nobel prizes in literature over the last hundred years, more than much larger countries such as the United States or the former Soviet Union.

Two good examples of France's many philosophical writers are Albert Camus and Jean-Paul Sartre. Underlying their work was the belief that human beings are plunged into an absurd world. They developed the philosophy of Existentialism, which holds that **«l'existence précède l'essence».** Existentialism tells us that we are responsible for making sense of our existence, every day, in every action we take, and that we are free

Camus.

Sartre et Simone de Beauvoir au café.

to choose our own actions. If we deny responsibility for our actions, blaming, for example, an outside influence, we are guilty of **la mauvaise foi** (*bad faith*).

Albert Camus (1913–1960) received his Nobel prize in 1957 for "having shed light on the problems posed today to the conscience of men." Born in Algeria, he was attracted to philosophy and writing from very early on. In works like ***L'Étranger*** or ***Le Mythe de Sisyphe,*** Camus portrayed a meaningless world against which individuals must struggle by using their passion for life and faith in their capacity to make a choice. In a later novel, ***La Peste*** (*The Plague*), Camus used plague as a metaphor for Nazism and called upon people to work together to fight evil. A man of conviction, he joined the **Résistance** during the Second World War and later headed the

newspaper ***Combat:*** «Je me révolte donc nous sommes.»

Jean-Paul Sartre (1905–1980) was first and foremost a philosopher but was equally involved in political combat, alongside his lifelong companion, writer Simone de Beauvoir. According to Sartre, Man must act upon History in order to shape it. Works like ***Les Chemins de la liberté*** or ***L'être et le néant*** (*Being and Nothingness*) illustrate this recurrent message in Sartre's writings. His plays such as ***Huis Clos*** (*No Exit*) or ***Le Diable et le Bon Dieu*** best present the idea of man's obligation to choose and shape his own fate in what he believed to be a godless world.

Awarded a Nobel prize in 1964, Sartre exercised his freedom and chose not to accept it, applying in his personal life the same set of values and beliefs he defined in his works.

http://www.wiley.com/aventure.html

Expliquez l'essentiel à votre partenaire. Choisissez un sujet et allez-y! Votre partenaire va accepter votre explication, la modifier ou y ajouter quelques détails.

1. Résumez en termes très généraux ce que vous savez sur la vie et les œuvres d'Albert Camus ou sur la vie et les œuvres de Jean-Paul Sartre.
2. La notion de choix est-elle essentielle dans la philosohie de Sartre? de Camus? Expliquez pourquoi.
3. Citez deux œuvres de Jean-Paul Sartre puis résumez et expliquez les concepts-clés *(key points)* sur lesquels ils fonctionnent.

Culture. Camus' **«Je me révolte donc nous sommes.»** is a reworking of the 17th century philosopher René Descartes' famous dictum **«Je pense, donc je suis.»,** in which Descartes affirmed the importance of reason and scientific thought, not blind belief, in human endeavor.

To learn more about Simone de Beauvoir, see p 454.

■ POUR COMMUNIQUER

Expressing hypotheses

II LES PROPOSITIONS AVEC *SI*

Si tu **as** de l'argent, tu **partiras** en week-end.
N'**oublie** pas de rendre ce livre si tu **vas** à la bibliothèque.
Si j'**étais** à ta place, je téléphonerais.
Benjamin et Caroline **seraient** heureux s'ils se **comprenaient** bien.

◆ To express hypotheses, use a **si** construction with the appropriate tense.

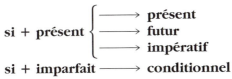

1. If the **si** clause uses the **présent,** the result clause may be in the **présent,** the **futur,** or the **impératif,** depending on the sense of the sentence.

   Si vous avez sommeil, vous **pouvez** dormir.
   Si vous partez tôt, vous **arriverez** en classe à l'heure.
   Si vous avez faim, **allez** au restaurant.

2. If the **si** clause uses the **imparfait,** the result clause should be in the **conditionnel.**

   Si tu étais à ma place, tu **pleurerais** aussi.

You may wish to discuss some of these concepts in English with your students (See the vous Êtes Branchés box on p. 438.) Explain the notion that people are free to shape their life and are responsible for their choices, or let students use their own knowledge of these authors to answer. Give students key vocabulary in French such as **choix, responsable, responsabilité, actes, destin, destinée monde sans Dieu...**

◆ The **si** clause can come first or second, and, in either case, the appropriate tenses must be used regardless of the order of the clauses.

Si Caroline **accepte** les idées de Benjamin, elle **sera** malheureuse.
Elle **répondra** à sa lettre, **si** elle a le temps.
Si Benjamin **réfléchissait**, il ne **serait** pas amoureux.
Tu ne **t'arracherais** pas les cheveux **si** tu **étais** dans ton état normal!

ACTIVITÉS

5. C'est dans sa nature! Papa adore donner des conseils à tous ses enfants. Aidez-le!

MODÈLE: Si tu manges tes légumes, tu / grandir bien
Si tu manges tes légumes, tu grandiras bien.

Les enfants réussiront à l'école s'ils / écouter leurs profs
Les enfants réussiront à l'école s'ils écoutent leurs profs.

1. Si tu te brosses les dents, tu / aimer aller chez le dentiste
2. Votre mère sera heureuse si vous / penser à son anniversaire
3. Si les enfants font leurs devoirs, ils / avoir de bonnes notes
4. Nous paierons vos études à la fac si vous / travailler bien
5. Si vous mangez vos épinards, vous / être très forts
6. Si vous vous levez assez tôt, nous / pouvoir arriver à l'école à l'heure
7. Vos grands-parents vous adoreront si vous / leur écrire souvent
8. Ta sœur te donnera sa voiture pour le week-end si tu / lui demander gentiment

6. Le monde parfait. Imaginez un monde idéal.

■ MOT À UTILISER: **guerre** *war*

MODÈLE: **S'il n'y avait plus de guerre, nous serions heureux.**
La vie serait belle si tous les enfants mangeaient tous les jours.

s'il n'y avait plus de criminels, on
si tout le monde était heureux, les gens
si nous respections les autres, nous
s'il n'y avait plus de guerres, nous
nous comprendrions les autres si nous
les gens écouteraient s'ils
vous auriez du temps libre si vous
la vie serait belle si tous les enfants

pouvoir vivre simplement
avoir le temps
les écouter
être heureux
refuser de se droguer
pouvoir sortir en sécurité
travailler moins
manger tous les jours

7. On n'est pas d'accord! Votre partenaire n'est jamais d'accord avec vous. Imaginez la conversation!

■ MOT À UTILISER: **prêter** *to lend*

MODÈLE: Tu as du temps libre. Tu as l'intention d'aller au cinéma.
> **—Si j'ai du temps libre, j'irai au cinéma.**
> **—Jamais de la vie! Si j'avais le temps, j'irais au théâtre!**

1. Nous sommes libres. Nous avons l'intention d'aller au restaurant.
2. Mon père ne travaille pas. Il a l'intention de partir à Las Vegas.
3. Ma meilleure amie vient me rendre visite. J'ai l'intention de faire des courses avec elle.
4. Je n'ai pas trop de travail. J'ai l'intention d'aller danser avec mon / ma petit(e) ami(e) toute la nuit.
5. Mes parents nous prêtent la voiture, nous avons l'intention d'aller à la plage.
6. Tu arrives à la maison après six heures. Tu as l'intention de manger avec nous.
7. Tes amis partent en vacances avec toi. Vous avez l'intention de visiter le Mexique.

8. À vous de vous exprimer. Finissez les phrases comme vous voulez. Attention aux temps!

1. Si j'ai le temps cette semaine, je...
2. Nous partirons pour Paris immédiatement si nous...
3. Si ma sœur me passe sa voiture pour le week-end, nous...
4. Vous irez danser dans votre discothèque favorite si...
5. Si je gagnais à la loterie nationale, je...
6. Mes parents seraient très heureux si nous...
7. Si je rencontrais la femme / l'homme de ma vie, je...
8. Je serais ravi(e) si...

Aimez-vous skier?

🎧 TROISIÈME ÉPISODE

(Quelques heures plus tard)...
Caroline a eu le temps de se calmer un peu. Julie est assise à côté d'elle. Elles prennent un thé ensemble et parlent de manière beaucoup plus raisonnable.

JULIE: Est-ce que tu te sens un peu mieux?
CAROLINE: Oui, un peu.
JULIE: Tu veux en parler?
CAROLINE: Oui, je pense que ça me fera du bien.

JULIE: As-tu parlé à Benjamin?
CAROLINE: Non, il n'en est pas question°.
JULIE: Tu es bien décidée? Tu ne veux pas l'appeler?
CAROLINE: Non, il est idiot. Et un vrai dictateur en plus! Il veut me dire comment vivre° ma vie! Il est complètement malade!
JULIE: Écoute, Caroline, regardons les choses objectivement. Penses-tu que Benjamin soit plus méchant° que les autres hommes?
CAROLINE: *(à contrecœur°)* Non!

il n'en est pas question *no way* / **vivre** *to live* / **plus méchant** *meaner* / **à contrecœur** *grudgingly*

Presentation. Before doing **Et Vous?,** you might want to give students the following vocabulary: **une dispute, se disputer, être fâché(e), s'excuser, s'expliquer.** You can tell them all the words are related to arguments and how to settle them.

AVEZ-VOUS COMPRIS?

1. Comment Caroline se sent-elle?
2. A-t-elle envie de parler avec Julie? et avec Benjamin? Expliquez.
3. Qui est Philippe?
4. Comparez Philippe et Benjamin (notez au moins trois choses).
5. Caroline accepte-t-elle de téléphoner à Benjamin? Pourquoi ou pourquoi pas?

442   **quatre cent quarante-deux**   **Chapitre 14**

JULIE: Est-ce qu'il est moins gentil que Philippe avec qui tu es sorti pendant deux ans?

CAROLINE: Tu sais très bien qu'on ne peut pas les comparer. Benjamin est beaucoup plus gentil... il est plus généreux, plus intelligent. Il travaille plus que Philippe n'a jamais travaillé. Il me comprend mieux! Mais quand même, il doit être aussi bête que° lui pour m'envoyer une lettre comme ça!

---

aussi bête que *as dumb as*

JULIE: Écoute-toi et réfléchis un peu! Tu le vois bien par toi-même. Benjamin est supérieur; il est bien meilleur que Philippe pour toi et, en plus tu l'aimes, grosse bécasse°! Alors? Est-ce que tu vas lui téléphoner, oui ou non?

CAROLINE: Non, c'est à lui° de me téléphoner!

JULIE: À lui? Mais comment veux-tu qu'il sache ce que tu ressens?° Il faut bien faire quelque chose enfin! Tu ne vas pas rester comme ça?

---

grosse bécasse *silly goose* / **c'est à lui** *it's up to him* / **ressens** *are feeling*

ET VOUS?

1. Vous disputez-vous quelquefois avec vos ami(e)s? Si oui, pourquoi?
2. Est-ce que vous continuez à parler à vos ami(e)s quand vous êtes furieux / furieuse?
3. Qui est la première personne à s'excuser après une dispute? vous ou vos ami(e)s?
4. Est-ce que vous acceptez toujours les excuses de vos ami(e)s quand ils / elles s'expliquent? Pourquoi ou pourquoi pas?
5. À votre avis, est-il préférable qu'une troisième personne vous aide à trouver une solution à votre dispute ou préférez-vous trouver une solution tout(e) seul(e)? Expliquez.

Caroline refuse de téléphoner à Benjamin pour parler de la lettre qu'il a écrite. Julie essaie de lui parler, mais Caroline ne veut pas l'écouter.

Julie devrait

a. composer le numéro de Benjamin et passer le téléphone à Caroline.
b. dire à Caroline d'écrire une lettre à Benjamin.
c. téléphoner à Benjamin elle-même.
d. Avez-vous une autre solution?

Justifiez votre réponse.

À VOUS DE JOUER

Vous avez vu Ghislaine, la petite amie de votre ami Stéphane, assise à la terrasse d'un café en tête à tête avec un homme que vous ne connaissez pas. Vous ne pouvez pas entendre ce qu'ils disent. Que faites-vous?

Moi, je

a. m'approche pour écouter discrètement leur conversation.
b. dis bonjour à Ghislaine et je lui demande de me présenter à l'homme.
c. rentre pour annoncer la nouvelle à Stéphane.
d. rentre et je ne dis rien à personne.
e. Avez-vous une autre solution?

Justifiez votre choix.

■ POUR COMMUNIQUER

Making comparisons

III   LE COMPARATIF

Benjamin est **plus beau que** Philippe.
Caroline répond **aussi bien que** Julie.
Benjamin a **autant de** bonnes qualités que Philippe.
Philippe comprend **moins que** Benjamin.

◆ To compare yourself, your possessions, or your abilities to others, use the comparative. Comparatives may be formed with adjectives, adverbs, nouns, or verbs.

◆ Comparative adjectives must agree with the first element in the comparison.

Caroline est **aussi belle que** Julie.
Benjamin est **plus beau que** Philippe.

◆ To show superiority, use **plus.** To show inferiority, use **moins.** The comparative may be followed by **que** to complete the comparison.

Nous sommes **plus / moins intelligents** (**que** toi).	*We are more/less intelligent (than you).*
Nous répondons **plus / moins lentement** (**que** toi).	*We answer more/less slowly (than you).*
Nous avons **plus / moins d'**amis (**que** toi).	*We have more/fewer friends (than you).*
Nous dormons **plus / moins** (**que** toi).	*We sleep more/less (than you).*

◆ To show equality, use **aussi** with adjectives and adverbs, and **autant** with nouns and verbs.

Nous sommes **aussi intelligents** (**que** toi).	*We are as intelligent (as you).*
Nous répondons **aussi lentement** (**que** toi).	*We answer as slowly (as you).*
Nous avons **autant d'amis** (**que** toi).	*We have as many friends (as you).*
Nous **dormons autant** (**que** toi).	*We sleep as much (as you).*

◆ With **plus, moins,** or **autant** + a noun, be sure to use **de (d')** before the noun. Add **que** before the person or thing being compared if you wish.

Elles ont **moins de temps libre.**
J'ai **plus d'amis que** toi.
Nous avons **autant de devoirs que** vous.

◆ Two irregular comparatives both mean *better.* Be careful to use them correctly. The comparative **adjective** *better* is **meilleur(e)(s).** The comparative **adverb** *better* is **mieux.**

Ces vins français sont bons, mais ces vins de Californie sont **meilleurs.**
Ce film est **meilleur que** l'autre.
Jean joue bien au tennis, mais Marc joue **mieux.**

> Since **meilleur** is an adjective, it must agree in number and gender with the noun(s) it modifies.

POUR S'EXPRIMER

Les relations personnelles

Ça va mal!

une dispute	*a fight; an argument*
un malentendu	*a misunderstanding*
se disputer	*to argue*
être déçu(e)	*to be disappointed*
être fâché(e)	*to be angry*
s'embrasser	*to kiss*
Il n'en est pas question!	*No way!*
Jamais de la vie!	*Never!*

Ça va mieux!

l'avenir	*the future*
s'excuser	*to apologize*
s'expliquer	*to explain*
se sentir mieux	*to feel better*
se réconcilier	*to make up*

ACTIVITÉS

 9. Vous disputez-vous? Vous faites un sondage pour votre classe de psychologie. Posez les questions suivantes à votre partenaire.

1. Est-ce que vos frères et sœurs se disputent plus que les frères et sœurs de vos amis?
2. Est-ce que vous êtes fâché(e) moins souvent que votre meilleur(e) ami(e)?
3. Est-ce que vous vous excusez aussi rapidement que votre meilleur(e) ami(e)?
4. Est-ce que votre mère est plus ou moins déçue que votre père quand vous oubliez leur anniversaire?
5. Est-ce que vous avez autant (plus / moins) de malentendus dans votre vie que votre meilleur(e) ami(e)?
6. Votre petit(e) ami(e) et vous, est-ce que vous vous embrassez plus ou moins souvent que d'habitude après une dispute?

10. Comparez-les. Donnez votre opinion en ce qui concerne les choses et les personnes suivantes. Faites tous les changements nécessaires.

MODÈLE: un lion / un tigre (féroce)
> **Un tigre est plus féroce qu'un lion.**
> OU **Un tigre est aussi féroce qu'un lion.**

> tu / moi (parler vite)
> **Tu parles moins vite que moi.**

1. les chats / les chiens (intelligent)
2. mes parents / mon petit(e) ami(e) et moi (se réconcilier vite)
3. je / ma mère (se sentir bien)
4. le Coca / le Pepsi (bon)
5. nous / les étudiants d'espagnol (comprendre bien le vocabulaire)
6. tu / moi (manger lentement)
7. je / mes amis (aller souvent au cinéma)
8. mes parents / mes professeurs (s'expliquer bien)

11. Pour mieux les connaître. Votre petit(e) ami(e) va rencontrer votre famille et vos amis. Comparez-vous à ces personnes.

MODÈLE: **Ma sœur, Monnet, a plus d'amis que moi.**

mon frère	avoir		amis
mes parents	acheter	plus de	disputes
mon (ma) meilleur(e) ami(e)	manger	moins de	musique
ma sœur	écouter	autant de	travail
	regarder		disques compacts
	faire		malentendus
			sport
			spaghettis
			émissions
			patience

You may want to ask students to justify their answers for Activité 10 if there is any disagreement among them.

12. Et ton ami(e)? Votre meilleur(e) ami(e) aimerait en savoir un peu plus sur votre petit(e) ami(e). Dites ce que vous et votre petit(e) ami(e) faites. Jouez les deux rôles avec un(e) partenaire.

T 82

MODÈLE:

> —**Mange-t-il / elle autant que toi?**
> —**Oui, il / elle mange autant que moi.**
> OU —**Non, il / elle mange plus / moins que moi.**

=

1

+

2

=

3

+

4

=

5

—

6

—

 13. Interview. Find out from your partner if he or she

1. is as intelligent as his or her best friend.
2. has as many friends as you.
3. has more classes than you.
4. speaks less often than you.
5. is prettier / more handsome than his or her brother or sister.
6. plays basketball better than his or her best friend.
7. goes out more often than his or her family.

Julie pense que cette situation est vraiment ridicule. Benjamin et Caroline s'aiment. Alors, Julie décide d'agir°. Elle téléphone à Benjamin et lui explique la situation.

agir *to act*

Benjamin, catastrophé°, prend le premier train et arrive, roses rouges et chocolat en main, chez Caroline. Pendant des heures, les deux amoureux se parlent, s'expliquent. Ils finissent par° s'embrasser et se réconcilier. Benjamin, qui a un examen de fin d'année à passer le lendemain, repart pour Grenoble.

catastrophé *devastated* / **finissent par** *end up*

AVEZ-VOUS COMPRIS?

1. Qu'est-ce que Julie décide de faire? Pourquoi?
2. Quelle est la réaction de Benjamin?
3. Qu'est-ce qu'il apporte à Caroline? Pourquoi?
4. Est-ce que Caroline et Benjamin se parlent? Quel est le résultat de leurs discussions?
5. Pourquoi Benjamin repart-il pour Grenoble?
6. Qu'est-ce que Caroline dit à Julie après le départ de Benjamin?
7. Julie dit «carpe diem» à Caroline. Pourquoi?

Julie et Caroline se retrouvent, encore une fois, et prennent un café.

CAROLINE: Tu sais, je ne sais pas comment te remercier. Sans ton coup de téléphone, Benjamin et moi, nous serions toujours fâchés! Tu avais raison! C'était vraiment idiot! Mais heureusement, tu as téléphoné! Et Benjamin est monté si vite. C'est l'homme le plus merveilleux de la terre! Il s'est montré le plus tendre et le plus délicat des amoureux...

JULIE: Oh là là. Hier, c'était le plus cruel, le moins compréhensif, le garçon le plus bête du monde, mais aujourd'hui, c'est l'homme le plus extraordinaire, le meilleur qui existe! L'amour... je n'y comprends rien. Tu es vraiment un peu bête, Caroline, tu sais! Benjamin t'aime, et tu l'aimes. Vous parlez d'une vie ensemble. Alors, carpe diem!° Profitez donc de la vie!

CAROLINE: Tu es plus sage que moi, Julie. Il va falloir que je° t'écoute plus souvent...

JULIE: Alors, là, ce n'est pas pour demain!°

carpe diem! Latin for *"seize the day!"* / **Il va falloir que je** *I'm going to have to* / **ce n'est pas pour demain!** *I'm not going to hold my breath!*

ET VOUS?

1. Quand vos amis se disputent, est-ce que vous essayez *(try)* de les calmer? Pourquoi ou pourquoi pas?
2. À votre avis, quand on veut s'excuser, est-il préférable de téléphoner, d'écrire une lettre ou de s'excuser en personne? Quels sont les avantages, les inconvénients de chaque méthode?
3. Que faites-vous quand vous voulez vous excuser?
4. Dites-vous ce que vous pensez à vos amis? Si oui, à quel(s) sujet(s)? Est-ce qu'ils vous écoutent?

VOUS ÊTES BRANCHÉS!

Louis Pasteur et Marie Curie: Deux Scientifiques Exceptionnels

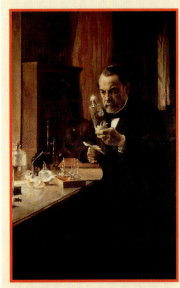

Louis Pasteur, homme de science.

Among the great French scientists, **Louis Pasteur** (1822–1895) and **Marie Curie** (1867–1934) occupy a very special place.

Born in Dole, Louis Pasteur revolutionized the field of medicine. Father of microbiology, he put an end to the theory, widely believed in his day, of **la génération spontanée** by demonstrating that it is the concentration of germs that causes microorganisms to appear. He went on to invent **la pasteurisation,** a process through which wine, beer, milk, and fruit juices can be heated up in an airtight container and kept safely for long periods of time. His remarkable work on infectious germs led to his discovery of the **vaccination par germe atténué,** a vaccination process which continues to be used even today. His method of preventing **la rage** (rabies), saved countless lives.

While Pasteur revolutionized medicine, Marie Curie turned the world of physics upside down. A young Polish woman, Marie Curie came to Paris where she studied chemistry and physics. Working with her husband, Pierre Curie, she discovered polonium and radium, which were used in radiation treatments to fight cancer. A woman of extraordinary intelligence, she was awarded *two* Nobel prizes. In 1903, she shared her first prize in physics with her husband, and in, 1911 she alone received a second Nobel prize in chemistry. To this day, she is the only woman who has received this supreme distinction. She is also the only woman to be buried in the **Panthéon,** the French "Hall of Heroes," for her work.

Marie Curie dans son laboratoire.

La génération spontanée is *abiogenesis,* or the idea that living organisms could arise from lifeless matter.

VOTRE Q. I. CULTUREL

 Expliquez l'essentiel à votre partenaire. Choisissez un sujet et allez-y! Votre partenaire va accepter votre explication, la modifier ou y ajouter quelques détails.

1. Résumez les découvertes de Louis Pasteur et de Marie Curie.
2. Nommez deux ou trois conséquences que les travaux de Pasteur et de Curie ont dans notre vie de tous les jours.

http://www.wiley.com/aventure.html

Making comparisons (continued)

IV **LE SUPERLATIF**

> Benjamin est **le plus bel homme de** la terre.
> C'est **le meilleur** homme qui existe.
> Julie a choisi la route **la moins difficile** pour réconcilier ses amis.
> Caroline comprend l'anglais **le plus vite** et **le mieux.**

◆ The superlative is used to compare someone or something to the rest of a group. Use it to express the idea of *the best, the worst, the most,* or *the least.*

◆ The superlative consists of the definite article (or a possessive adjective) followed by **plus** or **moins** and an adjective or adverb. Superlative adjectives agree in number and gender with the nouns they describe.

> **Ma meilleure amie** s'appelle Evelyne.
> **Mon meilleur ami** s'appelle Sam.

If an adjective normally comes *before* a noun, the superlative adjective also comes before the noun.

> Maryse est **la plus jolie femme** de la classe.
> Nous sommes **les plus petites femmes** de notre club.

If an adjective normally comes *after* a noun, the definite article is repeated after the noun and is followed by the superlative adjective.

> Robert est **l'homme le plus bavard** de la classe.
> Nous sommes **les femmes les plus intelligentes.**

Note: To say *in the class, in our club, in the world* after a superlative, use a form of **de** + the definite article.

> C'est le plus bel acteur **du monde.** *He's the most handsome actor in the world.*

◆ Superlatives can also be followed directly by a noun. As with the comparative, use **de** before the noun.

> William a **le moins d'argent**, mais il a **le plus d'amis.**

◆ The definite article is always **le** for the superlative of nouns or adverbs.

> J'ai **le moins de difficultés** en maths.
> Elles parlent **le plus vite** de tous mes amis.

◆ Two irregular superlatives both mean *the best*. Be careful to use them correctly. The superlative **adjective** *the best* is **le (la) (les) meilleur(e)(s).** The superlative **adverb** *the best* is **le mieux.**

> Benjamin est **le meilleur** joueur de tennis.
> Il joue **le mieux** de tous ses amis.
> Julie est **la meilleure** danseuse de sa classe.
> Elle danse **le mieux** de toutes ses amies.

ACTIVITÉS

14. À qui va-t-on décerner le César? Vous connaissez assez bien vos camarades de classe, et vous êtes prêt(e) à leur donner les prix qu'ils méritent. Répondez aux questions de votre partenaire.

Culture. Le César is the highest prize awarded at the Cannes Film Festival and is the European equivalent of an Oscar.

MODÈLE: généreux
> —**Qui est la fille la plus généreuse de la classe?**
> —**Michelle est la fille la plus généreuse.**

> grand
> —**Qui est le plus grand garçon de la classe?**
> —**Mark est le plus grand garçon.**

> bavard
> —**Qui est la personne la moins bavarde de la classe?**
> —**Kevin est la personne la moins bavarde.**

Even though the word **personne** is feminine in French, it may refer to either men or women. Make superlative adjectives agree with **la personne** rather than the subject of the sentence.

1. calme
2. impatient
3. amusant
4. travailleur

5. sportif
6. petit
7–10. d'autres questions

15. Dites ce que vous en pensez. Êtes-vous d'accord avec votre partenaire? Décidez.

■ MOT À UTILISER: **équipe** *team*

MODÈLE: Big Ben / la tour Eiffel / la Maison Blanche (joli / monument)
> —**La Maison Blanche est le plus joli monument.**
> —**Mais non, la tour Eiffel est le plus joli monument.**
> OU —**Bien sûr, la Maison Blanche est le plus joli monument.**

> *People / G.Q. / Elle* (intéressant / magazine)
> —***People* est le magazine le moins intéressant.**
> —**Mais non, *G.Q.* est le magazine le moins intéressant.**
> OU —**Bien sûr, *People* est le magazine le moins intéressant.**

Follow-up. If you like, have the students redo **Activité 14** using **du monde** instead of **de la classe.** You may also ask them to choose five more adjectives on their own to continue the activity.

Michael Jordan / Dennis Rodman / Tyus Edney (bon / joueur de basket)

—**Michael Jordan est le meilleur joueur de basket.**

—**Mais non, Tyus Edney est le meilleur joueur de basket.**

OU —**Bien sûr, Michael Jordan est le meilleur joueur de basket.**

1. les Oilers / les Rangers / les Kings (bon / équipe de hockey)
2. la musique classique / la musique punk / la musique folk (intéressant / musique)
3. la cuisine mexicaine / la cuisine française / la cuisine chinoise (cher / cuisine)
4. Lexus / BMW / Corvette (beau / voiture)
5. Brad Pitt / Antonio Banderas / Keanu Reeves (célèbre / acteur)
6. Emma Thompson / Cher / Jennifer Jason Leigh (célèbre / actrice)
7. les chiens / les chats / les rats (intelligent / animaux)
8. Paris / New York / Montréal (beau / ville)
9. la télévision / la lecture / le sport (amusant / distraction)

 16. C'est le meilleur! Tell your partner

1. who the best student is.
2. who sings the worst.
3. who the shortest actor is.
4. who the tallest basketball player is.
5. which restaurant near the campus is the best.
6. who the youngest person in his/her family is.
7. who has the most friends.

 **LECTURE**

LE DEUXIÈME SEXE

Reading Strategy: Reading for gist

Reading for gist means that you are looking for the heart or essence of a particular text. This technique is similar to scanning in that you move rapidly but thoroughly from one part of the passage to another to get to its main points. When you read the selection that follows, remember that you will be looking beyond individual vocabulary words to find the most central ideas.

Simone de Beauvoir (1908–1986) est souvent considérée comme la mère du féminisme. Son livre, ***Le deuxième sexe,*** publié en 1949, était une des premières œuvres en français à explorer le rôle de la femme dans la société. Aujourd'hui, le rôle que la femme joue ou doit jouer continue à être une question importante.

1. Lisez rapidement le paragraphe suivant. Ne vous inquiétez pas si vous ne comprenez pas tous les mots. N'oubliez pas que vous cherchez les idées centrales du passage. Quand vous aurez fini la lecture, écrivez deux ou trois phrases pour résumer ce que vous avez compris. Comparez avec un(e) partenaire pour voir si vous avez trouvé les mêmes idées.

Une scientifique au travail.

destines
forbids
servitude

heat; sexual activity

at a young age

births

Un des problèmes essentiels qui se posent à propos de la femme, c'est, avons-nous vu, la conciliation de son rôle reproducteur et de son travail producteur. La raison profonde qui à l'origine de l'histoire voue° la femme au travail domestique et lui interdit° de prendre part à la construction du monde, c'est son asservissement° à la fonction génératrice. Chez les femelles animales, il y a un rythme du rut° et des saisons qui assure l'économie de leurs forces; au contraire entre la puberté et la ménopause la nature ne limite pas les capacités de gestation de la femme. Certaines civilisations interdisent les unions précoces°; on cite des tribus indiennes où il est exigé qu'un repos d'au moins deux années soit assuré aux femmes entre leurs accouchements°; mais dans l'ensemble pendant de nombreux siècles la fécondité féminine n'a pas été réglementée.

Extrait, Simone de Beauvoir, **Le deuxième sexe.** vol. I, Editions Gallimard, 1949, renouvelé en 1976, p. 202.

Before having students discuss Question h. on the next page, be sure to warn them that it is quite controversial. Also make sure not to present your opinion, or otherwise

2. Répondez aux questions. Relisez le passage si vous voulez.

a. Est-ce qu'une femme devrait travailler à l'extérieur? Pourquoi ou pourquoi pas?

b. Est-ce qu'une femme devrait continuer à travailler si elle a des enfants?

c. À votre avis, y a-t-il des professions qui sont des «professions de femme» et d'autres métiers qui sont pour les hommes? Expliquez.

d. Quel est un des problèmes essentiels pour la femme selon de Beauvoir?

e. Historiquement, pourquoi les femmes sont-elles souvent obligées de faire du travail domestique au lieu de travailler à l'extérieur?

f. Comment les femelles animales conservent-elles leurs forces? Est-ce que les femmes ont cette même possibilité?

g. Que font certaines civilisations non-européennes (non-américaines) pour aider les femmes à conserver leur énergie? Que pensez-vous de ces solutions?

h. À votre avis, faut-il que la société réglemente la reproduction humaine? Pourquoi ou pourquoi pas?

influence the discussion according to your own beliefs. Rather, ask the students if they are aware of anywhere this happens, such as in France, where couples are *encouraged* to have more than one child, in China, where they are forbidden to have more than one, or in literature such as *1984* or *Brave New World*.

Expressing wishes, making polite requests, and giving advice   **Voir p. 432.**   RÉVISION ÉCLAIR

> Nous **pourrions** habiter aux États-Unis ou en France.
> Ça ne lui **plairait** pas.

Expressing hypotheses   **Voir p. 439.**

> **Si** elle **était** ma femme, je **serais** très heureux.
> **Allez** au restaurant **si** vous **avez** faim.

Making comparisons   **Voir p. 444.**

> Benjamin est **plus gentil que** la majorité des hommes.
> Il me comprend **mieux que** Philippe.

Making comparisons (continued)   **Voir p. 451.**

> C'est **l'homme le plus intelligent** du monde.
> Je te présente **ma meilleure amie.**

ÊTES-VOUS BRANCHÉS? _____

Mon journal. Vous savez maintenant que certains Français et Françaises ont reçu le Prix Nobel. Notez dans votre journal qui en a gagné un et quand. Expliquez aussi ce qu'ils / elles ont fait pour gagner ce prix. Donnez votre opinion sur les prix comme le Prix Nobel.

Y ÊTES-VOUS ARRIVÉS? _____

 A. Des comparaisons. Ressemblez-vous à votre partenaire? En quoi êtes-vous différent(e)? similaire? Parlez-en avec lui / elle. (Vous n'êtes pas obligé(e) de dire la vérité.)

MODÈLES: cassettes

—**Combien de cassettes as-tu?**
—**J'en ai trente. Et toi?**
—**J'en ai dix. Tu as plus de cassettes que moi.**

intelligent
—**Es-tu intelligent?**
—**Oui, je suis assez intelligent. Et toi?**
—**Je suis très intelligent. Tu es moins intelligent que moi.**

nager
—**Comment nages-tu?**
—**Je nage mal. Et toi?**
—**Moi aussi, je nage très mal. Tu nages aussi mal que moi.**

Objets	Qualités	Activités
argent	travailleur	chanter
compacts	paresseux	danser
cassettes	optimiste	lire
livres	bavard	parler
cartes de crédit	généreux	manger
exercices	sympathique	écrire

 B. Qu'en penses-tu? Demandez à votre partenaire ce qu'il / elle pense des personnes et des choses suivantes. Utilisez le superlatif.

MODÈLE: —**Que penses-tu de Michael Jordan?**
—**Je pense que c'est le meilleur joueur de basketball.**

1. Elvis (chanteur)
2. Dracula (vampire)
3. Madonna
4. Le Grand Canyon
5. La tour Eiffel
6. le chocolat
7. les vins de Californie
8. les films français

 C. Sondage. Ask your partner

1. what he or she will do this weekend if the weather is nice.
2. if he or she would like to go to the movies.
3. if he or she could help you with your homework.
4. what he or she will do after he or she finishes his or her studies.
5. who he or she would like to go out with.
6. if he or she would blush if he or she met the president of France.

(Lab) PRONONCIATION

[ə]

The symbol [ə] represents the sound that is sometimes referred to as "mute e" or schwa. Another name for this sound is "unstable e," since sometimes it is pronounced, and sometimes it is not. When it is pronounced, it sounds like the *u* in the English word *burn*. To determine where it is pronounced and where it is silent, follow the general rules below.

The letter e is pronounced as [ə]

When it occurs in the first syllable of a breath group:

> Demain, nous irons à Paris.
> Le livre de français est intéressant.

When it follows two consonant sounds and is followed by another consonant sound (the three-consonant rule):

vendredi	crevette
mercredi	faire le ménage
premier	

The letter e is silent

When it occurs at the end of a word:

chatte   tarte   italienne   voiture

When it occurs between single consonant sounds:

samedi	tu ne sais pas
la petite	heureusement

1. Listen to your professor or lab tape and repeat the following words, paying special attention to the [ə] sound.

regardez	te	le
petit	première	cela
je	que	mercredi

2. Now take out a sheet of paper and copy the following sentences. Listen to your professor or lab tape, and repeat each sentence. Every time you hear [ə] pronounced as in **je,** underline it. If the **e** is silent, draw a line through it.

a. Nous prenons le bus le samedi.
b. Je te verrai demain.
c. Elle ne sait pas si elle va acheter cette robe.
d. Ils prennent un litre de vin et des pommes de terre.
e. Je le ferai mercredi prochain.

Exprimer un désir, demander poliment

Aimerais-tu... / Aimeriez-vous...
  Would you like to . . .
Ça / cela m'arrangerait de...
  It would help me to . . .
Ça / cela vous arrangerait de...
  It would help you to . . .
Cela / ça me dérangerait de...
  *It would be a problem for
  me to . . .*

Ça me ferait plaisir de...   *It
  would make me happy to . . .*
Ce serait gentil de...   *It would be
  nice to . . .*
Serait-il possible de...   *Would it
  be possible to . . .*
Il serait possible de...   *It would
  be possible to . . .*

Je serais content(e) de...Je serais
  heureux / heureuse de...
  I would be happy to . . .
Je serais ravi(e) de...   *I would be
  delighted to . . .*
Pourrais-tu... / Pourriez-vous...
  Could you . . .
Voudrais-tu... / Voudriez-vous...
  Would you . . .

Les relations personnelles

Ça va mal!
une dispute   *a fight; argument*
un malentendu   *a misunderstanding*
se disputer   *to argue*
être fâché(e)   *to be angry*
être déçu(e)   *to be disappointed*
Il n'en est pas question!   *No way!*
Jamais de la vie!   *Never!*

Ça va mieux!
l'avenir   *the future*
s'expliquer   *to explain*
s'excuser   *to apologize*
se sentir mieux   *to feel better*
s'embrasser   *to kiss*
se réconcilier   *to make up*

Comparer les personnes et les choses

aussi (adj., adv.) que...   *as (adj.,
  adv.) as*
autant que...   *as much as*
autant de (nom) que...   *as
  many; much (noun) as*

meilleur(e)(s) que...   *better than
  (for nouns)*
mieux que...   *better than (for
  verbs)*
moins de (nom) que...   *fewer
  (noun) than*

moins (adj.) que...   *less than*
plus de (nom) que...   *more
  (noun) than*
plus (adj., adv.) que...   *(adj.) -er
  than; more (adv.) than*

Autres mots et expressions utiles

une équipe   *team*

une guerre   *war*

prêter   *to lend*

Chapitre 15 ◆ LA VIE EN ROSE

PRÉSENTATION ÉCLAIR

POUR COMMUNIQUER

Saying no (continued)
Talking about your activities (continued)
Giving more details (continued)
Talking about activities and expressing beliefs

POUR Y ARRIVER

La négation (suite)
Les verbes comme **ouvrir**
Les pronoms relatifs (suite)
Les verbes **voir** et **croire**

POUR S'ADAPTER À LA CULTURE

La carte d'identité et le permis de conduire
Argent, comptes en banque et chèques

Décidément cette fin d'année scolaire s'annonce bien° pour tout le monde. Caroline, ce n'est pas du tout difficile à comprendre, nage dans le bonheur°. Julie travaille très sérieusement et elle n'est pas mécontente non plus!°

Installée sur le sofa, Caroline prépare ses examens. Rien ne bouge° dans l'appartement quand, tout à coup, Caroline entend la porte s'ouvrir°. Julie rentre en chantant à tue-tête°.

CAROLINE: Julie, ça va bien?

---

s'annonce bien *is looking good* / **bonheur** *happiness* / **n'est pas mécontente non plus** *isn't unhappy either* / **rien ne bouge** *nothing moves* / **s'ouvrir** *to open* / **en chantant à tue-tête** *singing at the top of her lungs*

JULIE: Caroline, je suis aux anges!° J'ai une nouvelle géniale°. Tu ne me croiras jamais!°

CAROLINE: Serais-tu amoureuse? Alors, raconte vite, ça doit vraiment être génial parce que je ne t'ai jamais vue° comme ça...

JULIE: Écoute, écoute... Que tu es bête, non, je ne suis pas amoureuse... Est-ce que tu te souviens de Mme Villette? Eh bien, grâce à° elle, je vais passer l'année prochaine au Sénégal. Elle m'a aidée à décrocher un stage° super compétitif dans une compagnie internationale.

---

je suis aux anges! *I'm on cloud nine!* / **nouvelle géniale** *great news* / **Tu ne me croiras jamais!** *You'll never believe me!* / **vue** *seen* / **grâce à** *thanks to* / **décrocher un stage** *to get an internship*

AVEZ-VOUS COMPRIS?

1. Décrivez les actions et les sentiments de Caroline.
2. Qui rentre? Est-elle triste? Pourquoi?
3. Quelle nouvelle est-ce que Julie annonce à Caroline?
4. Comment a-t-elle eu ce stage?
5. Décrivez ce que Julie a l'intention de faire dans l'avenir.
6. Selon *(according to)* Caroline, pourquoi est-ce que Julie a réussi à avoir ce qu'elle voulait?
7. Où l'invite-t-elle ce soir? Pourquoi?

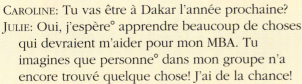

CAROLINE: Tu vas être à Dakar l'année prochaine?

JULIE: Oui, j'espère° apprendre beaucoup de choses qui devraient m'aider pour mon MBA. Tu imagines que personne° dans mon groupe n'a encore trouvé quelque chose! J'ai de la chance!

___

espère *hope* / **personne** *no one*

CAROLINE: Ce n'est pas de la chance; tu le mérites° bien. Tu as travaillé comme une folle cette année; tu as envoyé des dizaines de lettres et as eu beaucoup d'entretiens°. Je ne connais personne d'autre° qui a fait tout ça. Ce soir, je t'invite au restaurant! Décidément, on a vraiment des choses à fêter!!

___

mérites *deserve* / **entretiens** *interviews* / **personne d'autre** *nobody else*

ET VOUS?

1. Quand étudiez-vous en général? De quelle heure à quelle heure? Où?
2. Cette année, qu'allez-vous faire pendant les vacances d'été?
3. Quels sont les diplômes américains que vous désirez avoir dans les deux prochaines années? Dans l'avenir?
4. Avez-vous déjà cherché du travail? Quelle sorte de travail? Qu'avez-vous fait pour en trouver?
5. Avez-vous déjà fait un stage? Si oui, où et quand? Si non, aimeriez-vous en faire un? Pourquoi ou pourquoi pas?
6. Pensez-vous que les stages soient utiles? Pourquoi ou pourquoi pas?

Saying no (continued)

I **LA NÉGATION (SUITE)**

Dans l'appartement **rien ne** bouge.
Personne n'a trouvé de stage.
Ni tes amies françaises **ni** tes amies américaines **n'**ont travaillé
comme ça.

◆ You already know how to make a sentence negative using **ne... pas, ne...
jamais,** and **ne... pas du tout** (see Chapter 2). There are several other ways to
express negative meanings. They all include **ne** and a second element.

ne... rien	*nothing*	**ne... personne**	*nobody*
ne... pas encore	*not yet*	**ne... ni... ni**	*neither... nor*
ne... plus	*no longer;*	**ne... que**	*nothing but;*
	not anymore		*only*

Ne... pas encore and **ne... plus** work exactly the same way as **ne... pas.**

Vous **ne** travaillez **pas encore?**
Tu **n'**écouteras **plus** la radio!

◆ For **ne... que, que** is always placed directly before the word it limits.

Il **n'**y a **qu'**une solution.   *There's only one solution.*
Je **n'**ai mangé **qu'**un sandwich.   *I ate only one sandwich.*

◆ **Ne... rien** and **ne... personne** are negative expressions that can be used as
grammatical subjects or objects in a sentence. When used as a subject, **rien** and
personne are placed at the beginning of the sentence. Note that verbs are
always in the third person singular when **rien** and **personne** are the subjects.

Rien n'est difficile dans la vie.   *Nothing is difficult in life.*
Personne n'est encore là.   *Nobody is here yet.*

Otherwise, **rien** and **personne** normally follow the verb or preposition in the
présent.

Je **ne** regarde **personne.**	*I don't look at anyone.*
Je **ne** pense à **personne.**	*I don't think about anyone.*
Je **ne** comprends **rien.**	*I don't understand anything.*
Je **ne** pense à **rien.**	*I don't think about anything.*

In a compound tense, **personne** follows the past participle while **rien** precedes it.

| Je **n**'ai regardé **personne.** | *I didn't look at anyone.* |
| Je **n**'ai **rien** compris. | *I didn't understand anything.* |

◆ **Ne... ni... ni** is used to negate two things at once. As with **rien** and **personne,** put the **ne** before the verb. Place the **ni... ni...** around the negated items.

Ni Benjamin **ni** Caroline **ne** vont acheter de maison.	*Neither Benjamin nor Caroline is going to buy a house.*
Vous **n**'adorez **ni** le chocolat **ni** la vanille.	*You like neither chocolate nor vanilla.*
Elle **n**'aime **ni** son cousin Paul **ni** sa cousine Paulette.	*She likes neither her cousin Paul nor her cousin Paulette.*
As-tu un chien et un chat? J'ai **ni** chien **ni** chat.	*Do you have a dog or a cat? I have neither a dog nor a cat.*
As-tu mangé du poulet et des frites? Je **n**'ai mangé **ni** poulet **ni** frites.	*Did you eat chicken and fries? I didn't eat any chicken or fries.*

Note: The examples above show that the definite articles and possessive adjectives are retained in the negative, while the indefinite articles and partitives used in the affirmative are dropped in the negative.

POUR S'EXPRIMER

Le monde du travail

chercher un travail, un poste	*to look for a job*
chercher des renseignements	*to look for information*
écrire son curriculum vitae (c.v.)	*to write one's résumé*
écrire une lettre de recommandation	*to write a letter of recommendation*
un employeur	*employer*
un(e) employé(e)	*employee*
faire un stage	*to do an internship*
faire une demande d'emploi	*to put in an application; to apply*
une nouvelle	*bit of news*
passer une offre d'emploi	*to post a job offer; to place a want ad*
avoir un entretien	*to have a job interview*
un(e) stagiaire	*intern*

ACTIVITÉS

 1. Comment sont-ils? Dites à votre partenaire ce que ces personnes font ou ne font pas.

MODÈLE: **Je cherche un poste.**
Je n'ai pas encore d'entretiens.

un employeur		un stage
un professeur		une offre d'emploi
mes parents	avoir	une demande d'emploi
les étudiants	faire	un travail
nous	(ne pas)	passer	un poste
je	(ne jamais)	écrire	une place
un stagiaire	(ne plus)	chercher	un C.V.
tu	(ne pas du tout)	préparer	des renseignements
vous	(ne pas encore)	lire	un entretien
ma sœur / mon frère		une lettre de recommandation

 2. Je suis déprimé(e)! Vous vous sentez déprimé(e) et vous répondez de manière très négative à votre camarade. Attention à la place de la négation et au temps que vous utilisez.

MODÈLE: Tu veux quelque chose?
—**Non, je ne veux rien.**

Quelqu'un va venir te voir?
—**Non, personne ne va venir me voir!**

Tu as rencontré ton ami hier?
—**Non, je n'ai rencontré personne.**

As-tu entendu cette nouvelle?
—**Non, je n'ai rien entendu.**

1. Tu comprends bien tout ça?
2. Tu veux parler à quelqu'un?

3. Tu veux manger quelque chose?
4. Quelque chose te ferait plaisir?
5. Tes parents et toi, vous avez vu le docteur hier?
6. Tes ami(e)s t'ont aidé(e)?
7. Quelqu'un de nouveau est entré dans ta vie?

 3. Franchement, tu n'es pas drôle... Vous cherchez un(e) camarade de chambre. Mais il faut interviewer beaucoup de personnes avant de choisir la meilleure personne. Posez des questions à votre partenaire qui vous répondra négativement.

MODÈLE: aimer / les chiens et les chats
  —**Tu aimes les chiens et les chats?**
  —**Moi, je n'aime ni les chiens ni les chats!**

  Tes amis et ta famille / habiter ici
  —**Tes amis et ta famille habitent ici?**
  —**Ni mes amis ni ma famille n'habitent ici.**

1. vouloir / regarder la télévision et écouter la radio à minuit
2. aimer / faire tes devoirs et aller à la bibliothèque
3. tes livres et tes compacts disques / prendre beaucoup de place
4. adorer / la musique classique et les vieux films
5. ta sœur et ta / ton meilleur(e) ami(e) / venir te voir
6. garder / tes magazines et tes journaux
7. ta mère et ton père / téléphoner tôt le matin

 4. Interview. Posez les questions suivantes à votre partenaire qui va vous dire la vérité.

1. As-tu encore beaucoup d'énergie à l'université le vendredi?
2. Es-tu toujours en retard en cours de français? Pourquoi?
3. Est-ce que tu détestes deux ou trois personnes dans ce cours?
4. Manges-tu un steak frites à onze heures du soir?
5. Aimes-tu les petits pois et les asperges?
6. Es-tu toujours pessimiste?

DEUXIÈME ÉPISODE 🎧 `T 85`

Quelques heures plus tard, les deux filles ont fini leur travail et elles se préparent à sortir. Caroline a réservé une petite table sympa, et elles se dirigent° d'un pas énergique° vers° le restaurant parce qu'elles ont toutes les deux très faim. Caroline ouvre° la porte et la tient°.

CAROLINE: Vas-y Julie, après toi.

---

se dirigent *are walking* / **d'un pas énergique** *with a spring in their step* / **vers** *toward* / **ouvre** *opens* / **tient** *holds*

Julie et Caroline se mettent à table et entament une discussion° animée.

JULIE: Tu sais, cette année a été vraiment exceptionnelle. Quand je suis arrivée en France, d'abord, j'ai un peu souffert°; j'ai eu des difficultés à m'habituer à la vie, aux gens. Mais, maintenant ici, c'est presque chez moi; j'ai découvert° un nouveau pays, une autre façon° de penser et de vivre°. Je me sens tellement plus riche, et je voudrais te remercier de toute ton aide et de ton soutien° dans les bons et les mauvais moments. Tu te souviens de l'examen que j'ai failli râter?° Heureusement que tu étais là!

---

entament une discussion *start a conversation* / **souffert** *suffered* / **découvert** *discovered* / **façon** *way* / **vivre** *to live* / **soutien** *support* / **j'ai failli râter** *I almost missed*

AVEZ-VOUS COMPRIS?

1. Où vont les deux filles?
2. Décrivez l'année de Julie.
3. Qu'est-ce que Julie offre à Caroline? Pourquoi? À votre avis, est-ce une bonne idée? Justifiez votre point de vue.
4. Quelle bonne nouvelle est-ce que Caroline annonce à Julie?
5. Qu'est-ce que Julie en pense?
6. Qui va aider Caroline à préparer la fête? Pourquoi?

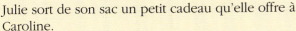

Julie sort de son sac un petit cadeau qu'elle offre à Caroline.

CAROLINE: Mais, qu'est-ce que c'est que ça?
Julie sourit° pendant que Caroline ouvre la petite boîte. Elle y découvre un stylo avec son nom gravé° sur le côté.
CAROLINE: Je suis vraiment touchée; je ne sais pas quoi dire... Elles mangent leur dessert en silence; puis, Caroline se décide à parler.

————————
sourit *smiles* / **gravé** *engraved*

CAROLINE: Tu sais, Julie, moi aussi j'ai une grande nouvelle à t'annoncer. Benjamin et moi, nous avons décidé de nous fiancer le mois prochain chez mes parents à Étretat...
JULIE: Ça alors! C'est la meilleure nouvelle de la journée. Je suis vraiment contente pour vous deux, et puis, je vais pouvoir y assister!°
CAROLINE: Absolument. En fait, je compte sur° toi. Après tout, c'est toi qui m'a mise dans cette situation. Sans ton coup de téléphone, Benjamin et moi, nous ne nous parlerions peut-être plus! Alors, tu vas m'aider à préparer la fête, n'est-ce pas?
JULIE: Caroline, rien ne pourrait me faire plus plaisir°.

————————
assister *attend* / **je compte sur** *I am counting on* / **rien ne pourrait me faire plus plaisir** *nothing could make me happier*

ET VOUS?

1. Où allez-vous souvent avec vos ami(e)s?
2. Comment s'est passée votre année scolaire?
3. Est-ce que vous avez une personne qui vous a beaucoup aidé(e) cette année? Si oui, comment allez-vous la remercier?
4. Avez-vous un(e) ami(e) qui se fiance cette année? Pensez-vous que c'est une bonne idée? Pourquoi ou pourquoi pas?
5. Que va-t-il / elle faire à cette occasion?

Culture. Étretat is a small community near **Rouen** on the English Channel. It is known for its lovely beaches and beautiful cliffs overlooking the water.

VOUS ÊTES BRANCHÉS!

La carte d'identité et le permis de conduire

Two documents are found in most French people's wallets: **une carte d'identité** *(a personal I.D. card)* and **un permis de conduire** *(a driver's license).*

Although a **carte d'identité** is not a compulsory document that every French person must have and carry, most people have one. It is very useful and allows its bearer to accomplish many administrative transactions with ease, paying by check, for example, as well as traveling freely without a passport throughout the **UE (Union Européenne).** Valid for ten years, a **carte d'identité** includes one's full name, date and place of birth, height, address, and picture as well as a **timbre fiscal** *(document fee stamp).*

The **permis de conduire** was instituted in France in 1922, it was modified in 1992 and is now known as a **permis de conduire à points.** People eighteen

Permis de conduire.

years of age or older who have passed the practical and theoretical examinations required are given a **permis de conduire** with 12 points. If driving code violations are committed, points are gradually taken off and the **permis de conduire** may be revoked. You may clean up your record by driving carefully for three years, or you may choose to attend paid classes similar to traffic school.

VOTRE Q. I. CULTUREL

Expliquez l'essentiel à votre partenaire. Choisissez un sujet et allez-y. Votre partenaire va accepter votre explication, la modifier ou y ajouter quelques détails.

1. Faites une liste des renseignements qui sont sur une carte d'identité.
2. Expliquez à votre partenaire à quoi sert une carte d'identité. Quelles sont les raisons d'en avoir une?
3. Résumez ce que vous savez sur le permis de conduire français. Comparez-le au permis de votre pays.

http://www.wiley.com/aventure.html

◼ POUR COMMUNIQUER

Talking about your activities (continued)

II LES VERBES COMME *OUVRIR*

Les personnes **offrent** souvent des cadeaux à leurs amis.
Caroline **ouvre** la porte du restaurant.
Julie **a** un peu **souffert** mais elle **a découvert** un nouveau pays.

◆ A few verbs end in **-ir** but are conjugated in the present tense like **-er** verbs.

ouvrir	
j'**ouvre**	nous **ouvrons**
tu **ouvres**	vous **ouvrez**
il / elle / on **ouvre**	ils / elles **ouvrent**
Passé composé: J'**ai** ouvert	

Grâce au français, je **découvre** des cultures différentes.
Tous les jours, nous **ouvrons** notre livre de français.

Thanks to French, I am discovering different cultures. Every day, we open our French book.

Note that the past participle of all these verbs ends in **-ert.**

Julie **a offert** un stylo à Caroline.
Nous avons **souffert** un peu au début du semestre.

Julie offered (gave) a pen to Caroline. We suffered a little at the beginning of the semester.

POUR S'EXPRIMER

Quelques verbes comme *ouvrir*			
couvrir	*to cover*	ouvrir	*to open*
découvrir	*to discover; to uncover*	recouvrir	*to re-cover; to cover up completely*
offrir	*to offer*	souffrir	*to suffer*

ACTIVITÉS

5. Est-ce logique? Mettez les verbes suivants à la bonne place: recouvrir, souffrir, offrir, ouvrir, découvrir, couvrir.

1. Au début de la classe, les étudiants _____ la porte et ils entrent très vite!
2. Les étudiants _____ quand ils _____ qu'ils ont un examen.
3. Leurs notes _____ leurs bureaux.
4. Le professeur est sympathique. Il _____ de relire les questions orales.
5. Au début du semestre, nous _____ nos livres.

 6. Découvrez votre partenaire! Quel type de personne est votre partenaire? Découvrez-le / la en lui posant ces quelques questions.

1. Es-tu bon(ne) en histoire? Sais-tu qui a découvert l'Amérique?
2. Es-tu optimiste ou pessimiste? Souffres-tu beaucoup dans tes cours ce trimestre / semestre?
3. Es-tu généreux / généreuse? Offres-tu souvent des cadeaux à tes amis? Quand leur as-tu offert quelque chose pour la dernière fois?
4. Es-tu poli(e)? Ouvres-tu la porte à tes parents? à tes professeurs? à une femme? à un homme? Pourquoi ou pourquoi pas?
5. Travailles-tu beaucoup? Prends-tu beaucoup de notes en français? Est-ce que tes notes recouvrent ton bureau à la maison?

1

2

Le grand jour est presque arrivé. Caroline organise les détails de dernière minute: sa robe, la montre qu'elle a achetée pour Benjamin, le foulard° que Benjamin va offrir à sa future belle-mère. Tout est là, elle est prête. Avec Julie, elles se préparent à partir et à aller chercher Benjamin qui les attend chez le fleuriste.

Tout à coup le téléphone sonne.

foulard *scarf*

CAROLINE: Allô, maman, c'est toi, ça va?
MME PERRIN: Bonjour ma chérie, ça va. Tu es prête?
CAROLINE: Oui, ne t'en fais pas°. Nous serons à la maison vers onze heures. Les invités n'arrivent pas avant une heure, non?
MME PERRIN: C'est très bien! Au fait°, peux-tu passer prendre les chaises dont° nous avons besoin chez ta cousine Cécile et t'arrêter chez Durand, le pâtissier à côté de l'église, pour y prendre le gâteau que j'ai commandé? Dis, tu vas bien, n'est-ce pas? Tu es heureuse?
CAROLINE: Mais bien sûr, maman!
MME PERRIN: C'est ce qui compte!° À tout à l'heure, Caroline! On vous attend!

ne t'en fais pas *don't worry* / **Au fait** *By the way* / **dont** *which* / **C'est ce qui compte!** *That's what counts!*

AVEZ-VOUS COMPRIS?

1. Qu'est-ce que Caroline doit faire avant d'aller chez sa mère?
2. Juste avant le départ de Caroline et Julie, qu'est-ce qui arrive?
3. Qu'est-ce que Mme Perrin demande à sa fille?
4. Comment Benjamin se sent-il? À votre avis, pourquoi?
5. Décrivez ce qui se passe quand les trois amis arrivent chez Mme Perrin.

3

4

Benjamin, Julie et Caroline se mettent en route°. Il fait un temps splendide. Ils bavardent gaiement ensemble. Benjamin, dont la cravate est un peu serrée, se sent nerveux, mais Caroline le rassure.

CAROLINE: Benjamin, sois tranquille, tout ira bien. Ils s'arrêtent° en route pour prendre les chaises et le gâteau. Benjamin, qui est assis devant, le tient° sur ses genoux. Julie, elle, a les chaises à côté d'elle.

———
se mettent en route *get going* / **s'arrêtent** *stop* / **tient** *holds*

Les voilà qui arrivent°. Bien sûr, tout le monde les attend. Mme Perrin dont la robe et le foulard sont très élégants, se précipite° pour ouvrir la porte. Benjamin, à son tour°, essaie de sortir très vite pour saluer sa future belle famille. Mais tout à coup, alors qu°'il se lève, la boîte du gâteau glisse, elle s'ouvre, et le miroir au chocolat° atterrit sur°... sa future belle-mère. Quelle catastrophe!

———
Les voilà qui arrivent. *Here they are.* / **se précipite** *rushes forward* / **à son tour** *meanwhile* / **alors que** *while* / **le miroir au chocolat** *a type of chocolate cake with shiny glaze, hence the name "mirror"* / **atterrit sur** *lands on*

Extension. You may want to ask students what they would say if they found themselves in situations similar to Benjamin's. Provide them with vocabulary such as **Pardon, excusez-moi, je suis désolé(e), Que je suis bête!,** or **Zut!**

ET VOUS?

1. Vous préparez-vous bien à l'avance ou attendez-vous jusqu'à la dernière minute quand vous sortez?
2. Quand vous rendez visite aux amis, leur apportez-vous un petit cadeau? Si oui, quel genre de cadeau?
3. Quand mettez-vous vos plus beaux habits? Y a-t-il des situations où il faut qu'on s'habille en complet *(suit)* ou en robe? Lesquelles?
4. Le week-end, comment vous habillez-vous? Et en semaine?

Le gâteau au chocolat que Benjamin apporte a taché *(stained)* la robe de Mme Perrin. Benjamin devrait

a. laver la robe de Mme Perrin avec un peu d'eau.
b. lui dire "désolé" et partir.
c. offrir de lui acheter une nouvelle robe.
d. offrir de faire nettoyer sa robe *(have her dress cleaned).*
e. Avez-vous une autre réponse?

Justifiez votre réponse.

À VOUS DE JOUER

Vous êtes chez des amis pour une grande fête. Vous portez un toast à vos amis, mais tout à coup, votre verre en cristal vous tombe de la main et se casse *(breaks).* Tout le monde vous regarde d'un air surpris. Que faites-vous? Moi, je

a. demande un autre verre et continue à porter mon toast
b. m'excuse, et offre d'acheter d'autres verres.
c. dis «Tant pis, on ne peut pas faire d'omelettes sans casser des œufs!»
d. Avez-vous une autre solution?

Justifiez votre réponse.

■ POUR COMMUNIQUER

Giving more details (continued)

III LES PRONOMS RELATIFS (SUITE)

> Le film **dont** je t'ai parlé passe au Cinéma Rex.
> Voilà le livre **dont** vous avez besoin.
> La robe **dont** elle a envie coûte trop cher.
> Le garçon **dont** la sœur habite en Israël parle hébreu.

◆ In Chapter 8, you learned that you can make a sentence more complex by using the relative pronouns **qui** and **que.** There is a third relative pronoun, **dont. Dont** is used to replace **de** + a noun or noun phrase. Some verbs and expressions followed by **de** are **avoir besoin de, avoir envie de, parler de,** and **s'occuper de.**

Voici le livre. Je t'ai parlé **du livre.**	→ Voici le livre **dont** je t'ai parlé. *Here's the book **(that)** I told you about.*
Elle a acheté des stylos. Elle avait besoin **de stylos.**	→ Elle a acheté les stylos **dont** elle avait besoin. *She bought the pens **(that)** she needed.*

◆ **Dont** is also used to indicate possession.

Nous écrivons au garçon. → Nous écrivons au garçon **dont** le père est
Son père est mort. mort.
*We're writing to the boy **whose** father died.*

ACTIVITÉS

 7. Conseiller matrimonial. Votre partenaire vous aide à faire le portrait de la personne de vos rêves. Répondez à ses questions en utilisant **qui, que,** ou **dont** dans toutes les réponses.

1. Désirez-vous connaître un homme / une femme qui parle une autre langue?
2. Aimez-vous les hommes / femmes qui sont snob?
3. Cherchez-vous quelqu'un avec qui vous pouvez faire du sport?
4. Désirez-vous rencontrer une personne que les autres admireront?
5. Voulez-vous sortir avec quelqu'un que tout le monde aime?
6. Sortiriez-vous avec une personne dont la religion est différente de la votre?

8. Voilà mon entourage! Caroline sort un album de famille pour présenter à Benjamin tous ses amis et les membres de sa famille.

MODÈLE: Grégoire / père / être médecin
Voilà Grégoire dont le père est médecin.

1. l'ami de maman / le fils / participer au marathon
2. Oncle Albert / la fille / être danseuse
3. Marilyne / la nièce / travailler à la banque
4. Cybille / la sœur / habiter aux U.S.A.
5. mon cousin / la moustache / être vraiment ridicule

9. Tout est relatif. Mettez le pronom relatif approprié **(qui, que, dont)** dans les phrases suivantes.

1. J'aime les animaux _____ sont petits.
2. Nous détestons la robe _____ tu as achetée.
3. Aimes-tu les fleurs _____ je t'ai envoyées?
4. C'est une amie _____ la mère travaille avec mon père.
5. As-tu vu le film _____ Spielberg a réalisé?
6. Cet homme, _____ j'ai oublié le nom, habite près de chez moi.

 10. Interview. Find out from your partner if he or she

1. knows a student who speaks Japanese or whose mother speaks Spanish.
2. wants to meet someone that you already know.
3. wants to eat at a restaurant that serves Chinese food.
4. has the book that you need.

QUATRIÈME ÉPISODE

Pour Benjamin, la journée a commencé difficilement! Heureusement sa future belle-mère l'a bien aidé à oublier ce malheureux faux-pas°. Elle a détaché° sa robe sans difficulté, et le beau foulard que Benjamin lui a donné a très bien remplacé celui° qu'elle portait.

___
malheureux faux-pas *unfortunate mistake* / **a détaché** *got the spot out* / **celui** *the one*

Maintenant la fête a commencé: les invités sont arrivés. Benjamin et Caroline forment un très beau couple. Tout le monde voit° bien qu'ils sont très amoureux l'un de l'autre°. À table, tout le monde discute, mange et s'amuse.

___
voit *sees* / **l'un de l'autre** *with each other*

AVEZ-VOUS COMPRIS?

1. Décrivez ce que Mme Perrin a fait pour aider Benjamin à oublier son faux-pas.
2. Quelle impression de Benjamin et de Caroline les invités ont-ils?
3. Résumez la discussion entre Julie et Caroline. Quels conseils (*advice*) est-ce que Julie donne à son amie?
4. Qu'est-ce qui se passe au moment du dessert? À votre avis, est-il important de suivre des traditions comme ça? Pourquoi ou pourquoi pas?

3

4

Pendant que Benjamin parle au petit cousin de Caroline, Julie en profite pour échanger quelques mots avec son amie.

JULIE: Alors, ça va? Tu es heureuse?

CAROLINE: Mais bien sûr!

JULIE: Au fait, vous avez décidé où vous allez vous installer?°

CAROLINE: L'année prochaine, je crois° qu'on va rester à Rouen pour que je finisse mes études. Mais après...

JULIE: Après, vous verrez° bien. Profite de ta journée, vous aurez tout le temps de vous décider.

***

vous installer *settle down* / **crois** *believe* / **verrez** *will see*

Enfin, on arrive au dessert. Benjamin se lève; il prend dans sa poche un écrin° et l'ouvre, en sort une très jolie bague° et l'offre à Caroline. Caroline, rouge de plaisir, donne à Benjamin une belle montre. Julie lève° son verre.

JULIE: Je voudrais porter° un toast au couple le plus merveilleux que je connaisse: «À Caroline et à Benjamin, beaucoup de bonheur°!»

***

écrin *jewelry box* / **bague** *ring* / **lève** *raises* / **porter** *propose* / **bonheur** *happiness*

ET VOUS?

1. Avez-vous déjà assisté aux fiançailles *(engagement party)* d'un(e) ami(e) ou d'un membre de votre famille? Si oui, décrivez la fête. Si non, imaginez les fiançailles parfaites.
2. En général, quelles sortes d'événements fêtez-vous dans votre famille? Comment les fêtez-vous?
3. Est-ce que quelqu'un vous a déjà offert un cadeau pour commémorer une occasion spéciale? Si oui, décrivez l'occasion et le cadeau. Si non, imaginez ce que vous aimeriez recevoir.
4. À votre avis, combien de temps un couple doit-il sortir ensemble avant de se fiancer? Avant de se marier? Expliquez.

VOUS ÊTES BRANCHÉS!

Argent, comptes en banque et chèques

As soon as you arrive in France, you will have to familiarize yourself with the money you will be handling.

La monnaie française *(French currency)* looks and feels different from American money. **Les pièces** *(coins)* made of metallic alloys are different in weight and composition from American coins and have the following values: **cinq centimes, dix centimes, vingt centimes, cinquante centimes, un franc, deux francs, cinq francs, dix francs,** and **vingt francs. Cinquante francs** and **cent francs** coins exist but are rare and are considered collector's items. **Les billets** *(bank notes)* are of different sizes and colors, so it is easy to distinguish each denomination. The composition of the paper they are printed on is a closely guarded secret kept by the **Banque de France,** which prints each note with a watermark, metallic strips, and small images to prevent counterfeiting.

All bank notes portray famous musicians, painters, scientists, writers, and philosophers, and pay tribute to French cultural life. Debussy, on the 20F note, was a composer. Other bills honor Quentin de la Tour and Delacroix, who were painters; Saint-Exupéry, a pilot and author; Montesquieu, a philosopher and writer; Pascal, a scientist, philosopher, and writer; and Pierre and Marie Curie, Nobel prize winners in physics and chemistry.

Billets, pièces, carte de crédit et chèque.

If you live and/or work in France for a long time, you will most likely need to open **un compte en banque** *(a bank account)*. Although most banking will feel very familiar, be careful when you fill out **un chèque français** *(a French check)*. In the United States, you usually indicate the name of the person the check is for and then, the amount of money the person is to receive. In France, you have to do the opposite. You need to indicate the amount of the check on the first and second lines, and you write the name of the person to whom you are writing the check on the third line.

VOTRE Q. I. CULTUREL

 Expliquez l'essentiel à votre partenaire. Choisissez un sujet et allez-y! Votre partenaire va accepter votre explication, la modifier ou y ajouter quelques détails.

1. Résumez tout ce que vous savez sur la monnaie en France.
2. En quoi l'argent français et l'argent américain sont-ils similaires? différents?
3. Indiquez la différence de présentation qui existe entre une formule de chèque en France et aux Etats-Unis.

http://www.wiley.com/aventure.html

Talking about your activities and expressing beliefs

IV LES VERBES *VOIR* ET *CROIRE*

Je **vois** que vous avez mon livre.
Benjamin et Caroline vont **voir** un film ce week-end.
Elles **croient** que leurs amis arriveront aujourd'hui.
Croyez-vous au Père Noël?
Je n'en **crois** pas mes yeux!

◆ **Voir** *(to see)* and **croire** *(to believe; to think)* are two very common irregular verbs.

voir	croire
je **vois**	je **crois**
tu **vois**	tu **crois**
il / elle / on **voit**	il / elle / on **croit**
nous **voyons**	nous **croyons**
vous **voyez**	vous **croyez**
ils **voient**	ils **croient**
past participle: **vu**	past participle: **cru**
futur: **verr-**	futur: **croir-**

Je **vois** deux hommes.   *I see two men.*
Vous **croyez** que Caroline et Benjamin   *You believe that Caroline and*
   seront contents.   *Benjamin will be happy.*

◆ Certain forms of the verb **voir** are often used idiomatically.

Papa, est-ce que je peux avoir un   *Daddy, can I have a dog?*
   chien?
   —Peut-être. **On verra.**   *—Maybe. We'll see.*

Voyons. D'abord je fais la   *Let's see. First I do the dishes, then*
   vaisselle, puis, la lessive...   *the laundry...*

Voyons! Qui a pris mes notes?   *Oh, come on! Who took my notes?*
Alors, vous comprenez le poème?   *So, do you understand the poem?*
   —Oui, **je vois** ce que le poète   *—Yes, I see what the poet*
   veut dire.   *means.*

◆ The verb **croire** may mean *to think, to be under the impression.*

> Tu **crois** que Pierre va arriver ce soir?
> —Je **crois** que oui.

> *Do you think (that) Pierre is going to arrive tonight?*
> —*I think so.*

> Est-ce qu'ils vont se marier cette année?
> —Je **crois** que non.

> *Are they going to get married this year?*
> —*I don't think so.*

◆ The verb **croire (en)** may mean *to believe (in).*

> Je **crois en toi.**   *I believe in you.*
> Elles **croient en** Dieu.   *They believe in God.*

Note: Two examples that use **au(x)** instead of **en** are given below:

> Les petits enfants **croient au Père Noël.**
> Croyez-vous **aux fantômes?**

> *Little children believe in Santa Claus.*
> *Do you believe in ghosts?*

ACTIVITÉS

POUR S'EXPRIMER	
Les relations humaines	
tomber amoureux	*to fall in love*
être amoureux	*to be in love*
les fiançailles	*engagement party*
se fiancer	*to get engaged*
le / la fiancé(e)	*fiancé/fiancée*
un écrin	*a jewelry case*
une bague	*a ring*
le mariage	*wedding ceremony; marriage*
le marié	*groom*
la mariée	*bride*
l'alliance	*wedding band/ring*
la cérémonie	*the ceremony*
un / une invité(e)	*a guest*
le bonheur	*happiness*
un conseiller matrimonial	*a marriage counselor*

11. Une mariée anxieuse. Sophie, une amie de Caroline, va se marier aujourd'hui. Mais est-ce que tout va bien se passer? Qu'est-ce que tout le monde pense?

MODÈLE: **Les parents croient que la cérémonie est splendide**

je			le jeune couple est amoureux
le fiancé			l'écrin est sur la table
la fiancé			la bague est belle
le marié			la montre du fiancé est superbe
la mariée	croire	que	le conseiller matrimonial est là
les parents	voir		la cérémonie est splendide
les beaux-parents			la nouvelle est extraordinaire
nous			le mariage est pour la vie
tu			les fiançailles sont superbes
tes amis et toi			le bonheur est pour la vie
			l'alliance est magnifique
			le couple s'est fiancé en juin
			le couple est tombé amoureux en janvier

12. Mini-sondage. Posez ces questions à cinq personnes de la classe. Soyez prêt(e) à partager vos réponses avec la classe. Attention aux temps.

MODÈLE: tes parents / voir un film / ce soir
Est-ce que tes parents voient un film ce soir?

1. ton frère / croire / en Dieu
2. tu / croire / au Père Noël
3. ton frère et toi / voir / souvent / vos amis
4. tes amis / voir / un film / le week-end prochain
5. ton professeur / voir / les étudiants qui arrivent en retard
6. tu / croire / en tes parents

13. Interview. Find out if your partner

1. used to believe in Santa when he or she was little.
2. will see a movie this weekend.
3. believes that he or she will get a good grade in French.
4. saw friends last night.
5. sees his or her parents very often.

FEMME NOIRE PAR LÉOPOLD SENGHOR

Reading Strategy: Identifying and explaining poetic imagery

Reading a poem is often quite different from reading a passage in prose. Poets often use colorful or evocative images to express ideas indirectly and to reach the reader on an emotional rather than a cognitive level. For example, instead of saying *I fell in love,* a poet might say *My heart was pierced by the arrows of Eros.* In the poem that follows, Senegalese poet Léopold Senghor (1906–   ), first Black member of the **Académie Française,** uses vivid imagery to express his thoughts.

1. Faites une liste d'un minimum de trois images poétiques que vous trouvez dans le poème **Femme noire,** puis essayez de les expliquer à un(e) partenaire.

Lab

Femme et enfant.

shadow / softness; covered

top / mountain pass / burned
stuns / plunging dive of an eagle

reduces / ashes
roots

Femme noire
Femme nue, femme noire
Vêtue de ta couleur qui est vie, de ta forme qui est beauté!
J'ai grandi à ton ombre°; la douceur° de tes mains bandait° mes yeux.
Et voilà qu'au cœur de l'Été et de Midi, je te découvre Terre
    promise, du haut° d'un col° calciné°
Et ta beauté me foudroie° en plein cœur, comme l'éclair d'un aigle°...

Femme nue, femme noire
Je chante ta beauté qui passe, forme que je fixe dans l'Éternel,
Avant que le Destin jaloux ne te réduise° en cendres° pour nourrir les
    racines° de la vie.

Culture. You may also want to share with your students Senghor's philosophy of **négritude,** which is defined as **l'ensemble des valeurs culturelles et spirituelles des Noirs.** (Petit Larousse illustré, 1990.)

There are many other images to be examined, but the following ones may be helpful in starting your discussion of the poem: **vêtue de ta couleur, de ta forme** (wearing only the clothing of her skin and form); **au cœur de l'Été et de Midi** (the heart of summer and noon, the hottest times of the year and day, respectively); **Terre promise** (Biblical reference of the Promised Land); **ta beauté me foudroie** (traditional "thunderstruck" image of love); **l'éclair d'un aigle** (swift diving of an eagle after its prey); **je chante ta beauté** (love brings forth praise in the form of song; cf. Songs of Solomon or Psalms); **le Destin... te réduise en cendres** (ashes to ashes, dust to dust; cycle of life).

2. Répondez aux questions suivantes.

a. De quoi ou de qui l'auteur parle-t-il dans ce poème?

b. Choisissez les qualités de la femme noire qui peuvent lui être attribuées d'après ce texte et justifiez votre choix.

_____ **1.** Elle est nue.
_____ **2.** Elle est noire.
_____ **3.** Elle est vie.
_____ **4.** Elle est morte.
_____ **5.** Elle est belle.
_____ **6.** Elle est douce.
_____ **7.** Elle est pleine de chaleur.
_____ **8.** Elle est éternelle.
_____ **9.** Elle est jalouse.
_____ **10.** Elle est racine de la vie.

c. À votre avis, qu'est-ce que cette femme noire représente?

d. Connaissez-vous d'autres poèmes qui évoquent les mêmes thèmes? Si oui, lesquels?

À VOS STYLOS

Writing Strategy: Writing a letter of inquiry for a job or internship

One day, you might be interested in working abroad. Although opportunities for students are quite limited, there may be a number of **stages** (internships) that are available.

Many require an application and/or documentation fee, and few positions offer a salary, but the experience can lead to job offers or further studies.

To begin your search for a **stage,** you will most likely need to write a letter of inquiry. In France, the letter of inquiry is usually handwritten. Some employers will examine your handwriting to decide whether or not to grant you **un entretien** (interview). Make sure your handwriting is legible and neat and avoid any flourishes. Carefully place your accents and make sure to end your letter with a simple signature.

Below is the letter of inquiry that Julie Lavalette wrote when she was seeking her internship. Look it over to get a feel for what should be included in such a letter.

Monsieur,

J'ai appris par mon professeur Mme Villette que votre entreprise recherche une jeune personne pour un stage non-rémunéré° de marketing d'une durée de deux mois.

Disponible° tout de suite, j'ai 21 ans et je viens de réussir ma troisième année d'université. Je suis dynamique, travailleuse et motivée, comme Mme Villette vous le dira. Je m'intéresse beaucoup à la vie de l'entreprise et j'aimerais avoir la possibilité de travailler avec vous. Je pourrais me présenter à votre bureau à Paris, à la date que vous m'indiquerez.

Veuillez agréer, Monsieur, l'expression de mes sentiments dévoués.

Julie Lavalette

To write your own letter of inquiry, follow the steps below.

1. Start your letter with **Monsieur, (Madame,).** Tell where you heard about the job, and what kind of position you are looking for.
2. List your background and qualifications for the job. For example, explain what kind of studies you have done, tell about your personal strengths, why you would be interested in the position, and your availability.
3. End your letter with **une formule de politesse** *(closing)* such as

    Veuillez agréer, Monsieur (Madame), l'expression de mes sentiments dévoués,

    OR **Veuillez agréer, Monsieur, (Madame), mes salutations respectueuses.**

    These are two expressions that will be useful to you in your job search.

You are now ready to write your own letter of inquiry. **À vos stylos!**

R E N C O N T R E S

Sénégalais et fier de l'être!

POPULATION: 8 730 508
SUPERFICIE: 196 190 km²
 (un peu plus petit que
 le Dakota du Sud)
CAPITALE: Dakar
LANGUES: français
 (officielle), wolof,
 pulaar, diola,
 mandingo

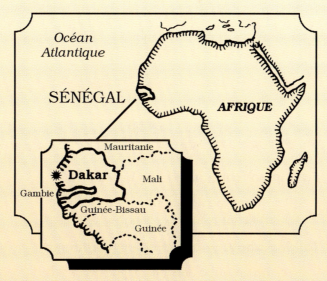

En quelques mots, qui êtes-vous?

Je m'appelle Abdoul Bakhayokho Seck et je viens d'une famille de musiciens qui habite à Saint-Louis, ancienne capitale du Sénégal. On a toujours gagné notre vie en chantant pour tous ceux qui veulent nous écouter.

Y a-t-il des musiciens sénégalais qui sont bien connus?

Mais bien sûr! Par exemple, Youssou'n'Dour a même fait un concert avec Peter Gabriel! Vous savez, la musique joue un rôle très important dans notre vie. Les griots, des hommes qui préservent nos traditions orales, sont encore très respectés dans notre société. Ils racontent notre histoire en parlant, chantant, et dansant avec les gens qui passent dans la rue.

Quelles sortes d'histoires racontent-ils?

Oh, ça dépend. Des fois, ils nous récitent des poèmes où les femmes plantent les arachides°, et quelquefois ils nous parlent des pauvres esclaves qui ont dû quitter à jamais notre pays. Vous avez peut-être entendu parler de la Maison des Esclaves dans l'île de Gorée?

peanuts

Oui. Alex Haley a raconté l'histoire d'un esclave, Kunta Kinte, dans son livre *Roots.* C'était un Sénégalais, n'est-ce pas?

Oui, plus précisément, un Mandingo. Au Sénégal, il y a pas mal de groupes ethniques, comme les Wolof, les Fulani, et les Serer. Finalement, il y a assez peu d'Européens qui sont restés ici après notre indépendance de la France en 1960. Bien que le français reste la langue officielle, nous sommes fiers de notre culture et de nos langues africaines.

Avez-vous une philosophie personnelle?

J'ai adopté l'idée de la négritude que notre premier président, Léopold Senghor, a proposée il y a soixante ans: N'oubliez pas que vous faites partie d'une grande race africaine et qu'il faut préserver vos valeurs spirituelles et culturelles.

QUELQUES QUESTIONS

1. Quelles sont deux ou trois groupes ethniques qui habitent au Sénégal?
2. Qu'est-ce qu'un griot? Quel rôle joue-t-il dans la société sénégalaise?

http://www.wiley.com/aventure.html

RÉVISION ÉCLAIR

Saying no (continued)　　Voir p. 462.

> **Personne ne** te parlera si tu es méchant.
> Je **n'**ai **rien** mangé ce matin.

Talking about your activities (continued)　　Voir p. 468.

> Benjamin **offre** une jolie bague à sa fiancée.
> Tu **souffriras** si tu ne travailles pas plus dur.
> Mme Perrin **a ouvert** son cadeau.

Giving more details (continued)　　Voir p. 472.

> Écoute la belle voix de cette fille **qui** chante.
> Les fleurs **que** j'ai vues étaient des pensées.
> C'est le garçon **dont** je t'ai parlé.

Talking about your activities and expressing beliefs　　Voir p. 477.

> Je **vois** que vous vous amusez bien.
> Ils n'en **croient** pas leurs yeux.

ÊTES-VOUS BRANCHÉS?

Mon journal. Pour faire partie de la société dans laquelle vous vivez, il faut un certain nombre de documents essentiels. Quels documents sont essentiels dans votre pays? Quels documents sont importants en France? À votre avis, est-il important d'avoir une carte d'identité nationale? Pourquoi ou pourquoi pas? Parlez aussi des différences et des similitudes que vous avez découvert entre l'argent de votre pays et l'argent français. À votre avis, est-il préférable de rendre hommage aux hommes politiques ou vaut-il mieux rendre hommage aux philosophes, aux écrivains, ou aux autres personnes? Justifiez votre réponse.

A. Les règles du jeu. *The rules of the game.* Your French professor has asked you and your classmates to come up with rules for the classroom and to write them up in French. When you have finished the first five rules, add three more of your own.

1. No one will smoke in class.
2. Students will eat nothing in class.
3. Neither the students nor the professor will be late.
4. Students will no longer speak English after the first week of class.
5. Students will never leave early.

B. Le prochain Spielberg? You are a brilliant young filmmaker. You have sent out a casting call looking for specific types of people and certain things for the film you would like to make. Choose who and/or what you need according to the type of film you are going to make. You may list more than three people or items.

MODÈLE: un western
    1. Je cherche un homme **que** le public connaît.
    2. Je cherche une femme **dont** la mère est Apache.
    3. Je cherche des acteurs **qui** aiment les chevaux.

1. un film d'amour
2. une comédie
3. un film d'aventure
4. un film d'épouvante *(horror)*
5. un western
6. un film de science-fiction

 C. La galanterie est-elle morte?

■ **MOTS À UTILISER: nourrir** *to feed* / **un SDF** *a homeless person*

Find out from your partner

1. when he or she opens the door for another person.
2. how he or she helps people who are suffering.
3. if he or she believes that it is necessary to offer money or jobs to the poor.
4. if he or she has ever covered a child who was cold.
5. if he or she has discovered how to feed people who are hungry.
6. what he or she does when he or she sees a homeless person.

> **SDF** stands for **sans domicile fixe,** the term most commonly used for homeless people in France.

 **PRONONCIATION**

SPEECH CHAINS

If you are having trouble repeating the whole sentence in one breath, you may break it up and repeat the smaller groupings before trying the whole sentence again. Look for words that fit together logically, such as subject-verb, when breaking a sentence into smaller parts. Remember that the stress rule you just learned applies to groups of *any length*.

Until now, you have been focusing on the specific sounds of French vowels or consonants, and the way they are pronounced in the environment of a particular word or phrase. This is a necessary step to speaking French fluently, but you need to take further steps if you are to become truly fluent.

In French words, all syllables receive equal stress except the last one, which should be just a little stronger than the rest. The same is true when words are linked or grouped together to form a "speech chain"; the last syllable of the *group* receives more stress than the other syllables. This rule applies to groups of any length: phrases, clauses, or whole sentences. It is called "level stressing," and works differently from stress in English, which goes up and down in different parts of a phrase or sentence.

1. Listen to your professor or lab tape and repeat the words below separately and then together in a sentence. When speaking the words individually, put a little more stress on the highlighted syllable of each one. Then when they occur in a phrase, put the emphasis on the highlighted syllable of the *entire* phrase.

a. pe**tite**   mai**son**   cam**pagne**
    Il a une petite maison de cam**pagne.**

b. a**vons**   fi**ni**   le**çons**
    Nous avons fini nos le**çons.**

c. néces**saire**   répé**ter**   vocabu**laire**
    Il est nécessaire de répéter le vocabu**laire.**

2. Go back to the reading on p. 480. Listen to your professor or lab tape as the poem **Femme noire** is read aloud. Listen carefully to the phrasing of the poem several times, then try to repeat the different lines, being careful to respect the musicality and breath groups of the speech chains that the poet has created.

Quelques expressions pour refuser ou nier

ne... ni... ni, ni... ni... ne *neither . . . nor*
ne... personne, personne... ne *no one; nobody*

ne... rien, rien... ne *nothing*
ne... que *only; hardly*

Le monde du travail

chercher des renseignements *to look for information*
chercher un travail, un poste *to look for a job*
écrire son curriculum vitae *to write one's résumé*
écrire une lettre de recommandation *to write a letter of recommendation*

faire une demande d'emploi *to put in an application; to apply*
faire un stage *to do an internship*
passer une offre d'emploi *to post a job offer; to place a want ad*
avoir un entretien *to have an interview*

un employeur *employer*
un(e) employé(e) *employee*
une nouvelle *bit of news*
un(e) stagiaire *intern*

Quelques verbes utiles

couvrir *to cover*
croire *to believe*
découvrir *to discover*

offrir *to offer*
ouvrir *to open*
recouvrir *to re-cover; to cover up completely*

souffrir *to suffer*
voir *to see*

Les relations humaines

une alliance *wedding band/ ring*
une bague *a ring*
le bonheur *happiness*
la cérémonie *ceremony*
un conseiller matrimonial *a marriage counselor*

un écrin *a jewelry case*
les fiançailles *engagement party*
le / la fiancé(e) *fiancé(e)*
un(e) invité(e) *a guest*
le marié *groom*

la mariée *bride*
le mariage *wedding ceremony*
se fiancer *to get engaged*
tomber amoureux / amoureuse *to fall in love*

Quelques pronoms relatifs

dont *whose; that; of which*

que *which; that*

qui *who; that*

Autres mots et expressions utiles

nourrir *to feed*   un SDF *homeless person*

APPENDICES
A. L'alphabet phonétique international

Consonnes

Symboles	Graphies possibles
[p]	**p**a**p**a, ta**p**is
[t]	**t**ante, gran**d** homme, quan**d** elle...
[k]	**q**uand, **c**ombien
[b]	**b**leu, trom**b**one
[d]	**d**e, atten**d**ent
[g]	**g**rand, lan**gu**e, se**c**onde
[m]	**m**on, co**mm**encer, problè**m**e
[n]	**n**on, mexicai**n**e, italie**nn**e
[ɲ]	campa**gn**e
[f]	**f**olle, **ph**oto, veu**f**
[v]	**v**oir, acti**v**e, neu**f** heures
[s]	**ç**a, **c**es, mer**c**i, **s**es, profe**ss**ion, na**t**ion, tenni**s**
[z]	**z**èbre, po**s**er
[ʃ]	**ch**ien, **sh**ort
[ʒ]	**j**e, a**g**ent, man**ge**ons
[l]	**l**à, be**ll**e
[ʀ]	**r**iz, peu**r**, hive**r**

Voyelles

Symboles	Graphies possibles
[i]	**i**ls, **y**
[e]	**e**t, voyag**é**, travaill**er**, n**ez**
[ɛ]	p**è**re, b**ei**ge, vil**ai**ne, b**ê**te, derni**è**re, **e**lle
[a]	t**a**, f**e**mme
[o]	tabl**eau**, h**au**t, v**o**s, r**o**se
[ɔ]	v**o**l, b**o**nne
[u]	n**ou**s, a**oû**t
[y]	l**u**ne, d**û**, **eu**
[ø]	v**eu**x, f**eu**, h**eu**reuse
[œ]	fl**eu**r, **œu**f, n**eu**f
[ə]	t**e**, s**e**rait, f**ai**sons
[ã]	**en**, qu**an**d, t**an**t, t**em**ps
[ɔ̃]	b**on**, t**om**ber, f**on**t
[ɛ̃]	p**ain**, f**in**, r**ien**, **im**possible, exam**en** sy**m**pathique, **un***, parf**um***

***un** and **um** are sometimes pronounced as [œ̃].

Semi-voyelles

Symboles	Graphies possibles
[w]	l**ou**is, **w**att
[ɥ]	n**u**it, m**u**et
[j]	trava**ille**, déta**il**, b**i**en, h**i**er, vo**y**ons, **y**aourt

Verbes réguliers

Infinitif	Présent	Passé composé	Imparfait
danser	je danse	j' ai dansé	je dansais
	tu danses	tu as dansé	tu dansais
	il danse	il a dansé	il dansait
	nous dansons	nous avons dansé	nous dansions
	vous dansez	vous avez dansé	vous dansiez
	ils dansent	ils ont dansé	ils dansaient
choisir	je choisis	j' ai choisi	je choisissais
	tu choisis	tu as choisi	tu choisissais
	il choisit	il a choisi	il choisissait
	nous choisissons	nous avons choisi	nous choisissions
	vous choisissez	vous avez choisi	vous choisissiez
	ils choisissent	ils ont choisi	ils choisissaient
attendre	j' attends	j' ai attendu	j' attendais
	tu atttends	tu as attendu	tu attendais
	il attend	il a attendu	il attendait
	nous attendons	nous avons attendu	nous attendions
	vous attendez	vous avez attendu	vous attendiez
	ils attendent	ils ont attendu	ils attendaient
se laver	je me lave	je me suis lavé(e)	je me lavais
	tu te laves	tu t'es lavé(e)	tu te lavais
	il se lave	il (elle) s'est lavé(e)	il se lavait
	nous nous lavons	nous nous sommes lavé(e)s	nous nous lavions
	vous vous lavez	vous vous êtes lavé(e)(s)	vous vous laviez
	ils se lavent	ils (elles) se sont lavé(e)s	ils se lavaient

B. Verbes

Futur	Conditionnel	Impératif	Subjonctif
je danserai	je danserais	danse	que je danse
tu danseras	tu danserais	dansons	que tu danses
il dansera	il danserait	dansez	qu'il danse
nous danserons	nous danserions		que nous dansions
vous danserez	vous danseriez		que vous dansiez
ils danseront	ils danseraient		qu'ils dansent
je choisirai	je choisirais	choisis	que je choisisse
tu choisiras	tu choisirais	choisissons	que tu choisisses
il choisira	il choisirait	choisissez	qu'il choisisse
nous choisirons	nous choisirions		que nous choisissions
vous choisirez	vous choisiriez		que vous choisissiez
ils choisiront	ils choisiraient		qu'ils choisissent
j' attendrai	j' attendrais	attends	que j' attende
tu attendras	tu attendrais	attendons	que tu attendes
il attendra	il attendrait	attendez	qu'il attende
nous attendrons	nous attendrions		que nous attendions
vous attendrez	vous attendriez		que vous attendiez
ils attendront	ils attendraient		qu'ils attendent
je me laverai	je me laverais	lave-toi	que je me lave
tu te laveras	tu te laverais	lavons-nous	que tu te laves
il se lavera	il se laverait	lavez-vous	qu'il se lave
nous nous laverons	nous nous laverions		que nous nous lavions
vous vous laverez	vous vous laveriez		que vous vous laviez
ils vous laveront	ils se laveraient		qu'ils se lavent

Verbes réguliers avec des changements orthographiques

Infinitif	Present	Passé composé	Imparfait
manger	je mange tu manges il mange nous mang**e**ons vous mangez ils mangent	j'ai mangé	je mang**e**ais nous mangions
Also: exiger, nager, neiger, voyager			
commencer	je commence tu commences il commence nous commen**ç**ons vous commencez ils commencent	j'ai commencé	je commen**ç**ais nous commencions
Also: divorcer			
préférer	je préf**è**re tu préf**è**res il préf**è**re nous préférons vous préférez ils préf**è**rent	j'ai préféré	je préférais
Also: espérer, exagérer, répéter, s'inquiéter			
acheter	j' ach**è**te tu ach**è**tes il ach**è**te nous achetons vous achetez ils ach**è**tent	j'ai acheté	j' achetais
Also: se lever, se promener			
appeler	j' appe**ll**es tu appe**ll**es il appe**ll**e nous appelons vous appelez ils appe**ll**ent	j'ai appelé	j'appelais
Also: s'appeler, épeler, se rappeler			
payer	je pa**i**e tu pa**i**es il pa**i**e nous pa**y**ons vous pa**y**ez ils pa**i**ent	j'ai payé	je pa**y**ais
Also: essayer, nettoyer			

Futur	Conditionnel	Impératif	Subjonctif
je mangerai	je mangerais	mange mangeons mangez	que je mange que nous mangions
je commencerai	je commencerais	commence commençons commencez	que je commence que nous commencions
je préférerai	je préférerais	préfère préférons préférez	que je préfère que nous préférions
j'achèterai	j'achèterais	achète achetons achetez	que j' achète que nous achetions
j'appellerai	j'appellerais	appelle appelons appelez	que j' appelle que nous appelions
je paierai	je paierais	paie payons payez	que je paie que nous payions

Verbes irréguliers

Infinitif	Présent	Passé composé	Imparfait
aller	je vais tu vas il va nous allons vous allez ils vont	je suis allé(e)	j'allais
apprendre (*see* **prendre**)			
s'asseoir	je m'assieds tu t'assieds il s'assied nous nous asseyons vous vous asseyez ils s'asseyent	je me suis assis(e)	je m'asseyais
avoir	j'ai tu as il a nous avons vous avez ils ont	j'ai eu	j'avais
boire	je bois tu bois il boit nous buvons vous buvez ils boivent	j'ai bu	je buvais
comprendre (*see prendre*)			
conduire	je conduis tu conduis il conduit nous conduisons vous conduisez ils conduisent	j'ai conduit	je conduisais

Futur	Conditionnel	Impératif	Subjonctif
j'irai	j'irais	va allons allez	que j' aille que nous allions
je m'assiérai	je m'assiérais	assieds-toi asseyons-nous asseyez-vous	que je m'asseye que nous nous asseyions
j'aurai	j'aurais	aie ayons ayez	que j' aie que nous ayons
je boirai	je boirais	bois buvons buvez	que je boive que nous buvions
je conduirai	je conduirais	conduis conduisons conduisez	que je conduise que nous conduisions

VERBES

Infinitif	Présent	Passé composé	Imparfait
connaître	je connais tu connais il connaît nous connaissons vous connaissez ils connaissent	j'ai connu	je connaissais
couvrir (*see* **ouvrir**)			
croire	je crois tu crois il croit nous croyons vous croyez ils croient	j'ai cru	je croyais
découvrir (*see* **ouvrir**)			
décrire (*see* **écrire**)			
devenir (*see* **venir**; *conjugated with* **être** *in the* **passé composé**)			
devoir	je dois tu dois il doit nous devons vous devez ils doivent	j'ai dû	je devais
dire	je dis tu dis il dit nous disons vous dites ils disent	j'ai dit	je disais
dormir (*see* **partir**; *conjugated with* **avoir** *in the* **passé composé**)			
écrire	j'écris tu écris il écrit nous écrivons vous écrivez ils écrivent	j'ai écrit	j'écrivais
être	je suis tu es il est nous sommes vous êtes ils sont	j'ai été	j'étais

Futur	Conditionnel	Impératif	Subjonctif
je connaîtrai	je connaîtrais	connais connaissons connaissez	que je connaisse que nous connaissions
je croirai	je croirais	crois croyons crovez	que je croie que nous croyions
je devrai	je devrais	dois devons devez	que je doive que nous devions
je dirai	je dirais	dis disons dites	que je dise que nous disions
j'écrirai	j'écrirais	écris écrivons écrivez	que j' écrive que nous écrivions
je serai	je serais	sois soyons soyez	que je sois que nous soyons

Infinitif	Présent	Passé composé	Imparfait
faire	je fais tu fais il fait nous faisons vous faites ils font	j'ai fait	je faisais
falloir	il faut	il a fallu	il fallait
lire	je lis tu lis il lit nous lisons vous lisez ils lisent	j'ai lu	je lisais

mentir (*see* **partir**; *conjugated with* **avoir** *in the* **passé composé**)

Infinitif	Présent	Passé composé	Imparfait
mettre	je mets tu mets il met nous mettons vous mettez ils mettent	j'ai mis	je mettais
mourir	je meurs tu meurs il meurt nous mourons vous mourez ils meurent	je suis mort(e)	je mourais
naître	je nais tu nais il naît nous naissons vous naissez ils naissent	je suis né(e)	je naissais

offrir (*see* **ouvrir**)

Infinitif	Présent	Passé composé	Imparfait
ouvrir	j' ouvre tu ouvres il ouvre nous ouvrons vous ouvrez ils ouvrent	j'ai ouvert	j'ouvrais

Futur	Conditionnel	Impératif	Subjonctif
je ferai	je ferais	fais faisons faites	que je fasse que nous fassions
il faudra	il faudrait	—	qu'il faille
je lirai	je lirais	lis lisons lisez	que je lise que nous lisions
je mettrai	je mettrais	mets mettons mettez	que je mette que nous mettions
je mourrai	je mourrais	meurs mourons mourez	que je meure que nous mourions
je naîtrai	je naîtrais	nais naissons naissez	que je naisse que nous naissions
j'ouvrirai	j'ouvrirais	ouvre ouvrons ouvrez	que j' ouvre que nous ouvrions

Infinitif	Présent	Passé composé	Imparfait
partir	je pars tu pars il part nous partons vous partez ils partent	je suis parti(e)	je partais
permettre (*see* **mettre**)			
pleuvoir	il pleut	il a plu	il pleuvait
pouvoir	je peux tu peux il peut nous pouvons vous pouvez ils peuvent	j'ai pu	je pouvais
prendre	je prends tu prends il prend nous prenons vous prenez ils prennent	j'ai pris	je prenais
promettre (*see* **mettre**)			
recevoir	je reçois tu reçois il reçoit nous recevons vous recevez ils reçoivent	j'ai reçu	je recevais
repartir (*see* **partir**)			
revenir (*see* **venir**)			
revoir (*see* **voir**)			
rire	je ris tu ris il rit nous rions vous riez ils rient	j'ai ri	je riais

Futur	Conditionnel	Impératif	Subjonctif
je partirai	je partirais	pars partons partez	que je parte que nous partions
il pleuvra	il pleuvrait	—	qu'il pleuve
je pourrai	je pourrais	— — —	que je puisse que nous puissions
je prendrai	je prendrais	prends prenons prenez	que je prenne que nous prenions
je recevrai	je recevrais	reçois recevons recevez	que je reçoive que nous recevions
je rirai	je rirais	ris rions riez	que je rie que nous riions

Infinitif	Présent	Passé composé	Imparfait
savoir	je sais tu sais il sait nous savons vous savez ils savent	j'ai su	je savais

sentir (*see* **partir**; *conjugated with* **avoir** *in the* **passé composé**)

servir (*see* **partir**; *conjugated with* **avoir** *in the* **passé composé**)

sortir (*see* **partir**)

souffrir (*see* **ouvrir**)

sourire (*see* **rire**)

se souvenir (*see* **venir**)

valoir (*see* **falloir**)

Infinitif	Présent	Passé composé	Imparfait
venir	je viens tu viens il vient nous venons vous venez ils viennent	je suis venu(e)je	je venais
voir	je vois tu vois il voit nous voyons vous voyez ils voient	j'ai vu	je voyais
vouloir	je veux tu veux il veut nous voulons vous voulez ils veulent	j'ai voulu	je voulais

Futur	Conditionnel	Impératif	Subjonctif
je saurai	je saurais	sache sachons sachez	que je sache que nous sachions
je viendrai	je viendrais	viens venons venez	que je vienne que nous venions
je verrai	je verrais	vois voyons voyez	que je voie que nous voyions
je voudrai	je voudrais	veuille veuillons veuillez	que je veuille que nous voulions

Vocabulaire

Français-Anglais

All of the active and most of the passive vocabulary found in this book is included in the following list. The numbers after each entry indicate the chapter in which the vocabulary first appeared. The symbol — shows the repetition of a key word. See the list of abbreviations for further information about the vocabulary items.

Abbreviations used in this glossary:

(adj) adjective
(adv) adverb
(f) feminine
(f, pl) feminine plural
(inv) invariable

(m) masculine
(m, pl) masculine plural
(n) noun
P Chapitre préliminaire
(pl) plural

(prep) preposition
(poss adj) possessive adjective
(pron) pronoun
(v) verb

A

à at, in, to 5; **— contrecœur** grudgingly 7; **— droite (de)** to the right (of) 5; **— gauche (de)** to the left (of) 5; **— l'aise** comfortable, at ease 13; **— l'appareil** on the phone, speaking 9; **— la fac** at school, at the university 4; **— l'heure** on time 1; **— la maison** at home 1; **— la prochaine** (see you) next time 10; **— la recherche** looking for 11; **— . . . heures** at . . . o'clock 4; **— midi** at noon P; **— minuit** at midnight P; **— quelle heure?** at what time? 4; **— tour de rôle** taking turns 7; **— tout à l'heure** (see you) later 8; **— tue-tête** at the top of one's lungs 15; **— vos marques** get ready 6; **— vos stylos** grab your pens 3; **être — to belong to 3
abord: d'— first 4
absolument absolutely 13
accompagner to accompany 8
achat *(m)* purchase 6
acheter to buy 5
actif/active active 1
activités *(f)* activities 4

adorer to adore 1
aéroport *(m)* airport 1
affaires *(f, pl)* business 13; **homme/femme d' —** *(m/f)* businessman/woman 4
afficher to show, display 3
Afrique *(f)* Africa 5
âge *(m)* age 3; **J'ai . . . ans.** I am— years old. 3; **Quel — as-tu?** How old are you? 3; **Quel — avez-vous?** How old are you?
agenda *(m)* datebook 7
agent d'assurance *(m)* insurance agent 4
agent immobilier *(m)* real-estate agent 4
agent de police *(m)* police officer 4
agent de voyage *(m)* travel agent 4
agir to act 14; **il s'agit de** it deals with, it's about 14
agneau *(m)* lamb 6
agrafeuse *(f)* stapler P
agrapher to staple 11
agréable pleasant 1
ah! Oh! 3; **— tiens!** Oh, look!
aïe ouch 9
aile*(f)* wing 8
ailleurs somewhere else 6; **d' —** in fact, furthermore

aimer to love 1; **— beaucoup** to like a lot; **— bien** to like; **— mieux** to like better, to prefer; **Aimerais-tu . . . ?** Would you like . . . ?; **Aimeriez-vous . . . ?** Would you like . . . ?
Algérie *(f)* Algeria 7
algérien(ne) Algerian 7
Allemagne *(f)* Germany 5
allemand(e) German 1
aller to go 5; **— en ville** to go to town; **Allez au tableau.** Go to the board.; **Allons-y!** Let's go!; **Comment allez-vous?** How are you?; **Je vais bien, merci.** I'm fine, thanks.
allô hello (on the telephone) 4
alliance wedding band 15
allocation familiale state allowance for children 3
s'allumer to light up 11
alors then, so 6; **— que** while, whereas (+ a clause)
améliorer to improve 9
américain(e) American 1
Amérique du Nord *(f)* North America 5
Amérique du Sud *(f)* South America 5

ami/amie *(m/f)* friend P; **meilleur(e) —** best friend 4

amour love 14

amoureux/amoureuse in love 13; **être amoureux/amoureuse (de)** to be in love (with); **tomber amoureux/amoureuse** to fall in love

amuse-gueule *(m)* finger food

s'amuser to have fun 10

an year 3; **Jour de l'An** *(m)* New Year's Day 4; **il y a quatre —** four years ago; **J'ai . . . —** I am . . . years old

ancêtre *(m)* ancestor 11

ange *(m)* angel; **être aux —** to be in heaven

anglais(e) English 1

Angleterre *(f)* England 5

animé(e) animated, lively 5

année *(f)* year 8; **toute l'-** all year long

anniversaire *(m)* birthday 4; **Joyeux —** Happy Birthday

annonce *(f)* ad 4; **petites annonces** classified ads

s'annoncer to announce, to tell 15; **ça s'annonce bien** it's looking good

Antarctique *(m)* Antarctic 5

antillais(e) West Indian 3

antiquaire *(m)* antique dealer 3

août August 4

appareil-photo *(m)* camera 2

appartement *(m)* apartment 2

appeler to call 1

s'appeler to be named P; **Comment t'appelles-tu?** What's your name?; **Comment vous appelez-vous?** What's your name?; **Il/Elle s'appelle...** His/her name is . . . ; **Je m'appelle** My name is . . .

apporter to bring 9

apprendre to learn 5

après after 5; **— demain** the day after tomorrow; **— -midi** *(m)* afternoon; **de l' — -midi** in the afternoon

s'approcher (de) to go up to 5

argent *(m)* money 7

s'arracher to pull out; **— les cheveux** to pull one's hair out

arranger to arrange 14; **Ça/cela vous arrangerait de . . .** It would help you to . . .

arrêt de bus *(m)* bus stop 4

s'arrêter to stop 8

arriver to arrive 1; **Qu'est-ce qui arrive?** What's happening?; **Qu'est-ce qui est arrivé?** What happened?

arroser to celebrate; **Ça s'arrose!** Let's celebrate!

Asie *(f)* Asia 5

asperge *(f)* asparagus 6

aspirine *(f)* aspirin 8

s'asseoir to sit down 10; **asseyez-vous** sit down; **assieds-toi** sit down; **je m'assieds** I sit down

assez (de) enough 6

assez rather 1; **assez bien** rather well; **assez mal** rather poorly

assis(e) seated 11

assistant(e) social(e) *(m/f)* social worker 4

assister (à) to attend 15

assortir to coordinate 3

attacher to tie down 13

attendre to wait (for) 1

attention attention; **faire —** to pay attention 4

attraper to catch 8

au (à, à la, à l', aux) at, to, in 5; **— fait** in fact; **— fond** at the back bottom; **— lieu de** instead of; **— lit** in bed; **— milieu de** in the middle of; **— revoir** good-bye; **— secours!** Help!

aujourd'hui today

aussi also 1; **— (adj) que** as . . . (adj) as . . .

aussitôt immediately 6; **— que** as soon as

Australie *(f)* Australia 5

autant as much as 14; **— que** as much; **— de (nom) que** as much (noun) as

auteur *(m)* author 10

auto *(f)* **(automobile)** car 5

automne *(m)* fall 4

autour de around 5

autre other 2

autrefois in the old days 11

aux (*see* **à**) at, in, to 5

avance *(f)* advance; **en —** early 1

avant before 7; **— hier** the day before yesterday

avec with 2

avenir *(m)* future 14

avenue *(f)* avenue 5; **sur l' —** on the avenue

avion *(m)* airplane 5

avis *(m)* opinion 5; **à mon/ton/votre** -in my/your opinion

avocat(e) *(m/f)* lawyer 4

avoir to have 3; **Avez-vous compris?** Did you understand?; **— . . . ans** to be . . . years old; **— besoin de** to need ; **— chaud** to be hot; **— envie de** to feel like; **— faim** to be hungry; **— froid** to be cold; **— honte (de)** to be ashamed of ; **— mal à . . .** (a part of the body) hurts; **— du mal à** to have difficulty; **— peur (de)** to be afraid (to); **— raison (de)** to be right (to); **— soif** to be thirsty; **— sommeil** to be sleepy; **— tort (de)** to be wrong (to) **— le droit (de)** to have the right (to); **— le trac** to have stage fright, to be scared; **— Qu'est-ce que tu as?** What's wrong?;

avril *(m)* April 4

B

bagage *(m)* luggage 13

bague *(f)* ring 15

baignoire *(f)* bathtub 4

bal populaire *(m)* dance 4

baladeur *(m)* Walkman 2

balancer to swing 13

banane *(f)* banana 6

bande dessinée, B.D. *(f)* comic strip 7

banque *(f)* bank 5; **à la —** at the bank 1

barque *(f)* small boat 7

bas/basse low 3

baseball *(m)* baseball 9

basketball *(m)* basketball 9

baskets *(f)* high tops 2

bateau *(m)* boat 5
bâti built 7
bâtiment building 8
batterie *(f)* drums 9
bavarder to chat 9
beau/bel/belle/beaux/belles beautiful 2; **beau-frère** brother-in-law; **Il fait beau** It's nice out
beaucoup a lot P; **— (de)** a lot (of) 6
bébé *(m)* baby 1
beige beige 2
belge Belgian 7
Belgique *(f)* Belgium 7
besoin *(m)* need 3; **avoir — de** to need
bête silly, stupid 4
bêtise *(f)* stupid thing, blunder 7; **dire des —** to say silly things
beurre *(m)* butter 6
bibliothèque *(f)* library 4
bicyclette *(f)* bicycle 5
bien well 1; **— à vous** yours truly; **— que** although; **Mais — sûr!** But of course!
bientôt soon 5; **à —** see you soon
bière *(f)* beer 1
billet *(m)* ticket 15
biologie *(f)* biology 2
bise *(f)* kiss; **grosses bises** love *(for closing a letter)*
blanc, blanche white 2
blé *(m)* wheat 6
bleu(e) blue 2
blond(e) blond 1
bœuf *(m)* beef 6
boire to drink 6
bois *(m)* wood 11
boisson *(f)* drink 1
boîte (de) *(f)* can (of) 6
bon (bonne) good 2; **bon marché** cheap, reasonnable
bonbon *(m)* candy 12
bonheur *(m)* happiness 15
bonjour hello P; **— Madame** Good morning/afternoon, ma'am ; **— Monsieur** Good morning/afternoon, sir; **— tout le monde** Good morning/afternoon everyone; **dire — (à)** to say hello (to)

bonsoir goodnight 9
borne *(f)* limit; **pas de —** no limits
bouche *(f)* mouth 8
boucherie *(f)* butcher shop 5
bouger to move 13
se bouger to get moving, to hurry 10
bouilloner to boil 13
boulangerie *(f)* bakery 4
boules *(f)* bocce ball, lawn bowling 9; **jouer aux boules** to play bocce ball
boulevard *(m)* boulevard 5; **sur le —** on the boulevard
boum *(f)* party 12
bouteille (de) *(f)* bottle (of) 6
boutique *(f)* boutique 8
branché(e) plugged in 1; **Vous êtes —!** You're in the know!
bras *(m)* arm 8
brave courageous 14
brie *(m)* brie (cheese) 6
brioche *(f)* bun 6
brosser to brush 10
se brosser to brush 10; **— les cheveux** to brush one's hair; **— les dents** to brush one's teeth
bruit *(m)* noise 2
brun(e) dark 2
bureau *(m)* desk, office P; **— des objets trouvés** lost and found 2; **— de poste** post office 5; **— de tabac** tobacco shop 5
bus *(m)* bus 5

C

ça (cela/, ce, c') this, that 1; **(Comment) — va?** How are you?; **C'est à qui?** To whom does it belong?; **C'est bien** That's fine; **C'est le . . .** Today is . . . (date); **C'est un/une . . .** It's a/an . . .
cacher to hide 12
cachet *(m)* pill 8
caddie *(m)* cart 11
cadeau *(m)* present 12
cadre *(m)* executive 4
café *(m)* coffee, café 1; **— au lait** coffee with milk; **— crème** coffee with cream
cahier *(m)* notebook P

calculatrice *(f)* calculator 2
calme calm 1
camarade de chambre *(m/f)* roommate 2
camembert camembert cheese 6
Cameroun *(m)* Cameroon 7
camerounais(e) Cameroonian 7
campagne *(f)* country(side) 9
campus *(m)* campus 2
Canada *(m)* Canada 5
canadien(ne) Canadian 1
carnet (de billets) *(m)* a book (of tickets) 2
carotte *(f)* carrot 6
carte *(f)* map 7; card 9; **— d'identité** I.D. card; **— postale** postcard; **écrire une — postale** to write a postcard
casser to break 13
se casser to break (up) 15
cassette *(f)* cassette 2
catastrophé(e) devastated 14
cauchemar *(m)* nightmare 6
caution *(f)* security deposit 4
ce, cet, cette, ces this, that, these, those 5
cela (ça) this, that 1
célibataire *(m/f)* single 1
celle(s) these, those 7
cent hundred 6
centime *(m)* cent 15
centre *(m)* center 4; **— commercial** shopping mall; **— ville** downtown
cercueil *(m)* casket 7
cérémonie *(f)* ceremony 15
cerise *(f)* cherry 6
certain(e) certain, sure 12
certainement certainly 9; **Mais —** (But) of course
c'est it is P
ceux these, those 12
chacun(e) each 10
chaise *(f)* chair P
chambre *(f)* room 2
chance *(f)* luck 3; **avoir de la —** to be lucky; **Bonne —!** Good luck!
chanson *(f)* song 9
chanter to sing 1
chanteur/chanteuse *(m/f)* singer 4
chapelure *(f)* bread crumbs 6

C

chaque each 11; — année each year

chargé(e) busy 10

charger to load 13

charges (f, pl) utilities 4

charmant(e) charming 12

chat/chatte (m/f) male/female cat 3

châtain (clair) (light) brown 6

chaud(e) hot 3; avoir — to be hot; Il fait — It's hot

chauffage (m) heat 4

chauffer to heat; Ça chauffe! Trouble's on the way!

chaussette (f) sock 2

chaussure (f) shoe 2

chef-d'œuvre (m) masterpiece 9

chemin (m) road, way 5

chemise (f) shirt 2

chemisier (m) blouse 10

chèque (m) check 15

cher, chère dear 2

chercher to look for 1

chéri(e) (m) (f) darling 14

cheveux (m, pl) hair 3; s'arracher les — to tear one's hair out 14

chez at (the house of) 3; chez moi at my house

chic chic 2; chic alors great 12

chien, chienne (f/m) dog 3

Chine (f) China 5

chinois(e) chinese 1

chocolat (m) chocolate 2; — noir dark chocolate; — chaud hot chocolate

choisir to choose 13

choix (m) choice 8

chose (f) thing 6; quelque — something

chut! shh! 3

chute (f) fall 5

cigarette (f) cigarette 2

cinéma (m) movie theater 4

cinq five p

cinquante fifty 3

citron (m) lemon 2; — pressé lemonade

clair(e) light 4

classe (f) class; en — , en cours in class

clé (f) key 9

clin d'œil (m) wink 12

Coca (m) coke 1

code bancaire (m) PIN, ATM code 12

cœur (m) heart 8; j'ai mal au — I feel nauseated; par — by heart

se coiffer to do one's hair

coiffeur (m) a hairdresser 10

coin (m) corner 4; au — (de) at the corner (of)

collant (m) pantyhose 2

combien how much, how many 1

commander to order 6

comme like, as 1; — prévu as planned; — (légumes) as a (vegetable)

commencer to begin 2

comment how, what 4; — allez-vous? How are you?; — t'appelles-tu? What's your name?; — vous appelez-vous? What's your name?; — ça va ? How's it going?; — sont-ils? What are they like?; — trouves-tu . . . What do you think (of) . . .

commode (f) a set of drawers, dresser 3

complet (m) suit 15

composer to dial 4; — un numéro to dial a number

composter (un billet) to punch/validate (a ticket)

comprendre to understand 5; Je ne comprends pas I don't understand; Avez-vous compris? Did you understand?

compris understood 1

comptable (m) accountant 4

compter to count 15; — sur to count on

conduire to drive 9

confier to confide 14

confiture (f) jam 6

confortable comfortable 2

confortablement comfortably 13

congés payés (m, pl) paid vacation 9

connaître to know 10

conseiller matrimonial (m) marriage counselor 15

conseil (m) advice 5

constamment constantly 13

conte de fée (m) fairy tale 11

content(e) happy 1; je serais — de . . . I would be happy to . . .

continent (m) continent 5

continuer to continue 5; continuez continue 5

convaincre to convince 13

convenir to agree 7

copain/copine (m/f) friend 9

coq au vin (m) chicken in a wine sauce 6

corde (f) rope 13

cordon bleu (m) a cordon bleu, a great cook 6

coréen(ne) Korean 1

corps (m) body 8; parties du — parts of the body

Côte d'Ivoire (f) Ivory Coast 7

côté (m) side 4; à — (de) near, next (to)

cou (m) neck 8

se coucher to go to bed 10

couler to run 13; J'ai le nez qui coule I have a runny nose 8

couleur (f) color 2; De quelle — . . . ? What color . . . ?

coupable guilty 8

couper to cut

se couper to cut oneself 10

courrier (m) mail 11

cours (m) lesson 7; — particulier private lesson; en — , in class

courses (f, pl) errands 4; faire des — to run errands

court(e) short 3

cousin/cousine (m/f) cousin 3

coût(m) cost 6

coûter to cost 6

couturier(m) (fashion) designer 10

couverture (f) blanket 13

couvrir to cover 15

craie (f) chalk; morceau de — (f) a piece of chalk

crayon (m) pen 5

crèche (f) day care center 3; — de Noël nativity scene

créer to create 14

croire to believe 15; **Je crois que oui** I think so; **Je crois que non** I don't think so

croissant (m) croissant 1

croque-monsieur (m) ham and cheese sandwich 1

cuillerée (de) (f) spoonful (of) 6

cuisine (f) kitchen 3

cultiver to cultivate 6

curriculum vitae (m) résumé 15; **écrire son —** to write one's résumé

D

d'abord first 4

d'accord OK 4; **être —** to be in agreement; **je (ne) suis (pas) —** I (don't) agree

d'ailleurs in fact, furthermore 11

d'habitude usually 11

dame (f) lady 4; **dames** (f, pl) checkers; **madame** (f) ma'am, Mrs., Ms. P

dans in 1; **— le vent** in style; **— deux semaines** in two weeks; **— dix minutes** in ten minutes

danser to dance 1

date (f) date P; **Quelle est la — aujourd'hui?** What's today's date?

de of, from 2; **— nouveau** again; **— rien** you're welcome

de la, du , de l', des of, from, some 6

se débrouiller to manage, to get by 10

début (m) beginning 7; **au —** at the beginning; **en — de** in the beginning of

décembre (m) December 4

décès (m) death 11

décider to decide 7

décision (f) decision 5; **prendre une —** to make a decision

découvrir to discover 15

décrire to describe 7

décrocher to pick up 10

déçu(e) disappointed 14; **être —** to be disappointed

dedans inside 13

défi (m) challenge 9

dehors outside 2

déjà already 7

déjeuner (m) lunch 6; **petit —** breakfast

deltaplane (m) hang glider 9; **faire du —** to go hang gliding 9

demain tomorrow 5; **après —** the day after tomorrow

demande (f) inquiry 15; **faire une — (d'emploi)** to fill out an application (for a job)

demander to ask 11; **— des conseils** to ask for advice; **— pardon** to ask for forgiveness

déménager to move 3

demi(e) half P; **et demi(e)** and a half, half past

dénicher to dig up, to find 8

dent (f) tooth 8

dépanner to fix 11

se dépêcher (de) to hurry 10

déprimé(e) depressed 8; **Je suis —** I am depressed

depuis since 13; **— que** since (+ clause)

déranger to disturb 14; **Cela/Ça me dérangerait de . . .** It would bother me to

dernier, dernière last 7; **le weekend dernier** last weekend; **la dernière fois** last time

derrière behind 4

des (see **de, de la, de l', du**) 1

dès que as soon as 13

désagréable unpleasant 1

descendre to go down 8

description (physique) (f) (physical) description 3

se déshabiller to undress 10

désirer to desire 12

désobéir to disobey 13

désolé(e) sorry 1; **être —** to be sorry

désordonné(e) messy 2

dessert (m) dessert 6

détente (f) relaxation 8

détester to hate 1

deux two P

deuxième second 4

devant in front of 4

devenir to become 7

deviner to guess 5

devoir to have to, must 12

devoir (m) duty, homework; **faire ses devoirs** to do one's homework; **Rendez vos devoirs.** Turn in your homework; **devrait** should

diable (m) devil 11

dieu (m) god 5; **Mon — !** My goodness!

différent(e) different 12

difficile difficult 3

difficilement with difficulty 13

dimanche (m) Sunday P

dîner (m) dinner 6

dîner to eat dinner 6

dire to say 7; **— au revoir** to say good-bye

se diriger to go (towards) 10

discipline (f) (school) subject 2

discuter to discuss 4

disponible available 15

dispute (f) argument 14

se disputer (avec) to argue (with) 10

disque compact (m) compact disc 2; **lecteur de disques compacts** (m) compact disc player

disquette (f) diskette 5

dissertation (f) term paper 7; **écrire une —** to write a paper

distributeur automatique (m) ATM 12

divorcé(e) divorced 1

divorcer to get a divorce

dix ten P

dix-huit eighteen P

dix-neuf nineteen P

dix-sept seventeen P

dizaine (de) (f) about ten 6

doigt (m) finger 8

dommage 12; **il est —** it's a shame

donc therefore 7

donner to give 7; **— un coup de main** to give a hand 11

dont which, whose 15

dormir to sleep 8

dos (m) back 8

doublé(e) dubbed 9
douceur (f) softness 15
douche (f) shower 2; **prendre une — ** to take a shower
douter to doubt 12
douteux, douteuse doubtful 12; **il est douteux** it's doubtful
douzaine (f) dozen 6
douze twelve P
droit (m) law 8; **avoir le — (de)** to have the right (to)
droit(e) right 5; **tout droit** straight ahead
drôle funny 11
dur hard 10

E

eau (f) (**eaux** pl) water 1; **— minérale** mineral water
échecs (m, pl) chess 9
économie (f) economy 2
écouter to listen 1; **écoutez** listen P
écrin (m) (jewel) case 15
écrire to write 7; **— un livre** to write a book; **Écrivez votre nom.** Write your name.
écrivain (m) writer 4
effacer to erase P; **Effacez le tableau.** Erase the board.
église (f) church 5
élégant(e) elegant 2
élevé(e) raised 7
elle (f) she 1
elles (f, pl) they 1
s'embrasser to kiss 10
émission (f) program 3
emploi du temps (m) schedule 4
employé(e) (m)/(f) employee 15
employeur (m) employer 15
en in, by, while 5; **— attendant** while waiting; **— auto, — voiture** by car; **— avance** early; **— de bonnes mains** in good hands; **— dix minutes** in ten minutes; **— face (de)** across (from) 4; **— retard** late; **Vous n'— avez plus?** You don't have any more?
en-cas (m) snack 1

enchanté(e) delighted P
encore still, yet 6; **— à boire?** more to drink?
s'endormir to fall asleep 10
endroit (m) place 10
énergique energetic 1
enfance (f) childhood 11
s'enfermer to close up 10
enfin finally 4
enseigner to teach 9
ensemble together P
ensuite then 4
entendre to hear 11
s'entendre (avec) to get along (with)
entre between 4
entrer to enter 1; **Entrez!** Come in!
entretien (m) interview; **passer un —** to have an interview 15
envers towards 12
envie (f) desire 3; **avoir — de** to feel like
envoyer to send 11
épeler to spell 1; **Épelez, s'il vous plaît.** Spell, please.
épicerie (f) grocery 4
épinards (m, pl) spinach 6
époque (f) time 11; **à cette époque-là** at that time
équipe (f) team 14
escalade (f) rock climbing 9; **faire de l' —** to go rock climbing
escalier (m) stairs 11
escargot (m) snail 6
espace non-fumeur (m) non-smoking area 2
Espagne (f) Spain 5
espagnol(e) Spanish 2
espérer to hope 8
essayer to try 10
essentiel essential 12; **il est —** essential
est is 1
est-ce que (question marker) 2
et and P; **— toi?** and you?; **— vous?** and you?
étage (m) floor 3; **le premier —** the second floor
États-Unis (m, pl) United States 5
été (m) summer 4

étoile (f) star 13; **à la belle —** outside, under the stars
étonnant(e) surprising 12; **il est —** it's surprising, astonishing
étonné(e) surprised 12; **être —** to be surprised
étourdi(e) scatter-brained 12
étranger (étrangère) foreign 5
être to be 1; **— à** to belong to; **— d'accord (avec)** to agree with; **Vous êtes d'où?** Where are you from?
étudiant(e) (m/f) student P
étudier to study 1
Europe (f) Europe 5
eux (to, at) them 4
éxagérer to exaggerate
examen (m) examination 2; **passer un —** to take an exam; **réussir à un —** to pass an exam; **échouer à un —** to fail an exam
excuser to forgive, to pardon 7; **Excusez-moi.** Excuse-me.
s'excuser to apologize 14
exemple (m) example 5
exiger to demand 12
expert-comptable (m) CPA 3
explication (f) explanation 7
expliquer to explain 11
s'expliquer to explain 14
exposé (m) oral report 12

F

fabriquer to make 5
fac (f) university 5; **à la —** at school
fâché(e) upset 14; **être —** to be upset, mad
facile easy 5
facilement easily 13
façon (f) way 15
facteur (m) mailman, postman 14
faculté (f) university 5; **à la —** at school
faim (f) hunger 3; **avoir —** to be hungry
faire to do, make 4; **— attention** to pay attention; **— connaissance** to meet; **— le . . .** to dial . . . ; **— du camping** to camp; **— les courses** to shop ; **— la cuisine**

to cook; **— du deltaplane** to go hang gliding; **— ses devoirs** to do one's homework; **— ses études** to do one's studies; **— la fête** to party; **— la grasse matinée** to sleep in; **— son lit** to make one's bed; **— le ménage** to do the housework; **— une promenade** to take a walk; **— les provisions** to go grocery shopping; **— la sieste** to take a nap ; **— du ski** to ski; **— du tennis** to play tennis; **— la vaisselle** to do the dishes; **— un voyage** to take a trip; **— du VTT** to go mountain-biking; **Fais comme chez toi!** Make yourself at home!; **Il fait chaud.** It's hot.; **Il fait froid.** It's cold.; **Ne te fais pas de souci!** Don't worry!

fait *(m)* fact 5; **au —** in fact

falloir to be necessary 6; **il faut** it is necessary; **il ne faut pas** one must not

famille *(f)* family 3

farine *(f)* flour 6

fatigué(e) tired 8; **Je suis —** I'm tired

fauteuil *(m)* armchair 3

faux/fausse false 1

faux-pas *(m)* blunder 15

femme *(f)* woman P; **une — d'affaires** a businesswoman

fenêtre *(f)* window P

fermé(e) closed P

fermer to close P; **Fermez votre livre.** Close your book.

fermier/fermière *(m/f)* farmer 11

fête *(f)* party 4; **faire la —** to party; **— du Travail** Labor Day; **— des Mères** Mother's Day

fêter to celebrate 12

feu *(m)* **(feux** *pl)* fire, traffic light 13; **au —** at the light

feuille *(f)* leaf 5; **— de papier** piece of paper

feutre (crayon-feutre) *(m)* felt-pen 5

février *(m)* February 4

fiançailles *(f, pl)* engagement 15

fiancé(e) engaged 1; **être —** to be engaged

fiancé(e) *(m/f)* fiancé(e) 15

se fiancer to get engaged 15

fiche *(f)* card 5

fichu *(slang)* missed 10; **c'est —** it's over

fidèle faithful 7

fièvre *(f)* fever 8; **J'ai de la —** I have a fever

fille *(f)* daughter, girl 3

film *(m)* film 2

fils *(m)* son 3

fin *(f)* end 5; **à la —** at the end

finir to finish 13

se fixer to settle 11

fleur *(f)* flower 12

fleuve *(m)* river 5

fois *(f)* time 7; **pour la dernière —** for the last time

follement in a crazy way 13

fonctionnaire *(m)* civil servant 4

fonctionner to function 1

fondre to melt 7

fondu melted 6

football *(m)* soccer 9; **— américain** *(m)* football

forme *(f)* shape 8; **Je suis en (pleine) —** . I feel great.

formidable great 1; **il est —** it's great

fou, folle crazy 9

frais, fraîche fresh 4

fraise *(f)* strawberry 6

français(e) French 1

France *(f)* France 5

franchement frankly 10

fréquemment frequently 13

frère *(m)* brother 3; **beau-frère** *(m)* brother-in-law

frites *(f, pl)* fries 6

froid(e) cold P; **avoir —** to be cold; **Il fait —** . It's cold.

fromagerie *(f)* cheese store 5

fromage *(m)* cheese 6

fruit *(m)* fruit 6

fumer to smoke 1

fumeur/fumeuse *(m)/(f)* smoker 2

furieux, furieuse furious 12; **être — to be mad**

fûté(e) smart, clever 10

gagner to earn, to win 7; **— à la loterie** to win the lottery; **— de l'argent** to earn money; **— sa vie** to earn one's living

garage *(m)* garage 3

garçon *(m)* boy, waiter 1

gare *(f)* station 1; **à la —** at the station

gars *(m)* guy 13

gâteau *(m)* cake 6

gauche left 5; **à —** to the left

général general 11; **en —** in general

génial(e) great, fantastic 8

genou *m* knee 8

gens *(m, pl)* people 5

gentil, gentille nice, pleasant 2; **Ce serait — (de) . . .** It would be nice (to) . . .

gentiment nicely, kindly 13

géographie *(f)* geography 2

glace *(f)* ice, ice-cream 2; **— à la vanille** vanilla ice-cream

glisser to glide 9

golf *(m)* golf 9

gomme *(f)* eraser 5

gorge *(f)* throat 8; **J'ai la — qui pique.** I have a scratchy throat.

gourmand(e) gourmand, food-lover 6

goût *(m)* taste 3

goûter to taste 12

grâce à thanks to 15

grand(e) tall, big 1

grand-mère *(f)* grandmother 3

grand-parents *(m, pl)* grandparents 3

grand-père *(m)* grandfather 3

grandir to grow 13

gras(se) fat 4; **faire la grasse matinée** to sleep in late

grippe *(f)* flu 8; **J'ai la —** . I have the flu.

gris(e) grey 2

gros(se) big, fat 2; **grosses bises** (lit.) big kisses; love (for closing a letter) 6

grossir to put on weight 13

gruyère *(m)* swiss cheese 6

guerre *(f)* war 7

guitare *(f)* guitar 9
gymnase *(m)* gymnasium 5

H

s'habiller to get dressed 10
habiter to live 1; **Où habites-tu?**
Where do you live?; **Où habitez-vous?** Where do you live?;
J'habite à . . . I live in . . .
habitude *(f)* habit 5; **d' —** usually;
avoir l' — de to be used to
hanche *(f)* hip 13
haricot vert *(m)* green bean 6
haut(e) high 15; **haute couture** *(f)*
high fashion 10
heure *(f)* hour P; **à tout à l'-** see
you later; **dans une —** in one
hour; **de bonne —** early; **Quelle
— est-il?** What time is it?; **Il est
une —** It's one o'clock; **Il est . . .
heure(s).** It's . . . o'clock.; **tout à
l'-** later, earlier
heureusement fortunately 12
heureux, heureuse happy 14; **Je
serais — de . . .** I would be
happy to . . .
hier yesterday 7; **— matin**
yesterday morning; **— soir** last
night
histoire *(f)* story 2; **Quelle — !**
What a story!
hiver *(m)* winter 4
hockey *(m)* hockey 9
homme *(m)* man P; **— d'affaire**
businessman
honnête honest 1
hors-d'œuvre *(m) (inv)* appetizer 6
hôtesse de l'air *(f)* (female) flight
attendant 4
huit eight P
hypermarché *(m)* huge
supermarket 5

I

ici here 13
idée *(f)* idea 9
il *(m)* he, it 1; needs**—y a** there is,
there are 3; **— faut** it's necessary
6; **— n'y en a plus.** There's none

left.; **— n'y a pas de quoi.**
You're welcome.; **— y a trois
mois** three months ago; **— y a
cinq semaines** five weeks ago;
Qu'est-ce qu' — y a? What's
wrong?; **— s'agit de . . .** it deals
with, it's about
ils *(m, pl)* they 1
immeuble *(m)* building 4
imperméable *(m)* raincoat 2
important important 12; **il est —** it
is important
impossible impossible 12; **il est —**
it's impossible; **Ça m'est — pour
l'instant.** I can't do this right
now.
incroyable incredible 1
indication *(f)* piece of information
indiquer to indicate 5
indispensable necessary 12; **il est
—** it's necessary
infirmier/infirmière *(m/f)* nurse 4
information *(f)* information, news
11
informatique *(f)* computer science
2
ingénieur *(m)* engineer 4
inquiet, inquiète worried 8
s'inquiéter to worry 10
s'installer to settle 2
instrument *(m)* instrument 9
intelligemment intelligently 13
intention *(f)* intention 8; **avoir l' —
de** to intend to
interdire to forbid 14
intéressant(e) interesting 2
intéresser to interest 9; **Ça
m'intéresse.** It interests me.
s'intéresser (à) to be interested in
10
intérieur inside 12; **à l' — de** inside
invité(e) *(m/f)* guest 15
inviter to invite 2
irlandais(e) Irish 5
Irlande *(f)* Ireland 5
irrésistible irresistible 1
Israël *(f)* Israel 5
israélien(ne) Israeli 5
Italie *(f)* Italy 5
italien(ne) Italian 5
ivoirien(ne) Ivorian 7

J

jamais never 2; **ne . . . —** never
jambe *(f)* leg 8
jambon *(m)* ham 1
janvier *(m)* January 4
Japon *(m)* Japan 5
japonais(e) Japanese 1
jardin *(m)* garden 11
jaune yellow 2
je I 1; **— peux vous aider?** Can I
help you?; **— voudrais . . .** I
would like . . . ; **— vais bien,
merci** I'm fine, thanks; **— vous
en prie.** You're welcome.
jean *(m)* jeans 2
jeudi *(m)* Thursday P
jeune young 2
joli(e) pretty 2
jouer to play 1; **À quoi jouez-vous?**
What (sport) do you play?; **De
quoi jouez-vous?** What
(instrument) do you play?
jouet *(m)* toy 11
jour *(m)* day 4; **— de l'An** New
Year's day; **— de semaine** week
day; **Quel — est-ce?** What day is
it?; **tous les —** every day
journal *(m)* newspaper 204
journée *(f)* day 8; **Bonne — !** Have
a good day!; **toute la —** all day
long
juger to judge 8
juillet *(m)* July 4
juin *(m)* June 4
jumeaux *(m, pl)* twins 10
jupe *(f)* skirt 2
jus *(m)* juice 1; **— d'orange** orange
juice
jusqu'à up to, as far as 5
justifier to justify 1; **Justifiez votre
choix** Justify your choice

K

kilo(gramme) de *(m)* kilo 6
kiosque *(m)* stand 4
kir *(m)* aperitif wine (white wine
and blackcurrant liqueur)

L

la (l') her, it 9
là there 3; **-bas** over there

laid(e) ugly 2

laine (*f*) wool 11

laisser to let 7; **laisse-moi tranquille** leave me alone

lait (*m*) milk 6; **un verre de —** a glass of milk

langue (*f*) language 3

lampe (*f*) lamp 3

lapin (*m*) rabbit 6

larme (*f*) tear 7

laver to wash 10

se laver to wash (oneself) 10

le/la/l'/les the 1

le (l') him, it, to him 9

leçon (*f*) lesson 7

lecteur de disques compacts (*m*) CD player 3

légume (*m*) vegetable 6

lendemain (*m*) the next day 13

lentement slowly 13

les them 9

lettre (*f*) letter 15; **écrire une — (de recommandation)** to write a letter (of recommendation)

leur their, to them 3

se lever to get up 10

librairie (*f*) bookstore 5

libre free 4

ligne (*f*) line 4

limonade (*f*) lemon-lime soda 1

lire to read 7; **— un livre** to read a book

lit (*m*) bed 3

litre (de) (*m*) liter 6

littérature (*f*) literature 2

livre (*m*) book P

loin (de) far (from) 4

loisirs (*m, pl*) leisure 8

longtemps for a long time 7; **il y a — ** a long time ago

lorsque when 13

louer to rent 4

loyer (*m*) rent 4

lui (to) him, it 4

lundi (*m*) Monday P; **C'est —** It's Monday

lunettes (*f, pl*) glasses 7

M

ma (*see* mon) my 3; **— chère amie** my dear friend 3

machine à laver (*f*) washing machine 4

Madame (*f*) ma'am, Mrs., Ms. P

Mademoiselle (*f*) Miss, Ms. P

magasin (*m*) store 5

magazine (*m*) magazine 7; **lire un —** to read a magazine

magnétoscope (*m*) VCR 3

mai (*m*) May 4

maigrir to lose weight 13

maillot de bain (*m*) bathing suit 13

main (*f*) hand 8; **J'ai mal à la — .** My hand hurts.

maintenant now P

mais but 1; **— oui** yes (emphatic); **— non** no (emphatic)

maison (*f*) house, home 1; **à la —** at home

maître, maîtresse (d'école) (*m*)/ (*f*) elementary school teacher 11

mal (*m*) soreness, pain 8; **avoir du — à** to have trouble (doing something); **avoir — à . . .** to be sore, to have a pain

malade sick 8; **Je suis — (comme un chien).** I'm (as) sick (as a dog).

malentendu (*m*) misunderstanding 14

malgré despite 13; **— tout** despite everything

malheureux, malheureuse unhappy 15

manger to eat 1

manquer to miss 9; **à ne pas —** not to be missed; **Tu me manques.** I miss you.; **Tu nous manques.** We miss you.

se maquiller to put on make-up 10

marche: se mettre en — to begin working 10

marcher to walk, to work (a machine) 6

mardi (*m*) Tuesday P

mari (*m*) husband 3

mariage (*m*) wedding 15

marié: le/la marié(e) (*m/f*) bridegroom, bride 15

marié(e) married 1

se marier (avec) to marry

Maroc (*m*) Morocco 7

marocain(e) Moroccan 1

marron brown 2

mars (*m*) March 4

matériel (*m*) equipment 13

mathématiques (*f, pl*) math 2

matin (*m*) morning 4; **du —** in the morning

matinal(e) morning person 12

matinée (*f*) (during the) morning 8; **toute la —** all morning long; **faire la grasse —** to sleep in, late

mauvais(e) bad 2; **Il fait — .** The weather is bad.

me (m') me, to me 9

mécontent(e) unhappy 15; **être —** to be unhappy

médecin (*m*) doctor 4

médicament (*m*) medicine 8

meilleur(e) best 4; **— ami(e)** best friend; **— que . . .** better than

membre (de la famille) (*m*) member (of the family) 3

même same, even 6

mensonge (*m*) lie 7; **dire des —** to tell lies

menthe (*f*) mint 2; **— à l'eau** mint syrup with water

mentir to lie 8

mer (*f*) sea 9

merci (*m*) thank you P; **dire —** to say thank you

mercredi (*m*) Wednesday P

mère (*f*) mother 3

mériter to deserve 8

mes (*see* mon) my 3

métro (*m*) metro, subway 5

mettre to put 4; **— la table** set the table; **se — (à)** to begin; **(se) — en marche** to start working; **se — sur son trente et un** put on one's Sunday best

meuble (*m*) a piece of furniture 3

meurtre (*m*) murder 8

mexicain(e) Mexican 1

Mexique (*m*) Mexico 5

midi (*m*) noon P; **Il est — .** It's noon.

Midi (*m*) the South 13

miel (*m*) honey 11

mieux better 14; **il vaut — que . . .** it is preferable that, better that . . .

milieu *(m)* middle 4; **au — (de)** in the middle (of)

mille thousand 6

milliard *(m)* billion 6

million *(m)* million 6

mince thin 1

minuit midnight P; **Il est — .** It's midnight.

minute *(f)* minute 3

moderne modern 1

modeste modest 1

moi me P

moins less 14; **— (adj) que . . .** less (adj) than; **— de (nom) que..**less, fewer (noun) than

moi me P; **— je vais bien**. *I'm* fine.

moins minus, less P; **— le quart** a quarter to (for telling time); **— vingt** twenty to

mois *(m)* month 4; **le — dernier** last month; **le — prochain** next month; **tous les —** every month

mon, ma, mes my 3; **— ami(e)** my friend; **— Dieu** my gosh (lit. my God)

monde *(m)* world; **tout le —** everyone

monnaie *(f)* money, change, currency 15

Monsieur *(m)* sir, Mr. P

montagne *(f)* mountain 9

monter to go up 8; **— dans** to get in, on

montre *(f)* watch 12

montrer to show 9

moralement morally, psychologically 7

morceau (de) *(m)* piece (of) 6; **un — de craie** a piece of chalk

mot *(m)* word P; **un petit —** a little note; **écrire un —** to write a word, note; **mots apparentés** cognates

moto *(f)* motocycle 5

mourir to die 8

mousse au chocolat *(f)* chocolate mousse 6

moyen *(m)* means 5; **— de transport** means of transportation

musée *(m)* museum 5

musique *(f)* music 2

N

nager to swim 1

naissance *(f)* birth 11

naître to be born 8

natation *(f)* swimming 9

nationalité *(f)* nationality 5

navré(e) devastated 7

ne not 2; **n'est-ce pas?** right? isn't it? **ne . . . jamais** never; **ne . . . ni . . . ni** neither . . . nor; **ne . . . pas** not; **ne . . . pas du tout** not at all; **ne . . . personne** no one, nobody; **ne . . . plus** no more, no longer; **ne . . . rien** nothing

nécessaire necessary 12; **il est — (que . . .)** it's necessary (that . . .)

négritude *(f)* negritude 15

neiger to snow P; **Il neige.** It's snowing. P

nettoyer to clean 12

neveu *(m)* nephew 3

neuf, neuve new P; **quoi de —** what's new?

nez *(m)* nose 8; **J'ai le — qui coule.** My nose is running.

ni neither 15; **ne . . . ni . . . ni** neither . . . nor . . . ; **ni . . . ni . . . ne** neither . . . nor . . .

nièce *(f)* niece 3

Noël *(m)* Christmas 4

noir(e) black 2

nom *(m)* name P; **Écrivez votre —.** Write your name.

nombre *(m)* number P

nommer to name 8

non no, not P; **plus** either, neither

nos our 3

notre our 3

note *(f)* note, grade 10; **prendre des notes** to take notes

nourrir to feed 15

nous we, us, to us 4

nouveau, nouvel, nouvelle(s), nouveaux new 2

nouvelle *(f)* a piece of news 15

novembre *(m)* November 4

nuit *(f)* night 8; **bonne —** good night

numéro (de téléphone) *(m)* (phone) number 4

O

obéir to obey 13

obligatoire compulsory 12; **il est —** it's compulsory, required, mandatory

obtenir to obtain 10

s'occuper (de) to take care (of) 10

octobre *(m)* October 4

œil (yeux) *(m)* eye 8; **Mon —** ! My foot!

œuf *(m)* egg 6

offre *(f)* offer 15; **passer une — d'emploi** to run a want ad

offrir to offer 12

oh là là oh no! wow! 14

ombre *(f)* shadow 15

omelette *(f)* omelet 1

on one, we, you, they, people 1; **— y va!** let's go!

oncle *(m)* uncle 3

onze eleven P

optimiste optimistic 1

orange *(f)* orange 6; **— pressée** fresh-squeezed orange juice

orange orange 2

ordinateur *(m)* computer 3

ordonnance *(f)* prescription 8

ordonné(e) tidy, neat 4

oreille *(f)* ear 8

oser to dare 13

où where P; **— est-elle?** Where is she?; **— donner de la tête** what to do first; **— habitez-vous?** Where do you live?

oublier to forget 7

ouf phew 1

oui yes P; **-, ça va.** Yes, I'm doing fine.

ouvert(e) open 15

ouvrir to open 15; **Ouvrez votre livre.** Open your book.

s'ouvrir to open 15

P

page *(f)* page 9

paillasson *(m)* doormat 12

pain *(m)* bread 6; **— complet** whole wheat bread; **petit —** roll

pané(e) breaded 6

panne *(f)* breakdown 11; **tomber en —** to break down

pantalon *(m)* pants 2

papier *(m)* paper 5

Pâques *(f, pl)* Easter 4

par by 9; **— terre** on the ground; **— semaine** per week

parc *(m)* park 4

parce que because 4

pardon pardon, sorry 4

parent *(m)* parent, relative 11

paresseux/paresseuse lazy 1

se parfumer to perfume oneself 10

parfum *(m)* perfume 2

parking *(m)* parking lot 4

parler to speak 1; **— à** to speak to; **— de** to speak/talk about

se parler to talk to each other 10

part (de) *(f)* piece (of) 6

partager to share 3

partie *(f)* part 8; **— du corps** body parts

partiel *(m)* midterm examination 10

partir to leave 8

partout everywhere 8; **J'ai mal —.** It hurts everywhere.

pas no, not 1; **ne . . . —** not; **ne . . . — du tout** not at all; **— encore** not yet; **— mal** not bad; **— tellement** not so; **— très bien** not very well

passé(e) last 7; **le weekend —** last weekend; **la semaine passée** last week

passer to pass, to spend, to take 3; **Que se passe-t-il?** What's happening?; **Que s'est-il passé?** What happened?; **— un examen** to take an examination; **— une semaine** to spend a week; **— chez** to drop by

se passer to happen 10

pastille *(f)* lozenge 8

patauger to paddle 11

pâte *(f)* pasta 6

pâtisserie *(f)* pastry shop 5

patron/patronne *(m/f)* boss 11

pauvre poor 1

payer to pay 7

pays *(m)* country 5

paysage *(m)* scenery 11

pêche *(f)* fishing 5

pêche *(f)* peach 6

pêcheur *(m)* fisherman 7

pendant during 11; **— combien de temps?** for how long?; **— que** while (+ clause)

pense-bête *(m)* reminder 12

pensée *(f)* thought 13

penser to think 5

perdre to lose 11

perdu(e) lost 5

père *(m)* father 3

permettre to allow 4

permis de conduire *(m)* driver's license 15

personnage *(m)* character 8

personne *(f)* person 1; **ne . . . —** no one, nobody; **— ne** nobody; **— d'autre** nobody else

pessimiste pessimistic 1

petit(e) small, little 1; **petit ami** *(m)* boyfriend; **petite amie** *(f)* girlfriend; **petites annonces** *(f, pl)* classified ads; **petit déjeuner** *(m)* breakfast; **petits-enfants** *(m, pl)* grandchildren; **petite-fille** *(f)* grandaughter; **petit-fils** *(m)* grandson; **petit gâteau** *(m)* individual pastry ; **Petit à petit, l'oiseau fait son nid.** Little by little, the bird makes its nest.; **petits pois** *(m, pl)* peas 6

pétrin *(m)* jam, mess 9; **dans le —** in a mess

peu (de) little few 2; **un — de** a little of; **un — de place** a little room

peur *(f)* fright 12; **avoir — (de)** to be afraid, scared (of)

peut-être maybe, perhaps 9

pharmacie *(f)* pharmacy 1

pharmacien/pharmacienne *(m/f)* pharmacist 4

piano *(m)* piano 9

pièce *(f)* room 3; **— (de monnaie)** coin; **— de théâtre** play; **lire une — de théâtre** to read a play

pied *(m)* foot 8

pierre *(f)* stone 7

pile sharp (time) 10

piquer to scratch, to sting 8; **J'ai la gorge qui pique.** I have a scratchy throat.

piscine *(f)* swimming pool 5

pizza *(f)* pizza 1

placard *(m)* closet 9

place *(f)* room, square 5; **sur la —** on the square; **un peu de —** a little room

plaire to please, to like P; **s'il vous plaît** please

plage *(f)* beach 9

plaisanter to tease, to joke around 6

plaisir *(m)* pleasure 9; **Avec —** With pleasure, gladly; **Ça me ferait — de . . .** It would make me happy to . . .

planche à voile *(f)* windsurfing board 9; **faire de la —** to go windsurfing

plante (verte) *(f)* plant 3

plat *(m)* dish 6

pleuvoir to rain P; **Il pleut.** It's raining.

plombier *(m)* plumber 4

plus plus P; **Il n'y en a —.** There's none left, there's no more.; **ne . . . —** no more, no longer; **— de (nom) que...** more than; **— (adj, adv) que . . .** more . . . than; **— tard** later

plutôt rather 9

poche *(f)* pocket 9

poêle *(f)* frying pan 6

poème *(m)* poem 7; **lire un —** to read a poem

poids *(m)* weight 5; **prendre du —** to put on weight

pointure *(f)* size 10

pois *(m, pl)* peas 6

poisson *(m)* fish 6

poitrine *(f)* chest 8

poivre *(m)* pepper 6

poli(e) polite 9

poliment politely 13

pomme *(f)* apple 6; **— de terre** *(f)* potato

pompiers *(m, pl)* firemen, fire department 11

porc *(m)* pork 6

porte (f) door P
portefeuille (m) wallet 7
porter to wear 2
poser to pose, to ask 11; **— une question** to ask a question
postal(e) postal; **carte postale** (f) postcard
possible possible 12; **Il est —** It's possible; **Il n'est pas —** It's not possible; **Serait-il — de . . .** Would it be possible to . . . ; **Il serait — de . . .** It would be possible to . . .
poste (f) post office 5; **bureau de — (m)** the post office
pot (m) pot 5; **prendre un —** to have a drink
poulet (m) chicken 6
pour for 6
pourquoi why 4
pouvoir can, to be able to 9; **Je ne peux pas** I can't (do it)
se précipiter to hurry, to rush 15
précoce precocious 14
préférable preferable 12; **Il est — de . . .** It's better to . . .
préférer to prefer 2
premier, première first 5
prendre to take, to make 5; **— une décision** to make a decision; **— des notes** to take notes; **— du poids** to put on weight; **— un pot** to have a drink
prénom (m) first name 3
préparer to prepare 3
se préparer to get ready 10
près (de) close to 4
présenter to introduce P; **Je te présente mon ami.** Let me introduce you to my friend. **Je vous présente mon amie.** Let me introduce you to my (female) friend.
presque almost 10
prêt(e)(à) ready (to) 9
prêter to lend 14
prêtre (m) priest 11
printemps (m) spring 4
prix (m) price 7
problème (m) problem 1

prochain(e) next 5; **la semaine/ l'année prochaine** next week/ year
prodige (m) prodigy 7
produit (m) product 6
professeur (m) teacher P
profession (f) profession 4
promenade (f) walk 4; **faire une — to take a walk
se promener to go for a walk, a stroll
promettre to promise 4
propre clean 2
provençal(e) from the Provence region 12
provisions (f, pl) grocery shopping 4; **faire les —** to go grocery shopping
psychologie (f) psychology 2
puis then 4
punir to punish 13

Q

quand when 1
quarante forty 3
quart (m) quarter P; **et —** quarter past; **moins le —** quarter to
quartier (m) neighborhood 4
quatorze fourteen P
quatre four P
quatre-vingt-dix ninety 3
quatre-vingt-onze ninety one 3
quatre-vingts eighty 3
que that, than 3; **ne . . . —** only; **Qu'est-ce qu'elle est petite!** It's so small!; **Qu'est-ce qu'ils ont?** What's the matter with them?; **Qu'est-ce que tu as?** What's the matter with you?; **Qu'est-ce que c'est?** What is it?; **Qu'est-ce qui ne va pas?** What's wrong?; **Qu'avez-vous retenu?** What do you recall?; **— faites-vous?** What are you doing?; **— faire?** What should one do?
quel(le)(s) what, which 3; **Quel âge avez-vous?** How old are you?; **Quel jour est-ce?** What's today?; **Quel bébé!** What a baby!; **Quelle est votre nationalité?** What is

your nationality?; **Quelle heure est-il?** What time is it?
quelque(s) some 6
quelque chose something 6
quelque part somewhere 6
quelqu'un someone 6
quelquefois sometimes 1
question (f) question 1; **Il n'en est pas — !** No way!
qui who 3; **— est-ce?** Who is it?
quinze fifteen P
quitter to leave 7
quoi what 7; **Il n'y a pas de — !** You're welcome!; **Quoi de neuf?** What's new? P

R

raccrocher to hang up 12
racine (f) root 7
raconter to tell 8
radio (f) radio 2
rafting (m) rafting 9; **faire du —** to go river rafting
raison (f) right, reason 3; **avoir —** to be right
Ramadan (m) Ramadan 4
ramener to bring back 8
randonnée (f) hike 9; **faire de la — to go hiking
ranger to put away 3
se rappeler to remember 6
rapidement quickly 13
rarement rarely 1
se raser to shave 10
rater to miss 12; **— un avion, train** to miss a plane, train
ravi(e) delighted 1; **Je serais — de . . .** I would be delighted to . . .
recette (f) recipe 12
recevoir to receive 12
recherche (f) research, search 11
récolte (f) crop, harvest 11
se réconcilier to make up, to reconcile 14
reconnaissant(e) grateful 12
recouvrir to cover 15
réfléchir to think (about) 13
réfrigérateur (m) fridge 4
refuser to refuse 2
regarder to look 1

régime *(m)* diet 6

règle *(f)* ruler 5

regrettable unfortunate 12; **il est —** it's unfortunate

regretter to regret, to be sorry 12

régulièrement regularly 13

remarquer to notice 9

remercier to thank 7; **— le ciel** to thank the heavens

remettre to give, to postpone 7

rencontre *(f)* meeting 5

rencontrer to meet 9

se rencontrer to meet each other 10

rendre to give, to turn in P; **Rendez vos devoirs.** Turn in your homework.; **— un petit service** to do (someone) a favor; **— visite à** to pay a visit to

se rendre à to go to 11

renfermer to close, to contain 13

renseignement *(m)* a piece of information 15; **chercher des —** to look for information

rentrée *(f)* back to school 5

rentrer to return, to go home 1

repartir to leave again 14

repas *(m)* meal 6

repêcher to fish out 13

répéter to repeat P; **Répétez, s'il vous plaît.** Repeat, please.

répondeur *(m)* answering machine 3

répondre to answer 11

se reposer to rest 8

résidence *(f)* residence, home 2; **— universitaire** dorm

ressentir to feel 14

restaurant *(m)* restaurant 4

rester to stay 6; **Il reste du poulet.** There's some chicken left.

retard *(m)* lateness 1; **en retard** (to be) late

retenir to retain 13

retenu(e) detained 12; **être —** to be detained

retirer to withdraw 12

retourner to return 8

retraite *(f)* retirement 13; **prendre sa —** to retire

retrouver to find again 13

se retrouver to find, to meet 10

réuni(e) gathered 13

réussir (à) to succeed (in) 13

rêve *(m)* dream 13

réveil *(m)* alarm (clock) 10

se réveiller to wake up 10

revenir to come back 7

révision *(f)* review 8

revoir to see again; **au revoir** good-bye

rez-de-chaussée *(m)* ground floor 3

rhume *(m)* cold 8; **J'ai un — .** I have a cold.

riche rich, wealthy 1

rien nothing 6; **de —** you're welcome; **ne . . . —** nothing ; **— ne** nothing

rigolo fun, funny 13

rime *(f)* rime 8

rire to laugh 13

robe *(f)* dress 2

roman *(m)* novel 7; **lire un —** to read a novel

ronfler to snore 10

roquefort *(m)* roquefort cheese 6

rose pink 2

Rosh Hashana Rosh Ha-Shana 4

rouge red 2

rougir to blush 13

rouler to drive along 11

route *(f)* road 5

roux/rousse red-haired 3

rue *(f)* street 5; **au coin de la —** at the corner (of the street); **dans la —** in the street

russe russian 1

Russie *(f)* Russia 5

S

sa (see son, ses) his, her 3

sac *(m)* bag, purse 2

sac à dos *(m)* backpack 2

sac de couchage *(m)* sleeping bag 13

saison *(f)* season 4

salade *(f)* salad 6; **— niçoise** mixed salad with tuna and olives

sale dirty 2

salé(e) salted, salty 6

salle *(f)* room 3; **— de classe** *(f)* classroom; **— à manger** *(f)* dining room; **— de séjour** *(f)* living room

salon *(m)* formal living room 3

salut *(m)* hello, hi P

salutations *(f, pl)* greetings

samedi *(m)* Saturday P

sandwich *(m)* sandwich 1; **— au fromage** cheese sandwich; **— au jambon** ham sandwich; **— au saucisson** salami sandwich

sans without 9; **— domicile fixe (SDF)** homeless

santé *(f)* health 8

santon *(m)* nativity scene figure 12

saumon *(m)* salmon 6

sauter to skip, to jump 12; **— au cou** to give a big hug

sauvé(e) saved 1

savoir to know 10; **— par cœur** to know by heart; **Je ne sais pas.** I don't know.

saxophone *(m)* saxophone 9

science *(f)* science 2; **— politiques** political science

sécher to dry 10

secouer to shake 10

seigle *(m)* rye 6

seize sixteen P

séjour *(m)* stay 3; **salle de —** living room

sel *(m)* salt 6

selon according to 6

semaine *(f)* week 4; **jours de la —** days of the week; **la — prochaine** next week; **la — dernière** last week ; **par —** per week; **toutes les semaines** every week

semestre *(m)* semester 7

Sénégal *(m)* Senegal 7

sénégalais(e) Senegalese 1

sensible sensitive 14

se sentir to feel 10; **Je ne me sens pas bien.** I don't feel well.; **— mieux** to feel better

sept seven P

septembre *(m)* September 4

sérieusement seriously 13
serrer to hold, to tighten 8
se serrer to hug; **— la main** to shake hands 8
serrure (f) lock 12
service (m) service, favor 5
serviette (m) napkin 5
servir to serve 8
ses (see son) his, her 3
seul(e) alone 3
sévère strict 1
short shorts 2
si if 1; **s'il vous plaît** please
siècle (m) century 5
sieste (f) nap; **faire la —** to take a nap
simple simple 1
six six P
ski (m) skiing 9; **— de fond** cross-country skiing; **faire du — de fond** to go cross-country skiing; **— nautique** water skiing; **faire du — nautique** to go water skiing
skier to ski 1
smoking (m) tuxedo 4
sœur (f) sister 3
sofa (m) couch, sofa 3
soi one (self) 4
soif (f) thirst 3; **avoir —** to be thirsty
soir (m) evening 4; **du —** in the evening; **ce —** tonight; **tous les soirs** every night
soirée (f) party 9; **toute la —** all evening long
soixante sixty
soixante et onze seventy-one
soixante-dix seventy
soixante-douze seventy-two
soldes (f, pl) sale 10; **en solde** on sale
soleil (m) sun P; **Il fait du — .** It's sunny.
sommeil (m) sleep 3; **avoir —** to be sleepy
son, sa, ses his, her 3
sondage (m) poll 3
sonner to ring 11
sonnette (f) doorbell 14
sorbet (m) sorbet 2

sortir to go out, to get out 1; **— avec** to date, to go out with
sortez get out, leave P
souci (m) worry 7; **Ne te fais pas de — .** Don't worry.
soudain suddenly 11
souffrir to suffer 15
souhaitable desirable 12; **il est —** it's desirable 12
souhaiter to wish 12
sous under 4
soutien (m) support 15
(se) sourire to smile 8
(se) souvenir (de) to remember 10
souvent often 1
spécialisation (f) major 7
stade (m) stadium 5
stage (m) internship 15; **faire un —** to do an internship
stagiaire (m/f) intern
stéréo (f) stereo 3
steward (m) (male) flight attendant 4
strophe (f) stanza 8
stylo (m) pen P
sucre (m) sugar 6
sucré(e) sweet 6
suffir to be enough 6; **ça suffit** it's enough
suisse Swiss 1
Suisse (f) Switzerland 5
suite (f) following/next 5; **tout de —** immediately
suivant(e) following/next 1
supermarché (m) supermarket 4
sur on 4
sûr(e) sure 1; **bien sûr** but of course; **il n'est pas sûr . . .** it's not certain . . .
surpris(e) surprised 12; **être —** to be surprised
sympathique nice, pleasant 1

T

TGV (Train à Grande Vitesse) (m) bullet train 1
ta (see ton, tes) your 3
tabac (m) tobacco 2; **bureau de —** tobacco shop
table (f) table 1; **mettre la —** set the table; **— basse** coffee table

tableau (m) chalkboard P; **Effacez le —** Erase the board; **— de bord** dashboard
tache (f) stain 2; **taches de rousseur** freckles 9
tâche (f) chore 4
tâcher to try, to attempt 15
taille (f) size 10
tant so much/many 7
tant que as long as 13
tante (f) aunt 3
tapis (m) rug 3
tapisserie (f) wallpaper 14
taquiner to tease 12
tard late 5; **plus —** later
tarte (aux pommes) (f) (apple) tart 6
tartine (f) slice of bread and butter 6
tasse (de) (f) cup (of) 6
tata (f) auntie 3
taxi (m) taxi 5
te (t') you, to you 9
T-shirt (m) tee-shirt 2
teindre to dye 10
télécarte (f) phone card 1
téléphone (m) telephone 3; **au —** on the phone
téléphoner (à) to phone, call 1
se téléphoner to call (each other) 10
télévision (télé) (f) television 3
témoin (m) witness 10
temps (m) time, weather P; **avoir le —** to have the time; **de — en —** from time to time; **emploi du —** schedule; **Quel — fait-il?** What's the weather like?; **tout le —** all the time
tendre tender 14
tendrement tenderly 13
tenir to hold 15
tennis (m) tennis 9; **jouer au —** to play tennis
tennis (f, pl) tennis shoes
tenter to try 13; **— sa chance** to try one's luck
terre (f) earth, ground 8
tes (see ton, ta) your 3
Têt (m) Tet 4
tête (f) head 8; **J'ai mal à la — .** I've got a headache.

thé *(m)* tea 1; **— au citron** tea with lemon; **— nature** plain tea

théâtre *(m)* theater 4

timide timid, shy 1

tirer to pull 7

toi you 1; **et — ?** what about you?

toilettes *(f, pl)* restroom 3

toit*(m)* roof 11

tomber to fall 8; **— en panne** to break down; **— amoureux, amoureuse** to fall in love

ton, ta, tes your 3

tort *(m)* wrong 3; **avoir —** to be wrong

tôt early 10

toujours always 1

tour *(m)* turn 7; **c'est votre — (de)** it's your turn (to)

tourner to turn 5

tourneur *(m)* stone turner 7

Toussaint *(f)* All Saint's Day 4

tousser to cough 8

tout, toute, tous, toutes all, every 8; **tout à coup** all of a sudden; **tout d'un coup** all of a sudden; **tout à fait** completely; **tout à l'heure** later; **à tout à l'heure** (see you) later; **tout le monde** every one; **tout de suite** immediately ; **tout le temps** all the time, constantly; **pas du tout** not at all

trac *(m)* nervousness 7; **avoir le —** to be nervous

train *(m)* train 5

traiteur *(m)* take-out restaurant, deli 12

trajet *(m)* trip 11

tranche (de) *(f)* slice (of) 6

tranquillement calmly 13

travail *(m)* job 15; **chercher un —** to look for a job

travailler to work 1

travailleur, travailleuse hardworking 2

traverser to cross 5; **traversez!** cross!

treize thirteen P

trente thirty P

très very P

triste sad 1

trois three P

trombone *(m)* trombone, paper clip 5

se tromper (de) to make a mistake 10

trompette *(f)* trumpet 9

trop too much 1; **— cher** too expensive; **— de** too much/many (noun)

trouver to find 1

se trouver to be located 4; **où se trouve . . . ?** where is . . . located?; **vous trouvez?** do you think so?

truite *(f)* trout 6

tu you 1

Tunisie *(f)* Tunisia 7

tunisien(ne) Tunisian 7

U

un, une a, an P

unité *(f)* unit 1

université *(f)* university 1

V

vacances (d'été) *(f, pl)* (summer) vacation 4; **Bonnes — !** Have a good vacation!; **en —** on vacation

vaisselle *(f)* dishes; **faire la —** to do the dishes

valoir to be worth 12; **il vaut mieux** it's better to . . .

valse *(f)* waltz 13

vanille *(f)* vanilla 2; **glace à la —** vanilla ice cream

vantard *(m)* show-off 12

vaut is worth 12; **il — mieux** it's better

veau *(m)* veal 6

veille *(f)* eve, day before 4

vélo *(m)* bicycle 5

vendeur, vendeuse *(m)* *(f)* salesman, saleswoman 10

vendre to sell 11

vendredi *(m)* Friday P

venir to come 8; **venir de (+ infinitive)** to have just . . .

vent *(m)* wind P; **Il fait du — .** It's windy.

ventre *(m)* belly 8; **J'ai mal au — .** I have a stomach ache.

vérité *(f)* truth 7; **dire la —** to tell the truth

verre *(m)* glass 6; **en —** made of glass; **— de vin blanc** glass of white wine; **— de vin rouge** glass of red wine

vers around, toward 15; **— sept heures** around seven o'clock; **se diriger —** to go towards

vers *(m)* verse 8; **— libre** free verse

verser to pour 7

vert(e) green 2

veste *(f)* jacket 2

vêtement *(m)* article of clothing 2

veuf/veuve widowed 1

viande *(f)* meat 6

vie *(f)* life 7; **C'est la — !** That's life!; **Jamais de la vie!** Never!; **gagner sa —** to earn a living

vieillir to get old 13

Viêt-nam *(m)* Vietnam 7

vietnamien(ne) Vietnamese 1

vieux/vieil/vieille(s)/vieux old 2; **une vieille fille** an old maid

vilain, vilaine bad, naughty 3

ville *(f)* town 5

vin *(m)* wine 6

vingt P twenty

vingt et un twenty-one P

vingt-deux twenty-two P

violet(te) violet 2

violon *(m)* violin 9

visage *(m)* face 8

visite *(f)* visit 11; **rendre — à** to visit (someone)

visiter to visit (something) 11

vite quickly 5

vitrine *(f)* store window 10

vivre to live 5

voici here is/this is 3

voilà there is (are)/that is P; **— mon ami Paul.** That's my friend Paul.

voile *(f)* sail 9; **faire de la —** to go sailing

voir to see 9

voisin/voisine *(m)* *(f)* neighbor 7

voiture *(f)* car 5; **en —** by car

voix *(f)* voice 5

volleyball *(m)* volleyball 9

Vocabulaire

Anglais-Français

A

a, an un(e)
able: be — to pouvoir
about de, il s'agit de
absolutely absolument
ache: I — everywhere j'ai mal partout
accompany accompagner
according to selon
accountant comptable (m)
across (from) en face (de)
act agir
active actif, active
activity activité (f)
actor acteur (m)
actress actrice (f)
adore adorer
advertisement petite annonce, publicité (f)
advice (piece of) conseil (m)
afraid: be — avoir peur
Africa Afrique (f)
after après
afternoon après-midi (m); **in the — ** l'après-midi
again encore, de nouveau
age (n) âge (m)
age (v) vieillir
ago il y a; **five weeks —** il y a cinq semaines
agree (with) être d'accord avec
agreed d'accord
ahead droit; **straight —** tout droit
airport aéroport (m)
alarm clock réveil (m)
Algeria Algérie (f)
Algerian algérien(ne)
all tout(es), tous; **— of a sudden** tout d'un coup; **— Saints' Day** Toussaint (f); **— the time** tout le temps
allow laisser, permettre
almost presque

alone seul(e); **leave me —** laissez-moi tranquille
already déjà
also aussi
always toujours
American américain(e)
amuse amuser, s'amuser
amusing amusant(e)
ancestor ancêtre (m)
and et; **— you?** Et vous?
angel ange (m)
angry fâché(e); **be —** être fâché; **get — ** se fâcher
answer répondre; **answering machine** répondeur (m)
Antarctica Antarctique (f)
apartment appartement (m); **— building** immeuble (m)
appetizer hors-d'œuvre (m, inv)
apple pomme (f)
apply (for a job) faire une demande (d'emploi)
appointment rendez-vous (m)
approximately à peu près
April avril (m)
argue se disputer
argument dispute (f)
arm bras (m)
armchair fauteuil (m)
around vers; **— ten** dizaine (f)
arrive arriver
article of clothing vêtement (m)
as comme, aussi; **— . . . —** aussi . . . que; **— a (vegetable)** comme (légume); **— long —** tant que; **— many, — much** autant de; **— many, — much . . . —** autant de . . . que; **— planned** comme prévu; **— soon —** aussitôt que
Asia Asie (f)
ashamed honteux, honteuse; **be —** avoir honte
ask demander; **— (a question)**

poser une question; **— for advice** demander un conseil
asleep: fall — s'endormir
aspirin aspirine (f)
asparagus asperge (f)
at à, chez; **— the antique dealer** chez l'antiquaire; **— the end** à la fin, au bout de (la rue); **— the lost and found** au bureau des objets trouvés; **— the top of one's lungs** à tue-tête; **— the university** à la fac, à l'université; **— what time?** à quelle heure?; **— which** à quel(le); **— . . . o'clock** à . . . heure(s)
athletic sportif, sportive
ATM distributeur automatique (m)
attend assister à, aller à (la fac)
attention: pay — faire attention
August août (m)
aunt tante (f); **auntie** tata (f)
Australia Australie (f)
author auteur (m)
available disponible
avenue avenue (f); **on . . . —** sur l'avenue . . .
away: right — tout de suite

B

baby bébé (m)
back to school rentrée (f)
back (n) dos (m)
back (v): **come —** revenir; **give —** rendre; **go —** retourner; **— then** à cette époque-là
backpack sac à dos (m)
bad mauvais(e); **it's — weather** il fait mauvais; **that's (it's) too —** c'est dommage
badly mal
bakery boulangerie (f)
bald chauve
banana banane (f)

bank banque *(f)*
banknote billet *(m)*
bar bar *(m)*
baseball baseball *(m)*
basketball basket-ball *(m)*
bathing suit maillot de bain *(m)*
bathroom, restroom; salle de bains *(f)*; toilettes *(f, pl)*
bathtub baignoire *(f)*
be être; **— able to** pouvoir; **— afraid** avoir peur; **— ashamed** avoir honte; **— better** valoir mieux; **— born** naître; **— cold** avoir froid; **— hot** avoir chaud; **— hungry** avoir faim; **— interested in** s'intéresser à; **— located** se trouver; **— looking good** s'annoncer bien; **— lucky** avoir de la chance; **— necessary** falloir (il faut); **— nervous** avoir le trac; **— right (to)** avoir raison (de); **— sleepy** avoir sommeil; **— sore** avoir mal à; **— sorry** regretter; **— thirsty** avoir soif; **— wrong** avoir tort; **— . . . years old** avoir . . . ans
beach plage *(f)*
bean haricot *(m)*
beautiful beau/belle
because parce que
bed lit *(m)*; **go to —** se coucher
bedroom chambre *(f)*
beef bœuf *(m)*
beer bière *(f)*
before avant
begin commencer
beginning début *(m)*; **in the —** au début
behind derrière
beige beige
Belgian belge
Belgium Belgique *(f)*
believe (in) croire (à)
belong to être à
beside, next to à côté de
best meilleur(e)(s); **— friend** meilleur(e) ami(e); **the —** le, la, les meilleur(e)(s)
better than . . . mieux/ meilleur(e)(s) que

between, among entre
beverage boisson *(f)*
bicycle bicyclette *(f)*, vélo *(m)*
big grand(e)
bike vélo *(m)*
bill *(paper money)* billet *(m)*; *(check in a restaurant)* addition *(f)*
billion milliard *(m)*
biology biologie *(f)*
birth naissance *(f)*
birthday anniversaire *(m)*; **Happy —** Joyeux Anniversaire
black noir(e)
blanket couverture *(f)*
blond blond(e)
blouse chemisier *(m)*
blue bleu(e)
blush rougir
board planche *(f)*; **chalk —** tableau *(m)*; **erase the —** effacez le tableau; **surf —** planche *(f)* (de surf)
boat bateau *(m)*
body corps *(m)*; **parts of the —** parties du corps
book livre *(m)*; **— of tickets** carnet *(m)*
bookstore librairie *(f)*
bored: to be — s'ennuyer
boring ennuyeux (ennuyeuse)
born né(e); **be —** naître; **I was —** je suis né(e)
boss patron *(m)*, patronne *(f)*
both les deux
bottle (of) bouteille (de) *(f)*
boulevard boulevard *(m)*; **on . . . — sur le boulevard . . .**
bowling: lawn — pétanque *(f)*, boules *(f, pl)*
box boîte *(f)*
boy garçon *(m)*
boyfriend copain, petit ami *(m)*
bread pain *(m)*; **— and butter** tartine *(f)*; **breaded** pané(e)
break casser/se casser
breakdown panne *(f)*; **to have a (mechanical) —** tomber en panne
breakfast petit déjeuner *(m)*
bride mariée *(f)*

Brie cheese brie *(m)*
bring apporter; **— back** ramener
brother frère *(m)*
brother-in-law beau-frère *(m)*
brown brun(e)
brunette brune *(f)*
brush *(n)*: **hair —** brosse à cheveux *(f)*; **tooth —** brosse à dents *(f)*;
brush *(v)* brosser; **to — one's hair, teeth** se brosser les cheveux, les dents
building bâtiment *(m)*
bus bus *(m)*; **— stop** arrêt de bus *(m)*
business affaires *(f, pl)*, commerce *(m)*
businessman homme d'affaires *(m)*
businesswoman femme d'affaires *(f)*
busy occupé(e), chargé(e); **— schedule** emploi du temps chargé *(m)*
but mais
butcher shop boucherie *(f)*; **pork —** charcuterie *(f)*
butter beurre *(m)*
buy acheter
by en, par; **— car** en voiture; **— plane** par avion; **— the way** au fait

C

café, coffee shop café *(m)*
cake gâteau *(m)*
calculator calculatrice *(m)*
call appeler
calm calme, tranquille
calmly calmement, tranquillement
Camembert cheese camembert *(m)*
camera appareil-photo *(m)*
Cameroon Cameroun *(m)*
Cameroonian camerounais(e)
campus campus *(m)*
can *(n)* boîte *(f)*
can *(v)* pouvoir
Canada Canada *(m)*
Canadian canadien(ne)
candy bonbon *(m)*
car voiture, auto *(f)*

card carte *(f)*; **credit —** carte de crédit *(f)*; **note —** fiche *(f)*; **post —** carte postale *(f)*
cards (game) cartes *(f, pl)*
care (worry) s'inquiéter de
carrot carotte *(f)*
carry porter
cartoon BD, bande dessinée *(f)*
casket cercueil *(m)*
cassette cassette *(f)*
cat chat *(m)*; **female —** chatte
catch attraper
CD player lecteur de disques compacts *(m)*
celebrate fêter, arroser
celebration fête *(f)*; **That calls for a —!** Ça s'arrose!
century siècle *(m)*
ceremony cérémonie *(f)*
certainly certainement
certified public accountant expert — comptable *(m)*
chair chaise *(f)*
chalk craie *(f)*
chalkboard tableau *(m)*
challenge défi *(m)*
change *(n)* monnaie *(f)*; **Do you have — for . . . ?** Avez-vous de la monnaie pour . . . ?
change *(v)* changer
character personnage *(m)*
charming charmant(e)
chat bavarder
cheap bon marché *(inv)*
check *(n)* chèque *(m)*; addition *(f)*
check *(v)* vérifier
checkers dames *(f, pl)*
cheese fromage *(m)*; **— sandwich** sandwich au fromage *(m)*; **— shop** fromagerie *(f)*
chemistry chimie *(f)*
cherry cerise *(f)*
chess échecs *(m, pl)*
chest poitrine *(f)*; **— of drawers** commode *(f)*
chic chic, stylish
chicken poulet *(m)*; **— in wine sauce** coq au vin *(m)*
child enfant *(m)*
childhood enfance *(f)*

China Chine *(f)*
Chinese chinois(e)
chocolate chocolat *(m)*; **— mousse** mousse au chocolat *(f)*; **dark —** chocolat noir; **hot —** chocolat chaud
choice choix *(m)*
choose choisir
chore tâche ménagère *(f)*
Christmas Noël *(m)*
church église *(f)*
cigarette cigarette *(f)*
city ville *(f)*
civil servant fonctionnaire *(m)*
class classe *(f)*; **in —** en classe
classified ad petite annonce *(f)*
classroom salle de classe *(f)*
clean propre
climbing escalade *(f)*; **to go —** faire de l'escalade
close *(prep)* près de
close *(v)* fermer
closet placard *(m)*
clothes vêtements *(m, pl)*
Coca-Cola Coca *(m)*
coffee café *(m)*; **— table** table basse *(f)*; **— with cream** café crème; **— with milk** café au lait
coin pièce *(f)*
cold *(adj)* froid(e); **it's — weather** il fait froid; **be —** avoir froid
cold *(n)* rhume *(m)*; **I've got a —** j'ai un rhume
color couleur *(f)*; **What — is (are) . . . ?** De quelle couleur est (sont) . . . ?
come venir; **— back** revenir; **— in** entrer; **Where do you — from?** D'où venez-vous?
comfortable confortable; **be —** être à l'aise
comfortably confortablement
comic strip BD, bande dessinée *(f)*
compact disk, CD disque compact *(m)*
completely complètement
computer ordinateur *(m)*; **— science** informatique *(f)*
constantly constamment

continent continent *(m)*
continue continuer
cook *(n)* chef *(m)*; **an excellent —** cordon bleu *(m)*
cook *(v)* faire la cuisine
cookie (petit) gâteau sec *(m)*
cooking cuisine *(f)*
corner coin *(m)*; **at, on the — (of)** au coin de
cost *(n)* prix *(m)*
cost *(v)* coûter
couch sofa *(m)*
cough tousser
cough toux *(f)*
count compter; **— one's blessings** remercier le ciel
couple couple *(m)*
country pays *(m)*
countryside campagne *(f)*, paysage *(m)*
course cours *(m)*; **of —** bien sûr
cousin cousin *(m)*/cousine *(f)*
cover *(n)* couverture *(f)*
cover *(v)* couvrir, recouvrir
crazy fou (folle); **in a — way** follement
cream crème *(f)*
create créer
credit card carte de crédit *(f)*
croissant croissant *(m)*
cross traverser; **— the street** traverser la rue
cross-country skiing ski de fond *(m)*; **to go —** faire du ski de fond
cry pleurer
cultivated cultivé(e)
cup (of) tasse (de) *(f)*
currency monnaie *(f)*
cut couper; **— oneself** se couper

D

dance *(n)* bal *(m)*
dance *(v)* danser
dangerous dangereux, dangereuse
dare *(n)* défi *(m)*
dare *(v)* oser
dark noir; **— chocolate** chocolat noir
darling chéri(e)
darn (it) zut

date (*n*) date (*f*); **What is today's — ?** Quelle est la date aujourd'hui?

date (someone) (*v*) sortir avec

datebook agenda (*m*)

daughter fille (*f*)

day jour (*m*); **— after tomorrow** après demain; **— before yesterday** avant hier; **all — long** toute la journée; **every —** tous les jours; **Have a nice — !** Bonne journée!; **New Year's —** Jour de l'An (*m*); **What — is it?** Quel jour est-ce?

daycare center crèche (*f*)

dead mort(e)

dear cher, chère

death mort (*f*)

December décembre (*m*)

decent décent(e)

decide décider

decision décision (*f*); **to make a —** prendre une décision

definitely absolument

deli traiteur (*m*)

delighted ravi(e); **I'd be — to . . .** Je serais ravi(e) de . . .

demand exiger

den salon (*m*)

department store grand magasin (*m*)

departure départ (*m*)

depend dépendre, compter sur; **that depends** ça dépend

depressed déprimé(e); **be —** être déprimé(e)

describe décrire

deserve mériter

desirable désirable, souhaitable; **it would be —** il serait souhaitable

desk bureau (*m*)

dessert dessert (*m*)

detained retenu(e); **to be — (delayed)** être retenu(e)

detest détester

devastated navré(e)

devil diable (*m*)

dial composer (un numéro)

die mourir

diet régime (*m*)

different différent(e)

dining room salle à manger (*f*)

dinner dîner (*m*); **to eat —** dîner

dirty sale

disappointed déçu(e); **be —** être déçu(e)

discreet discret, discrète

dish plat (*m*)

dishes vaisselle (*f, s*); **do the —** faire la vaisselle

dishwasher lave-vaisselle (*m*)

diskette disquette (*f*)

disobey désobéir

divorce divorcer

divorced divorcé(e)

do faire; **— a little favor** rendre un petit service **— one's hair** se coiffer; **— one's homework** faire ses devoirs; **— the housework** faire le ménage; **What should I — ?** Que faire?

doctor médecin (*m*)

dog chien (*m*); **female —** chienne (*f*)

door porte (*f*)

door mat paillasson (*m*)

doorbell sonnette (*f*)

doubt douter

doubtful douteux, douteuse; **it's —** il est douteux

downtown centre ville (*m*)

dozen douzaine (*f*)

dream (*n*) rêve (*m*)

dream (*v*) rêver

dress robe (*f*)

dressed: get — s'habiller

drink (*n*) boisson (*f*)

drink (*v*) boire; **to have a —** prendre un pot

drive conduire; **— along** rouler

driver's license permis de conduire (*m*)

drop by passer chez

drugstore pharmacie (*f*)

drums batterie (*f, s*)

dubbed doublé(e)

during pendant

E

each chaque

ear oreille (*f*)

early tôt, en avance

earn gagner; **— a living** gagner sa vie

easily facilement

Easter Pâques (*f*)

easy facile

eat manger; **— dinner** dîner; **— lunch** déjeuner

economics économie (*f*)

egg œuf (*m*)

eight huit

eighteen dix-huit

eighty quatre-vingts

elegant élégant(e)

else d'autre

employee employé(e)

employer employeur (*m*), patron(ne)

end fin (*f*)

end up finir par

energetic énergique

engaged fiancé(e)

engagement fiançailles (*f, pl*)

engineer ingénieur (*m*)

England Angleterre (*f*)

English anglais(e)

enough (of) assez (de)

enter entrer

equipment matériel (*m*)

erase effacer; **— the board** effacez le tableau

eraser gomme (*f*)

errands courses (*f*)

essential essentiel(le); **it is —** il est essentiel

Europe Europe (*f*)

eve (day before) veille (*f*)

even même

evening soir (*m*); **all — long** toute la soirée; **every —** tous les soirs; **in the — , at night** le soir; **this — , tonight** ce soir

every tout(e)(s), tous; **— day** tous les jours; **— night** tous les soirs; **— week** toutes les semaines; **— year** tous les ans

everybody tout le monde

everyone tout le monde

everything tout (*pron inv*)

everywhere partout; **I ache —** J'ai mal partout

exam examen (*m*)

example exemple *(m)*; **for —** par exemple
excellent excellent(e)
executive cadre *(m)*
exciting passionnant(e)
excuse me pardon
expenses frais *(m, pl)*
expensive cher, chère
explanation explication *(f)*
eye œil *(m)*; **eyes** yeux *(m, pl)*; **my — hurt** j'ai mal aux yeux
eyeglasses lunettes *(f, pl)*

F

face visage *(m)*
faded passé
fairy tale conte de fée *(m)*
faithful fidèle
fall *(n)* automne *(m)*
fall *(v)* tomber; **— asleep** s'endormir
false faux
familiar: be — with connaître
family famille *(f)*
fantastic formidable
far (from) loin (de)
farmer fermier *(m)*, fermière *(f)*
fashion designer couturier *(m)*
fast vite, rapide, rapidement
fat gros(se); **get —** grossir
father père *(m)*
father-in-law beau-père *(m)*
favor service *(m); do a —* rendre un service
favorite préféré(e)
fear peur *(f)*
February février *(m)*
feed nourrir, donner à manger
feel sentir, se sentir; **— like** avoir envie de
felt-tip pen feutre, crayon-feutre *(m)*
fever fièvre *(f)*; **I have a —** j'ai de la fièvre
few peu de; **a —** quelques
fiancé(e) fiancé(e)
fifteen quinze
fifty cinquante
fight *(n)* dispute *(f)*
fight *(v): —* **with (each other)** se disputer

finally enfin
find trouver
fine bien
finger doigt *(m)*; **— food** amuse-gueule *(m, inv)*
finish finir
fire feu *(m)*; **— department, — men** pompiers *(m)*
first premier, première; **— (of all)** d'abord; **— name** prénom *(m)*
fish poisson *(m)*
fisherman pêcheur *(m)*
fishing pêche *(f)*; **go —** aller à la pêche
five cinq
fix réparer
flavor parfum *(m)*
flight vol *(m)*
flight attendant hôtesse (de l'air) *(f)*, steward *(m)*
floor (of a building) étage *(m)*; **on the first —** au premier étage; **ground —** rez-de-chaussée *(m)*; **on the —** par terre
flour farine *(f)*
flower fleur *(f)*
flu grippe *(f)*
following suivant(e)
food cuisine *(f)*
foot pied *(m)*
football football américain *(m)*
for depuis, pendant, pour; **— rent** à louer
forbid interdire
forbidden interdit(e)
foreign étranger, étrangère
forget oublier
fortunately heureusement
fortune teller voyante *(f)*
forty quarante
found trouvé(e); **be —** se trouver; **lost and —** bureau des objets trouvés *(m)*
four quatre
fourteen quatorze
franc franc *(m)*
France France *(f)*
frankly franchement
freckle tache de rousseur *(f)*
free libre; **— verse** vers libre *(m)*

French français(e); **— fries** frites *(f)*; **in —** en français
frequently fréquemment
fresh-squeezed pressé(e); **— lemonade** citron pressé *(m)*; **— orange juice** orange pressée *(f)*
Friday vendredi *(m)*
friend ami(e); **best —** meilleur(e) ami(e)
from de
front: in — of devant
fruit fruit *(m)*
frying pan poêle *(f)*
fun amusant(e); **have —** s'amuser
funny amusant(e), drôle, bizarre
furious furieux, furieuse; **be —** être furieux, furieuse
furniture meubles *(m, pl)*
future avenir *(m)*

G

game jeu *(m)*
garage garage *(m)*
garden jardin *(m)*
general: in — en général
generous généreux, généreuse
geography géographie *(f)*
German allemand(e)
Germany Allemagne *(f)*
get: — along s'entendre; **— angry** se fâcher; **— dressed** s'habiller; **— engaged** se fiancer; **— fat** grossir; **— going** s'en aller; **— into** monter dans; **— married** se marier; **— ready** se préparer; **— up** se lever
gift cadeau *(m)*
girl jeune fille *(f)*
give (to) donner (à); **— back** rendre; **— a hand** donner un coup de main
gladly volontiers
glass verre *(m)*; **— of** un verre de
glasses (eye) lunettes *(f, pl)*
glide glisser
go aller; **— camping** faire du camping; **— home** rentrer; **— out** sortir; **— toward** s'approcher
goat chèvre *(f)*; **— cheese** chèvre *(m)*
golf golf *(m)*

good bon/bonne; — **afternoon** bonjour; — **evening** bonsoir; — **looking** beau, belle; — **morning** bonjour

good-bye au revoir

government employee fonctionnaire (m)

grade note (f)

grandchilds petits enfants (m, pl)

granddaughter petite fille (f)

grandfather grand-père (m)

grandmother grand-mère (f)

grandparent grand-parent (m)

grandson petit fils (m)

gray gris

great formidable, génial; **it's —** c'est formidable

green vert(e); — **beans** haricots verts (m)

greetings salutations (f)

grocery store épicerie (f)

groom marié (m)

ground terre (f); — **floor** rez-de-chaussée (m); **on the —** par terre

guest invité(e)

guilty coupable

guitar guitare (f)

guy gars (m)

gymnasium gymnase (m)

H

habit habitude (f); **to be in the — of** avoir l'habitude de

hair cheveux (m, pl); — **dresser** coiffeur (m), coiffeuse (f)

half demi(e); — **past** et demi(e)

ham jambon (m); — **sandwich** sandwich au jambon (m); — **and cheese sandwich with bechamel sauce** croque-monsieur (m)

hand main (f); **my — hurts** j'ai mal à la main

handsome beau

hang up raccrocher

hang glider deltaplane (m); **to go hang-gliding** faire du deltaplane

happen se passer; **What happened?** Qu'est-ce qui s'est passé?; **What's happening?** Qu'est-ce qui se passe?

happiness bonheur (m)

happy content(e)/heureux (heureuse); **I'd be — to . . .** Je serais content(e) de . . .

hard (adv) dur

hard-working travailleur (travailleuse)

hardly guère

harvest récolter

hat chapeau (m)

hate détester

have avoir; — **dinner** dîner; — **fun** s'amuser; — **just . . .** venir de; — **lunch** déjeuner; — **the right** avoir le droit;; — **something to drink** prendre quelque chose à boire; — **to** devoir; — **trouble (doing something)** avoir du mal à

he il/lui

head tête (f)

headache mal de tête (m); **I have a headache** J'ai mal à la tête

hear entendre

heart cœur (m); **by —** par cœur

heat (for a house) (n) chauffage (m)

heat (v) chauffer

heaven: be in — être aux anges

hello bonjour; **say —** dire bonjour

help aider; **Help!** Au secours!

her (poss adj) sa, ses, son

her (pron) elle, lui

here ici

here is, here are voici/voilà

hi salut

high-tops baskets (f, pl)

hide cacher

high fashion haute couture (f)

hiking randonnée (f); **to go —** faire de la randonnée

him le, lui

hip hanche (f)

his sa, ses, son

history histoire (f)

hockey hockey (m)

hold tenir, retenir

holiday fête (f)

home maison (f); **at the — of** chez; **go —** rentrer

homeless: — person SDF (sans domicile fixe) (m)

homework devoir (m); **do one's —** faire ses devoirs

honest honnête

honey miel (m)

hope espérer

hot chaud(e); **be —** avoir chaud; — **chocolate** chocolat chaud (m); **It's —** Il fait chaud

hour heure (f); **an — ago** il y a une heure

house maison (f); **at, to the —** à la maison/chez

housework ménage (m); **do the —** faire le ménage

how comment; — **are you?** Comment allez-vous?; — **'s it going?** Comment ça va?; — **much, many** combien (de); — **old are you?** Quel âge avez-vous?

hundred cent

hungry: be — avoir faim

hurry se dépêcher

hurt avoir mal (à); **my hand hurts** j'ai mal à la main

husband mari (m)

I

I je

I. D. card carte d'identité (f)

ice cream glace (f)

idea idée (f)

if si

imbecile imbécile (m)

immediately tout de suite, immédiatement

impatient impatient(e)

important important(e); **it's — that** il est important que

impossible impossible; **it's —** c'est impossible; **that's — for me** cela m'est impossible

improve faire des progrès

in à, dans, en; — **the back** au fond; — **bed** au lit; — **the classroom** dans la classe; — **fact** au fait; — **a fix** dans le pétrin; — **front (of)** devant; — **good hands** en bonnes mains; — **a little while** tout à l'heure; — **the meantime**

entre temps; **— the middle of** au milieu de; **— the old days** autrefois; **— the past** autrefois; **— spite** malgré; **— spite of everything** malgré tout; **— ten minutes** dans dix minutes; **— two weeks** dans deux semaines

incredible incroyable

inexpensive bon marché

information renseignement *(m)*; **to look for —** chercher des renseignements

inside dedans

instead (of) au lieu de

insurance assurance *(f)*; **— agent** agent d'assurance *(m)*

intelligent intelligent(e)

intelligently intelligemment

interested: be — in s'intéresser à

interesting intéressant(e)

intern stagiaire *(m)*

internship stage *(m)*; **do an —** faire un stage

interview entretien *(m)*; **have an —** passer un entretien

introduce présenter; **I'd like to — you to my friend Paul** Je voudrais vous presenter mon ami Paul

invite inviter

Ireland Irlande *(f)*

Irish irlandais(e)

irresistible irrésistible

Israel Israël *(m)*

Israeli israélien(ne)

it cela, ça, il, elle

it is c'est, il est; **— a . . .** c' est un(e) . . . ; **— about** il s'agit de; **— cold** il fait froid; **— hot** il fait chaud; **— important** il est important; **— necessary** il faut, il est nécessaire; **— nice weather** il fait beau; **— over** c'est fini; **— raining** il pleut; **— snowing** il neige; **— the . . . (date)** c'est le . . . ; **— your turn** c'est votre tour

Italian italien(ne)

Italy Italie *(f)*

its sa, son, ses

Ivory Coast Côte d'Ivoire *(f)*

J

jacket veste *(f)*

jam confiture *(f)*

January janvier *(m)*

Japan Japon *(m)*

Japanese japonais(e)

jeans jean *(m)*

jewelry box écrin *(m)*

job travail *(m)*, situation *(f)*; **look for a —** chercher un travail

judge juger

juice jus *(m)*; **orange —** jus d'orange *(m)*

July juillet *(m)*

jump sauter

June juin *(m)*

just: have — venir de

justify justifier; **— your choice** justifiez votre choix

K

keep garder; **— going** continuer

key clé *(f)*

kid around plaisanter

kilo(gram), ~ 2.2 lbs. kilo(gramme) *(m)*

kind *(adj)* gentil(le)

kind *(n)* sorte *(f)*; **what — (of)?** quelle sorte (de)?

kiss *(n)* (grosse) bise *(f)*

kiss (each other) *(v)* s'embrasser

kitchen cuisine *(f)*

knee genou *(m)*

know connaître, savoir; **I don't —** je ne sais pas; **— by heart** savoir par cœur

Korea Corée *(f)*

Korean coréen(ne)

L

Labor Day Fête du Travail *(f)*

lady dame *(f)*

lamb agneau *(m)*

lamp lampe *(f)*

language langue *(f)*

last dernier, dernière; **— name** nom de famille *(m)*; **— night** hier soir; **the — time** la dernière fois

late tard, en retard; **be —** être en retard; **it is —** il est tard

later plus tard; **see you —** à tout à l'heure

laugh rire

law droit *(m)*

lawn bowling boules, pétanque *(f)*

lawyer avocat(e)

lazy paresseux (paresseuse)

learn apprendre

least le, la, les moins; **at —** au moins

leave laisser, partir, quitter; **leave again** repartir; **— me alone** laisse(z)-moi tranquille

left gauche *(f)*; **on the —** à gauche; **there are three . . . left** il reste trois . . .

leg jambe *(f)*

leisure activities loisirs *(m)*

lemon citron *(m)*

lemon-lime soda limonade *(f)*

lemonade citron pressé *(m)*

lend prêter

less moins

lesson leçon *(f)*

let laisser, permettre; **let's go** allons-y; **let's see** voyons; **let's sit down** asseyons-nous

letter lettre *(f)*; **— of recommendation** lettre de recommendation

library bibliothèque *(f)*

license: driver's — permis de conduire *(m)*

lie mentir

life vie *(f)*; **Not on your —!** Jamais de la vie!; **That's —!** C'est la vie!

light *(adj)* clair; **light brown** châtain clair

light *(n)* lumière *(f)*

light up s'allumer

like *(prep)* comme

like *(v)* aimer; **— a lot** aimer beaucoup; **— very much** aimer bien; **I would —** je voudrais

line ligne *(f)*

listen écouter

liter (of) litre (de) *(m)*

literature littérature *(f)*

little petit(e), peu (de); **a —** un peu (de); **— by —** petit à petit, peu à peu

live habiter; **Where do you — ?** Où habitez-vous?
lively vif (vive)
living room salle de séjour *(f)*
loan prêter
located: be — se trouver
lock serrure *(f)*
long long (longue); **a — time** longtemps; **a — time ago** il y a longtemps; **how — . . . ?** depuis/ pendant combien de temps . . . ?; **no longer** ne . . . plus
look (at) regarder; **— for** chercher
lose perdre; **— weight** maigrir, perdre du poids
lot: a — (of) beaucoup (de)
love *(n)* amour *(m)*; **— (closing a letter)** grosses bises, je t'embrasse
love *(v)* aimer, adorer; **be in —** être amoureux (amoureuse); **fall in —** tomber amoureux (amoureuse); **I — you** je t'aime
lover (of) amateur (de) *(m)*
low bas(se); **lower** plus bas(se)
lozenge pastille *(f)*
luck chance *(f)*
lucky: be lucky avoir de la chance
lunch déjeuner *(m)*; **eat —** prendre le déjeuner, déjeuner

M

ma'am madame
madly follement
magazine magazine *(m)*
mail *(n)* courrier *(m)*
mail *(v)* envoyer
mailman facteur *(m)*
major (in school) spécialisation *(f)*
make faire; **— a decision** prendre une décision; **— a mistake** faire une erreur, se tromper; **— one's bed** faire son lit; **— oneself at home** faire comme chez soi
make-up maquillage *(m)*; **to put on —** se maquiller
mall centre commercial *(m)*
man homme *(m)*
manners étiquette *(f)*

many beaucoup (de); **how —** combien (de); **so —** tant (de); **too —** trop (de)
map carte *(f)*; **city —** plan *(m)*
March mars *(m)*
market marché *(m)*; **super —** supermarché *(m)*
marriage mariage *(m)*; **— counselor** conseiller matrimonial *(m)*
married marié(e); **get —** se marier
marry se marier
masterpiece chef-d' œuvre *(m)*
match allumette *(f)*
math mathématiques *(f, pl)*
matter: What's the — ? Qu'est-ce qu'il y a? Qu'est-ce que tu as?
May mai *(m)*
may: — I help you? Je peux vous aider?
maybe peut-être
me me, moi
meal repas *(m)*
mean méchant(e)
means moyen *(m)*; **— of transportation** moyens de transport
meantime entre temps
meat viande *(f)*
medicine médicament *(m)*
meet rencontrer, se retrouver
meeting rendez-vous *(m)*
melt fondre; **melted** fondu
member membre *(m)*
menu carte *(f)*, menu *(m)* (fixed price)
messy désordonné(e)
Mexican mexicain(e)
Mexico Mexique *(m)*
middle milieu *(m)*; **in the — of** au milieu de
midnight minuit *(m)*
midterm partiel *(m)*
milk lait *(m)*
million million *(m)*
mineral water eau minérale *(f)*
mint menthe *(f)*
minute minute *(f)*
miss manquer; **I — you** tu me manques; **— a train** manquer,

rater un train; **not to be missed** à ne pas manquer
Miss Mademoiselle (Mlle)
mistake faute, erreur *(f)*; **make a —** se tromper, faire une faute
misunderstanding malentendu *(m)*
modern moderne
modest modeste
Monday lundi *(m)*
money argent *(m)*
month mois *(m)*; **every —** tous les mois; **monthly allowances** allocations (familiales) *(f)*
more encore, plus; **no — . . .** plus de . . .
morning matin *(m)*; **in the —** le matin; **all — long** toute la matinée; **every —** tous les matins
Moroccan marocain(e)
Morocco Maroc *(m)*
most la plupart ; **the —** la, le, les plus
mother mère *(f)*; **Mother's Day** Fête des Mères *(f)*
mother-in-law belle-mère *(f)*
motorcycle moto *(f)*
mouse souris *(f)*
mountain montagne *(f)*
mountain bike VTT *(m)*; **to go off-road biking** faire du VTT
mouth bouche *(f)*
move déménager ; **— around** bouger
movie film *(m)*; **— theater** cinéma *(m)*
murder meurtre *(m)*
Mr. Monsieur (M.)
Mrs. Madame (Mme)
much beaucoup; **how —** combien (de); **not —** pas grand-chose, pas beaucoup; **so —** tant de; **too —** trop (de)
museum musée *(m)*
mushroom champignon *(m)*
music musique *(f)*
must devoir, il faut; **one — not** il ne faut pas
my ma, mon, mes; **— goodness** mon Dieu

naive naïf, naïve

name nom *(m)*; **my — is . . .** je m'appelle. . .; **What is your — ?** Comment vous appelez-vous?; **write your —** écrivez votre nom

nap sieste *(f)*; **take a —** faire la sieste

napkin serviette *(f)*

nasty méchant(e)

nationality nationalité *(f)*; **What is your — ?** Quelle est votre nationalité?

nativity scene crèche *(f)*; **— figure** santon *(m)*

naturally naturellement

naughty vilain(e); **— girl** vilaine *(f)*

near près (de)

necessary nécessaire; **it is —** il est nécessaire, il faut

neck cou *(m)*

need *(n)* besoin *(m)*

need *(v)* avoir besoin de

neighbor voisin(e)

neighborhood quartier *(m)*

neither ne . . . ni . . . ni, non plus

nephew neveu *(m)*

nervous nerveux, nerveuse, anxieux, anxieuse; **be —** être nerveux, avoir le trac

never jamais (ne . . . jamais)

new nouveau, nouvel, nouvelle, neuf, neuve; **— Year's Day** Jour de l'An *(m)*; **What's — ?** Quoi de neuf?

news informations, nouvelles *(f, pl)*

newspaper journal *(m)*

newsstand kiosk *(m)*

next prochain(e), ensuite, puis; **— door** à côté; **— to** à côté de; **— week** la semaine prochaine; **— weekend** le week-end prochain; **— year** l'année prochaine ; **the — day** lendemain *(m)*

nice sympathique, gentil(le), agréable; **Have a — day!** Bonne journée!; **It's — weather.** Il fait beau.; **It would be — to . . .** Il serait agréable de . . .

nicely gentiment

niece nièce *(f)*

night nuit *(f)*

nightmare cauchemar *(m)*

nine neuf

nineteen dix-neuf

ninety quatre-vingt-dix

no non; *(emphatic)* mais non!; **— longer** ne . . . plus; **— more** ne . . . plus; **— one** personne ; **— smoking area** espace non-fumeur

noise bruit *(m)*

noon: it's — il est midi

nor ne . . . ni . . . ni, non plus

north nord *(m)*; **— America** Amérique du Nord *(f)*

nose nez *(m)*; **I have a runny —** j'ai le nez qui coule

not pas, ne (n') . . . pas; **— anyone** ne . . . personne ; **— anything** ne . . . rien; **— at all** pas du tout, de rien; **— ever** ne . . . jamais; **— much** pas beaucoup; **— really** pas vraiment; **— yet** pas encore

note note *(f)*, petit mot *(m)*; **take notes** prendre des notes, noter

notebook cahier *(m)*

nothing (ne) rien

notice remarquer

novel roman *(m)*

November novembre *(m)*

now maintenant

number numéro, nombre, chiffre *(m)*; **telephone —** numéro de téléphone *(m)*

nurse infirmier, infirmière

O

obey obéir

obligatory obligatoire

obtain obtenir

occupy occuper

o'clock heure(s); **at . . . —** à . . . heure(s); **it is . . . —** il est . . . heure(s)

October octobre *(m)*

of de; **— course** bien sûr

offer *(n)* offre *(f)*

offer *(v)* offrir

office bureau *(m)*; **post —** bureau de poste *(m)*

officer: police — agent de police *(m)*

often souvent

okay d'accord

old vieux, vieil, vieille; **— maid** vieille fille *(f)*, **How — are you?** Quel âge avez-vous?

omelet omelette *(f)*

on sur; **— the corner** au coin; **— the first floor** au rez-de-chaussée; **— the floor** par terre; **— the ground** par terre; **— the phone** au téléphone; **— time** à l'heure

one *(number)* un(e); **— hundred** cent; **— by —** un(e) à un(e)

one *(pron)* on; **no —** ne . . . personne

oneself soi

onion oignon *(m)*

only *(adj)* seul(e)

only *(adv)* seulement, ne . . . que

open *(adj)* ouvert(e)

open *(v)* ouvrir; **— your book** ouvrez votre livre

operate fonctionner

opinion avis *(m)*; **in my (your, etc.) —** à mon (votre, etc.) avis

opposite contraire *(m)*

optimist optimiste *(m/f)*

optimistic optimiste *(m/f)*

or ou

oral oral(e); **— report** exposé *(m)*

orange *(adj)* orange *(inv)*

orange *(n)* orange *(f)*; **— juice** jus d'orange *(m)*; **— soda** Orangina *(m)*

order *(n)* ordre *(m)*, commande *(f)*

order *(v)* commander

original original(e)

other autre

ouch aïe

our notre, nos

outfit ensemble *(m)*

outside dehors

over fini(e); **— there** là-bas

owe devoir

P

page page (f)
pain: have a — avoir mal (à)
pal copain (m), copine (f)
pants pantalon (m, s.)
pantyhose collant (m, s.)
paper papier (m); **term —** dissertation (f)
pardon (me) excusez-moi, pardon
parents parents (m, pl)
park parc (m)
parking lot parking (m)
party (n) fête (f), boum (f) (fam)
party (v) faire la fête
pass (an exam) réussir (à un examen)
pasta pâtes (f, pl)
pastry pâtisserie (f); **— shop** pâtisserie (f)
patient (adj) patient(e)
pay payer; **— attention** faire attention
peach pêche (f)
peas petits pois (m, pl)
pen stylo (m)
pencil crayon (m)
people gens (m, pl), on
pepper poivre (m)
per par
perhaps peut-être
permit permettre
person personne (f) (for a male or female)
pessimist pessimiste (m/f)
pessimistic pessimiste (m/f)
pharmacist pharmacien (m), pharmacienne (f)
pharmacy pharmacie (f)
phone (n) téléphone (m); **— card** télécarte (f)
phone (v) téléphoner
photo photo (f)
physical physique ; **— description** description physique (f)
piano piano (m)
pie tarte (f); **apple —** tarte aux pommes
piece (of) morceau (de) (m)
PIN code bancaire (m)
pink rose

pity dommage (m), pitié (f); **it's a —** c'est dommage
pizza pizza (f)
place (n) endroit, lieu (m)
place (v) mettre
plane avion (m)
plant plante (f); **green —** plante verte
play (n) pièce (f)
play (v) jouer
please s'il vous plaît, s'il te plaît
pleased to meet you enchanté(e)
pleasure plaisir (m)
plumber plombier (m)
plus plus
pocket poche (f)
poem poème (m)
police officer agent de police (m)
polite poli(e)
politely poliment
political science sciences politiques (f, pl)
poor pauvre
poorly mal
popular populaire; **— song** chanson populaire (f)
pork porc (m); **— butcher's** charcuterie (f)
possible possible; **it is —** il est possible, c'est possible; **it would be — to . . .** il serait possible de . . . ; **would it be — to . . .** serait-il possible de . . .
post office bureau de poste (m)
postcard carte postale (f)
potato pomme de terre (f)
pour verser
precocious précoce
prefer préférer
preferable préférable; **it would be — to** il serait mieux de
prepare préparer
prescription ordonnance (f)
pretty joli(e)
price prix (m)
priest prêtre (m)
private privé(e); **— lesson** leçon particulière (f)
product produit (m)
profession profession (f)

professor professeur (m)
program programme (m); **television —** émission (f)
promise promettre
psychologically moralement
psychology psychologie (f)
punch (a ticket) composter (un billet)
punish punir
purchase (n) achat (m)
purchase (v) acheter
purple violet(te)
put mettre; **— away** ranger; **— to bed** coucher; **— on clothing** mettre, s'habiller; **— on perfume** se parfumer; **— on weight** grossir

Q

quarter quart (m); **a — past** et quart; **a — to** moins le quart
question question (f); **ask a —** poser une question
quickly vite, rapidement

R

rabbit lapin (m)
radio radio (f)
rafting rafting (m); **go river —** faire du rafting
rain (n) pluie (f)
rain (v) pleuvoir; **it's raining** il pleut
raincoat imperméable (m)
raise lever
Ramadan Ramadan (m)
rarely rarement
rather assez, plutôt
read lire
ready (to) prêt(e) (à)
real estate agent agent immobilier (m)
really vraiment
reasonable raisonnable
recall rappeler
receive recevoir
recently récemment
recipe recette (f)
recommendation recommandation (f); **letter of —** lettre de recommandation (f)

red rouge; **turn red** rougir
redhead (red-haired) roux, rousse
refrigerator réfrigérateur *(m)*
regularly régulièrement
relatives parents *(m, pl)*
relaxing reposant(e)
reluctantly à contrecœur
remain rester
remember se rappeler, se souvenir (de)
reminder pense-bête *(m)*
rent *(n)* loyer *(m)*
rent *(v)* louer
repeat répéter
request demande *(f)*; **make a —** demander
research recherche *(f)*; **do —** faire des recherches
responsibility responsabilité *(f)*
rest *(n)* reste *(m)*
rest *(v)* se reposer
restaurant restaurant *(m)*
restroom toilettes *(f, pl)*
résumé résumé *(m)*, curriculum vitae *(m)*
retire prendre sa retraite
retirement retraite *(f)*
return rendre, rentrer, retourner, revenir
review *(n)* révision *(f)*
review *(v)* réviser
rhyme rime *(f)*
right *(adj)* droit(e)
right *(n)* droit *(m)*; **— ?** n'est-ce pas? **— away** tout de suite; **be —** avoir raison; **have the —** avoir le droit; **to the — (of)** à droite (de);
ring *(n)* bague *(f)*; **wedding —** alliance *(f)*
ring *(v)* sonner
river rivière *(f)*
road route *(f)*
roll *(n)* petit pain *(m)*
roll *(v)* rouler
roof toit *(m)*
room salle *(f)*, pièce *(f)*; **bathroom** salle de bains *(f)*; **bedroom** chambre *(f)*; **classroom** salle de classe *(f)*; **dining —** salle à

manger *(f)*; **hotel —** chambre *(f)*; **living —** salle de séjour *(f)*
roommate camarade de chambre *(m/f)*
root racine *(f)*
rope corde *(f)*
Roquefort cheese roquefort *(m)*
Rosh Hashana Rosh Ha-Shana *(m)*
rug tapis *(m)*
ruler règle *(f)*
run courir, couler
runny qui coule; **I have a — nose** j'ai le nez qui coule
rush se dépêcher (de)
Russia Russie *(f)*
Russian russe
rye seigle *(m)*

S

sad triste
sailing voile *(f)*; **go —** faire de la voile
salad salade *(f)*; **green —** salade verte *(f)*
sale soldes *(f, pl)*; **on —** en solde
salesman vendeur *(m)*
saleswoman vendeuse *(f)*
salmon saumon *(m)*
salt sel *(m)*
salty salé(e)
same même
sandwich sandwich *(m)*
Saturday samedi *(m)*
sausage saucisse *(f)*
save sauver
saxophone saxophone *(m)*
say dire
scarf foulard *(m)*
scatter-brained étourdi(e)
schedule emploi du temps *(m)*, horaire *(m)*
school école *(f)*
schoolteacher instituteur, institutrice
science science *(f)*; **computer —** informatique *(f)*
sea mer *(f)*
season saison *(f)*
seated assis(e)
second deuxième

security deposit caution *(f)*
see voir; **— again** revoir; **— you later** à tout à l'heure
seem sembler
sell vendre
semester semestre *(m)*
send envoyer
Senegal Sénégal *(m)*
Senegalese sénégalais(e)
sensitive sensible
separate séparer
September septembre *(m)*
serious sérieux, sérieuse
seriously sérieusement
service service *(m)*
set (the table) mettre (la table)
settle s'installer
seven sept
seventeen dix-sept
seventy soixante-dix
seventy-one soixante et onze
seventy-two soixante-douze
shadow ombre *(f)*
shame honte *(f)*, dommage *(m)*; **It's a —** C'est dommage
shape forme *(f)*; **be in great —** être en forme
share partager
sharp *(for time)* pile
shave se raser
she elle
sheet (of paper) feuille (de papier) *(f)*
sherbet sorbet *(m)*
shh chut
shirt chemise *(f)*
shoes chaussures *(f, pl)*; **— size** pointure *(f)*
shop boutique *(f)*; **cheese —** fromagerie *(f)*; **tobacco —** (bureau de) tabac *(m)*
shopping courses *(f, pl)*; **— cart** caddie *(m)* **— center** centre commercial *(m)*; **go —** faire les courses
short court(e), petit(e) *(for a person)*
shorts short *(m, s.)*
shoulder épaule *(f)*
show *(n)* spectacle *(m)*

S

show (v) montrer
show-off vantard(e)
shower douche (f); **take a —** prendre une douche
shut fermer, se fermer
shy timide
sick malade; **be — (as a dog)** être malade (comme un chien)
silly bête; **— things** bêtises (f, pl)
simple simple
since depuis, puisque
sing chanter
singer chanteur, chanteuse
single célibataire, seul(e)
sir monsieur
sister sœur (f)
sister-in-law belle-sœur (f)
sit down s'asseoir; **Sit down!** Asseyez-vous!
six six
sixteen seize
sixty soixante
size taille (f)
skate patiner
ski (v) skier; **go water skiing** faire du ski nautique; **go cross-country skiing** faire du ski de fond
skis (n) skis (m, pl)
skirt jupe (f)
sleep dormir; **— late** faire la grasse matinée
sleeping bag sac de couchage (m)
slice (of) tranche (de) (f)
slip glisser
slow lent(e)
slowly lentement
small petit(e)
smart intelligent(e); **— one** futé(e)
smile (n) sourire (m)
smile (v) sourire; **— at each other** se sourire
smoke (n) fumée (f)
smoke (v) fumer; **no smoking area** espace non-fumeur (m)
snack en-cas (m)
snail escargot (m)
snore ronfler
snow (n) neige (f)
snow (v) neiger; **It's snowing.** Il neige.

so alors, si; **— many** tant (de); **— much** tant (de)
soccer football (m)
social worker assistant social (m)/assistante sociale (f)
socks chaussettes (f, pl)
soda coca (m); **lemon-lime —** limonade (f); **orange —** Orangina (m)
sofa sofa (m)
some quelques, des, en
someone quelqu'un
something quelque chose (m)
sometimes quelquefois
somewhat assez
somewhere quelque part; **— else** ailleurs
son fils (m)
song chanson (f)
soon bientôt; **see you —** à bientôt
sore: **be —** avoir mal (à); **I have a — throat.** J'ai mal à la gorge.
sorry désolé(e); **be —** être désolé(e), regretter; **I'm sorry.** Je suis désolé(e).
soup soupe (f)
south sud; **— America** Amérique du Sud (f)
Spain Espagne (f)
Spanish espagnol(e)
speak (to) parler (à); **— to each other** se parler
spell épeler
spend (money) dépenser (de l'argent); **— time** passer (du temps)
spinach épinards (m, pl)
splash around patauger
spoon cuillère (f)
spoonful (of) cuillerée (de) (f)
spring printemps (m)
square: **public —** place (f); **on the — ** sur la place
stadium stade (m)
stain (n) tache (f)
stain (v) tacher
stair escalier (m)
stamp timbre (m)
stand up se lever
stand up! levez-vous!
stanza strophe (f)

staple agrafe (f)
stapler agrafeuse (f)
star étoile (f); **under the stars** à la belle étoile
start commencer
state état (m)
station station; **gas —** station service (f); **train —** gare (f)
stay rester
steak steak (m)
step-father beau-père (m)
step-mother belle-mère (f)
stereo stéréo (f)
still encore, toujours
stomach estomac (m)
stone pierre (f)
stop (n) arrêt (m); **bus —** arrêt de bus (m)
stop (v) (s')arrêter
store magasin (m); **department —** grand magasin (m); **grocery —** épicerie (f); **— window** vitrine (f)
story (of a building) étage (m); (tale) histoire (f)
stove cuisinière (f)
straight droit; **— ahead** tout droit
strawberry fraise (f)
street rue (f); **in the —** dans la rue
strict sévère
stringbeans haricots verts (m, pl)
student étudiant(e)
studies (n) études (f, pl)
study (n) bureau (m)
study (v) étudier
stylish chic
subway métro (m)
succeed réussir
suddenly tout d'un coup, tout à coup
suffer souffrir
sugar sucre (m)
suit complet (m); **bathing —** maillot de bain (m)
summer été (m)
sun soleil (m); **— glasses** lunettes de soleil (f, pl); **It's sunny.** Il fait du soleil.
Sunday dimanche
supermarket supermarché (m)
support soutenir

sure sûr(e), bien sûr

surprise surprise *(f)*

surprised: be surprised être surpris(e)

surprising étonnant(e)

survey sondage *(m)*

sweater pull(over) *(m)*

Sweden Suède *(f)*

Swedish suédois(e)

sweet sucré(e) *(for food)*, doux, douce *(for people)*

swim nager

swimming natation *(f)*

swimming pool piscine *(f)*

swing balancer

Swiss suisse ; **— cheese** emmenthal *(m)*

Switzerland Suisse *(f)*

T

table table *(f)*; **coffee —** table basse *(f)*; **set the —** mettre la table

tablet cachet *(m)*

take prendre; **— back** reprendre; **— an exam** passer un examen; **— a nap** faire la sieste; **— notes** prendre des notes; **— a trip** faire un voyage; **— a walk, ride** faire une promenade;

take-out restaurant traiteur *(m)*

talkative bavard(e)

tall grand(e)

taste *(n)* goût *(m)*

taste *(v)* goûter

taxi taxi *(m)*

tea thé *(m)*

teach enseigner

teacher professeur *(m)*; **elementary school —** instituteur *(m)*, institutrice *(f)*

team équipe *(f)*

teardrop larme *(f)*

tease taquiner

tee-shirt tee-shirt *(m)*

teeth dents *(f, pl)*

telephone *(n)* téléphone *(m)*; **— booth** cabine *(f)*; **— call** appel *(m)*; **— card** télécarte *(f)*; **— number** numéro de téléphone *(m)*; **on the —** au téléphone

telephone *(v)* téléphoner

television télévision *(f)*

tell dire ; **— about** parler de; **— a story** raconter une histoire;

ten dix; **about — (items)** dixaine *(f)*

tender tendre

tenderly tendrement

tennis tennis *(m)*; **— shoes** tennis *(f, pl)*

term semestre *(m)* (trimestre *(m)*); **— paper** dissertation *(f)*

test examen *(m)*

Têt Tet (Vietnamese New Year)

thank remercier, dire merci à ; **— you** merci ; **thanks to** grâce à

that *(adj)* ce, cet, cette

that *(pron)* ce, cela, ça; **That's enough.** Ça suffit.; **That's good, fine.** Ça va.

that *(relative pron)* qui, que;

the le, la, l', les

theater théâtre *(m)*

their leur(s)

them elles, eux, les, leur

then alors, ensuite, puis

there là, y; **over —** là-bas; **— is/ are** il y a, voilà

therefore alors, donc

these *(adj)* ces

they elles, eux, ils, on

thin mince

thing chose *(f)*; **(my) things** (mes) affaires *(f, pl)*

think penser, croire, trouver; **What do you — of . . ?** Comment trouvez-vous . . . ?; **Do you think so?** Vous croyez?; **I think so.** Je crois que oui.

thirsty: be — avoir soif

thirteen treize

thirty trente

this *(adj)* ce, cet, cette; **— is . . .** c'est . . .

those *(adj)* ces

thought idée *(f)*

thousand mille *(inv)*

three trois

throat gorge *(f)*; **I have a sore —.** J'ai mal à la gorge.

Thursday jeudi *(m)*

ticket billet *(m)* *(train)*, ticket *(m)* *(metro or tram)*

tidy ordonné(e)

tie cravate *(f)*

tights collant *(m, s.)*

time fois *(f)*, heure *(f)*, temps *(m)*; **all the —** tout le temps, constamment; **at that —** à cette époque-là; **for the last —** pour la dernière fois; **from — to —** de temps en temps; **have the —** avoir le temps; **on —** à l'heure; **What — is it?** Quelle heure est-il?

tired fatigué(e)

to à

tobacco tabac *(m)*; **— shop** (bureau de) tabac *(m)*

today aujourd'hui

together ensemble

tomato tomate *(f)*

tomorrow demain; **day after —** après-demain; **see you —** à demain

tonight ce soir

too aussi; **that's — bad** c'est dommage; **— bad** dommage; **— many** trop (de); **— much** trop (de);

tooth dent *(f)*

toothbrush brosse à dents *(f)*

top haut *(m)*

tour visite *(f)*, tour *(m)*

toward vers

tower tour *(f)*

town ville *(f)*; **— hall** mairie *(f)*

toy jouet *(m)*

traffic light feu *(m)*

train train *(m)*; **— station** gare *(f)*

travel voyager; **— agent** agent de voyage *(m)*

traveler voyageur *(m)*

trip voyage *(m)*

trombone trombone *(m)*

trout truite *(f)*

true vrai(e)

truly vraiment

trumpet trompette *(f)*

truth vérité *(f)*; **tell the —** dire la vérité

try essayer; **— on (clothing)** essayer (un vêtement)

Tuesday mardi *(m)*

Tunisia Tunisie *(f)*

Tunisian tunisien(ne)

turn tourner; **— in (your homework)** rendre (vos devoirs); **— on (the TV)** mettre la télé; **— red** rougir

tuxedo smoking (m)

twelve douze; **about —** douzaine (f)

twenty vingt

twin jumeau/jumelle

two deux

U

ugly laid(e)

unbelievable incroyable

uncertain pas sûr(e), incertain(e)

uncle oncle (m)

under sous

understand comprendre; **I don't —** je ne comprends pas

undress se déshabiller

unfortunate malheureux, malheureuse

unhappy malheureux, malheureuse; **be —** être malheureux, malheureuse

United States États-Unis (m, pl)

university université (f), faculté (fac) (f); **at the —** à la fac

unmarried célibataire

unpleasant désagréable

until jusqu'à

unusual bizarre

up: get — se lever; **go —** monter

us nous

usually d'habitude

utilities charges (f, pl)

V

vacation vacances (f, pl); **have a good —** bonnes vacances; **on —** en vacances; **summer —** vacances d'été

vanilla vanille (f); **— ice cream** glace à la vanille (f)

VCR magnétoscope (m)

veal veau (m)

vegetable légume (m)

very très; **— well** très bien

Vietnam Viêt-nam (m)

Vietnamese vietnamien(ne)

violet violet(te)

violin violon (m)

visit (n) visite (f)

visit (v) visiter; **— (someone)** rendre visite (à quelqu'un)

voice voix (f)

volleyball volley-ball (m)

voyage voyage (m)

W

wait (for) attendre

waiter garçon (m)

waitress serveuse (f)

wake réveiller; **— up** se réveiller

walk (n) promenade (f); **go for a —** faire une promenade, se promener

Walkman baladeur (m)

wallet portefeuille (m)

wallpaper tapisserie (f)

waltz valse (f)

want vouloir, désirer, avoir envie de

war guerre (f)

warehouse supermarket hypermarché

wash laver, se laver

washing machine machine à laver (f)

watch (n) montre (f)

watch (v) regarder

water eau (f); **mineral —** eau minérale (f); **— skiing** ski nautique (m); **go — skiing** faire du ski nautique

waterfall cascade (f), chute d'eau (f)

way chemin (m), route (f); **by the —** au fait

we nous

wear porter

weather temps (m), météo (f); **What's the — like?** Quel temps fait-il?

wedding mariage (m); **— band** alliance

Wednesday mercredi (m)

week semaine (f); **every —** toutes les semaines; **per —** par semaine; **two weeks** quinze jours, deux semaines

weight poids (m); **gain —** grossir,

prendre du poids; **lose —** maigrir, perdre du poids

well bien; **fairly —** assez bien; **very —** très bien; **— then** alors

what (adj) quel(le); (pron) que, qu'est-ce que, qu'est-ce qui; **— a baby!** Quel bébé!; **— about you?** Et vous? Et toi?; **— are they like?** Comment sont-ils?; **— (did you say)?** Comment?; **— do you think (of). . .?** Que pensez-vous de . . .? Comment trouvez-vous . . .?; **— should I do?** Que faire?; **— 's happening?** Qu'est-ce qui se passe?; **— 's new?** Quoi de neuf?; **— 's that?** Qu'est-ce que c'est?; **— 's the matter?** Qu'est-ce qui ne va pas?, Qu'est-ce que tu as?; **— 's your name?** Comment vous appelez-vous? Comment t'appelles-tu?; **— time is it?** Quelle heure est-il?

wheat blé (m)

when quand

where où; **— do you live?** Où habitez-vous? ; **— are . . . ?** Où se trouvent . . .?; **— is . . . ?** Où se trouve . . . ?

whew! ouf!

which quel(le)(s)

while pendant que; **a little —** tout à l'heure

white blanc, blanche

who qui; **— is it?** Qui est-ce?

whole tout(e); **whole-grain bread** pain complet (m)

whose (pron) dont; **— is it?** C'est à qui?

why pourquoi

widow veuve (f)

widower veuf (m)

wife femme (f)

win gagner

wind vent (m)

windy: It's windy. Il fait du vent.

window fenêtre (f)

windsurfer planche à voile (f); **go windsurfing** faire de la planche à voile

wine vin (m)

wing aile (f)

wink clin d' œil *(m)*
winter hiver *(m)*
wish vouloir, désirer, souhaiter
with avec; **— difficulty** difficilement
withdraw retirer
without sans
witness témoin *(m)*
woman femme *(f)*
wonder se demander
wood bois *(m)*
woods bois *(m)*
wool laine *(f)*
word mot *(m)*

work *(n)* travail *(m)*
work *(v)* travailler
workbook cahier *(m)*
world monde *(m)*; **take a trip around the —** faire le tour du monde; **the whole —** le monde entier
worried inquiet, inquiète
worry *(n)* souci *(m)*
worry *(v)* s'inquiéter; **Don't — .** Ne t'en fais pas.
would: I — like . . . je voudrais
write écrire
writer écrivain *(m)*

wrong faux, fausse; **be wrong** avoir tort

Y

year an *(m)*, année *(f)*; **all —** toute l'année; **I'm . . . years old** j'ai . . . ans; **four years ago** il y a quatre ans
yellow jaune
yes oui; *(emphatic)* mais oui
yesterday hier
you vous, tu, toi, te
young jeune
your votre, vos, ta, ton, tes

Photo Credits

Preliminary Chapter
Opener: Stuart Cohen/Comstock, Inc. Page 4 (top): Greg Meadors/Stock, Boston. Page 4 (center and on the right): Stuart Cohen/Comstock, Inc. Page 4 (center): R. Lucas/The Image Works. Page 4 (bottom): Bruno Maso/Photo Researchers. Page 6: Stephanie Maze/Woodfin Camp & Associates. Page 8: M. Antman/The Image Works. Page 12: Stuart Cohen/Comstock, Inc.

Chapter 1
Opener: F. Hache/Explorer. Page 18 (top): David Barnes/The Stock Market. Page 18 (bottom): Jean-Luc Bohin/Explorer. Page 32: Photo by M. Reynaud, courtesy France Telecom. Page 35: Courtesy Café Orbital, Paris. Page 40: Courtesy Rail Europe, Inc.

Chapter 2
Opener: Ulrike Welsch/Ulrike Welsch Photography. Page 48 (left): Painting by Claude Monet, Musée d'Orsay, Paris; Scala/Art Resource, NY. Page 48 (right): Bohin/Explorer. Page 64: Gilles Bassignac/Gamma Liaison.

Chapter 3
Opener: Peter Menzel. Page 80 (center): ©LDG Productions/The Image Bank. Page 80 (top right): N. Godinh PhU/Explorer. Page 88: Ghislaine Bras/Rapho.

Chapter 4
Opener: Peter Menzel. Page 118 (top left): Owen Franken/Stock, Boston. Page 118 (top and center): P. Parrot/Sygma. Page 118 (top right): ©Gutierrez/Explorer. Page 118 (bottom left): Blair Seitz/Photo Researchers. Page 118 (bottom right): Spectrum/Bavaria/Viesti Associates, Inc. Page 122: Lee Snider/The Image Works. Page 126: Greg Meadors/Stock, Boston. Page 130: Owen Franken/Stock, Boston.

Chapter 5
Opener: David Ball/The Stock Market. Page 156 (left): Mark Antman/The Image Works. Page 156 (top right): F. Ancellet/Rapho. Page 165: David Ball/The Stock Market. Page 168: David Barnes/The Stock Market. Page 170: Archive Photos. Page 173: Courtesy L'Office de Tourisme de Grenoble. Page 174: Courtesy Association Touristique Régionale de Charlevoix. Page 175: Photo by Majeau Sylvain, courtesy Institut de Tourisme et d'Hotellerie du Quebec.

Chapter 6
Opener: M. Everton/The Image Works. Page 188: R. Lucas/The Image Works. Page 193: Michael Busselle/Tony Stone Images/ New York, Inc. Page 196: ©Roux/Explorer. Page 205 (top): P. Quittemelle/Stock, Boston. Page 205 (center): Brauner/StockFood America.

Chapter 7
Opener: Ulrike Welsch/Ulrike Welsch Photography. Page 214: ©Plassart/Explorer. Page 217: Stuart Cohen/Comstock, Inc. Page 226 (left): David Simson/Stock, Boston. Page 226 (right): Nicholas DeVore/Tony Stone Images/ New York, Inc. Page 226 (center): Owen Franken/Stock, Boston. Page 230: Dailloux/Rapho. Page 235: Ben Simmons/The Stock Market. Page 236: Peter Stone/Black Star.

Chapter 8
Opener: Paddy Eckersley/Tony Stone Images/ New York, Inc. Page 248 (top right): Cathlyn Melloan/Tony Stone Images/ New York, Inc. Page 248 (bottom left): Henri Simon/Explorer. Page 255: Niels van Iperen/Retna. Page 262 (top left): Jean-Marc Truchet/Tony

Stone Images/ New York, Inc. Page 262 (top and center): David Ball/The Stock Market. Page 262 (top right): Jean-Marie Truchet/Tony Stone Images/ New York, Inc. Page 262 (center and left): Reproduced with permission of The Louvre. Page 262 (center): John Lamb/Tony Stone Images/ New York, Inc. Page 262 (center and right): David H. Endersbee/Tony Stone Images/ New York, Inc.

Chapter 9
Opener: Richard Lucas/The Image Works. Page 276 (top left): R. Lucas/The Image Works. Page 276 (top and center): Curt Fischer/Tony Stone Images/ New York, Inc. Page 276 (top right): Owen Franken /Stock, Boston. Page 276 (left and center): Peter Menzel. Page 276 (center): Owen Franken/Stock, Boston. Page 286 (center): Jacques Langevin/Sygma. Page 286 (top right): Patrick Zachmann/Magnum Photos, Inc. Page 302: ©A.S.K. /Viesti Associates, Inc.

Chapter 10
Opener: Peter Menzel. Page 314: Owen Franken/Stock, Boston. Page 324: David Simson/ Stock, Boston. Page 328: ©1994 Alexandra & Pierre Boulat/Material World/Peter Menzel. Page 332: Reproduced with permission of *Maxi*, January 30, 1994, p. 6.

Chapter 11
Opener: W. Bokelberg/The Image Bank. Page 345: Michael Busselle/Tony Stone Images/ New York, Inc. Page 355: P. Caron/Sygma. Page 358 (left): Vince Streano/Tony Stone Images/ New York, Inc. Page 358 (right): Zefa/The Stock Market. Page 364: Edouard Berne/Tony Stone Images/ New York, Inc.

Chapter 12
Opener: D. Herman/Explorer. Page 370: Stuart Cohen/Comstock, Inc. Page 381: Comstock, Inc. Page 384 (top left): J.M. Charles/Rapho. Page 384 (center): Ulrike Welsch/ Ulrike Welsch Photography. Page 384 (top right): ©M. Le Coz/Explorer.

Chapter 13
Opener: M. Serraillier/Rapho. Page 404: ©De Richemond/The Image Works. Pages 414-415: Sygma Photo News. Pages 422-423: Reproduced with permission of Alpha Bâteau, Vallon Pont d'Arc. Page 423 (bottom): Rene van der Meer/World View/Tony Stone Images/ New York, Inc. Page 424: Robert Fried/Stock, Boston.

Chapter 14
Opener: David Simson/Stock, Boston. Page 434 : Reproduced with permission of La Française des Jeux. Courtesy La Française des Jeux. Page 435: Olivier Martell/Black Star. Page 438 (left): ©Keystone Paris/Sygma. Page 438 (right): Bruno Barbey/Magnum Photos, Inc. Page 441: ©Joe Viesti/Viesti Associates, Inc. Page 450 (top): ©A. Wolf/Explorer. Page 450 (right): ©Coll. Lausat/Explorer. Page 454: ©Abbas/Magnum Photos, Inc.

Chapter 15
Opener: R. Lucas/The Image Works. Page 468: Stuart Cohen/Comstock, Inc. Page 476: P.Wysocki/Explorer. Page 480: Dennis Purse/Photo Researchers.

Text and Realia Credits

Chapter 1: Page 40: Documents appartenant à la SNCF. Tous droits de reproduction réservés. SNCF: Reprinted by permission.

Chapter 2: Page 72: Reprinted by permission of Tim Restaurant Chinois; Crêperie Gwenaelle; L'Équateur Restaurant Tex-Mex.

Chapter 3: Page 104: Reprinted by permission of Dunod Éditeur.

Chapter 5: Page 173: Reprinted by permission of the Office du Tourisme, Grenoble; Page 174: Reprinted by permission of the Association Touristique régionale de Charlevoix.

Chapter 6: Page 205: Adapted from "Sachez cuisiner—Sachez recevoir," Zurich 1983; © Verlag Das Beste, Stuttgart, 1991, 1983. Reprinted by permission.

Chapter 7: Page 235: Pham Duy Khiêm: "Le Cristal d'amour," in *Légendes des terres sereines*. © Mercure de France, 1951. Reprinted by permission.

Chapter 8: Page 268: Jacques Prévert, "Paris at Night," in *Paroles*. © Éditions Gallimard, 1946. Reprinted by permission.

Chapter 9: Page 299: Reprinted by permission of Dunod Éditeur.

Chapter 10: Page 332: "La croix rouge vous écoute," *Maxi,* No. 378, 24 janvier 1995, © Éditions Bauer. Reprinted by permission.

Chapter 11: Page 362: Reprinted by permission of Budget Rent a Car International Inc.

Chapter 12: Page 395: "La chandeleur, Fête des lumières," *Journal Français d'Amérique,* 20 janvier-2 février 1995. Reprinted by permission.

Chapter 13: Pages 422–423: Reprinted by permission of Alpha Bateaux.

Chapter 14: Page 454: From Simone de Beauvoir, *Le deuxième sexe.* © Éditions Gallimard, 1976, 1949. Reprinted by permission.

Chapter 15: Page 480: Léopold Senghor, «"Femme Noire" Chants d'ombre» in (Œuvre Poétique, © Éditions du Seuil, 1990. Reprinted by permission.

Index

imperative, 282
position of object pronouns with, 296–297, 373
of reflexive verbs, 322–323
imperfect, 310, 341–342
-**ger** verbs, 343
-**ir** verbs, 410
vs. **passé composé,** 359
impersonal
expressions, 393
pronouns, 20
indefinite article, 32–33, 463
avoir and, 81
indirect object pronouns, 352–353
interrogation, 70–71, 100
interrogative adjectives, 102
interrogative expressions, 101–102, 126
intonation, 70
inversion, 71, 348
immediate future and, 157
used to ask question, 100
-**ir** verbs, 410, 468–469

J

jouer, à, de, 287

L

language, levels of, 4
le, la, les. *See* definite articles
liaison, 42
lire, 215

M

marital status, 28
meilleur
vs. **mieux,** 445
-**même,** 129
mentir, 244
mettre, 137
moins, 444, 451

N

nationalities, 29, 149, 177, 240
negation, 56, 202–203, 462–463
imperative sentences, 282, 297
partitive in, 190
passé composé sentences, 231, 264, 291
with reflexive verbs, 316, 322
n'est-ce pas, 70
numbers, 6, 97, 199

O

object pronouns. *See* direct object pronouns; indirect object pronouns
orders, giving, 282
où, 127
ouvrir, 468–469

P

partir, 244
partitive articles, 190, 463
passé composé
position of adverbs, 416
with **avoir,** 230–231, 410
with **être,** 264
negative, 231, 264
of reflexive verbs, 329–330
vs. imperfect, 359
past participle
agreement of, 264, 290–291, 330, 372
irregular, 266
-**re** verbs, 348
past tenses. *See* immediate past; imperfect; **passé composé**
pendant, 343, 420
plus, 451
possessive adjectives, 88–89
pourquoi, 127
pouvoir, 277–278
subjunctive of, 392
prendre, 157, 282
idiomatic expressions with, 158
imperfect of, 342
vs. **boire,** 182
professions, 130
prepositions, 134–135
pronouns. *See also* direct object pronouns; impersonal pronouns; relative pronouns; stress pronouns; subject pronouns
direct object, 289–290
order of, 371–372
position with imperative, 296–297

Q

quand, 38, 126, 405
quantity
expressions of, 196–197
tout expressing, 258

que
in comparisons, 444
interrogative pronoun, 101–102
relative pronoun, 250
used with obligation and desire expressions, 386
quel, interrogative adjective, 101–102
questions. *See also* interrogative expressions
asking. *See* interrogation; intonation; inversion
passé composé, 231
with reflexive verbs, 316
qui
interrogative pronoun, 101–102
relative pronoun, 250
quoi, 102

R

reflexive verbs, 315–316
imperative of, 322–323
passé composé of, 329–330
relative pronouns, 250, 472–473
-**re** verbs, 348
rien, 462

S

savoir, 310
subjunctive of, 392
seasons, 119
servir, 244
si, 406
clauses with, 439–440
sortir, 244
stress pronouns, 128–129, 220
subject pronouns, 19
subjunctive
expressing emotion and doubt, 392–393
expressing obligation and desire, 386–387
superlative, 451–452

T

time
dates, 233
days, months, seasons, 119–120
expressions of, 232, 420
telling, 7, 13, 114–115
tout, 258–259